Studies in International Investment Law

edited by
Prof. Dr. Marc Bungenberg, LL.M., Universität des Saarlandes
Prof. Dr. Dr. h.c. Stephan Hobe, LL.M., Universität zu Köln
Prof. Dr. August Reinisch, LL.M., Universität Wien
Prof. Dr. Andreas R. Ziegler, LL.M., Universität Lausanne

Volume 41

Niclas Landmann

Legitimate Expectations and Fair-and-Equitable-Treatment under the Energy Charter Treaty

A Comparative Analysis of the Renewable Energy Cases

Nomos

facultas

DIKE

Onlineversion
Nomos eLibrary

The Deutsche Nationalbibliothek lists this publication in the Deutsche Nationalbibliografie; detailed bibliographic data are available on the Internet at http://dnb.d-nb.de

a.t.: Köln, Univ., Diss., 2021

ISBN 978-3-8487-8654-1 (Nomos Verlagsgesellschaft mbH & Co. KG, Baden-Baden, Print)
ISBN 978-3-7489-3025-9 (Nomos Verlagsgesellschaft mbH & Co. KG, Baden-Baden, ePDF)
ISBN 978-3-7089-2232-4 (facultas Verlag, Wien)
ISBN 978-3-03891-427-3 (Dike Verlag, Zürich / St. Gallen)

British Library Cataloguing-in-Publication Data
A catalogue record for this book is available from the British Library.

ISBN 978-3-8487-8654-1 (Nomos Verlagsgesellschaft mbH & Co. KG, Baden-Baden, Print)
ISBN 978-3-7489-3025-9 (Nomos Verlagsgesellschaft mbH & Co. KG, Baden-Baden, ePDF)
ISBN 978-3-7089-2232-4 (facultas Verlag, Wien)
ISBN 978-3-03891-427-3 (Dike Verlag, Zürich / St. Gallen)

Library of Congress Cataloging-in-Publication Data
Landmann, Niclas
Legitimate Expectations and Fair-and-Equitable-Treatment under the Energy Charter Treaty
A Comparative Analysis of the Renewable Energy Cases
Niclas Landmann
370 pp.
Includes bibliographic references.

ISBN 978-3-8487-8654-1 (Nomos Verlagsgesellschaft mbH & Co. KG, Baden-Baden, Print)
ISBN 978-3-7489-3025-9 (Nomos Verlagsgesellschaft mbH & Co. KG, Baden-Baden, ePDF)
ISBN 978-3-7089-2232-4 (facultas Verlag, Wien)
ISBN 978-3-03891-427-3 (Dike Verlag, Zürich / St. Gallen)

1st Edition 2022

To my parents
I will always owe you my heartfelt gratitude

Preface

This thesis was accepted as a doctoral dissertation by the Faculty of Law of Cologne University in September 2021. Arbitral jurisprudence and legal literature up until February 2021 were taken into account.

This work could not have been realised without the support of numerous people. I would like to take this opportunity to express my sincere gratitude.

First of all, my special thanks goes to my doctoral supervisor Prof. Dr. Dr. h.c. Stephan Hobe, who was always eager to offer his help as well as wise words of guidance. Despite his numerous doctoral students, he always found time to listen to and respond to any type of enquiry. His doctoral seminars provided an excellent opportunity for the exchange of ideas.

Second, I would also like to thank Prof. Dr. Julian Scheu for the speedy completion of the second opinion. Moreover, I would like to thank him for establishing the study group on a possible ISDS reform and the creation of a Multilateral Investment Court at the International Investment Law Centre Cologe (IILCC). This academic journey has been most exciting and will hopefully see further continuation.

Third, I would like to thank Prof. Dr. Dr. Rainer Hofmann, who has been a driving force behind my academic career. Not only did he write the recommendation that enabled me to study Investment Treaty Arbitration under Prof. Dr. Kaj Hobér at Uppsala University, he also brought the topic of this dissertation to my attention and kindly recommended me to Prof. Hobe.

Additionally, my thanks go to all the members of the IILCC's doctoral network, who proofread my dissertation and became equally passionate about the joys of investment law.

I would also like to thank all of my friends who supported my work with great commitment, many discussions, critical questions and, above all, tireless encouragement. I thank all my "old" friends, who even developed a mild interest in investment law after one of my enthusiastic (and sometimes tiresome) lectures on this topic. And I thank all my "new" friends, who I only met working in this incredible field full of incredible people.

Finally, I owe the deepest gratitude to my parents. Although writing a doctoral dissertation is a famously lonely endeavour, they always supported me with all of their energy, had my back unconditionally, and enabled me to walk the long path that eventually lead to the publication of this work.

Rodenbach, October 2021, Niclas Landmann

Table of Content

Table of Abbreviations

AEEG	Italian *Autorità per l'energia elettrica e il gas*
AU	Italian *Autorizzazione Unica*
BIT	Bilateral Investment Treaty
CETA	Comprehensive Economic and Trade Agreement between the EU and Canada of 30 October 2016
CJEU	Court of Justice of the European Union
CNE	Spanish National Energy Commission
CNE Reports	Public Reports issued by CNE
COMESA	Investment Agreement for the Common Market for Eastern and Southern Africa of 23 May 2007
CPI	Consumer Price Index
CSP	Concentrated Solar Power
CSR	Corporate Social Responsibility
Destinazione Italia Decree	Italian LD No. 145/2013 of 23 December 2013
DIA	Italian *Denuncia di Inizio Attivitci*
EC	European Commission
ECHR	European Charter of Human Rights
ECT	Energy Charter Treaty
ECtHR	European Court of Human Rights
EL	Spanish Energy Law of 27 November 1997
Energy Account	Series of so-called "Conto Energia" decrees implemented by the Italian Ministry of Economic Development
ERO	Czech Energy Regulatory Office
EU	European Union
FDI	Foreign Direct Investment
FET	Fair and Equitable Treatment
FIP	Feed-in Premium
FIT	Feed-in Tariff
FPS	Full Protection and Security
FTA	Free Trade Agreement
GSE	Italian *Gestore dei Servizi Energetici*
GSE Convention	Private contract concluded between renewable energy producers and the GSE

IBA	International Bar Association
ICJ	International Court of Justice
ICSID	International Centre for Settlement of Investment Disputes
ICSID Convention	International Convention on the Settlement of Investment Disputes between States and Nationals of Other States of 14 October 1966
IDEA	Spanish Institute for Energy Diversification and Savings
IEA	International Energy Agency
IFC	International Finance Corporation
IIA	International Investment Agreement
ILC	International Law Commission
Intra-EU dispute	Dispute between an investor from the EU and a Member State of the EU
IPA	Investment Protection Agreement
ISDS	Investor-State Dispute Settlement
LD	Italian Legislative Decree
Mauritius Convention	United Nations Convention on Transparency in Treaty-based Investor-State Arbitration of 10 December 2014
MIGA	Multilateral Investment Guarantee Agency
NAFTA	North America Free Trade Agreement
NEL	Spanish New Energy Law of 26 December 2013
OECD	Organisation for Economic Co-operation and Development
PANER 2011-2020	Spanish National Action Plan for Renewable Energy 2011-2020
PCIJ	Permanent Court of International Justice
PER 2005-2010	Spanish Plan for Renewable Energies 2005-2010
PPA	Power Purchase Agreement
PV	Photovoltaic
RAIPRE	Administrative Registry for Electrical Power Generating Units
RD	Spanish Royal Decree
RDL	Spanish Royal Decree Law
Romani Decree	Italian LD 28/2011 of 3 March 2011
Spalma Incentivi Decree	Italian LD 91/2014, converted into law by Law 116/2014 of 11 August 2014

TVPEE	Tax on the value of the production of electrical energy, introduced by Spanish Law 15/2012 of 21 April 2012.
UNCITRAL	United Nations Commission on International Trade Law
UNCTAD	United Nations Conference on Trade and Development
UNFCCC	United Nations Framework Convention on Climate Change
VCLT	Vienna Convention on the Law of Treaties
WTO	World Trade Organization

Executive Summary

The Fair and Equitable Treatment Standard (FET) has been a highly undetermined concept ever since investors began relying on it as an individual protective right under international investment agreements (IIAs). The notion of legitimate expectations emerged in the early 2000s as a key aspect of the FET Standard and to counter the vagueness that coincides with it. This development has greatly benefitted from the cases against the Argentine Republic in the aftermath of its financial crisis between 1998-2002. While arbitral jurisprudence on the notion of legitimate expectations has developed immensely during this phase, the application of the standard is still characterized by legal uncertainty. Legal uncertainty, in turn, does not only adversely affect investors in their business decisions and states in their right to regulate but also undermines the legitimacy of investment law and its dispute resolution mechanisms as a whole. This legal uncertainty partly derives from the issue that the notion of legitimate expectations is now firmly rooted in international investment law but has seen inconsistency in its application in arbitral jurisprudence.

The question, therefore, is whether the new generation of arbitral decisions, emerging under the renewable energy cases under the Energy Charter Treaty (ECT), follow a system of soft precedent, which allows the further refinement of the requirements for the investors' legitimate expectations. This analysis focuses on 1) the conduct presented by the host states which has been qualified as grounds for legitimate expectations, 2) the level of due diligence which arbitral tribunals required from investors, and 3) the intensity of the state's measures that eventually violated the reliance of the investors. Within this analysis, the focus is set on the highly controversial question of whether the legal framework may serve as a basis for legitimate expectations. The case is made that recent arbitral jurisprudence accepted the legal framework as a basis for some sort of legitimate expectations. The intensity of the expectations is then determined by the additional conduct of the state based on the particular facts of the individual case. A sufficiently specific legal framework may invoke the expectations in investors that it will not be fundamentally and drastically altered which would undermine the premises on which sufficiently diligent investors based their business decisions. If the host states make supporting representations that are mapping out a certain policy with regard to an individual or a group of investors, the expectations may further be narrowed down. The investors, on the other hand, must assess the economic environment in the host state carefully and consider warning signs that may indicate a change in trend in the host state's conduct, which may eventually result in the alteration or abolishment of the prevailing legal framework. Since states are afforded a wide margin of discretion by their right to regulate, the legal framework can never be interpreted as a freezing-commitment. The right to regulate derives from state sovereignty and must duly be considered when evaluating a state's actions. Therefore, the measures implemented in the host state must also have a significant impact on the profitability of the investment. Regarding the profitability, which internal rates of return tribunals deem "reasonable" in context of the commitments of the host states and their legitimate aim to reduce excessive gains to the detriment of the public, are also analysed.

The analysis of the case law aims to demonstrate that arbitral jurisprudence, despite the different possible outcomes in light of the individual facts or the case, has formed a common understanding of certain subcategories of the notion of legitimate expectations in many respects. Lastly, it is argued that the acceptance of the legal framework as a basis for a minimum standard of protection against regulatory change is not unduly restricting the states' right to regulate and maintains a sizable margin of discretion.

Introduction

Investment law, in contrast to other areas of international commercial law, in particular international trade law or international monetary law, consists of a multitude of bilateral, regional and multilateral treaties. Hence, the legal issues arising in connection with transnational investments are not governed by a uniform regime, but must be solved on the basis of over 3,000 international investment agreements (IIAs) that set out in their entirety the current Investor-State Dispute Settlement (ISDS) system.[1] One of the most commonly invoked IIAs in recent times is the Energy Charter Treaty (ECT).[2] The ECT is a multilateral investment protection framework, which was signed in December 1994 and entered into legal force in April 1998.[3] There are currently 55 Signatories and Contracting Parties to the Treaty, including the European Union (EU).[4] The scope of the ECT encompasses the protection of foreign investments, non-discriminatory conditions for trade in energy materials, products and energy-related equipment, the resolution of disputes between participating states and between investors and host states, as well as the promotion of energy efficiency, and attempts to minimise the environmental impact of energy production and use.[5]

Although the ECT was relatively unpopular and rarely relied on by investors at its inception, there has been a marked increase in cases brought under its ambit within recent years.[6] The ECT was originally designed to

---

1 Hobe, 'The Development of the Law of Aliens and Emergence of General Principles of Protection under International Law' in Bungenberg and others (eds), *International Investment Law: A Handbook* (Nomos 2015), p. 14.

2 *See* UNCTAD, 'World Investment Report 2019', UNCTAD Series on Issues in International Investment Agreements II (United Nations 2019), p. 103.

3 Energy Charter Secretariat, *The Energy Charter Treaty: A Reader's Guide* (2002), p. 8.

4 Although Australia, Russia, and Norway have not ratified the ECT, *see* <https://www.energycharter.org/process/energy-charter-treaty-1994/energy-charter-treaty/> (accessed 3 May 2021).

5 Hobér, 'Overview of Energy Charter Treaty Cases' in Scherer and Amirfar (eds), *International Arbitration in the Energy Sector* (OUP 2018), para. 8.03.

6 Hobér, *Overview of Energy Charter Treaty Cases*, para. 8.08; Orsat Miljenić, 'Energy Charter Treaty – Standards of Investment Protection' (2018) 24(83) Croatian International Relations Review 52, p. 53. *See* a full list of Investment Dispute

create a safe environment for Western capital flowing into Eastern privatisation projects.[7] Currently, its application has evolved from investment disputes concerning Eastern fossil fuel sources and power plants to investments in the renewable energy sector.[8] Disputes regarding investments in the renewable energy sector, including but not limited to, actions taken by Spain, Italy and the Czech Republic, in the aftermath of the 2007/2008 financial crisis make up the majority of ECT cases brought within the past decade.[9] A comparison has been drawn between the impact of the renewable energy cases on the development of investment arbitration practice and the multiple arbitration proceedings against Argentina for measures taken by the host state to counter its financial crisis in the late 1990s and early 2000s.[10] This influx of disputes mainly arose as a result of the alteration or abolishment of incentives offered by host states to promote investments in the renewable energy sector, as a reaction to the reduced state budget caused by the financial crisis. The investors based their claims on a violation of the obligations under Part III of the ECT, mainly the violation of the Standard of Fair and Equitable Treatment (FET standard) pursuant to Article 10(1) ECT.[11]

The FET standard has become the most popular and most controversial standard of protection in investment treaties due to its broad and vague language.[12] Statistics indicate that most investor claims are won on the ba-

---

Settlement Cases at <https://energycharter.org/what-we-do/dispute-settlement/all-investment-dispute-settlement-cases/> (accessed 3 May 2021).

7 Happ, 'The Energy Charter Treaty' in Bungenberg and others (eds), *International Investment Law: A Handbook* (Nomos 2015), p. 241.

8 Benson, Yim and Orlowski, 'The Energy Charter Treaty' in Rowley, Bishop and Kaiser (eds), *The Guide to Energy Arbitrations* (Second Edition, Law Business Research Ltd 2017), p. 30.

9 Patrizia and others, 'Investment Disputes Involving the Renewable Energy Industry Under the Energy Charter Treaty' in Rowley, Bishop and Kaiser (eds), *The Guide to Energy Arbitrations* (Second Edition, Law Business Research Ltd 2017), p. 48-52; Benson, Yim and Orlowski, *The Energy Charter Treaty*, p. 45.

10 Gallagher, 'ECT and Renewable Energy Disputes' in Scherer and Amirfar (eds), *International Arbitration in the Energy Sector* (OUP 2018), para. 11.02.

11 Patrizia and others, *Investment Disputes Involving the Renewable Energy Industry Under the Energy Charter Treaty*, p. 52-57.

12 Kläger, "Fair and Equitable Treatment' and Sustainable Development' in Cordonier Segger, Gehring and Newcombe (eds), *Sustainable Development in World Investment Law* (Global Trade Law Series vol. 30, Kluwer Law International 2010), p. 241.

sis of a breach of the FET standard.[13] Despite the efforts of international investment law scholars and practitioners, the scope of the protection under FET provisions remains a standard that is "none too clear and precise".[14] In further definition efforts, the notion of legitimate expectation was developed by arbitral jurisprudence as a key aspect of the FET standard. The notion migrated from domestic laws and other fields of international law into investment law in the early 2000s and has gained further significance ever since.[15] Today, the existence of the notion of legitimate expectations in international investment law is accepted by arbitral jurisprudence and also explicitly incorporated in new generations of IIAs concluded by the EU.[16]

At its core, the notion of legitimate expectations covers the question of whether and to what extent public statements or administrative decisions can be relied on by investors.[17] Further, the notion includes the principle of sustainable development, which requires states to strike a balance between the interests of the investors in a stable and predictable legal

---

13 UNCTAD, 'World Investment Report 2016', UNCTAD Series on Issues in International Investment Agreements II (United Nations 2016), p. 107; UNCTAD, 'World Investment Report 2019', p. 104. Recent developments demonstrate that this still holds true today, *see* Ch. 3.

14 Enron Corporation and Ponderosa Assets, L.P. v. The Argentine Republic, Award, 22 May 2007 ICSID Case No. ARB/01/3, para. 256.

15 Maynard, 'Legitimate Expectations and the Interpretation of the 'Legal Stability Obligation'' (2016) 1(1) Eur Invest Law Arbitr Rev 99, p. 101; Potestà, 'Legitimate Expectations in Investment Treaty Law: Understanding the Roots and the Limits of a Controversial Concept' (2013) 28(1) ICSID Review 88, p. 88. Most notable in the development of the notion of legitimate expectations are the decisions in Metalclad Corporation v. The United Mexican States, Award, 30 August 2000 ICSID Case No. ARB(AF)/97/1, Técnicas Medioambientales Tecmed, S.A. v. The United Mexican States, Award, 29 May 2003 ICSID Case No. ARB (AF)/00/2, Waste Management, Inc. v. United Mexican States, Award, 30 April 2004 ICSID Case No. ARB(AF)/00/3, MTD Equity Sdn. Bhd. and MTD Chile S.A. v. Republic of Chile, Award, 25 May 2004 ICSID Case No. ARB/01/7, Occidental Exploration and Production Company v. The Republic of Ecuador Final, Award, 1 July 2004 LCIA Case No. UN3467.

16 *See* Hobe, *The Development of the Law of Aliens and Emergence of General Principles of Protection under International Law*, p. 18. *For example* Article 8.10(4) of the Comprehensive and Economic Trade Agreement (CETA) (2016); 2.5(4) EU-Vietnam Investment Protection Agreement (IPA) (2019); 2.4(3) EU-Singapore IPA (2018).

17 ibid, p. 18.

framework and the right of the host state to regulate.[18] However, tribunals have rarely attempted to delve deeper into the systematics of the legitimate expectations, outside the scope of their specific cases, to provide for a cohesive body of case law on the concept.[19] This partial lack of a common legal systematic raises issues concerning the legitimacy of arbitral jurisprudence beyond simple legal uncertainty. Scholars such as *Kläger* claim that the FET standard may have become a "black box" that might contain unwanted surprises for host states.[20] The lack of a general international court or committee, acting as an appellate authority in investment law, only serves to add to the legal uncertainty.[21]

A number of tribunals acknowledged that "a recognized goal of international investment law is to establish a predictable, stable legal framework for investments".[22] Tribunals giving due regard to previous decisions on similar issues is a decisive factor for the establishment of such a predictable framework in international investment law.[23] However, a role equal to a legislative body in international law has been rejected on the grounds that arbitral tribunals owe primary allegiance to the parties and not to the international community.[24] Nonetheless, a lack of consistency and pre-

18 Hobe, *The Development of the Law of Aliens and Emergence of General Principles of Protection under International Law*, p. 19; Kläger, *'Fair and Equitable Treatment' in International Investment Law* (CUP 2011), p. 195; Potestà, 'Legitimate Expectations in Investment Treaty Law: Understanding the Roots and the Limits of a Controversial Concept', p. 113.

19 Potestà, 'Legitimate Expectations in Investment Treaty Law: Understanding the Roots and the Limits of a Controversial Concept', p. 89. With regard to the earliest cases that applied the notion of legitimate expectations *see* Snodgrass, 'Protecting Investors' Legitimate Expectations - Recognizing and Delimiting a General Principle' (2006) 21(1) ICSID Review 1, p. 17.

20 Kläger, *'Fair and Equitable Treatment' and Sustainable Development*, p. 242.

21 Cheng, 'Precedent and Control in Investment Treaty Arbitration' (2007) 30(4) Fordham International Law Journal 1014, p. 1030.

22 Suez, Sociedad General de Aguas de Barcelona, S.A. and Vivendi Universal, S.A. v. The Argentine RepublicRepublic, Decision on Liability, 30 July 2010 ICSID Case No. ARB/03/19, para. 189. *Also agreeing*: Saipem S.p.A. v. The People's Republic of Bangladesh, Award, 30 June 2009 ICSID Case No. ARB/05/07, para. 90.

23 Suez, Sociedad General de Aguas de Barcelona, S.A. and Vivendi Universal, S.A. v. The Argentine RepublicRepublic, Decision on Liability, 30 July 2010 ICSID Case No. ARB/03/19, para. 189; Saipem S.p.A. v. The People's Republic of Bangladesh, Award, 30 June 2009 ICSID Case No. ARB/05/07, para. 90.

24 Romak S.A. (Switzerland) v . The Republic of Uzbekistan, Award, 26 November 2009 PCA Case No. AA280, para. 171. *See also* Part I 2) of the Introduction.

dictability negatively influences both the actual legitimacy and the public's perceptions of the legitimacy of investment treaty arbitral awards.[25]

Apart from the negative influence of legal uncertainty on the legitimacy of ISDS, economic issues arise as well from diverging arbitral decisions. Consistency is needed in order for investors to evaluate the risk associated with an investment.[26] States, on the other side, need to adjust their regulatory amendments to the requirements of international obligations.[27] Moreover, legal certainty has a strong influence on the transition from fossil fuels to renewable energy sources. Foreign direct investment (FDI) is of immense importance for the development of the renewable energy sector.[28] This transition again is not only important for economic growth, but essential to minimise the human-made impact on global climate change.

These legal and economic issues pose major hindrances to FDI and international investment protection.[29] The only practical approach available to counter this legal uncertainty is to analyse and compare the decisions of courts and investment tribunals, with regard to the FET standard and their approach to the issue of the legitimate expectations of an investor. It needs to be explored whether arbitral jurisprudence establishes some degree of cohesiveness and consistency in its interpretation and application of the notion of legitimate expectations. The cases in the aftermath of the Argentinian financial crisis have contributed greatly to the development of the FET standard.[30] Although not all decisions were consistent, tribunals

---

25 Franck, 'The Legitimacy Crisis in Investment Treaty Arbitration: Privatizing Publlic International Law through Inconsistent Decisions' (2005) 73 Fordham Law Review 1521, p. 1558; Cheng, 'Precedent and Control in Investment Treaty Arbitration', p. 1015; Norton, 'The Role of Precedent in the Development of International Investment Law' (2018) 33(1) ICSID Review 280, p. 290.

26 Gallagher, *ECT and Renewable Energy Disputes*, para. 11.54.

27 Ibid, para. 11.54.

28 *See* "Impact of the Regulatory Changes", Part III of the Introduction.

29 Sussman, 'The Energy Charter Treaty's Investor Protection Provisions: Potential to Foster Solutions to Global Warming and Promote Sustainable Development' in Cordonier Segger, Gehring and Newcombe (eds), *Sustainable Development in World Investment Law* (Global Trade Law Series vol. 30, Kluwer Law International 2010), p. 516.

30 Decisive landmark decision have been, inter alia, BG Group Plc. v. The Argentine Republic, Award, 24 December 2007 UNCITRAL; El Paso Energy International Company v. The Argentine Republic, Award, 31 October 2011 ICSID Case No. ARB/03/15; CMS Gas Transmission Company v. The Argentine Republic, Award, 21 May 2005 ICSID Case No. ARB/01/8; Sempra Energy International v. The Argentine Republic, Award, 28 September 2007 ICSID Case No. ARB/02/16; Siemens A.G. v. The Argentine Republic, Award, 17 January 2007 ICSID Case

assessing the scope of the FET standard regularly refer to the jurisprudence that has been developed in these cases.[31] The Argentinian cases also served as a basis for the advancement of the FET standard and the notion of legitimate expectations in legal academia.[32] The plethora of cases in the renewable energy sector are deemed to be an important ingredient towards a more consistent case law and offers a unique opportunity for an overarching legal analysis and comparison of decisions based on the FET standard.[33] Not only are the claims based on the same legal grounds—including the violation of the FET standard pursuant to Article 10(1) ECT —but also deal with the same or at least similar acts attributable to the host states.[34]

Hence, the current circumstances form a solid basis for an extensive legal comparison of reoccurring themes and abstract holdings by investment tribunals. In turn, this allows for the distillation of generally valid requirements to diminish the legal uncertainty regarding the protection of the FET standard under the ECT and other IIAs.

In summary, the aim of this research is to find common requirements pursuant to which legitimate expectations can be formed and subsequently violated. Thus, the leading research question must be: Is there a system

---

No. ARB/02/8; Total S.A. v. The Argentine Republic, Award, 27 November 2013 ICSID Case No. ARB/04/01; LG&E Energy Corp. LG&E Capital Corp. and LG&E International, Inc. v. The Argentine Republic, Decision on Liability, 3 October 2006 ICSID Case No. ARB/02/1; Mobil Exploration and Development Inc. v. The Argentine Republic, Decision on Jurisdiction and Liability, 10 April 2013ICSID Case No. ARB/04/16; National Grid P.L.C. v. The Argentine Republic, Award, 3 November 2008 UNCITRAL; Azurix Corp. v. The Argentine Republic, Award, 14 July 2006 ICSID Case No. ARB/01/12; Abaclat and Others v. The Argentine RepublicRepublic, Decision on Jurisdiction and Admissibility, 4 August 2011 ICSID Case No. ARB/07/5.

31 *See for example* Charanne and Construction Investments v. Kingdom of Spain, Award, 21 January 2016 SCC Case No. V 062/2012, para. 501, 502; Blusun S.A. Jean-Pierre Lecorcier and Michael Stein v. Italian Republic, Award, 27 December 2016 ICSID Case No. ARB/14/3, para. 363; Jürgen Wirtgen, Stefan Wirtgen, Gisela Wirtgen and JSW Solar (zwei) GmbH & Co. KG v. Czech Republic, Award, 11 October 2017 PCA Case No. 2014-03, para. 409.

32 *See* for example Yannaca-Small, 'Fair and Equitable Treatment Standard: Recent Developments' in August Reinisch (ed), *Standards of Investment Protection* (OUP 2008); Tudor, *The Fair and Equitable Treatment Standard in the International Law of Foreign Investment* (OUP 2008); Kläger, *'Fair and Equitable Treatment' in International Investment Law*; Potestà, 'Legitimate Expectations in Investment Treaty Law: Understanding the Roots and the Limits of a Controversial Concept'.

33 Hobér, *Overview of Energy Charter Treaty Cases*, para. 8.89.

34 Gallagher, *ECT and Renewable Energy Disputes*, para. 11.29.

of soft precedent in international investment law regarding the breach of the FET standard and the violation of legitimate expectations under the ECT, and can requirements be deduced from such system? If so, does such *jurisprudence constante* raise concerns regarding its interference with state sovereignty and the states' right to regulate?

I. Premises and Methodology of the Research

In order to further define the term of legitimate expectations, the following Sections of this Chapter will give an overview of the main issues in connection with the components of the legitimate expectations, the development, and impacts of the regulatory changes in the renewable energy sector. Subsequent to this, the concepts of the FET standard and the legitimate expectations will be dealt with in the abstract.[35] In doing so, the components and the purpose of the legal concept of the legitimate expectations will be explored and particular aspects, such as the commitment on the side of the state and the due diligence requirement for the investor, will be discussed.[36] Additionally, the states' right to regulate and the competing interests of the investors, as well as the application of the principle of proportionality in the balancing act within the assessment of the legitimacy of the expectations, will be reviewed.[37] The main part of the analysis includes an in-depth review of the background of the renewable energy cases and the decisions of the respective tribunals.[38] This Section investigates the events triggering the disputes and provoking the states' behaviour as well as providing a thorough analysis of the legal framework and its alteration for the three main respondent states Spain, Italy, and the Czech Republic. Such an in-depth analysis is crucial to understand which acts of the states the tribunals deemed to create legitimate expectations and which acts were deemed to violate those expectations.

The decisions will be categorized, in order to find case groups that allow drawing conclusions for specific requirements with respect to the conduct of the host state, as well as the due diligence of the investor. Said case groups will then be compared, with a specific examination of any possible contradictions within the decisions and whether they form a solid

35 Ch. 1 and 2.
36 Ch. 2 I-III.
37 Ch. 2 IV.
38 Ch. 3.

system of soft precedent, on which future investors and states may rely.[39] Therefore the aim is not to second-guess the tribunals' legal appreciation of the facts of the given case, but to identify a common understanding of the notion of legitimate expectations and its individual requirements.

The corresponding results will then be compared to previous arbitral decisions regarding the FET standard. The aim of this exercise is to assess whether recent decisions follow an older line of precedent or if there are any new trends discernible, regarding the FET standard under the ECT and other investment treaties. Lastly, the conclusive evidence will be summarised to formulate requirements that an investor has to demonstrate in order to prove a violation of the FET standard.[40] Before commencing the analysis, however, the basic premises and the methodology of the research, in regard to the validity of awards as the legal source, must first be laid out.

1) Arbitral Awards as a Legal Source

The "classic" sources in international law, that were combined in Article 38 of the Statute of the International Court of Justice (ICJ), are: Treaty, custom, general principles of law, judicial decisions, and teachings of the most highly qualified publicists.[41] However, judicial decisions and the teachings of the most highly qualified publicists of the various nations only act as a subsidiary means for the determination of rules of law.[42] Al-

39 Ch. 4.

40 Ch. 5.

41 Article 38(1) ICJ Statute: "The Court, whose function is to decide in accordance with international law such disputes as are submitted to it, shall apply: a) international conventions, whether general or particular, establishing rules expressly recognized by the contesting states; b) international custom, as evidence of a general practice accepted as law; c) the general principles of law recognized by civilized nations; d) subject to the provisions of Article 59, judicial decisions and the teachings of the most highly qualified publicists of the various nations, as subsidiary means for the determination of rules of law." *See also* Hugh W A Thirlway, *The Sources of International Law* (Second Edition, 2019).

42 Cheng, 'Precedent and Control in Investment Treaty Arbitration', p. 1027; Jose G Muñoz, 'El precedente en el derecho internacional de inversiones: el valor argumentativo de decisiones arbitrales previas' (2018) 22(22) IU, p. 90.

though arbitral awards are no judicial decisions *stricto sensu*, it is acknowledged that they may also qualify as a subsidiary means of interpretation.[43]

Arbitral tribunals have the task of interpreting standards of international law.[44] They consistently derive detailed rules from these rather broad or even vague norms.[45] This gap shows that arbitral tribunals seem to have a *de facto* broad margin of discretion when interpreting international investment law. Despite such a broad margin of discretion and having only subsidiary status as means of interpretation, arbitral decisions and the rules promulgated by the tribunals are often taken as guidelines.[46]

Thus, the first question for every research in international investment law is "what value an arbitral award bears as a legal source?". The question stems from the major flaw that arbitral awards are decisions of a privately constituted tribunal, convened to solve a private conflict, whose decisions only have *inter partes* effect.[47] Thus, two main problems can be identified: The availability and the legal value of arbitral awards as a source of law.[48]

The lack of available awards is concerning, as one is only afforded a fragmented picture of the arbitration practice, thus hindering an exhaustive analysis of the empirical evidence. In general, awards are confidential due to the private nature of the proceedings. The "flaw" of confidentiality has, however, gradually been remedied over the past decade. For example, the International Centre for Settlement of Investment Disputes (ICSID) publishes all awards, though only with the consent of the parties. In the case of denial of consent by both parties, it is either common practice that

---

43 Schill, 'Sources of International Investment Law: Multilateralization, Arbitral Precedent, Comparativism, Soft Law' in Besson and d'Aspremont (eds), *The Oxford Handbook of the Sources of International Law* (OUP 2018), p. 1103.

44 Viñuales, 'Sources of International Investment Law: Conceptual Foundations of Unruly Practices' in Besson and d'Aspremont (eds), *The Oxford Handbook of the Sources of International Law* (OUP 2018), p. 1080, 1086; Norton, 'The Role of Precedent in the Development of International Investment Law', p. 283, 290.

45 Viñuales, *Sources of International Investment Law: Conceptual Foundations of Unruly Practices*, p. 1080, 1086; Norton, 'The Role of Precedent in the Development of International Investment Law', p. 283, 290.

46 *For example* the so called „Salini Criteria" named after the decision of Salini Costruttori S.p.A. and Italstrade S.p.A. v. Kingdom of Morocco Decision on Jurisdiction, 23 June 2001 Case No. ARB/00/4 in which they were first applied in.

47 Schill, 'Sources of International Investment Law: Multilateralization, Arbitral Precedent, Comparativism, Soft Law' in Besson and d'Aspremont (eds), *The Oxford Handbook of the Sources of International Law* (OUP 2018), p. 1104.

48 Hobér and Dahlquist Cullborg, *Investment Treaty Arbitration: Problems and Exercises* (Edward Elgar Publishing 2018), p. 4.

one of the parties releases the award for publication in a journal[49] or the Centre publishes excerpts of the tribunal's legal reasoning promptly after an award has been rendered[50]. In general, however, awards can only be obtained without the parties' consent, if the respective institute publishes the awards following a policy of transparency, one of the parties leaks theaward, or they become subject to a challenge before a national court, in which that court has to give the public access to the matter of the proceedings.[51] Therefore, there is a concern regarding the unknown number of unpublished and unregistered *ad-hoc* arbitration decisions. Even so, if the parties chose to apply the United Nations Commission on International Trade Law (UNCITRAL) arbitration rules, the UNCITRAL Rules on Transparency also find application in investor-state disputes based on IIAs concluded on or after 1 April 2014, unless the parties to the treaty have agreed otherwise.[52] Furthermore, the United Nations Convention on Transparency in Treaty-based Investor-State Arbitration (Mauritius Convention) aims to extend the application of the UNCITRAL Rules on Transparency to any ISDS arbitration, whether or not initiated under the UNCITRAL Arbitration Rules.[53] The Mauritius Convention has, however, not yet reached the broad support among the international community to have a significant impact on transparency in ISDS.[54] Notwithstanding all this, the availability of awards does not constitute as severe an issue for academic research, in the field of investment law, as anticipated. On the one hand, the trend towards the publication of awards is evident when taking into consideration that the majority of all known recent decisions in the renewable energy sector have been published. On the other hand,

49 ICSID Secretariat, 'Possible Improvements of the Framework for ICSID Arbitrations' (2004), para. 11 <https://icsid.worldbank.org/sites/default/files/Possible%20Improvements%20of%20the%20Framework%20of%20ICSID%20Arbitration.pdf> (accessed 3 May 2021).

50 Article 48(5) of the ICSID Convention (1966); Article 48(4) of the ICSID Arbitration Rules (2006).

51 Hobér, *Investment Treaty Arbitration*, p. 4.

52 Article 1(4) UNCITRAL Arbitration Rules (2013); Article 1(1) UNCITRAL Rules on Transparency (2013).

53 Article 2 of United Nations Convention on Transparency in Treaty-based Investor-State Arbitration (Mauritius Convention) (2014).

54 United Nations Convention on Transparency in Treaty-based Investor-State Arbitration of 10 December 2014 has currently 23 signatory states. In only 6 of these states, the Convention was ratified and entered into force. *See* <https://uncitral.un.org/en/texts/arbitration/conventions/transparency/status> (accessed 3 May 2021).

even if they remained confidential, a number of arbitration institutions allow limited access to otherwise confidential awards for researchers.[55]

The second issue regarding the value of arbitral awards, as a source of legal authority, derives from a possible lack of legitimacy and binding precedent in international investment law. To start with, arbitral tribunals draw their legitimacy exclusively from the consent of the parties. Thus, one could argue that the value of an award as a legal source "only" amounts to that of scholarly writing. This is further perpetuated by the fact that there is no binding precedent in investment law.[56] Consequently, the interpretation of international law by an arbitral tribunal and its considerations cannot be taken for granted. Furthermore, the insufficient provision of reasoning within earlier awards is an additional concern, which hinders the traceability of a tribunal's deliberations.[57] However, tribunals have shifted to a more explanatory approach recently, which improves the analysis of the legal reasoning underlying the tribunal's decisions.[58] In particular, the recent decisions under the ECT have become increasingly sophisticated, which aids in the legal analysis of the awards.

2) Precedent in International Investment Law

Coherent case law strengthens the predictability of arbitral decisions and enhances their legal authority and persuasiveness.[59] Arbitral awards, however, take effect only *inter partes* and thus cannot compel any subsequent

55 *For example* Appendix II Article 1(5) International Chamber of Commerce (ICC) Rules of Arbitration (2017).

56 This will be dealt with in Section 2 of this Chapter.

57 *For example*, the Tribunal in Nykomb Synergetics Technology Holding AB v. The Republic of Latvia, SCC, Award, 16 December 2003 SCC only issued an award with a length of only 45 pages and limited its reasoning on the breach of Article 10(1) ECT to one paragraph (p. 34) which was of little guidance on the interpretation of the ECT for future tribunals. *See thereto also* Gallagher, *ECT and Renewable Energy Disputes*, para. 11.17.

58 Potestà, 'Legitimate Expectations in Investment Treaty Law: Understanding the Roots and the Limits of a Controversial Concept', p. 121.

59 Cheng, 'Precedent and Control in Investment Treaty Arbitration', p. 1015; Commission, 'Precedent in Investment Treaty Arbitration' (2007) 24(2) Journal of International Arbitration 129, p. 134; Dolzer and Schreuer, *Principles of International Investment Law* (Second Edition, OUP 2012), p. 33.

tribunals to follow the same line of decision.[60] Therefore, there is no principle of stare decisis in investment law.[61] This notwithstanding, tribunals consistently reach out to the findings of other tribunals to substantiate their decision.[62] While not formally binding, the fact that both the tribunal itself and the counsel appearing before it often cite and rely on prior decisions, one may come to the conclusion that there is at least a system of "soft precedent" in investment treaty arbitration.[63] Such an approach stems from the rule of law itself, which demands that "like cases should be decided alike, unless a strong reason exists to distinguish the current case from previous ones".[64] Thus, it has been acknowledged that a tribunal must provide reasoned justification, if they are to depart from the established precedent in a certain area.[65] Beyond that, tribunals have be-

---

60 Commission, 'Precedent in Investment Treaty Arbitration', p. 134; Dolzer and Schreuer, *Principles of International Investment Law*, p. 33; Romak S.A. (Switzerland) v . The Republic of Uzbekistan, Award, 26 November 2009 PCA Case No. AA280, para. 171.

61 Norton, 'The Role of Precedent in the Development of International Investment Law', p. 280; Cheng, 'Precedent and Control in Investment Treaty Arbitration', p. 1016; Kyla Tienhaara and Christian Downie, 'Risky Business? The Energy Charter Treaty, Renewable Energy, and Investor-State Disputes' (2018) 24(3) Global Governance 451, p. 459; AES Corporation v. The Argentine RepublicRepublic, Decision on Jurisdiction, 26 April 2005 ICSID Case No ARB/02/17, para. 23(d).

62 Norton, 'The Role of Precedent in the Development of International Investment Law', p. 285; Muñoz, 'El precedente en el derecho internacional de inversiones: el valor argumentativo de decisiones arbitrales previas', p. 90, characterising the interaction between arbitral tribunals through awards as "judicial dialogue".

63 Commission, 'Precedent in Investment Treaty Arbitration' (2007) 24(2) Journal of International Arbitration 129, p. 141; Norton, 'The Role of Precedent in the Development of International Investment Law', p. 280; McLachlan, Shore and Weiniger, *International Investment Arbitration: Substantive principles* (Oxford International Arbitration Series, Second Edition, OUP 2017), p. 70–76.

64 Suez, Sociedad General de Aguas de Barcelona, S.A. and Vivendi Universal, S.A. v. The Argentine RepublicRepublic, Decision on Liability, 30 July 2010 ICSID Case No. ARB/03/19, para. 189; AWG Group Ltd. v. The Argentine Republic, Decision on Liability, 30 June 2010 ICSID Case No. ARB/03/19, para. 189; Daimler Financial Services AG v Argentine Republic, Award, 22 August 2012 ICSID Case No. ARB/05/1, para. 52; Burlington Resources Inv. v. Republic of Ecuador Decision on Jurisdiction, 2 June 2010 ICSID Case No. ARB/08/5, para. 100. *See also* Schill, *Sources of International Investment Law: Multilateralization, Arbitral Precedent, Comparativism, Soft Law*, p. 1104, 1105.

65 Saipem S.p.A. v. Bangladesh Decision on Jurisdiction and Recommendation on Provisional Measures, 21 March 2007 ICSID Case No. ARB/05/07, para. 67; International Thunderbird Gaming Corporation v. The United Mexican States

gun to develop investment law beyond the scope of mere interpretation.[66] Furthermore, it is noteworthy that oftentimes investment tribunals are constituted from the same tribunal members. In the recent renewable energy cases, there have been a number of arbitrators, who were appointed in two or more cases.[67] While those arbitrators do not always share identical views on all aspects of a given case, they at least have a broadly consistent understanding of the main structural features and substantive principles of international investment law, which offers a basis for consistent decisions and some degree of legal predictability, if not certainty.[68]

As demonstrated, a system of "soft precedent" is demanded by the rule of law, as a self-contained principle, and it is also important to maintain the trust in the established system of ISDS through arbitration. In the past, discrepancies and inconsistencies occasionally arose between decisions of different tribunals.[69] The prime examples of inconsistent decisions, which was quoted as "the ultimate fiasco in investment arbitration", are the cases of *Lauder v. Czech Republic* and *CME v. Czech Republic*, in which both the shareholder and a subsidiary initiated proceedings against the Czech Republic, on the basis of the same factual background.[70] A comparable

---

Separate Opinion of Thomas Wälde, 26 January 2006 UNCITRAL, para. 16; Burlington Resources Inv. v. Republic of Ecuador Decision on Jurisdiction, 2 June 2010 ICSID Case No. ARB/08/5, para. 100. *See also* Schill, *Sources of International Investment Law: Multilateralization, Arbitral Precedent, Comparativism, Soft Law*, p. 1104.

66 Schill, *Sources of International Investment Law: Multilateralization, Arbitral Precedent, Comparativism, Soft Law*, p. 1105; Muñoz, 'El precedente en el derecho internacional de inversiones: el valor argumentativo de decisiones arbitrales previas', p. 90.

67 To name just a few: Guido Santiago Tawil in *Charanne, Isolux, and STEAG v. Spain*; Claus von Wobeser in *Charanne* and *Isolux v. Spain*; Dupuy in *InfraRed* and *STEAG v. Spain*; Giorgio Sacerdoti in *Greentech* and *CEF Energia v. Italy* as well as *Portigon v. Spain*; Klaus Reichert in *CEF Energia* and *VC Holding II v. Italy*; Gary Born and Peter Tomka in *Wirtgen* and *Antaris* and Wirtgen *v. Czech Republic*. *See also* Gallagher, *ECT and Renewable Energy Disputes*, para. 11.25-11.28.

68 Schill, *Sources of International Investment Law: Multilateralization, Arbitral Precedent, Comparativism, Soft Law*, p. 1102; Norton, 'The Role of Precedent in the Development of International Investment Law', p. 300.

69 Hobér, *Overview of Energy Charter Treaty Cases*, para. 8.89; Cheng, 'Precedent and Control in Investment Treaty Arbitration', p. 1034.

70 CME Czech Republic B.V. v. The Czech Republic Final, Award, 14 March 2013, and Ronald S. Lauder v. The Czech Republic, Award, 3 September 2001 UNCITRAL. *See also* Levashova, *The Right of States to Regulate in International Investment Law: The Search for Balance Between Public Interest and Fair and Equitable Treatment* (Wolters Kluwer Law & Business 2019), p. 90, footnote 516.

risk did not materialise in *Blusun v. Italy*[71] and *Eskosol v. Italy*[72], in which *Blusun* was a majority shareholder of *Eskosol* and both tribunals reached a similar conclusion.[73] However, the risk of diverging decisions can still be found in the cases of *Antin v. Spain*[74] and *Portigon v. Spain*[75], in which Portigon financed, inter alia, the investments of Antin.

Therefore, it is of crucial importance to analyse whether investment arbitration has evolved into a coherent system of "soft precedent", in regard to the FET standard.

3) Method of Analysis

Overall, the reliance on non-binding precedent by subsequent tribunals illustrates how investment treaty tribunals move from mere institutions that settle individual investment disputes to makers of international investment law.[76] Despite their *de jure* limitation to the individual cases, arbitral decisions determine *de facto* how investment treaties are interpreted, and investment disputes decided. Hence, their practical impact on the jurisprudence in international investment law is far greater than their limited status as subsidiary means for the determination of rules of law accorded to them in Article 38(1)(d) ICJ Statute.[77]

Furthermore, notwithstanding the non-binding nature of awards, the legal arguments relied on by the tribunals bear substantive value on their

71 Blusun S.A. Jean-Pierre Lecorcier and Michael Stein v. Italian Republic, Award, 27 December 2016 ICSID Case No. ARB/14/3.

72 Eskosol S.p.A. in liquidazione v. Italian Republic, Award, 4 September 2020 ICSID Case No. ARB/15/50.

73 *See* Ch. 3 III 2) b) (1) (2).

74 Antin Infrastructure Services Luxembourg S.à.r.l. and Antin Energia Termosolar B.V. v. Kingdom of Spain, Award, 15 June 2018 ICSID Case No. ARB/13/31.

75 Portigon AG v. Kingdom of Spain Pending Proceeding ICSID Case No. ARB/17/15.

76 Schill, *Sources of International Investment Law: Multilateralization, Arbitral Precedent, Comparativism, Soft Law*, p. 1106; Norton, 'The Role of Precedent in the Development of International Investment Law', p. 300.

77 Schill, *Sources of International Investment Law: Multilateralization, Arbitral Precedent, Comparativism, Soft Law*, p. 1106; Commission, 'Precedent in Investment Treaty Arbitration', p. 130; Norton, 'The Role of Precedent in the Development of International Investment Law', p. 298-301.

own and can be valid beyond the scope of the parties' dispute.[78] Thus, the legal arguments of the respective tribunals will be reviewed and analysed in the abstract. Emphasis will be put on the question of whether the legal argument provided by tribunals is comprehensible or whether it must be criticized. Arbitral decisions must, therefore, be taken with a "grain of salt". A new rule established by a tribunal is not true merely because an arbitral tribunal has reasoned so. Rather, the reasoning itself must be reviewed and evaluated, and it must be taken into account whether subsequent tribunals accepted this line of argument.[79]Depending on the evaluation of the reasoning and the acceptance in international investment law practice, awards must be given different weight.[80] If a rule is set out by an arbitral tribunal and followed by subsequent tribunals, it transforms the rule from the decision of a private tribunal to the opinion of multiple experts in international law within the meaning of Article 38(1)(d) ICJ Statute and thus increases the integrity of the ruling.[81]

Furthermore, arbitral decisions only paint a fragmented picture, as their reasoning is fact-specific. Most tribunals limit their investigation to those single elements of the principle in question, which are useful to the resolution of a given dispute.[82] Accordingly, the Tribunal in *CEF v. Italy* concurred "principles have to be adapted to the specificity of each case and that in this field previous awards and decisions may properly be looked at as useful (re-) statements of the law, but do not represent binding precedents".[83] Thus, it is necessary to find first distinguishing different fact-specific decisions of the multitude of tribunals, and combine their

78 Prior decisions have been characterised as "helpful" (Azurix Corp. v. The Argentine Republic, Award, 14 July 2006 ICSID Case No. ARB/01/12, para. 391), "instructive" (Liberian Eastern Timber Corporation v Republic of Liberia, Award, 31 March 1986 ICSID Case No ARB/83/2, para. 16.11), and "persuasive" (Metalclad Corporation v. The United Mexican States, Award, 30 August 2000 ICSID Case No. ARB(AF)/97/1, para. 108).

79 Cheng, 'Precedent and Control in Investment Treaty Arbitration', para. 1030; also suggesting a quantitative and qualitative citation analysis of investment treaty awards, decisions, and orders *see* Commission, 'Precedent in Investment Treaty Arbitration', p. 143, 144.

80 Hobér, *Investment Treaty Arbitration*, p. 5; Gazzini, *Interpretation of International Investment Treaties* (Hart Publishing 2016), p. 296, 297.

81 Norton, 'The Role of Precedent in the Development of International Investment Law', p. 292, 293.

82 Palombino, *Fair and Equitable Treatment and the Fabric of General Principles* (T.M.C. Asser Press 2018), p. 13, 14.

83 CEF Energia B.V. v. Italian Republic, Award, 16 January 2019 SCC Arbitration No. 2015/158, para. 185.

differing reasonings.[84] This, in turn, allows for a view of the whole picture, eliminating contradictory rulings.[85]

Henceforth, the approach used in this evaluation will be (1) the schematic portrayal of the underlying legal concepts in the abstract, based on the prior case law, (2) an in-depth review of the so far concluded cases in the renewable energy sector, and (3) an overarching comparison of the tribunals' conclusions with earlier decisions, both under and outside the ECT, in order to find case groups. Finding case groups may make it possible to identify a "red line", common thread, or repetitive schemes in the holdings of the different tribunals, which allow drawing conclusions for the international investment jurisprudence.[86]

II. Open Questions in the Development of the Notion of Legitimate Expectations

The concept of legitimate expectations can be found in various systems of international law.[87] The content of the notion is, however, undefined and interpreted differently under each system.[88] Legitimate expectations under the FET standard are influenced by the conduct of the host state and of the investor respectively. Host states must, on the one hand, have acted in a manner that invoked certain expectations in investors.[89] Investors, on

84 Dolzer, 'Fair and Equitable Treatment: Today's Contours' (2014) 12(1) Santa Clara Journal of International Law 7, p. 15, 16; Valenti, 'The Protection of General Interests of Host States in the Application of the Fair and Equitable Treatment Standard' in Giorgio Sacerdoti and others (eds), *General Interests of Host States in International Investment Law* (CUP 2014), p. 33.

85 Dolzer, 'Fair and Equitable Treatment: Today's Contours', p. 15, 16; Valenti, *The Protection of General Interests of Host States in the Application of the Fair and Equitable Treatment Standard*, p. 33.

86 The Standard of Fair and Equitable Treatment has been found one of the few examples in international arbitration in which there can be found a clear progression among the decisions of investment tribunals, G. Kaufmann-Kohler, 'Arbitral Precedent: Dream, Necessity or Excuse?' (2007) 23(3) Arbitration International 357, p. 371-373.

87 *For example* in EU law and under the European Charter of Human Rights (ECHR), *see* Ch. 1 II.

88 Kläger, 'Fair and Equitable Treatment A Look at the Theoretical Underpinnings of Legitimacy and Fairness' (2010) 11(3) The Journal of World Investment & Trade 435, p. 441.

89 Potestà, 'Legitimate Expectations in Investment Treaty Law: Understanding the Roots and the Limits of a Controversial Concept', p. 113; Mairal, 'Legitimate

the other hand, cannot rely blindly on the alleged commitments by the host states. Rather, they must gather all relevant information on the investment environment in the host state, in order to make an informed and reasonable investment decision.[90] While this may seem obvious from the outset, three main issues can be identified with the creation of legitimate expectations and their violation, depending on the circumstances of the case.

1) What are the Requirements for a Commitment by the State?

It is undisputed that an investor can rely legitimately on a contractual guarantee or a promise of the host state.[91] Such undertakings and representations by state authorities form the strongest basis for legitimate expectations.[92] However, investors and states rarely conclude investment contracts guaranteeing certain rights.[93] More often, investors allege they received guarantees from the state, by undergoing a registration process with an administrative authority or by unilateral declarations. Such unilateral declarations may include assurances by high ranking state authorities or simple advertisements. However, legitimate expectations may, under certain circumstances, also be based on more general conduct on the side

---

Expectations and Informal Administrative Representations' in Schill (ed), *International Investment Law and Comparative Public Law* (OUP 2010), p. 439; Graham Mayeda, 'Playing Fair: The Meaning of Fair and Equitable Treatment in Bilateral Investment Treaties' (2007) 41(2) Journal of World Trade Law, Economics, Public Policy 273, p. 276.

90 Palombino, *Fair and Equitable Treatment and the Fabric of General Principles*, p. 91; Viñuales, 'Investor Diligence in Investment Arbitration: Sources and Arguments' (2017) 32(2) ICSID Review - Foreign Investment Law Journal 346, p. 362; Levashova, *The Right of States to Regulate in International Investment Law*, p. 116.

91 Potestà, 'Legitimate Expectations in Investment Treaty Law: Understanding the Roots and the Limits of a Controversial Concept', p. 100, 101; Palombino, *Fair and Equitable Treatment and the Fabric of General Principles*, p. 91; Urbaser SA and Consorcio de Aguas Bilbao Bizkaia, Bilbao Biskaia Ur Partzuergoa v The Argentine Republic, Award, 8 December 2016 ICSID Case No ARB/07/26, para. 627.

92 Dolzer and Schreuer, *Principles of International Investment Law*, p. 145; Potestà, 'Legitimate Expectations in Investment Treaty Law: Understanding the Roots and the Limits of a Controversial Concept', p. 100, 101.

93 Investment contracts have often been proven inadequate when dealing with sovereign states, *see* Simões, 'When Green Incentives Go Pale: Investment Arbitration and Renewable Energy Policymaking' (2017) 45(2) The Denver journal of international law and policy 251, p. 254.

of the state.[94]State officials may announce a particular policy, relevant for investors, or make public declarations that clarify the object and purpose of an investor-friendly legal framework.[95] Naturally, investors that observe the host states conduct will rely on such general representations in their investment decision, although these representations are not directed exclusively at a given individual investor. Especially the latter type of conduct may induce certain expectations among investors, in spite of the fact that host states may not have intended to legally bind themselves under international investment law.[96] This raises the question of what conduct of the state can be deemed sufficient to constitute a commitment on which investors may legitimately base their expectations.

2) Can the Legal Framework Create Legitimate Expectations?

In the absence of or in addition to representations by state authorities, investors will also be inclined to vest their reliance in the provisions of the law governing the investment.[97] The legal framework is a special case of general representations, as it is basically addressed to all persons within its scope, and not to individual investors. Although the regulatory framework is a major point of consideration for investors conducting an investment, it is disputed whether laws and regulations on their own can produce legitimate expectations.[98] Among other things, this is contested on the basis of the fact that the addressees of legislative representation are an unknown number of potential investors and not a single entity.[99] It, therefore, lacks the character of a "specific commitment" on which investors may base

94 Dolzer and Schreuer, *Principles of International Investment Law*, p. 115.

95 Palombino, *Fair and Equitable Treatment and the Fabric of General Principles*, p. 97.

96 Mairal, *Legitimate Expectations and Informal Administrative Representations*, p. 414.

97 Simões, 'When Green Incentives Go Pale: Investment Arbitration and Renewable Energy Policymaking', p. 253; Palombino, *Fair and Equitable Treatment and the Fabric of General Principles*, p. 110; Tienhaara and Downie, 'Risky Business? The Energy Charter Treaty, Renewable Energy, and Investor-State Disputes', p. 458.

98 *See* in detail Ch. 2 III 2) e) and Ch. 4 I 2) b).

99 Snodgrass, 'Protecting Investors' Legitimate Expectations - Recognizing and Delimiting a General Principle', p. 34.

their expectations.[100] Thus the question to be answered in regard to the issue is, whether there is support, based on the practice of investment law, whereby the legal framework itself can create legitimate expectations.

3) How much Due Diligence Must an Investor Apply?

The investors' due diligence is a key consideration in assessing the reasonableness or legitimacy of investors' expectations.[101] As already addressed, the legal framework and the conduct of the host state form the basis for the investors' investment decisions. These decision to invest must be reasonable and follow the ideal of an experienced business person.[102] Hence, the investors are obligated to take action and conduct research before investing in a foreign economy and may not blindly rely on representations by the host state.[103] This research is commonly known as due diligence. The degree of the investors' due diligence can play a role at different stages of investment proceedings: Jurisdiction, admissibility, merits, and quantum.[104] While due diligence is not an entirely new concept, it is only recently that tribunals have tried to carve out the requirements for the application of a proper due diligence analysis.[105] The level of due diligence required strongly correlates with the clarity or the unambiguousness (or the lack thereof) of the host state's acts and cannot be analysed in isolation.[106] Thus, the question is which factors need to be taken into account, to assess how much due diligence an investor in the energy sector needs to

---

100 CEF Energia B.V. v. Italian Republic, Award, 16 January 2019 SCC Arbitration No. 2015/158, para. 222; Belenergia S.A. v. Italian Republic, Award, 6 August 2019 ICSID Case No. ARB/15/40, para. 580.

101 Viñuales, 'Investor Diligence in Investment Arbitration: Sources and Arguments', p. 362.

102 International Thunderbird Gaming Corporation v. The United Mexican States Separate Opinion of Thomas Wälde, 26 January 2006 UNCITRAL, para. 47; Joseph Charles Lemire v. Ukraine Decision on Liability, 14 January 2010 ICSID Case No. ARB/06/18, para. 285; Alasdair Ross Anderson et al v. Republic of Costa Rica, Award, 19 May 2010 ICSID Case No. ARB(AF)/07/3, para. 58. *See also* OECD, *Guidelines for Multinational Enterprises, 2011 Edition* (OECD 2011), p. 58.

103 Levashova, *The Right of States to Regulate in International Investment Law*, p. 166.

104 Viñuales, 'Investor Diligence in Investment Arbitration: Sources and Arguments', p. 355.

105 ibid, p. 347.

106 Levashova, *The Right of States to Regulate in International Investment Law*, p. 167.

conduct, in order to have legitimate expectations and thus be within the ambit of the FET standard under Article 10(1) ECT.

III. The Impact of Regulatory Measures on the Renewable Energy Sector

The disputes in the renewable energy sector and their outcome are of immense relevance not only for the investors, but also on a political and environmental scale. The sustainable development of the renewable energy sector is important, as it allows a transition from fossil fuels, as the world's primary source of energy, to renewable energy sources, which in turn could help halt the climate change crisis.

The adoption of the Kyoto Protocol in 1997 by 191 states and the EU constituted the first step towards a more sustainable energy sector and triggered the events, which eventually initiated the events disputed in the renewable energy cases. The Kyoto Protocol is an international agreement linked to the United Nations Framework Convention on Climate Change (UNFCCC), which binds its parties by setting emission reduction targets.[107] In order to comply with the regulations set out in the Kyoto Protocol, the EU adopted the Directive 2001/77/EC on the promotion of the use of energy from renewable sources.[108] The EU recognised that it would be necessary to incentivise investment in the renewable energy sector through state subsidies. Thus, the mandatory national targets were set for each EU Member State regarding renewable energy production, through the Directive 2009/28/EC[109]. In accordance with the directives,

---

107 Kyoto Protocol of 11 December 1997, <https://unfccc.int/process-and-meetings/the-kyoto-protocol/what-is-the-kyoto-protocol/what-is-the-kyoto-protocol> (accessed 3 May 2021). *See also* Baetens, 'The Kyoto Protocol in Investor-State Arbitration: Reconciling Climate Change and Investment Protection Objectives' in Cordonier Segger, Gehring and Newcombe (eds), *Sustainable Development in World Investment Law* (Global Trade Law Series vol. 30, Kluwer Law International 2010), p. 686-690.

108 Directive 2001/77/EC of the European Parliament and of the Council of 27 September 2001 on the promotion of electricity produced from renewable energy sources in the internal electricity market, preamble recital no. 1. <https://eur-lex.europa.eu/legal-content/EN/TXT/?uri=CELEX%3A32001L0077> (accessed 3 May 2021). Renewable energy sources are, inter alia, biomass, wind, geothermal, hydraulic, maritime and solar technologies.

109 Directive 2009/28/EC of the European Parliament and of the Council of 23 April 2009 on the promotion of the use of energy from renewable sources and amending and subsequently repealing Directives 2001/77/EC and

the Member States introduced different benefits such as Feed-in Tariffs (FITs), Feed-in Premiums (FIPs), Green Certificates, quota obligations, loans, subsidies, net-metering or tax exemptions.[110] Most commonly used were FITs and FIPs accompanied by tax exemptions. Such support schemes reduce financial and regulatory risk by guaranteeing investors a fixed price for their produced energy over a certain period of time.[111]

This trend, however, was soon to come to a halt: The global economic crisis in 2007/2008 forced economically weaker Member States into a recession and led them to alter their support schemes.[112] At the same time, the massive investments in the renewable energy sector fostered the development of renewable energy technologies, which made the market prices for renewable energy production facilities fall dramatically.[113] While new investors were no longer depending on high subsidies, investors at the beginning of the renewable energy boom had much higher up-front costs than subsequent investors. The amendments reduced the revenue of solar energy power plants by up to 66%, which in the most extreme cases led to the abandonment of the projects.[114] Investments in the energy sector differ from other forms of investment, epitomised by large upfront-investments and a lengthy period between the initial commitment and the first returns.[115] Hence, renewable energy power plants are reliant on a stable

---

2003/30/EC, <https://eur-lex.europa.eu/legal-content/EN/ALL/?uri=CELEX%3A32009L0028> (accessed 3 May 2021).

110 Restrepo, 'Modification of Renewable Energy Support Schemes Under the Energy Charter Treaty: Modification of Renewable Energy Support Schemes Under the Energy Charter Treaty: Eiser and Charanne in the Context of Climate Change' (2017) 8(1) Goettingen Journal of International Law 101, p. 102. *See also* Ilaria Espa, 'Promoting Renewables in the Energy Union: Current Strategies and the Challenges Ahead' (2017) 2(1) Eur Invest Law Arbitr Rev 225, p. 232-235.

111 Tienhaara and Downie, 'Risky Business? The Energy Charter Treaty, Renewable Energy, and Investor-State Disputes', p. 457.

112 Simões, 'When Green Incentives Go Pale: Investment Arbitration and Renewable Energy Policymaking', p. 258-260.

113 Espa, 'Promoting Renewables in the Energy Union: Current Strategies and the Challenges Ahead', p. 226.

114 *For example* Eiser Infrastructure Limited and Energía Solar Luxembourg S.à.r.l. v. Kingdom of Spain, Award, 4 May 2017 ICSID Case No. ARB/13/36, para. 389. *See also* Ch. 4 III 3) c).

115 Baltag, *The Energy Charter Treaty: The Notion of Investor* (International Arbitration Law Library, Wolters Kluwer Law & Business; Kluwer Law International 2012), p. 2; Patrizia and others, *Investment Disputes Involving the Renewable Energy Industry Under the Energy Charter Treaty*, p. 47.

legal framework, over a period of possibly decades, in order to recoup their initial costs and make a profit.

The failure of many early investment projects, due to the amended support schemes, scared away potential new investors and put a halt to the advancement of the renewable energy sector in Europe. This, however, was contradictory to the aims of the Kyoto Protocol and the Directives 2001/77/EC and 2009/28/EC, which were to lower the emission of greenhouse gases, slow the climate change and reduce global warming at an average temperature increase of 1,5° Celsius. Climate change, on the other hand, will not be stopped without drastically limiting the rising greenhouse gas emissions from the energy sector. Such a cut in emissions will only be achieved, if the transition to renewable and clean energy sources happens as soon as possible.[116] The international community has recognised that there is an urgent need to stop unsustainable, inefficient and wasteful patterns of traditional economic growth and replace them with so-called "green growth"[117], in order to avoid environmental drawbacks.[118] Therefore, renewable energies are a vital tool for sustainable development, but they have not reached a level of efficiency (yet) in which they would fully substitute themselves.[119]

The massive investments in the renewable energy sector in the past have already decreased the cost of wind and solar power significantly, and made renewable energy sources a real and affordable competitor for fossil-fuelled power plants.[120] Already today renewable energies account for more than 20% of the global electricity supply.[121] Notwithstanding the massive devel-

---

116 IPPC, 'Special Report "Global Warming 1,5 °C" (Summary for Policy Makers)' (IPPC Publishing 2019) <https://www.ipcc.ch/sr15/> (accessed 3 May 2021).

117 *See* Vávra, Cudlínová and Miloslav, 'Green Growth from the Viewpoint of the Czech Republic' in Vávra, Lapka and Cudlínová (eds), *Current challenges of Central Europe* (Varia vol 29. Univ. Karlova Filozoficka Fak 2015), Ch. 2.

118 The World Bank, 'Inclusive Green Growth: The Pathway to Sustainable Development' (The World Bank 2012) <https://openknowledge.worldbank.org/bitstream/handle/10986/6058/9780821395516.pdf?sequence=1> (accessed 3 May 2021).

119 Vávra, Cudlínová and Miloslav, *Green Growth from the Viewpoint of the Czech Republic*, p. 113.

120 International Renewable Energy Agency, 'Renewable Power Generation Costs in 2019' (IRENA 2020), p. 12 <https://www.irena.org/publications/2020/Jun/Renewable-Power-Costs-in-2019> (accessed 3 May 2021).

121 International Energy Agency, 'Energy Technology Perspectives 2014: Harnessing Electricity's Potential' (2014), p. 11 <https://cleanenergysolutions.org/sites/default/files/documents/2014_05_12_iea_energy_technology_perspectives_webinar_transcript.pdf> (accessed 3 May 2021). In Germany on average even 40% <https://www.umweltbundesamt.de/themen/

opments of the last decade, the International Energy Agency (IEA) still estimated in 2014 that an additional 44 trillion USD in investment is required to transition the energy sector to renewable energy sources.[122] A large portion of this sum must be acquired through FDI.[123] Recently, many countries acquired FDI participation on a large scale in the search for the development of renewable energy sources.[124] The future demand for investment capital, however, can only be satisfied, if international investors find a stable and transparent investment environment.[125] In 2014, The European Commission (EC) authorised *Ecofys* to issue a report which evaluated the EU Member States' progress in fostering the renewable energy sector. The 2014 Ecofys Report came to the conclusion that a significant amount of EU Member States would fail to meet their prescribed targets, if the current policies and measures remained in place, with Spain being likely to miss the renewable energy goals by up to 30%.[126] Hence, the unfavourable investment environment is the main obstacle, when it comes to FDI in the renewable energy sector. The ECT aims to create a

---

klima-energie/erneuerbare-energien/erneuerbare-energien-in-zahlen> (accessed 3 May 2021); Tienhaara and Downie, 'Risky Business? The Energy Charter Treaty, Renewable Energy, and Investor-State Disputes', p. 452.

122 International Energy Agency, 'Energy Technology Perspectives 2014: Harnessing Electricity's Potential'(2014), p. 11, 14 <https://cleanenergysolutions.org/sites/default/files/documents/2014_05_12_iea_energy_technology_perspectives_webinar_transcript.pdf> (accessed 3 May 2021); Tienhaara and Downie, 'Risky Business? The Energy Charter Treaty, Renewable Energy, and Investor-State Disputes', p. 452.

123 Karl, 'FDI in the Energy Sector: Recent Trends and Policy Issues' in Eric d Brabandere and Gazzini (eds), *Foreign Investment in the Energy Sector: Balancing Private and Public Interests* (Nijhoff International Investment Law Series, Brill 2014), p. 10.

124 Mbengue and Raju, 'Energy, Environment and Foreign Investment' in Eric d Brabandere and Gazzini (eds), *Foreign Investment in the Energy Sector: Balancing Private and Public Interests* (Nijhoff International Investment Law Series, Brill 2014), p. 173.

125 Sussman, *The Energy Charter Treaty's Investor Protection Provisions: Potential to Foster Solutions to Global Warming and Promote Sustainable Development*, p. 527; Elizabeth Trujillo, 'Balancing Sustainability, the Right to Regulate, and the Need for Investor Protection: Lessons from the Trade Regime' (2018) 59(8) Boston College Law Review 2735, p. 2758, 2759.

126 Frauenhofer, EEG, BBH, IASA, SEI, 'Final Report on Renewable Energy Progress and Biofuels Sustainability' (Ecofys 2014), p. 50, 51 (more recent reports have not been issued at the time of the writing).

favourable investment environment and thus promotes the development of the renewable energy sector.[127]

Nonetheless, creating a favourable and yet stable and sustainable investment environment has proven to be a difficult task. The recent cases in the renewable energy sector show that some countries offered very favourable conditions to foreign investors in the past, only to find out later that they did not secure a sufficient share in the profits or experienced other negative social or environmental consequences.[128] The consequence of the incentive programs, which meant a reduced risk for the investors, entailed the inherent risk of successive amendment or repeal. [129] Apart from financial risks, the risk of a change in public policy around renewable energies poses the most severe threat to investments in the renewable energy sector.[130] The underlying cases of this research made apparent that changes in government or unexpected cost escalations can undermine political support for incentive schemes and lead to their alteration or complete abolishment.[131] This, in turn, not only endangers the investors' interests, but also the entire investment.

Traditionally, investment protection and environment protection are perceived to have friction points.[132] This stems from the fact that environmental protection measures tend to limit or diminish the development of an investment.[133] In the case of renewable energy sources, however, investment protection and environmental protection go hand in hand. While renewable energies will, in the long run, become more cost-efficient and hence make fossil fuel-based energies eventually obsolete, inventive

127 Sussman, 'The Energy Charter Treaty's Investor Protection Provisions: Potential to Foster Solutions to Global Warming and Promote Sustainable Development' in Cordonier Segger, Gehring and Newcombe (eds), *Sustainable Development in World Investment Law* (Global Trade Law Series vol. 30, Kluwer Law International 2010), p. 532; doubtful after extensive analysis: Kyla Tienhaara and Christian Downie, 'Risky Business? The Energy Charter Treaty, Renewable Energy, and Investor-State Disputes'(2018) 24(3) Global Governance 451, p.461

128 *See* Ch. D III.

129 Karl, *FDI in the Energy Sector: Recent Trends and Policy Issues*, p. 28.

130 Tienhaara and Downie, 'Risky Business? The Energy Charter Treaty, Renewable Energy, and Investor-State Disputes', p. 457; Sussman, *The Energy Charter Treaty's Investor Protection Provisions: Potential to Foster Solutions to Global Warming and Promote Sustainable Development*, p. 528.

131 Tienhaara and Downie, 'Risky Business? The Energy Charter Treaty, Renewable Energy, and Investor-State Disputes', p. 457.

132 Mbengue and Raju, *Energy, Environment and Foreign Investment*, p. 176.

133 Baetens, *The Kyoto Protocol in Investor-State Arbitration: Reconciling Climate Change and Investment Protection Objectives*, p. 699-701.

programs and support schemes are in the transition period and important to kick-start the change to renewable energies.[134] This also means that FITs and FIPs will only be needed for the transition period and do not pose a long-term threat to the host states' economy.[135] In the meantime, international investment practices have a duty to further define the requirements an investor must fulfil in order to be protected by the ECT. Only with legal certainty investments in the renewable energy sector will flourish and further negative impacts on the environment be counteracted.

134 Overview of the different energy sources and their cost-efficiency: Tienhaara and Downie, 'Risky Business? The Energy Charter Treaty, Renewable Energy, and Investor-State Disputes', p. 457. *See also* Hernández-Moro and Martínez-Duart, 'Analytical model for solar PV and CSP electricity costs: Present LCOE values and their future evolution' (2013) 20 Renewable and Sustainable Energy Reviews 119, p. 130.

135 Tienhaara and Downie, 'Risky Business? The Energy Charter Treaty, Renewable Energy, and Investor-State Disputes', p. 457.

Pursuant to Article 26(6) ECT, tribunals trying investment disputes shall decide the issues in accordance with the ECT, as well as applicable rules and principles of international law.[136] The ordinary meaning of the term "principles of international law" is "the legal principles derived from all sources of international law".[137] To qualify as a principle of international law, the principle must be recognised by the majority of the legal systems.[138] It follows that a tribunal assessing a dispute in international investment law does not only have to take into account substantive rights and obligations afforded by the investment treaty, but must also be aware of the very basic principles in international law. This provision complies with the requirement of systemic integration enshrined in Article 31(3)(c) VCLT.[139] The exact content of substantive rights and obligations of the ECT, as well as principles of international law, however, are often undefined and subject to dispute.

This already makes the discretion of tribunals in an ECT dispute evident. They exercise their margin of discretion when examining whether an investor is protected by the rights accorded under the ECT. The ECT contains in Part III, inter alia, the right of the investor against unlawful expropriation and the violation of the FET standard.[140] While the question of unlawful expropriation regards whether a specific right of the investor was taken[141], the FET standard simply asks whether the investor suffered

136 Baltag, *The Energy Charter Treaty*, p. 25.

137 The definition was established by the Tribunal in accordance with Article 31(1) VCLT in Suez, Sociedad General de Aguas de Barcelona, S.A. and Vivendi Universal, S.A. v. The Argentine RepublicRepublic, Decision on Liability, 30 July 2010 ICSID Case No. ARB/03/19, para. 185. *See also* Palombino, *Fair and Equitable Treatment and the Fabric of General Principles*, p. 185.

138 Gazzini, 'General Principles of Law in the Field of Foreign Investment' (2009) 10(1) The Journal of World Investment & Trade 103, p. 105; Levashova, *The Right of States to Regulate in International Investment Law*, p. 98; Mairal, *Legitimate Expectations and Informal Administrative Representations*, p. 415.

139 Lo, *Treaty Interpretation under the Vienna Convention on the Law of Treaties: A New Round of Codification* (Springer 2017), p. 216, 217.

140 Energy Charter Secretariat, *The Energy Charter Treaty*, p. 21, 22, 23.

141 Dolzer and Schreuer, *Principles of International Investment Law*, p. 101.

from unfair and/or discriminatory treatment by the host state[142]. Due to its broad scope of application, the FET standard has become the most important standard in investment law, being the grounds that offered the highest chance of success in investor claims today.[143] It is considered the manifestation of "normative equity".[144] Equity as a legal notion serves as the benchmark of substantive justice and offers a judge or tribunal the tool to incorporate equity considerations into the decision, thereby factoring in the specific circumstances of the individual case at hand.[145]

With a broad scope of application and the non-binding nature of arbitral awards for subsequent tribunals, also comes legal uncertainty for investors and states respectively.[146] Hence the FET standard's flexibility is its strength and at the same time its weakness.[147] Nevertheless, flexibility is necessary to accommodate the many unpredictable constellations involved in international investment transactions.[148] On the flipside, excessive legal uncertainty can lead to miscalculations on the part of the state and/or investors, jeopardising the investment or the credibility and financial interests of the host state.[149] Thus the nature, abstract content, as well as the legal specifics of the FET standard under the ECT, need to be assessed.

---

142 Palombino, *Fair and Equitable Treatment and the Fabric of General Principles*, p. 22.

143 UNCTAD, 'World Investment Report 2016', p. 107; UNCTAD, 'World Investment Report 2019', p. 104. *See also* Kläger, *'Fair and Equitable Treatment' and Sustainable Development*, p. 241; Sipiorski, *Good Faith in International Investment Arbitration* (Oxford International Arbitration Series, 2019), para. 9.04; Maynard, 'Legitimate Expectations and the Interpretation of the 'Legal Stability Obligation'', p. 99.

144 Palombino, *Fair and Equitable Treatment and the Fabric of General Principles*, p. 2, 3.

145 ibid, p. 2, 3.

146 Sipiorski, *Good Faith in International Investment Arbitration*, para. 9.05; Kläger, *'Fair and Equitable Treatment' and Sustainable Development*, p. 242.

147 Sipiorski, *Good Faith in International Investment Arbitration*, para. 9.05; Kläger, *'Fair and Equitable Treatment' and Sustainable Development*, p. 242.

148 *See* 2 IV 1).

149 *See* 2 IV 2).

I. Interpretation of Provisions Including the Fair and Equitable Treatment Standard

The predominant tool for treaty interpretation is the Vienna Convention on the Law of Treaties from 1969 (VCLT). Almost all Member States of the ECT are signatories to the VCLT.[150] However, the rules of the VCLT reflect and develop rules of customary international law and therefore also apply in its relevant parts to the Contracting Parties of the ECT that did not sign the VCLT.[151] International investment tribunals regularly rely on the rules set out in the VCLT to clarify the broad and rather vague FET standard, within the ECT or other investment treaties.[152] Thus, the ECT's provisions and especially the FET standard must be construed in accordance with the rules of interpretation in Article 31 and Article 32 VCLT.

Article 31 provides that a treaty shall be interpreted in good faith in accordance with the ordinary meaning to be given to the terms of the treaty, in their context and in light of its object and purpose. The ordinary meaning is the starting point for every treaty interpretation.[153] Together with the context, a treaty's object and purpose a key aspect of the construction of international treaties.[154] The object is referred to as the "subject matter subjected to the treaty", whereas the purpose of the treaty refers to the "aim of the norm".[155] Those key features need to be interpreted in good faith. The good faith principle is connected to the principle of *pacta sunt servanda* and requires the states to obey a standard of honesty, loyalty, and fair dealing, in short of morality, in international conduct.[156]

---

150 Only non-overlap: Norway, France, Rumania, Turkey, Iceland, Afghanistan, Belarus, Russia, and the EU.

151 Weeramantry, *Treaty Interpretation in Investment Arbitration* (vol 1, OUP 2012), para. 2.22; Lo, *Treaty Interpretation under the Vienna Convention on the Law of Treaties*, Chs. 3.3-3.4; Dörr and Schmalenbach, *Vienna Convention on the Law of Treaties*, Article 4, para. 4.

152 Viñuales, *Sources of International Investment Law: Conceptual Foundations of Unruly Practices*, p. 1080; Gazzini, *Interpretation of International Investment Treaties*, p. 64.

153 Lo, *Treaty Interpretation under the Vienna Convention on the Law of Treaties*, p. 153, 154.

154 Gazzini, *Interpretation of International Investment Treaties*, p. 67.

155 Levashova, *The Right of States to Regulate in International Investment Law*, p. 81; Kolb, *Good Faith in International Law* (Hart Publishing 2017), p. 145.

156 Weeramantry, *Treaty Interpretation in Investment Arbitration*, para. 3.21; Dörr and Schmalenbach, *Vienna Convention on the Law of Treaties*, Article 26, para. 15.

The *pacta sunt servanda* principle, in turn, is a fundamental cornerstone of treaty law.[157] While good faith is seldom invoked independently, it is an overarching international law principle that must always be considered, in interpreting treaty standards.[158] A major application of the good faith principle in the renewable energy cases can be found in the interpretation of the taxation carve-out in Article 21(1) ECT.[159] The object and purpose jointly refer to the ultimate aim that a treaty intends to achieve.[160] The object and purpose of the ECT are, according to Article 2, to establish a legal framework to promote long-term cooperation in the energy field, based on complementarities and mutual benefits. This aim needs always to be considered when interpreting the rights and obligations under the ECT. Additionally, interpreters of an international treaty are compelled to consider the conduct of the parties subsequent to an agreement.[161]

Only if the interpretation pursuant to Article 31 VCLT leaves the meaning of the relevant treaty clause ambiguous or obscure, or leads to a result which is manifestly absurd or unreasonable, such that recourse may be had to the preparatory work of the treaty and the circumstances of its conclusion as a supplementary means of interpretation in accordance with Article 32 VCLT.[162] This differs from the traditional approach to interpreting statutes of national law. An extensive interpretation or an analogical interpretation can, therefore, be contrary to the VCLT.[163] The legislative history or the legislator's intent documented in the preparatory work only have the status of a supplementary means of interpretation. In contrast, preparatory work is often used under domestic legal systems to define the content of a law. Thus, it is necessary to bear in mind that treaties need to be construed differently than statutory provisions in domestic legal orders.

---

157 Dörr and Schmalenbach, *Vienna Convention on the Law of Treaties* (Springer Berlin Heidelberg 2018), Article 26, para. 20.

158 Kolb, *Good Faith in International Law*, p. 35, 36.

159 *See for example* Antaris Solar and Dr. Michael Göde v. Czech Republic, Award, 2 May 2018 PCA Case No. 2014-01, para. 223, 224; Voltaic Network GmbH v. Czech Republic, Award, 15 September 2019 PCA CASE No 2014-20, para. 266, 267; Eiser Infrastructure Limited and Energía Solar Luxembourg S.à.r.l. v. Kingdom of Spain, Award, 4 May 2017 ICSID Case No. ARB/13/36, para. 287; Novenergia II - Energy & Environment (SCA), SICAR v. The Kingdom of Spain, Award, 15 February 2018 SCC Case No. V 2015/063, para. 521.

160 Lo, *Treaty Interpretation under the Vienna Convention on the Law of Treaties*, p. 180, 181.

161 Article 31(3)(b) VCLT.

162 Weeramantry, *Treaty Interpretation in Investment Arbitration*, para. 4.02.

163 Lo, *Treaty Interpretation under the Vienna Convention on the Law of Treaties*, p. 23.

II. Fair and Equitable Treatment as an Overarching International Law Principle

The FET standard is almost universally accepted and used in investment law.[164] The concept derives from general international law and is most commonly invoked in investment arbitration.[165] Over 95% of the investment treaties in existence bind their signatories to accord FET to foreign investors.[166] Despite its omnipresence, the FET standard remains an indeterminate legal concept. This could be related to the fact that investors have only begun to rely on the FET standard in compensation claims since the late 1990s and the early 2000s, although the concept of the FET has existed for much longer in investment protection treaties.[167] Protection of international investment has for a long time been considered a diplomatic task between the home state of the investor and the host state of the investment.[168] Hence, when states started to establish investor rights through investment treaties, the standard was considered simply a political signal in the text of agreements. Only over time, it has revealed its potential to restrict the sovereignty of the host states more than any of the other rule found in IIAs.[169]

Today, the FET standard is generally viewed as an autonomous standard that is not limited to a treaty or a set of treaties.[170] Apart from its character-

164 McLachlan, Shore and Weiniger, *International Investment Arbitration*, p. 289; Peter D Cameron, *International Energy Investment Law: The Pursuit of Stability* (OUP 2010), Part I, Ch. 4, para. 4.59.

165 Fanou and Tzevelekos, 'Shared Territory of the ECHR and International Investment Law' in Yannick Radi (ed), *Research Handbook on Human Rights and Investment* (Research Handbooks in International Law Series 2018), p. 122.

166 Dumberry, 'Has the Fair and Equitable Treatment Standard Become a Rule of Customary International Law?' (2016) J Int Disp Settlement 155-178, p. 156, 157.

167 Kalicki and Medeiros, 'Fair, Equitable and Ambiguous: What Is Fair and Equitable Treatment in International Investment Law?' (2007) 22(1) ICSID Review 24, p. 24; Paparinskis, *The International Minimum Standard and Fair and Equitable Treatment* (OUP 2013), p. 112; Gaukrodger, 'The Balance Between Investor Protection and the Right to Regulate in Investment Treaties' (2017) OECD Working Papers on International Investment, p. 5.

168 *See* Hobe, *The Development of the Law of Aliens and Emergence of General Principles of Protection under International Law*, p. 8-11.

169 *See* Kläger, *'Fair and Equitable Treatment' in International Investment Law*, p. 155-163.

170 Técnicas Medioambientales Tecmed, S.A. v. The United Mexican States, Award, 29 May 2003 ICSID Case No. ARB (AF)/00/2, para. 155; MTD Equity Sdn. Bhd.

ization as the manifestation of normative equity, it is partly perceived to be rooted in the good faith principle of international law or the rule of law itself.[171] Hence, it is argued that the plentiful and consistent state practice has already or will eventually transform the FET standard into a new and autonomous rule of customary international law.[172] While the threshold for becoming customary international law does not yet seem to have been reached, it illustrates the overarching character of the FET standard extending beyond the scope of the respective treaty. The FET standard gains further complexity due to the fact that it is included in thousands of investment treaties. Most of these treaties have an open formulation of the FET standard and belong to a plurality of legal regimes, which are in turn interpreted differently by different tribunals.[173] Three types of "classic" FET provisions can be found in international investment treaties: The first type solely establishes the obligation to afford fair and equitable treatment without further references.[174] The second type combines the obligation to afford FET with a reference to international law.[175] The third type correlates the FET obligation with other standards of treatment, such as

and MTD Chile S.A. v. Republic of Chile, Award, 25 May 2004 ICSID Case No. ARB/01/7, para. 111–112; Saluka Investments B.V. v. The Czech Republic Partial, Award, 17 March 2006 UNCITRAL, para. 309; Joseph Charles Lemire v. Ukraine Decision on Liability, 14 January 2010 ICSID Case No. ARB/06/18, para. 284; Knoll-Tudor, 'The Fair and Equitable Treatment Standard and Human Rights Norms' in Dupuy, Petersmann and Francioni (eds), *Human Rights in International Investment Law and Arbitration* (OUP 2009), p. 318.

171 Dupuy, 'Unification Rather Than Fragmentation of International Law? The Case of International Investment Law and Human Rights Law' in Dupuy, Petersmann and Francioni (eds), *Human Rights in International Investment Law and Arbitration* (OUP 2009), p. 52; Sipiorski, *Good Faith in International Investment Arbitration*, para. 9.04.

172 Hobe, *The Development of the Law of Aliens and Emergence of General Principles of Protection under International Law*, p. 18; Tudor, *The Fair and Equitable Treatment Standard in the International Law of Foreign Investment* (OUP 2008), p. 85. Critical thereto: Palombino, *Fair and Equitable Treatment and the Fabric of General Principles*, p. 32; Dumberry, 'Has the Fair and Equitable Treatment Standard Become a Rule of Customary International Law?', p. 177.

173 Levashova, *The Right of States to Regulate in International Investment Law*, p. 5; Dumberry, 'Has the Fair and Equitable Treatment Standard Become a Rule of Customary International Law?', p. 157.

174 Knoll-Tudor, *The Fair and Equitable Treatment Standard and Human Rights Norms*, p. 313.

175 Ibid, p. 313.

Most Favoured Nation provisions, National Treatment, or Full Protection and Security (FPS).[176]

Despite the variety of possible implementations and additions, the FET standard has certain key elements that are not only recurring in investment treaties, but are also found in other international law systems, such as human rights law.[177] Human rights are generally perceived as conceptually similar to principles of investment protection.[178] Both systems address the asymmetrical legal relationship between sovereign states and individuals, and provide for individual and neutral fora for the enforcement of the granted rights.[179] The European Court of Human Rights (ECtHR) particularly acknowledged the notion of legitimate expectations.[180] The notion of legitimate expectations can also be found in EU law.[181] If used correctly, the requirement of systemic integration enshrined in Article 31(3)(c) VCLT compels a tribunal or any judicial body assessing the FET stan-

---

176 Ibid, p. 313.

177 *For example* non-discrimination (Article 14), the abuse of rights (Articles 17 and 18), the Fair Trial Principle (Article 6), and Just Satisfaction (Article 41) of the European Charter of Human Rights (ECHR). *See also* Fanou and Tzevelekos, *Shared Territory of the ECHR and International Investment Law*, p. 123.

178 Dupuy, *Unification Rather Than Fragmentation of International Law? The Case of International Investment Law and Human Rights Law*, p. 49; Knoll-Tudor, *The Fair and Equitable Treatment Standard and Human Rights Norms*, p. 335; Hirsch, 'Investment Tribunals and Human Rights: Divergent Paths' in Dupuy, Petersmann and Francioni (eds), *Human Rights in International Investment Law and Arbitration* (OUP 2009), p. 98; Wood, 'Political Risk or Political Right? Reconciling the International Legal Norms of Investment Protection and Political Participation' (2015) 30(3) ICSID Review 665, p. 667.

179 Dupuy, *Unification Rather Than Fragmentation of International Law? The Case of International Investment Law and Human Rights Law*, p. 49; Knoll-Tudor, *The Fair and Equitable Treatment Standard and Human Rights Norms*, p. 335; Hirsch, *Investment Tribunals and Human Rights: Divergent Paths*, p. 98; Wood, 'Political Risk or Political Right? Reconciling the International Legal Norms of Investment Protection and Political Participation', p. 667.

180 ECtHR Judgment *Centro Europa 7 srl and di Stefano v. Italy,* 7 June 2012 Application No. 38433/09, para. 173.

181 *See for example* CJEU Judgment *HLH Warenvertriebs GmbH and Orthica BV v Germany,*9 June 2005 C-17/03, para. 73; CJEU Judgment *Atlanta v European Community,*14 October 1999 C-104/97 P, para. 52; CJEU Judgment *Di Lenardo and Dilexport,*15 July 2004 C-37/02 and C-38/02, para. 70; CJEU Judgment *Marks & Spencer plc v Commissioners of Customs & Excise,*11 July 2002 Case C-62/00; para. 46; CJEU Judgment *Grundstückgemeinschaft Schloßstraße GbR v Finanzamt Paderborn,*8 June 2000 C-396/98, para. 47.

dard to construe those key elements uniformly regardless of the treaty or system of international law they are applied in.

III. The Fair and Equitable Treatment Standard in Abstract

In general, the obligation to provide FET is broad and overarching and leaves arbitral tribunals a wide margin of discretion in the interpretation of the standard.[182] A wide margin of discretion is crucial to determine what conduct is fair and equitable on the facts of the particular case.[183] This lack of normative content of the FET standard, however, also raised criticism from commentations.[184] Thus, the content of the FET standard must be further examined.

1) The Ordinary Meaning of "Fair and Equitable"

Every tribunal assessing the content of the FET standard must backtrack to the very roots of the FET standard of the respective treaty provision by examining the ordinary meaning of the wording, pursuant to Article 31(1) VCLT. In their common understanding, the terms "fair" and "equitable", as used in investment treaties, mean "just", "even-handed", "unbiased", "legitimate", as well as "reasonable".[185] This indicates that

182 Titi, *The Right to Regulate in International Investment Law* (Studien zum Internationalen Investitionsrecht, Nomos 2014), stating that the FET standard requires by its "very nature" a balancing of interests, p. 277. *See also* Levashova, *The Right of States to Regulate in International Investment Law*, p. 104, 105.

183 Mondev International Ltd. v United States of America, Award, 11 October 2002 ICSID Case No. ARB(AF)/99/2, para. 118; Knoll-Tudor, *The Fair and Equitable Treatment Standard and Human Rights Norms*, p. 318.

184 Schill, 'Fair and Equitable Treatment, the Rule of Law, and Comparative Public Law' in Schill (ed), *International Investment Law and Comparative Public Law* (OUP 2010), p. 151; Kalicki and Medeiros, 'Fair, Equitable and Ambiguous: What Is Fair and Equitable Treatment in International Investment Law?', p. 25.

185 MTD Equity Sdn. Bhd. and MTD Chile S.A. v. Republic of Chile, Award, 25 May 2004 ICSID Case No. ARB/01/7, para. 113; Azurix Corp. v. The Argentine Republic, Award, 14 July 2006 ICSID Case No. ARB/01/12, para. 360; Siemens A.G. v. The Argentine Republic, Award, 17 January 2007 ICSID Case No. ARB/02/8, para. 290. *See also* Tudor, *The Fair and Equitable Treatment Standard in the International Law of Foreign Investment*, p. 128.

equitable treatment is characterized by equity or fairness.[186] Accordingly, the conduct of the host state is deemed a violation of the FET standard, if it is grossly unfair, unjust or involves a lack of due process leading to an outcome that offends judicial propriety.[187] In general, the plain meaning of the terms "fair and equitable" does not provide much assistance in the interpretation of the standard.[188] Nonetheless, arbitral tribunals have been further defining the content of the FET standard through their jurisprudence by finding groups and clusters of subgroups with more refined contours.[189]

Some of these subgroups were identified in the prohibition of harassment, coercion, abuse of power, arbitrary or inconsistent conduct, and the violation of the investors' legitimate expectations by failure to offer a stable and predictable legal framework.[190] A state may also violate the FET standard by performing actions that fall far below international standards or are even subjective bad faith[191] or by failing to provide due process to investors[192].

---

186 Parkerings-Compagniet AS v. Republic of Lithuania, Award, 11 September 2007 ICSID Case No. ARB/05/8, para. 276.

187 Total S.A. v. The Argentine Republic, Decision on Liability, 27 December 2010 ICSID Case No. ARB/04/01, para. 129; Waste Management, Inc. v. United Mexican States, Award, 30 April 2004 ICSID Case No. ARB(AF)/00/3, para. 98.

188 Ioan Micula, Viorel Micula, S.C. European Food S.A, S.C. Starmill S.R.L. and S.C. Multipack S.R.L. v. Romania, Award, 11 December 2013 ICSID Case No. ARB/05/20, para. 504; Saluka Investments B.V. v. The Czech Republic Partial, Award, 17 March 2006 UNCITRAL, para. 297; Levashova, *The Right of States to Regulate in International Investment Law*, p. 78.

189 Dolzer, 'Fair and Equitable Treatment: Today's Contours', p. 15; Kläger, *'Fair and Equitable Treatment' and Sustainable Development*, p. 242; Maynard, 'Legitimate Expectations and the Interpretation of the 'Legal Stability Obligation'', p. 99, 100.

190 Rusoro Mining Ltd. v. Bolivarian Republic of Venezuela, Award, 22 August 2016 ICSID Case No. ARB(AF)/12/5, para. 524; Joseph Charles Lemire v. Ukraine Decision on Liability, 14 January 2010 ICSID Case No. ARB/06/18, para. 284; Sipiorski, *Good Faith in International Investment Arbitration*, para. 9.06.

191 Ian Brownlie and James Crawford, *Brownlie's Principles of Public International Law* (Ninth Edition, 2019), p. 529; Alex Genin, Eastern Credit Limited, Inc. and A.S. Baltoil v. The Republic of Estonia, Award, 25 June 2001 ICSID Case No. ARB/99/2, para. 367.

192 Biwater Gauff (Tanzania) Ltd. v. United Republic of Tanzania, Award, 24 July 2004 ICSID Case No. ARB/05/22, para. 602; Joseph Charles Lemire v. Ukraine Decision on Liability, 14 January 2010 ICSID Case No. ARB/06/18, para. 284; Loewen Group, Inc. and Raymond L. Loewen v. United States of America, Award, 26 June 2003 ICSID Case No. ARB(AF)/98/3, para. 132. *See also* Dupuy,

2) Unjust and Arbitrary Treatment

Additionally, a manifest failure of natural justice in judicial proceedings or a complete lack of transparency and candour in the administrative process, amounting to unjust and arbitrary treatment was found to be contrary to the states' FET obligation.[193] The threshold for "unjust" or "arbitrary" treatment is unclear since it has to be assessed on a case-by-case basis. Some tribunals have gone so far as to demand that the state has to act in "such an unjust or arbitrary manner that the treatment rises to the level that is unacceptable".[194] Most tribunals, however, associate arbitrariness simply with unreasonable and improper conduct and use these terms interchangeably, as it will be demonstrated in the analysis *infra*.[195] In more recent investment treaties and investment protection provisions, the adjectives "manifest" or "evident" were incorporated in order to set a higher threshold for the determination as to which treatment must be deemed as arbitrary.[196] Such additions are often used in the wording of a provision to express that investment tribunals should recognise a high threshold regarding the violation of the FET standard.[197] However, this seems to be redundant and more of a safety precaution than an additional requirement, since investment tribunals have regularly demonstrated cau-

---

Unification Rather Than Fragmentation of International Law? The Case of International Investment Law and Human Rights Law, p. 51 and Knoll-Tudor, *The Fair and Equitable Treatment Standard and Human Rights Norms*, p. 323.

193 Waste Management, Inc. v. United Mexican States, Award, 30 April 2004 ICSID Case No. ARB(AF)/00/3, para. 98; Urbaser SA and Consorcio de Aguas Bilbao Bizkaia, Bilbao Biskaia Ur Partzuergoa v The Argentine Republic, Award, 8 December 2016 ICSID Case No ARB/07/26, para. 845.

194 S.D. Myers, Inc. v. Government of Canada Partial, Award, 13 November 2000 UNCITRAL, para. 263; Saluka Investments B.V. v. The Czech Republic Partial, Award, 17 March 2006 UNCITRAL, para. 297; Tulip Real Estate and Development Netherlands B.V. v. Republic of Turkey, Award, 10 March 2014 ICSID Case No. ARB/11/28, para. 401.

195 *See* Ch. 2 IV 3) b). *See also* Kriebaum, 'Arbitrary/Unreasonable or Discriminatory Measures' in Bungenberg and others (eds), *International Investment Law: A Handbook* (Nomos 2015), p. 792, 793.

196 *For example* Article 8.10(2) CETA (2016) provides in an exhaustive list that a party breached the FET standard if a measure or series of measures constitutes "*manifes*t arbitrariness" or "discrimination on *manifestly*" wrongful grounds (emphasis added).

197 UNCTAD, 'Fair and Equitable Treatment' UNCTAD Series on Issues in International Investment Agreements II (United Nations 2012), p. 110.

tion and thorough consideration when finding a breach of the obligation to afford FET.[198]

3) Transparency and Predictability

States must act in a way that enables investors to adjust their business decisions to the host state's policies. Therefore, states must be open about their agenda and make available information on the status of laws, regulations, as well as relevant policies and justifications for decisions by their own governmental bodies.[199] Accordingly, a change in the state's policy does not amount to a violation of the FET standard, if the relevant information had been publicly available and the changes thus foreseeable.[200] Hence, transparency interplays with the due diligence obligation of the investors to base their investment decision on all relevant information.

4) Discrimination Against Foreign Investors

The arbitral practice in international investment law is undetermined, whether the prohibition of discriminatory measures is part of the FET standard or a conceptually different right.[201] Some investment treaties, such as the ECT, explicitly refer to the prohibition of discrimination.[202] However, even without the explicit reference to non-discrimination in

---

198 Kläger, 'Revising Treatment Standards— Fair and Equitable Treatment in Light of Sustainable Development' in Hindelang and Krajewski (eds), *Shifting Paradigms in International Investment Law* (OUP 2016), p. 75.

199 Técnicas Medioambientales Tecmed, S.A. v. The United Mexican States, Award, 29 May 2003 ICSID Case No. ARB (AF)/00/2, para. 154; Saluka Investments B.V. v. The Czech Republic Partial, Award, 17 March 2006 UNCITRAL, para. 499; Parkerings-Compagniet AS v. Republic of Lithuania, Award, 11 September 2007 ICSID Case No. ARB/05/8, para. 295; Ioan Micula, Viorel Micula, S.C. European Food S.A, S.C. Starmill S.R.L. and S.C. Multipack S.R.L. v. Romania, Award, 11 December 2013 ICSID Case No. ARB/05/20, para. 825. *See also* Levashova, *The Right of States to Regulate in International Investment Law*, p. 216.

200 Parkerings-Compagniet AS v. Republic of Lithuania, Award, 11 September 2007 ICSID Case No. ARB/05/8, para. 304.

201 Kriebaum, *Arbitrary/Unreasonable or Discriminatory Measures*, p. 806; Kläger, *'Fair and Equitable Treatment' and Sustainable Development*, p. 247.

202 *See* Ch. 1 IV.

investment treaties, tribunals have found a violation of the FET standard in instances of discrimination against foreign investors.[203]

In general, the FET has not been interpreted to be limited to a specific form of discrimination. Instead, discrimination relevant for the violation of the obligation to provide FET may be based on nationality, race, religion and political affiliation.[204] However, the FET standard, in contrast to the explicit national treatment obligation, does not prohibit every kind of unequal treatment of national and foreign investors.[205] Rather, states may provide privileges to national investors, if there is a reasonable explanation for the unequal treatment.[206] Thus, the differentiation in treatment between foreign and national investors does not constitute a violation of the FET standard, if it is not arbitrary and reasonably justified.[207] The possibility for a state to reasonably justify the discrimination against foreign investors consequently leads tribunals to rarely base their decision on discriminatory treatment alone.[208] Instead, tribunals further base their decision on accompanying circumstances, such as unfairness or ambiguity in the states' conduct in general.[209]

---

203 Saluka Investments B.V. v. The Czech Republic Partial, Award, 17 March 2006 UNCITRAL, para. 309; Biwater Gauff (Tanzania) Ltd. v. United Republic of Tanzania, Award, 24 July 2004 ICSID Case No. ARB/05/22, para. 602; Joseph Charles Lemire v. Ukraine Decision on Liability, 14 January 2010 ICSID Case No. ARB/06/18, para. 284. *See also* Hobe, *The Development of the Law of Aliens and Emergence of General Principles of Protection under International Law*, p. 19.

204 Kriebaum, *Arbitrary/Unreasonable or Discriminatory Measures*, p. 798; Levashova, *The Right of States to Regulate in International Investment Law*, p. 212.

205 International Thunderbird Gaming Corporation v. The United Mexican States Separate Opinion of Thomas Wälde, 26 January 2006 UNCITRAL, para. 103; Kläger, *'Fair and Equitable Treatment' in International Investment Law*, p. 103.

206 Diehl, *The Core Standard of International Investment Protection: Fair and Equitable Treatment* (International Arbitration Law Library, 2012), p. 452, 453; Levashova, *The Right of States to Regulate in International Investment Law*, p. 213.

207 Saluka Investments B.V. v. The Czech Republic Partial, Award, 17 March 2006 UNCITRAL, para. 313, 437; Electrabel S.A. v. Republic of Hungary, Award, 25 November 2015 ICSID Case No. ARB/07/19, para. 175; Kriebaum, *Arbitrary/Unreasonable or Discriminatory Measures*, p. 804, 805; Levashova, *The Right of States to Regulate in International Investment Law*, p. 213.

208 Bonnitcha, *Substantive Protection under Investment Treaties: A Legal and Economic Analysis* (Cambridge studies in international and comparative law), Ch. 4.3.2; Levashova, *The Right of States to Regulate in International Investment Law*, p. 213.

209 Bonnitcha, *Substantive Protection under Investment Treaties: A Legal and Economic Analysis* (Cambridge studies in international and comparative law), Ch. 4.3.2; Levashova, *The Right of States to Regulate in International Investment Law*, p. 213.

5) The Obligation of Treatment in Good Faith

With regard to the application of the good faith principle in international investment law, most tribunals and scholars hold the view that the violation of the FET standard does not necessarily require conduct in bad faith.[210] Therefore, a state may treat foreign investors unfairly and inequitably, without intending to do so. Nonetheless, proof of a good faith effort by the state in regard to the implementation of measures infringing investors interest may "counter-balance instances of disregard of legal or regulatory requirements".[211]

6) Consistency and Legitimate Expectations

Separate branches of the government are required to act free from ambiguity and in a consistent manner.[212] Inconsistent behaviour can, on the one hand, be characterized by the notion of *venire contra factum proprium*, which derives from the good faith principle and stipulates that a state may not deviate from its previous practice to the detriment of an investor,

---

210 Mondev International Ltd. v United States of America, Award, 11 October 2002 ICSID Case No. ARB(AF)/99/2, para. 116; Técnicas Medioambientales Tecmed, S.A. v. The United Mexican States, Award, 29 May 2003 ICSID Case No. ARB (AF)/00/2, para. 153; Siemens A.G. v. The Argentine Republic, Award, 17 January 2007 ICSID Case No. ARB/02/8, para. 299; CMS Gas Transmission Company v. The Argentine Republic, Award, 21 May 2005 ICSID Case No. ARB/01/8, para. 280; Mobil Exploration and Development Inc. v. The Argentine Republic, Decision on Jurisdiction and Liability, 10 April 2013 ICSID Case No. ARB/04/16, para. 937; Schreuer, 'Fair and Equitable Treatment in Arbitral Practice' (2005) 6(3) The Journal of World Investment & Trade 357-386, p. 357; Sipiorski, *Good Faith in International Investment Arbitration*, para. 9.13. In contrast, the Tribunal in *Alex Genin* seemed to require bad faith for a violation of the FET standard, Alex Genin, Eastern Credit Limited, Inc. and A.S. Baltoil v. The Republic of Estonia, Award, 25 June 2001 ICSID Case No. ARB/99/2, para. 371.

211 Gami Investments, Inc. v.The United Mexican States Final, Award, 15 November 2004 UNCITRAL, para. 97, with reference to the decision in Waste Management, Inc. v. United Mexican States, Award, 30 April 2004 ICSID Case No. ARB(AF)/00/3.

212 Técnicas Medioambientales Tecmed, S.A. v. The United Mexican States, Award, 29 May 2003 ICSID Case No. ARB (AF)/00/2, para. 153, 154; Bayindir Insaat Turizm Ticaret Ve Sanayi A.S. v. Islamic Republic of Pakistan, Award, 27 August 2009 ICSID Case No. ARB/03/29, para. 237. *See also* Ch. 2 IV 2).

which has legitimately relied on the previous declaration or practice of that state.[213] On the other hand, inconsistent behaviour can be characterized by the "lack of answers on issues where disagreement existed, its silence in light of an aggravating situation, the delivery of inconsistent administrative decisions, and continued legislative changes".[214] Nevertheless, the FET standard must leave sufficient flexibility to the states, so that they are still able to exercise their right to regulate in order to safeguard the public interest.[215] Hence, arbitral tribunals should not act as an additional instance in administrative law disputes and may only find a violation of the FET standard, if the misconduct of the state is sufficiently serious.[216] Otherwise, any minor misconduct by a public official could lead to the assumption of jurisdiction by an investment tribunal.[217] However, this would exceed the purpose of investment treaties, compelling states to only compensate for similarly severe legal infringements as expropriation. Such an "international appellate body" would interfere too much with the right of states to regulate their internal affairs, in particular through administrative jurisdiction.[218]

This notwithstanding, investment disputes regularly occur in conjunction with regulatory acts by the authorities and changes within the host states legal framework. Therefore, tribunals find themselves in the difficult position of having to decide whether the states' conduct violated the obligation to provide FET or whether the states acted in accordance

---

213 The notion is also comparable to the doctrine of estoppel in common law, *see* Parchomiuk, 'The Protection of Legitimate Expectations in Administrative Law: A Horizontal Perspective' (2017) 10(2) Baltic Journal of Law & Politics 1, p. 6 and Dolzer and Schreuer, *Principles of International Investment Law*, p. 132.

214 Mairal, *Legitimate Expectations and Informal Administrative Representations*, p. 438. *See also* Saluka Investments B.V. v. The Czech Republic Partial, Award, 17 March 2006 UNCITRAL, para. 305, 351.

215 *See* Ch. 2 IV 1).

216 Philip Morris Brands Sàrl et. al. v. Oriental Republic of Uruguay, Award, 8 July 2016 ICSID Case No. ARB/10/7, para. 418; International Thunderbird Gaming Corporation v. The United Mexican States Separate Opinion of Thomas Wälde, 26 January 2006 UNCITRAL, para. 14.

217 International Thunderbird Gaming Corporation v. The United Mexican States Separate Opinion of Thomas Wälde, 26 January 2006 UNCITRAL, para. 14; Liman Caspian Oil BV and NCL Dutch Investment BV v. Kazakhstan, Award, 22 June 2010 ICSID Case No. ARB/07/14, para. 274; S.D. Myers, Inc. v. Government of Canada Partial, Award, 13 November 2000 UNCITRAL, para. 261.

218 Miljenić, 'Energy Charter Treaty – Standards of Investment Protection', p. 63, 64; Liman Caspian Oil BV and NCL Dutch Investment BV v. Kazakhstan, Award, 22 June 2010 ICSID Case No. ARB/07/14, para. 274.

with their right to regulate. An act may even be within the ambit of the state's right to regulate under international law, if the conduct amounts to administrative malpractice from a domestic law standpoint.[219] Hence, the right to regulate conflicts with the obligation to provide a stable and predictable legal framework, to the extent of what a diligent investor at the time of the investment could legitimately expect.[220] Not surprisingly, the right of states to regulate is progressively moving into the focus of the arbitral practice and state reforms are developing as a decisive factor in the assessment of the FET standard.[221]

The right to regulate closely interacts with the notion of the investors' legitimate expectations.[222] The assessment of whether an investor's expectations were legitimate has been acknowledged as a key element of the FET standard by a host of tribunals.[223] Apart from its application in the FET standard, the notion of legitimate expectations is also used to assess whether an indirect expropriation took place.[224] Although both claims are

---

219 *See for example* Philip Morris Brands Sàrl et. al. v. Oriental Republic of Uruguay, Award, 8 July 2016 ICSID Case No. ARB/10/7, para. 418; S.D. Myers, Inc. v. Government of Canada Partial, Award, 13 November 2000 UNCITRAL, para. 261.

220 Metalclad Corporation v. The United Mexican States, Award, 30 August 2000 ICSID Case No. ARB(AF)/97/1, para. 99; Técnicas Medioambientales Tecmed, S.A. v. The United Mexican States, Award, 29 May 2003 ICSID Case No. ARB (AF)/00/2; Occidental Exploration and Production Company v. The Republic of Ecuador Final, Award, 1 July 2004 LCIA Case No. UN3467, para. 154; Occidental Exploration and Production Company v. The Republic of Ecuador Final, Award, 1 July 2004 LCIA Case No. UN3467, para. 191; CMS Gas Transmission Company v. The Argentine Republic, Award, 21 May 2005 ICSID Case No. ARB/01/8, para. 274, 276.

221 Kalicki and Medeiros, 'Fair, Equitable and Ambiguous: What Is Fair and Equitable Treatment in International Investment Law?', p. 24; Total S.A. v. The Argentine Republic, Decision on Liability, 27 December 2010 ICSID Case No. ARB/04/01, para. 129.

222 *See* Ch. 2 IV 1).

223 *See for example* Saluka Investments B.V. v. The Czech Republic Partial, Award, 17 March 2006 UNCITRAL, para. 499; Biwater Gauff (Tanzania) Ltd. v. United Republic of Tanzania, Award, 24 July 2004 ICSID Case No. ARB/05/22, para. 602; Suez, Sociedad General de Aguas de Barcelona, S.A. and Vivendi Universal, S.A. v. The Argentine RepublicRepublic, Decision on Liability, 30 July 2010 ICSID Case No. ARB/03/19, para. 222. *See also* Hobe, *The Development of the Law of Aliens and Emergence of General Principles of Protection under International Law*, p. 18.

224 *See* Metalclad Corporation v. The United Mexican States, Award, 30 August 2000 ICSID Case No. ARB(AF)/97/1, para. 107; Técnicas Medioambientales

often raised jointly, most of the claims are successful because tribunals conclude that a breach of the FET standard has occurred.[225] States are by no means barred from introducing any change to their laws and regulations.[226] However, they have agreed to honour what the investors justifiably expected at the time they made their investment, by entering into the respective investment treaty entailing the FET provision.[227] In order to determine whether the states have honoured the legitimate expectations of the investors, the rights and obligations at stake must be set into relation by using a balancing test.[228] The balancing test requires the analysis of the purpose, nature and objectives of the measures challenged, and an evaluation of whether they are proportional, reasonable and not discriminatory.[229] The exact contours of this balancing test will be depicted in detail in the next Chapter of this study.[230]

7) Addressees of the Fair and Equitable Treatment Obligation

Under international law, the state is seen as a whole and therefore the FET standard binds all branches of government.[231] Therefore, the violation of the FET standard may arise from administrative acts targeting the investors or their investments directly, from judicial decisions that are addressed directly at the investor or the investment personally, as well as from legislation or regulation.[232] The administrative acts can be adopted by the

---

Tecmed, S.A. v. The United Mexican States, Award, 29 May 2003 ICSID Case No. ARB (AF)/00/2, para. 149; International Thunderbird Gaming Corporation v. The United Mexican States, Award, 26 January 2006 UNCITRAL, para. 147, 166. *See also* Dolzer and Schreuer, *Principles of International Investment Law*, p. 115, 116.

225 Potestà, 'Legitimate Expectations in Investment Treaty Law: Understanding the Roots and the Limits of a Controversial Concept', p. 98.

226 Ibid, p. 113.

227 *See* Ch. 2 IV 1) and 2).

228 Tudor, *The Fair and Equitable Treatment Standard in the International Law of Foreign Investment*, p. 128, 129.

229 Total S.A. v. The Argentine Republic, Decision on Liability, 27 December 2010 ICSID Case No. ARB/04/01, para. 162. *See also* Ch. 2 III 3).

230 Ch. 2. IV 3).

231 Dolzer and Schreuer, *Principles of International Investment Law*, p. 219; Kläger, *'Fair and Equitable Treatment' in International Investment Law*, p. 158.

232 Rusoro Mining Ltd. v. Bolivarian Republic of Venezuela, Award, 22 August 2016 ICSID Case No. ARB(AF)/12/5, para. 523.

government or its agencies respectively. No distinction is made between acts of the administrative, the legislative, or the judicative branch of the government.[233] Furthermore, there is no exhaustive list of state actions, which are held to be infringing the investors' rights. Hence, legislation and regulation can either be aimed at citizens in general or investors and investments in particular.

8) The Basic Aspects of the Fair and Equitable Treatment Standard

In conclusion, arbitral practise demonstrates that the FET standard is comprised of (1) due process and the prohibition of coercion and harassment, (2) the prohibition of unjust or arbitrary treatment, (3) transparency and predictability of the host state's conduct, (4) prohibition of discrimination, and (5) a reasonable degree of consistency in light of the investors' legitimate expectations.[234] Said elements elevate the FET standard to be characterised as "a broad behavioural direction or an indeterminate concept", which offers a broad margin of discretion for the arbitral tribunal due to its flexibility.[235] The flexibility allows the standard to adapt to a variety of circumstances, create a link between law and society, and set conformity requirements between national law and international law.[236] Given the overall importance and its predominant role in this understanding of the FET, the subsequent research will centre around the notion of the legitimate expectations and the act of balancing between the states' right to regulate and the investors' interest in a stable business environment.

IV. Legal Specifics under the Energy Charter Treaty

It is almost universally accepted that that Article 10(1) ECT refers to the FET standard known in international investment law.[237] Although the

---

233 ibid, para. 523.

234 Coming to a similar conclusion: Dolzer, 'Fair and Equitable Treatment: Today's Contours', p. 15; Valenti, *The Protection of General Interests of Host States in the Application of the Fair and Equitable Treatment Standard*, p. 33; Miljenić, 'Energy Charter Treaty – Standards of Investment Protection', p. 55.

235 Knoll-Tudor, *The Fair and Equitable Treatment Standard and Human Rights Norms*, p. 318.

236 ibid, p. 318.

237 Miljenić, 'Energy Charter Treaty – Standards of Investment Protection', p. 55.

FET standard is a principle of international law, the interpretation of the ECT, in accordance with Article 31(1) VCLT also demands that the ordinary meaning, as well as the context and its object and purpose, must be considered.[238] Thus, the term must be interpreted within the context of the various rights and responsibilities, together with all the conditions and limitations to which the Contracting Parties agreed.[239] The special feature of the FET provision in the ECT lies in the fact that it is extraordinarily detailed and supplemented by explanations, annexes and reservations. This makes it theoretically possible for signatory states to "tailor" the FET provision to their own needs.[240] However, issues that have moved into the focus of the EU and its Member States recently, such as the right to regulate, have not been addressed during the adoption of the ECT.

Some investors[241] relied on the word "stable" and tried to argue that Article 10(1) ECT includes a special stabilisation guarantee. In general, it is recognized that stable and equitable conditions are part of the FET standard under the ECT.[242] Nonetheless, the investors' argument did not succeed before the respective tribunals. It was held that the word "stable" in Article 10(1) ECT rather relates to the framework within which the investment takes place, which by definition is subject to change as it adapts to new circumstances.[243] The FET standard under the ECT may only be

---

238 *See* Hobe, *The Development of the Law of Aliens and Emergence of General Principles of Protection under International Law*, p. 18.

239 AWG Group Ltd. v. The Argentine Republic, Decision on Liability, 30 June 2010 ICSID Case No. ARB/03/19, para. 214. *See also* Ch. 1 I.

240 Knoll-Tudor, *The Fair and Equitable Treatment Standard and Human Rights Norms*, p. 315.

241 Inter alia Eiser Infrastructure Limited and Energía Solar Luxembourg S.à.r.l. v. Kingdom of Spain, Award, 4 May 2017 ICSID Case No. ARB/13/36, para. 357; Charanne and Construction Investments v. Kingdom of Spain, Award, 21 January 2016 SCC Case No. V 062/2012, para. 293; Antaris Solar and Dr. Michael Göde v. Czech Republic, Award, 2 May 2018 PCA Case No. 2014-01, para. 267.

242 Happ, *The Energy Charter Treaty*, p. 245; Plama Consortium Limited v. Republic of Bulgaria, Award, 27 August 2008 ICSID Case No. ARB/03/24, para. 173; Electrabel S.A. v. Republic of Hungary, Award, 25 November 2015 ICSID Case No. ARB/07/19, para. 7.73; The PV Investors v. Kingdom of Spain Final, Award, 28 February 2020 PCA Case No. 2012-14, para. 567; Hydro Energy 1 S.A.R.L. and Hydroxana Sweden AB v. The Kingdom of Spain, Decision on Jurisdiction, Liability and Directions on Quantum, 9 March 2020 ICSID Case No. ARB/15/42, para. 548.

243 AES Summit Generation Limited et. al. v. The Republic of Hungary, Award, 23 September 2010 ICSID Case No. ARB/07/22, para. 9.3.29; Plama Consor-

interpreted to protect the reasonable and justifiable expectations of the investors, if such were created in that regard by the host state.[244] Such interpretation corresponds with the recently expressed view of the EU in its negotiation directive at the modernisation of the ECT.[245]

Although the preamble of the ECT also mentions the promotion of long-term cooperation, this is not suggesting that the treaty is conceived as enhancing the particular stability required for such cooperation.[246] In general, fundamental stability in the essential characteristics of the legal regime relied upon by investors in making long-term investments is protected at the core of the ECT's FET standard clause.[247] However, the states

---

tium Limited v. Republic of Bulgaria, Award, 27 August 2008 ICSID Case No. ARB/03/24, para. 173.

244 Plama Consortium Limited v. Republic of Bulgaria, Award, 27 August 2008 ICSID Case No. ARB/03/24, para. 219; also cited, inter alia, by Foresight and others v. Kingdom of Spain Final, Award, 14 November 2018 SCC Case No. V 2015/150, para. 354; Eiser Infrastructure Limited and Energía Solar Luxembourg S.à.r.l. v. Kingdom of Spain, Award, 4 May 2017 ICSID Case No. ARB/13/36, para. 381. Critical with regard to this interpretation but eventually conceding that a different interpretation may not change the outcome: Hydro Energy 1 S.A.R.L. and Hydroxana Sweden AB v. The Kingdom of Spain, Decision on Jurisdiction, Liability and Directions on Quantum, 9 March 2020 ICSID Case No. ARB/15/42, para. 549 and Cavalum SGPS v. Kingdom of Spain, Decision on Jurisdiction, Liability and Directions on Quantum, 31 August 2020 ICSID Case No. ARB/15/34, para. 403, 437.

245 "In line with the EU reformed approach on investment protection, it should be clarified that investment protection provisions cannot be interpreted as a commitment by the Parties not to change their laws, including in a manner that may negatively affect the investor's expectations of profits", Council of the EU, Negotiating Directives for the Modernisation of the Energy Charter Treaty, 2 July 2019, p. 3 <https://data.consilium.europa.eu/doc/document/ST-10745-2019-ADD-1/en/pdf> (accessed 3 May 2021). *See also* Council of the EU, Press Release, 15 July 2019 <https://www.consilium.europa.eu/en/press/press-releases/2019/07/15/council-adopts-negotiation-directives-for-modernisation-of-energy-charter-treaty/> (accessed 3 May 2021).

246 Eiser Infrastructure Limited and Energía Solar Luxembourg S.à.r.l. v. Kingdom of Spain, Award, 4 May 2017 ICSID Case No. ARB/13/36, para. 378.

247 Eiser Infrastructure Limited and Energía Solar Luxembourg S.à.r.l. v. Kingdom of Spain, Award, 4 May 2017 ICSID Case No. ARB/13/36, para. 382; RREEF Infrastructure (G.P.) Limited and RREEF Pan-European Infrastructure Two Lux S.à.r.l. v. Kingdom of Spain, Decision on Responsibility and on the Principles of Quantum, 30 November 2018 ICSID Case No. ARB/13/30, para. 315; Antin Infrastructure Services Luxembourg S.à.r.l. and Antin Energia Termosolar B.V. v. Kingdom of Spain, Award, 15 June 2018 ICSID Case No. ARB/13/31, para. 533; Novenergia II - Energy & Environment (SCA), SICAR v. The Kingdom of

are only barred from introducing regulatory changes, if they committed themselves to refrain from doing so. Therefore, it has to be interpreted as a reinforcement of the FET standard and does—in the absence of a stabilization provision or other assurance—not give rise to a legitimate expectation of stability.[248] Rather, sentences one and two of the first paragraph need to be read in conjunction and form an FET obligation to encourage and create stable, equitable, favourable and transparent conditions for foreign investors.[249]

In detail, the second sentence of Article 10(1) demands that such conditions (as in the first sentence) shall include a commitment to accord FET to protected investments at all times. The wording differs from most BITs and does not obligate the states to accord to FET directly, but simply to create such conditions. By doing so, the ECT imposes a due diligence standard on states and decouples measures that could amount to unfair treatment from strict liability.[250] States are therefore only liable, if they should have acted in a certain manner, but failed to do so. In addition to this, the reference to transparency was construed to obligate states to openly inform the public, i.e. potential investors, about intended changes in policy, laws, judicial decisions, and administrative regulations that may significantly affect investments.[251] Overall, this conduct should enable investors to "adequately plan their investments and, if needed, engage the host state in

Spain, Award, 15 February 2018 SCC Case No. V 2015/063, para. 654, 694; OperaFund Eco-Invest SICAV PLC and Schwab Holding AG v. Kingdom of Spain, Award, 6 September 2019 ICSID Case No. ARB/15/36, para. 508; Stadtwerke München GmbH and others v. Kingdom of Spain, Dissenting Opinion Kaj Hobér, 2 December 2019 ICSID Case No. ARB/15/1, para. 9.

248 Ioan Micula, Viorel Micula, S.C. European Food S.A, S.C. Starmill S.R.L. and S.C. Multipack S.R.L. v. Romania, Award, 11 December 2013 ICSID Case No. ARB/05/20, para. 666; AES Summit Generation Limited et. al. v. The Republic of Hungary, Award, 23 September 2010 ICSID Case No. ARB/07/22, para. 9.3.29-9.3.30; Eiser Infrastructure Limited and Energía Solar Luxembourg S.à.r.l. v. Kingdom of Spain, Award, 4 May 2017 ICSID Case No. ARB/13/36, para. 362; Novenergia II - Energy & Environment (SCA), SICAR v. The Kingdom of Spain, Award, 15 February 2018 SCC Case No. V 2015/063, para. 646; Masdar Solar & Wind Cooperatief U.A. v. Kingdom of Spain, Award, 16 May 2018 ICSID Case No. ARB/14/1, para. 484.

249 Charanne and Construction Investments v. Kingdom of Spain, Award, 21 January 2016 SCC Case No. V 062/2012, para. 476-477.

250 For a contrary opinion *see* Happ, *The Energy Charter Treaty*, p. 249.

251 Happ, *The Energy Charter Treaty*, p. 248; Electrabel S.A. v. Republic of Hungary, Award, 25 November 2015 ICSID Case No. ARB/07/19, para. 7.79.

dialogue about protecting their legitimate expectations".[252] A specific reference to transparency in investment treaties has also been interpreted to impose the duty on the authorities to clarify misunderstandings.[253] However, tribunals have concluded that the reference to transparency under the ECT is not an independent obligation, but rather a simple illustration of the FET standard and its obligation to respect the investors' legitimate expectations.[254]

Moreover, tribunals interpreting the FET standard under ECT requirements, have also taken recourse to the arbitral jurisprudence under other investment treaties.[255] The plentiful case law is considered to have added specific meaning and content to the standard, which can also be used to construe the FET obligation stipulated in the ECT.

Nonetheless, tribunals concluded that the FET standard in the ECT does not contain any reference to the minimum standard for treatment of aliens under customary international law.[256] This finding is contrary to the view expressed by tribunals interpreting various FET provisions found in BITs, which concluded that the FET standard does indeed afford the minimum standard of protection acknowledged in international law.[257] However, the

---

252 Electrabel S.A. v. Republic of Hungary, Award, 25 November 2015 ICSID Case No. ARB/07/19, para. 7.79.

253 *See* Metalclad Corporation v. The United Mexican States, Award, 30 August 2000 ICSID Case No. ARB(AF)/97/1, para. 76. Suggesting the application of the aforementioned holding in the interpretation of the ECT: Happ, *The Energy Charter Treaty*, p. 248.

254 Novenergia II - Energy & Environment (SCA), SICAR v. The Kingdom of Spain, Award, 15 February 2018 SCC Case No. V 2015/063, para. 568; Isolux Netherlands, BV v. Kingdom of Spain Final, Award, 17 July 2016 SCC Case V2013/153, para. 764; Foresight and others v. Kingdom of Spain Final, Award, 14 November 2018 SCC Case No. V 2015/150, para. 361; Hydro Energy 1 S.A.R.L. and Hydroxana Sweden AB v. The Kingdom of Spain, Decision on Jurisdiction, Liability and Directions on Quantum, 9 March 2020 ICSID Case No. ARB/15/42, para. 552.

255 Plama Consortium Limited v. Republic of Bulgaria, Award, 27 August 2008 ICSID Case No. ARB/03/24, para. 164; Stati and others v. Kazakhstan, Award, 19 December 2013 SCC Case No. 116/2010, para. 943.

256 Belenergia S.A. v. Italian Republic, Award, 6 August 2019 ICSID Case No. ARB/15/40; para. 568; SunReserve Luxco Holdings v. Italian Republic Final, Award, 25 March 2020 SCC Arbitration V (2016/32), para. 672.

257 Alex Genin, Eastern Credit Limited, Inc. and A.S. Baltoil v. The Republic of Estonia, Award, 25 June 2001 ICSID Case No. ARB/99/2, para. 367; Ronald S. Lauder v. The Czech Republic, Award, 3 September 2001 UNCITRAL, para. 292; Occidental Exploration and Production Company v. The Republic of Ecuador Final, Award, 1 July 2004 LCIA Case No. UN3467, para. 188.

minimum standard and the FET standard are closely related. Due to their close relationship, the outcome of the application of the two standards will be most likely be substantively the same.[258] Therefore, the question of whether fair and equitable treatment is or is not added to the minimum treatment requirement under international law must not be decided from a practical standpoint.[259] Hence, the FET standard under the ECT does not significantly vary from the overarching principle of international law identified in Section II of this Chapter[260].

The third sentence of Article 10(1) combines a variation of the FPS standard with the non-discrimination standard.[261] The FET standard and the FPS standard are considered two distinct standards of protection under the ECT, dealing with two different types of protection for foreign investors.[262] Nonetheless, there are no known awards in which tribunals found a violation of the FPS standard.[263] Furthermore, the standard of non-discrimination may overlap with the FET standard, but has to be viewed as a separate standard of protection.[264]

In comparison, the FET standard under the ECT requires the states to be particularly forthcoming with information and take an active part in the protection of the legitimate expectations of the investor, instead of merely refraining from acting contrary to them. Beyond that, the substantial provisions of the ECT do not differ from the rights provided by the FET standard under regular BITs.[265]

---

258 Azurix Corp. v. The Argentine Republic, Award, 14 July 2006 ICSID Case No. ARB/01/12, para. 364, 365; Saluka Investments B.V. v. The Czech Republic Partial, Award, 17 March 2006 UNCITRAL, para. 295; Siemens A.G. v. The Argentine Republic, Award, 17 January 2007 ICSID Case No. ARB/02/8, para. 293; CMS Gas Transmission Company v. The Argentine Republic, Award, 21 May 2005 ICSID Case No. ARB/01/8, para. 284.

259 Azurix Corp. v. The Argentine Republic, Award, 14 July 2006 ICSID Case No. ARB/01/12, para. 364.

260 Ch. 1 II.

261 Happ, *The Energy Charter Treaty*, p. 249.

262 Electrabel S.A. v. Republic of Hungary, Award, 25 November 2015 ICSID Case No. ARB/07/19, para. 7.80.

263 Benson, Yim and Orlowski, *The Energy Charter Treaty*, p. 40.

264 Benson, Yim and Orlowski, *The Energy Charter Treaty*, p. 41; ESPF Beteiligungs GmbH et. al. v. Italian Republic, Award, 14 September 2020 ICSID Case No. ARB/16/5, para. 698.

265 Coming to the same conclusion: Electrabel S.A. v. Republic of Hungary, Award, 25 November 2015 ICSID Case No. ARB/07/19, para. 7.79.

Chapter 2: Legitimate Expectations as the Core Element of Fair and Equitable Treatment

The term "legitimate expectations" was first introduced into investment law by arbitral tribunals in the early 2000s and has gained further significance ever since.[266] However, tribunals failed to develop detailed systematics of the legitimate expectations, in particular under which circumstances investors' expectations may be considered legitimate.[267] The lack of efforts to further define the notion may seem odd, considering the dominant role of the concept and the fact that investment treaties rarely contain any specific references to legitimate expectations.[268] Only recently, the notion of legitimate expectations has been explicitly included in investment treaties.[269]

Nonetheless, principles similar to the notion of legitimate expectations can be found in various domestic legal orders, predating its introduction in investment law. Stemming from the principle of good faith and the rule of law, the notion can be found in different legal traditions, in particular,

---

266 Maynard, 'Legitimate Expectations and the Interpretation of the 'Legal Stability Obligation'', p. 101, Potestà, 'Legitimate Expectations in Investment Treaty Law: Understanding the Roots and the Limits of a Controversial Concept', p. 88, 89. For a detailed case law overview *see* Snodgrass, 'Protecting Investors' Legitimate Expectations - Recognizing and Delimiting a General Principle', p. 4-11.

267 Potestà, 'Legitimate Expectations in Investment Treaty Law: Understanding the Roots and the Limits of a Controversial Concept', p. 89. *See also* Nitish Monebhurrun, 'Gold Reserve Inc. v. Bolivarian Republic of Venezuela Enshrining Legitimate Expectations as a General Principle of International Law?' (2015) 32(5) Journal of International Arbitration 551, p. 553, 554.

268 Potestà, 'Legitimate Expectations in Investment Treaty Law: Understanding the Roots and the Limits of a Controversial Concept', p. 90; Gaukrodger, 'The Balance Between Investor Protection and the Right to Regulate in Investment Treaties', p. 26.

269 *For example* Article 8.10(4) CETA (2016), Article 2.4(3) EU-Singapore IPA (2018); Article 2.5(4) of the EU-Vietnam IPA (2019).

German[270] and French[271] administrative law, according to which expectations may be reasonably or legitimately created by the acts and constant representations of the state.[272] The concept of legitimate expectations has also migrated from the domestic legal traditions of the EU Member States into the jurisprudence of the CJEU[273] and of the ECtHR[274]. Additionally, the notion of legitimate expectations has also been acknowledged by the World Trade Organization (WTO), but linked primarily to the good faith principle.[275] This leads to the conclusion that in any developed and democratic legal system, private parties' legitimate expectations are safeguarded, at least to some degree.[276] This also allows drawing inspiration in regard to the interpretation, clarification and a better understanding of the notion of legitimate expectations and other public law concepts from more developed domestic legal systems.[277]

---

270 *"Vertrauensschutz"*, *see* Calmes-Brunet, 'Rechtssicherheit und Vertrauensschutz im Verwaltungsrecht: Ein Vergleich zwischem deutschem und französischem Recht' (2014) 54(12) Juristische Schulung 1077, p. 1077-1081.

271 *"Confiance Légitime"*, *see* Dupuy, 'La ′Protection de l'Attente Légitime des Parties au Contrat: Etude de Droit International des Investissements à la Lumière du Droit Comparé' (Dissertation (Ph.D) Paris-Panthéon-Assas 30 November 2007), p. 92-102.

272 Gold Reserve Inc. v. Bolivarian Republic of Venezuela, Award, 22 September 2014 ICSID Case No. ARB(AF)/09/1, para. 576; Monebhurrun, 'Gold Reserve Inc. v. Bolivarian Republic of Venezuela Enshrining Legitimate Expectations as a General Principle of International Law?', p. 556; Potestà, 'Legitimate Expectations in Investment Treaty Law: Understanding the Roots and the Limits of a Controversial Concept', p. 93-96.

273 *See for example* CJEU Judgment *HLH Warenvertriebs GmbH and Orthica BV v Germany,*9 June 2005 C-17/03, para. 73; CJEU Judgment *Atlanta v European Community,*14 October 1999 C-104/97 P, para. 52; CJEU Judgment *Di Lenardo and Dilexport,*15 July 2004 C-37/02 and C-38/02, para. 70.

274 *See for example* ECtHR Judgment *Centro Europa 7 srl and di Stefano v. Italy,* 7 June 2012 Application No. 38433/09, para. 173.

275 India—Patent Protection for Pharmaceutical and Agricultural Chemical Products Report of the Appellate Body, 19 December 1997 WT/DS50/AB/R, para. 41; European Communities—Customs Classification of Certain Computer Equipment, Report of the Appellate Body Report of the Appellate Body, 5 June 1998 WT/DS62/AB/R, WT/DS67/AB/R, WT/DS68/AB/R, para. 80. For an in-deph review *see* Marion Panizzon, *Good Faith in the Jurisprudence of the WTO: The protection of Legitimate Expectations, Good Faith Interpretation and Fair Dispute Settlement* (Studies in International Trade Law vol 4, Hart 2006).

276 Palombino, *Fair and Equitable Treatment and the Fabric of General Principles*, p. 86.

277 Schill, *Fair and Equitable Treatment, the Rule of Law, and Comparative Public Law*, p. 154. *See also* Total S.A. v. The Argentine Republic, Decision on Liability,

In addition, the advanced jurisprudence regarding legitimate expectations and concerning indirect expropriation has been sampled multiple times as guidelines for the application of the notion in the FET standard.[278] Despite its broad acceptance today, it was partially questioned whether legitimate expectations have no grounds in international law and are merely a tool of interpretation.[279] Nevertheless, the majority of tribunals and scholars accepts that the notion of legitimate expectations stems from general principles of law, as referred to in Article 38(1)(c) of the ICJ Statute, and forms the central component of the FET standard.[280]

Notwithstanding that there are other subcategories of the FET standard, the legitimate expectations of the investors are the turning point in most cases.[281] However, the notion of legitimate expectations is difficult to apply due to its missing links in the wording of FET provisions and its sole origin in jurisprudence.[282] Therefore, a thorough analysis of the notions purpose and components is necessary.

---

27 December 2010 ICSID Case No. ARB/04/01, para. 128-130, also cited by Toto Costruzioni Generali S.p.A. v. The Republic of Lebanon, Award, 7 June 2012 ICSID Case No. ARB/07/12, para. 166.

278 Dolzer and Schreuer, *Principles of International Investment Law*, p. 115, 145.

279 Dupuy, *La 'Protection de l'Attente Légitime des Parties au Contrat*, p. 396; MTD Equity Sdn. Bhd. and MTD Chile S.A. v. Republic of Chile Decision on Annulment, 21 March 2007 ICSID Case No. ARB/01/7, para. 67.

280 *See for example* Gold Reserve Inc. v. Bolivarian Republic of Venezuela, Award, 22 September 2014 ICSID Case No. ARB(AF)/09/1, para. 575–576; Técnicas Medioambientales Tecmed, S.A. v. The United Mexican States, Award, 29 May 2003 ICSID Case No. ARB (AF)/00/2, para. 154; Total S.A. v. The Argentine Republic, Decision on Liability, 27 December 2010 ICSID Case No. ARB/04/01, para. 128; Toto Costruzioni Generali S.p.A. v. The Republic of Lebanon, Award, 7 June 2012 ICSID Case No. ARB/07/12, para. 166; LG&E Energy Corp. LG&E Capital Corp. and LG&E International, Inc. v. The Argentine Republic, Decision on Liability, 3 October 2006 ICSID Case No. ARB/02/1, para. 127; MTD Equity Sdn. Bhd. and MTD Chile S.A. v. Republic of Chile, Award, 25 May 2004 ICSID Case No. ARB/01/7, para. 114; Occidental Exploration and Production Company v. The Republic of Ecuador Final, Award, 1 July 2004 LCIA Case No. UN3467, para. 185; Dolzer and Schreuer, *Principles of International Investment Law*, p. 145, Potestà, 'Legitimate Expectations in Investment Treaty Law: Understanding the Roots and the Limits of a Controversial Concept', p. 121; Monebhurrun, 'Gold Reserve Inc. v. Bolivarian Republic of Venezuela Enshrining Legitimate Expectations as a General Principle of International Law?', p. 560, 651.

281 *See above* Ch. 1 III 2)-5).

282 Knoll-Tudor, *The Fair and Equitable Treatment Standard and Human Rights Norms*, p. 327.

I. Purpose of the Legitimate Expectations: Balancing Legal Interests

The concept of legitimate expectations represents the specific features of the *venire contra factum proprium* principle and is, therefore, a manifestation of the good faith principle in international law.[283] It follows from the principle of good faith and the rule of law that states may not act inconsistently towards private individuals.[284] In particular, they may not change their expressed positions on a particular matter, without an objective reason. This also includes an obligation to thoroughly consider the interests of investors in light of their basic expectations.[285] In the early stages of the legitimate expectation's development, a rather stiff pattern was used to determine whether legitimate expectations were violated.[286] This approach, however, was strongly criticized because of its extreme demands on the states' conduct and its inflexibility.[287]

---

283 Total S.A. v. The Argentine Republic, Decision on Liability, 27 December 2010 ICSID Case No. ARB/04/01, para. 111; Foresight and others v. Kingdom of Spain Final, Award, 14 November 2018 SCC Case No. V 2015/150, para. 362; Sipiorski, *Good Faith in International Investment Arbitration*, para. 9.04, 9.08; Kläger, *'Fair and Equitable Treatment' in International Investment Law*, p. 130; Parchomiuk, 'The Protection of Legitimate Expectations in Administrative Law: A Horizontal Perspective', p. 6.

284 Total S.A. v. The Argentine Republic, Decision on Liability, 27 December 2010 ICSID Case No. ARB/04/01, para. 129; Monebhurrun, 'Gold Reserve Inc. v. Bolivarian Republic of Venezuela Enshrining Legitimate Expectations as a General Principle of International Law?', p. 556; Potestà, 'Legitimate Expectations in Investment Treaty Law: Understanding the Roots and the Limits of a Controversial Concept', p. 93-96.

285 The Tribunal in *TecMed* held that the principle of good faith contained in the FET standard "requires the Contracting Parties to provide to international investments treatment that does not affect the basic expectations that were taken into account by the foreign investor to make the investment", Técnicas Medioambientales Tecmed, S.A. v. The United Mexican States, Award, 29 May 2003 ICSID Case No. ARB (AF)/00/2, para. 154.

286 The Tribunal in *TecMed* outlined a pattern of conduct with respect to the foreign investor or its investments, which primarily reflected the elements of the FET standard analysed above in Ch. 1 III, Técnicas Medioambientales Tecmed, S.A. v. The United Mexican States, Award, 29 May 2003 ICSID Case No. ARB (AF)/00/2, para. 154.

287 UNCTAD, 'Fair and Equitable Treatment', p. 65; McLachlan, Shore and Weiniger, *International Investment Arbitration*, p. 315; MTD Equity Sdn. Bhd. and MTD Chile S.A. v. Republic of Chile Decision on Annulment, 21 March 2007 ICSID Case No. ARB/01/7, para. 67; Biwater Gauff (Tanzania) Ltd. v. United Republic of Tanzania, Award, 24 July 2004 ICSID Case No. ARB/05/22,

Instead, an approach developed that identified the notion of legitimate expectations as a distinct subcategory of the FET standard.[288] Under this progressive interpretation, the question must be asked whether states created expectations in investors, and whether the reasonable reliance on these expectations was violated by subsequent state conduct.[289] To assess, whether a violation occurred, tribunals have weighed the investors' legitimate expectations against the states' duty to regulate its legal framework in the public interest.[290] Thus, the aim of legitimate expectations is to balance between the right of the state to regulate on one side, the duty to accord FET on the other side, and consequently, to provide the investor with a stable legal framework.[291] Such a concept allows for a more subtle approach to provide a case-specific remedy, as compared to the more drastic "all-or-nothing" approach inherent in the concept of direct or indirect expropriation through regulatory measures.[292] Whereas tribunals under an expropriation claim only have the option to deny or accept that an unlaw-

---

para. 600; El Paso Energy International Company v. The Argentine Republic, Award, 31 October 2011 ICSID Case No. ARB/03/15, para. 343.

288 *Thomas Wälde* elaborated in his separate opinion that the notion of the legitimate expectations has developed "from an earlier function as a subsidiary interpretative principle to reinforce a particular interpretative approach chosen to its current role as a self-standing subcategory and independent basis for a claim under 'fair and equitable standard'", International Thunderbird Gaming Corporation v. The United Mexican States Separate Opinion of Thomas Wälde, 26 January 2006 UNCITRAL, para. 37.

289 In the context of the North American Free Trade Agreement (NAFTA), the Tribunal in *Thunderbird* held that the concept of legitimate expectations relates to a situation where a state's conduct "creates reasonable and justifiable expectations on the part of an investor (or investment) to act in reliance on said conduct, such that a failure [...] to honour those expectations could cause the investor (or investment) to suffer damage" International Thunderbird Gaming Corporation v. The United Mexican States, Award, 26 January 2006 UNCITRAL, para. 147.

290 *See for example* Saluka Investments B.V. v. The Czech Republic Partial, Award, 17 March 2006 UNCITRAL, para. 301, 302, 305; Total S.A. v. The Argentine Republic, Decision on Liability, 27 December 2010 ICSID Case No. ARB/04/01, para. 121; Joseph Charles Lemire v. Ukraine Decision on Liability, 14 January 2010 ICSID Case No. ARB/06/18, para. 285.

291 Coop and Seif, 'ECT and State's Right to Regulate' in Scherer and Amirfar (eds), *International Arbitration in the Energy Sector* (OUP 2018), para. 10.02; Peter Muchlinski, "Caveat Investor'? The Relevance of the Conduct of the Investor Under the Fair and Equitable Treatment Standard' (2006) 55(3) ICLQ 527, p. 532.

292 International Thunderbird Gaming Corporation v. The United Mexican States Separate Opinion of Thomas Wälde, 26 January 2006 UNCITRAL, para. 37.

ful taking of a right had occured, the FET standard and the notion of the legitimate expectations allow a balance between the rights and interests at stake. This circumstance comes into play particularly in the review of administrative decisions, in which the fine line between the lawful exercise of the administrative discretion and the unlawful abuse of power must be drawn, in a careful analysis of the facts and circumstances, and a balancing of the rights at stake.[293]

The rights at stake are the investors' interest in maintaining a given legal situation, on the one side, and the states' inherent power to regulate in the public interest, on the other side. By striking a fair balance, a stable investment environment is created, which can be relied on by the investors in their assessments and business decisions.[294] The balancing test, when applied in a legitimate expectation setting, has been originally imported from domestic law. Almost all domestic legal systems have developed some degree of balancing test for the rights at stake in a particular case.[295] This interpretative approach gives states the necessary freedom to address the core issues of public interest. At the same time, it allows the tribunals to make a case-by-case decision based on the level of commitment of the host state and to balance the opposing rights and interests.

Before discussing the exact approach with regard to the balancing of opposing rights and interests *infra*[296], it is necessary to determine the relevant time of the investment and further contour the notion of legitimate expectations by examining the different components which may give rise to legitimate expectations.

---

293 As observed by the Tribunal in *Total v. The Argentine Republic*, the notion of legitimate expectations "appears to be applicable mostly in respect of administrative acts and protects an individual from an incoherent exercise of administrative discretion, or excess or abuse of administrative powers", Total S.A. v. The Argentine Republic, Decision on Liability, 27 December 2010 ICSID Case No. ARB/04/01, para. 129.

294 Palombino, *Fair and Equitable Treatment and the Fabric of General Principles*, p. 87; Potestà, 'Legitimate Expectations in Investment Treaty Law: Understanding the Roots and the Limits of a Controversial Concept', p. 113.

295 *See* 2 IV 3).

296 *See* 2 IV 3).

II. Time for the Determination of Legitimate Expectations

The legitimacy of the investors' expectations must be evaluated at the time the investment was made.[297] Commitments after the investment have been conducted cannot be taken into consideration.[298] Hence, determining the exact time of the investment is critical to the success of the investors' claim under the FET standard.[299] Assessing the time when the investment was in fact made might be more difficult, depending on the size of the investment in the actual case.[300] Conducting a larger investment project will transcend through various stages: Starting from negotiations, due diligence, internal corporate decisions, over external contractual commitments, financing, acquisition, construction, registration, and start-up, as well as the first generation of revenues.[301] Investments may also be structured in consecutive executive stages. If there are binding commitments predating one of these consecutive stages, they may nonetheless apply for future stages of the investment.[302] Hence, a change in the regulatory framework might be more apparent at a subsequent stage than at the start of the initial investment negotiations.[303] At an advanced stage, however, the investors might have already dispensed substantial amounts of capital

297 Schreuer and Kriebaum, 'At What Time Must Legitimate Expectations Exist?' (2012) Transnational Dispute Management 265, p. 268.

298 Duke Energy Electroquil Partners & Electroquil S.A. v. Republic of Ecuador, Award, 18 August 2008 ICSID Case No. ARB/04/19, para. 365.

299 Novenergia II - Energy & Environment (SCA), SICAR v. The Kingdom of Spain, Award, 15 February 2018 SCC Case No. V 2015/063, para. 532; RREEF Infrastructure (G.P.) Limited and RREEF Pan-European Infrastructure Two Lux S.à.r.l. v. Kingdom of Spain, Decision on Responsibility and on the Principles of Quantum, 30 November 2018 ICSID Case No. ARB/13/30, para. 391.

300 Schreuer and Kriebaum, 'At What Time Must Legitimate Expectations Exist?', p. 269.

301 Novenergia II - Energy & Environment (SCA), SICAR v. The Kingdom of Spain, Award, 15 February 2018 SCC Case No. V 2015/063, para. 538, also cited by Cavalum SGPS v. Kingdom of Spain, Decision on Jurisdiction, Liability and Directions on Quantum, 31 August 2020 ICSID Case No. ARB/15/34, para. 451.

302 *See* Sempra Energy International v. The Argentine Republic, Award, 28 September 2007 ICSID Case No. ARB/02/16 and Belenergia S.A. v. Italian Republic, Award, 6 August 2019 ICSID Case No. ARB/15/40 in which the investment took place in different instalments. *See also* SunReserve Luxco Holdings v. Italian Republic Final, Award, 25 March 2020 SCC Arbitration V (2016/32), para. 718.

303 In Isolux Netherlands, BV v. Kingdom of Spain Final, Award, 17 July 2016 SCC Case V2013/153 and Belenergia S.A. v. Italian Republic, Award, 6 August 2019 ICSID Case No. ARB/15/40 the respective tribunals deemed the investments to

into the investment and are not able to reverse their business decision. Therefore, the time of the investment cannot be generalised, but it has to be assessed on a case-by-case basis. If the investment is conducted in different stages, the legitimate expectations must be assessed at the time of every step towards the creation, expansion, development or reorganization of the investment.[304]

Some tribunals took the decision to invest as the crucial time for the determination of the investors' legitimate expectations, i.e. the time from which on the investors had "irreversibly committed" themselves to the investment.[305] Such points of irreversible commitment were considered, for example, when the investor had acquired a 100% interest in the company holding the energy plants[306] or when the bank financing contracts have been concluded[307]. An irreversible commitment was also found when the construction contract was concluded and the installation work for the power plant was stated.[308]

be conducted at time in which the change in the regulatory framework was already apparent.

304 Schreuer and Kriebaum, 'At What Time Must Legitimate Expectations Exist?', p. 270, 276.

305 Novenergia II - Energy & Environment (SCA), SICAR v. The Kingdom of Spain, Award, 15 February 2018 SCC Case No. V 2015/063, para. 539; SunReserve Luxco Holdings v. Italian Republic Final, Award, 25 March 2020 SCC Arbitration V (2016/32), para. 767.

306 Novenergia II - Energy & Environment (SCA), SICAR v. The Kingdom of Spain, Award, 15 February 2018 SCC Case No. V 2015/063, para. 539; Isolux Netherlands, BV v. Kingdom of Spain Final, Award, 17 July 2016 SCC Case V2013/153, para. 783; SunReserve Luxco Holdings v. Italian Republic Final, Award, 25 March 2020 SCC Arbitration V (2016/32), para. 768; Cavalum SGPS v. Kingdom of Spain, Decision on Jurisdiction, Liability and Directions on Quantum, 31 August 2020 ICSID Case No. ARB/15/34, para. 451, 452.

307 When the respondent alleged that the date of investment was the conclusion of the bank financing contracts, this contention has not been rebutted by the tribunal, NextEra Energy Global Holdings B.V. and NextEra Energy Spain Holdings B.V. v. Kingdom of Spain, Decision on Jurisdiction, Liability and Quantum Principles, 12 March 2019 ICSID Case No. ARB/14/11, para. 499.

308 I.C.W. Europe Investments Limited v. The Czech Republic, Award, 15 May 2019 PCA CASE No 2014-22, para. 549; Voltaic Network GmbH v. Czech Republic, Award, 15 September 2019 PCA CASE No 2014-20, para507; WA Investments-Europa Nova Limited v. The Czech Republic, Award, 15 May 2019 PCA CASE No 2014-19, para. 590.

III. Components of the Legitimate Expectations

Although legitimate expectations are naturally subjective, the question of whether they are legally protected under the FET standard must be assessed objectively.[309] Legitimate expectations are not subjective hopes and perceptions, and must not be frivolous or unrealistic.[310] Rather, they must be based on objectively verifiable facts.[311] Neither is the notion of legitimate expectations synonymous with a simply reasonable business judgement, as even reasonable business decisions involve taking and accepting certain risks.[312] Hence, a tribunal has to determine the facts and circumstances on an objective basis, and balance the different rights accordingly.[313] Such facts and circumstances can (arguably) be found in the host state's legal framework, and in any undertakings and representations made explicitly or implicitly by the host state.[314] Additionally, the circumstances in which an investment was made are crucial to determine the legitimacy and reasonableness of the expectations.[315] This also includes the

309 Maynard, 'Legitimate Expectations and the Interpretation of the 'Legal Stability Obligation'', p. 103; Garcia-Castrillon, 'Spain and Investment Arbitration - The Renewable Energy Explosion' in Armand de Mestral (ed), *Second Thoughts: Investor-State Arbitration between Developed Democracies* (Centre for International Governance Innovation 2017), p. 293; Coop and Seif, *ECT and State's Right to Regulate*, para. 10.78; Invesmart v. Czech Republic, Award, 26 June 2009 UNCITRAL, para. 250.

310 Dolzer and Schreuer, *Principles of International Investment Law*, p. 145; Maynard, 'Legitimate Expectations and the Interpretation of the 'Legal Stability Obligation'', p. 103.

311 Ibid, p. 103.

312 Schreuer and Kriebaum, 'At What Time Must Legitimate Expectations Exist?', p. 265; Maynard, 'Legitimate Expectations and the Interpretation of the 'Legal Stability Obligation'', p. 103.

313 Dolzer, 'Fair and Equitable Treatment: Today's Contours', p. 20; Tudor, *The Fair and Equitable Treatment Standard in the International Law of Foreign Investment*, p. 217.

314 Dolzer and Schreuer, *Principles of International Investment Law*, p. 145; Invesmart v. Czech Republic, Award, 26 June 2009 UNCITRAL, para. 250-258.

315 Maynard, 'Legitimate Expectations and the Interpretation of the 'Legal Stability Obligation'', p. 103; Duke Energy Electroquil Partners & Electroquil S.A. v. Republic of Ecuador, Award, 18 August 2008 ICSID Case No. ARB/04/19, para. 340; El Paso Energy International Company v. The Argentine Republic, Award, 31 October 2011 ICSID Case No. ARB/03/15, para. 360.

prevailing situation in the host state in which the investment was made, and with due regard to the host states' rights.[316]

In general, expectations are born and become legitimate, i.e. protected by international obligations, because of the existence of reliance by the investors on the representations made by the host state.[317] Claims for compensation for the violation of legitimate expectations regularly arise out of changes or alterations to the initial representations made by the host state to an individual or a group of investors.[318] On the part of the investors, reliance requires that investors prove proper due diligence, i.e. that certain expectations were reasonable in the light of the legal and factual investment environment in the host state.[319]

Thus, the main aspects of the concept of legitimate expectations are representation, reliance, and subsequent frustration based on the aforementioned requirements.[320] Under what circumstances a state made a binding

---

316 Maynard, 'Legitimate Expectations and the Interpretation of the 'Legal Stability Obligation'', p. 103. *See for example* Generation Ukraine, Inc. v. Ukraine, Award, 16 September 2003 ICSID Case No. ARB/00/9, para. 20.37; Methanex Corporation v. United States of America Final, Award, 3 August 2005 UNCITRAL, Part 4, Ch. D, para. 9,10.

317 The Tribunal in *Invesmart* analysed the prevailing investment practice at the time and set out "six propositions" relevant to the assessment of legitimate expectations:
(a) the expectations must be objectively reasonable;
(b) a contract can be a source of evidence about expectations;
(c) expectations must be generated by state conduct directed to the investor;
(d) expectations are to be shaped by the investor's burden of performing its own due diligence in vetting the investment;
(e) expectations must be based on the host state's legal regulatory regime; and
(f) investors must respect the allocation of functions across governmental departments, preventing one organ from binding another,
Invesmart v. Czech Republic, Award, 26 June 2009 UNCITRAL, para. 249-258. *See also* Maynard, 'Legitimate Expectations and the Interpretation of the 'Legal Stability Obligation'', p. 104; Monebhurrun, 'Gold Reserve Inc. v. Bolivarian Republic of Venezuela Enshrining Legitimate Expectations as a General Principle of International Law?', p. 560, 561. While all of named aspects play a role in determining the frustration of legitimate expectations, the questions of whether the state had made specific representations to the investor prior to the investment and whether the state has failed to offer a stable and predictable legal framework are the principal points in the recent renewable energy cases.

318 Levashova, *The Right of States to Regulate in International Investment Law*, p. 114.

319 Viñuales, 'Investor Diligence in Investment Arbitration: Sources and Arguments', p. 362.

320 *Knoll-Tudor* defines general criteria for the assessment of the legitimacy of the expectations as "the type of conduct necessary to generate expectations that

commitment via a representation and whether investors relied on such representations reasonably in light of their due diligence, will be further assessed in this Section.

1) Content of the Investors' Legitimate Expectations

Regarding the content of the representation, states may commit to anything which they deem important to the investor. The only limitation is that the aim sought with the commitment is reasonable and attainable from the perspective of an objective third person. In general, the burden of proof with regard to the exact content and its correct interpretation of a state representation lies with the investors.[321] Even so, states may not "evade" liability by using vague language.[322] Rather, the representation must be precise and unambiguous.[323] The transparency aspect of the FET can also compel authorities to clarify misunderstandings based on their communication.[324] Hence, misunderstandings as a result of ambiguous communication on the side of state officials must be borne by

become legitimate by an authority of the host state; the level of the expectations have to be reasonable and justifiable in light of the conduct; and there has to be a causal link between the failure to respect these expectations and the damage suffered by the investor", Knoll-Tudor, *The Fair and Equitable Treatment Standard and Human Rights Norms*, p. 327. This view is also reflected in recent arbitral jurisprudence, *see* Antaris Solar and Dr. Michael Göde v. Czech Republic, Award, 2 May 2018 PCA Case No. 2014-01, para. 360(3); RREEF Infrastructure (G.P.) Limited and RREEF Pan-European Infrastructure Two Lux S.à.r.l. v. Kingdom of Spain, Decision on Responsibility and on the Principles of Quantum, 30 November 2018 ICSID Case No. ARB/13/30, para. 388; CEF Energia B.V. v. Italian Republic, Award, 16 January 2019 SCC Arbitration No. 2015/158, para. 235; SunReserve Luxco Holdings v. Italian Republic Final, Award, 25 March 2020 SCC Arbitration V (2016/32), para. 695; ESPF Beteiligungs GmbH et. al. v. Italian Republic, Award, 14 September 2020 ICSID Case No. ARB/16/5, para. 644.

321 Tudor, *The Fair and Equitable Treatment Standard in the International Law of Foreign Investment*, p. 138.

322 Mairal, *Legitimate Expectations and Informal Administrative Representations*, p. 429.

323 Mairal, *Legitimate Expectations and Informal Administrative Representations*, p. 429. *See for example* Marvin Roy Feldman Karpa v. United Mexican States, Award, 16 December 2002 ICSID Case No. ARB(AF)/99/1, para. 123–127.

324 Metalclad Corporation v. The United Mexican States, Award, 30 August 2000 ICSID Case No. ARB(AF)/97/1, para. 76.

the states.[325] This notwithstanding, the subsequent conduct of parties to an agreement may provide evidence of the intent of the parties.[326] This, however, is only an evidentiary rule, which should not be confused with the fact that the relevant time for determining the legitimate expectation is the time of the investment.

On the lower end, the very core of every investors' expectations is the expectation of a reasonable return.[327] Thus, a fine line must be drawn between protecting the investors' legitimate trust and assuming an unjustified state guarantee against the typical investment risk that expectations of profitability are not met.[328] Only if investors can prove that they relied on the representations made by the state, may their expectations form the basis for a claim to compensation based on the violation of legitimate expectations and the FET standard.[329]

2) Aspects of the Commitment of the State

Tribunals assessing the concept of legitimate expectations have often stressed the fact that the right of the host state to adapt the legal framework to changing circumstances can, under regular circumstances, only be barred by specific commitments.[330] If an authority represents the state in

325 International Thunderbird Gaming Corporation v. The United Mexican States Separate Opinion of Thomas Wälde, 26 January 2006 UNCITRAL, para. 88; Metalclad Corporation v. The United Mexican States, Award, 30 August 2000 ICSID Case No. ARB(AF)/97/1, para. 76; Occidental Exploration and Production Company v. The Republic of Ecuador Final, Award, 1 July 2004 LCIA Case No. UN3467, para. 184; Azurix Corp. v. The Argentine Republic, Award, 14 July 2006 ICSID Case No. ARB/01/12, para. 91.

326 Mairal, *Legitimate Expectations and Informal Administrative Representations*, p. 439.

327 Selivanova, 'Changes in Renewables Support Policy and Investment Protection under the Energy Charter Treaty: Analysis of Jurisprudence and Outlook for the Current Arbitration Cases' (2018) 33(2) ICSID Review - Foreign Investment Law Journal 433, p. 442, 447.

328 Diehl, *The Core Standard of International Investment Protection*, para. 386.

329 Copper Mesa Mining Corporation v. Republic of Ecuador Award PCA No. 2012-2, para. 6.61.

330 *See* Potestà, 'Legitimate Expectations in Investment Treaty Law: Understanding the Roots and the Limits of a Controversial Concept', p. 113; Mairal, *Legitimate Expectations and Informal Administrative Representations*, p. 439; Mayeda, 'Playing Fair: The Meaning of Fair and Equitable Treatment in Bilateral Investment Treaties', p. 276.

a specific, precise, unambiguous, and unqualified manner, it will normally create the reasonable expectation within the addressee of the representation, that the authority will act in the prescribed way.[331] Thus, a host state which acts intentionally to create expectations for potential investors, with respect to particular treatment or comportment, should abide by these commitments.[332] The analogy of a merchant who makes a contract or agreement with the intent not to perform can be used to illustrate when a state acted unfairly, hence violating the legitimate expectations of the investor.[333] As initially outlined, the very core of this reasoning can be traced back to the principle of good faith, i.e. the rule of *venire contra factum proprium*, which bans contradictory behaviour.[334] This requires states to abide by representations made by and attributable to a competent state authority, which are capable of creating expectations within the investor.[335] In a temporal dimension, the extent of the investor's reliance on state representations must be assessed in context and light of how the officials actually dealt with the investor at the time of the investment.[336]

The commitments relevant under international investment law can be distinguished into two types: specific commitments and commitments of a

---

331 Schønberg, *Legitimate Expectations in Administrative Law* (OUP 2000), p. 125.

332 Metalclad Corporation v. The United Mexican States, Award, 30 August 2000 ICSID Case No. ARB(AF)/97/1, para. 85, 89; Campbell, 'House of Cards: The Relevance of Legitimate Expectations under Fair and Equitable Treatment Provisions in Investment Treaty Law' (2013) 30(4) Journal of International Arbitration 361, p. 367.

333 Stadtwerke München GmbH and others v. Kingdom of Spain, Award, 2 December 2019 ICSID Case No. ARB/15/1, para. 257.

334 Mairal, *Legitimate Expectations and Informal Administrative Representations*, p. 422, 423; Sipiorski, *Good Faith in International Investment Arbitration*, para. 9.04, 9.08; Kläger, *'Fair and Equitable Treatment' and Sustainable Development*, p. 130; Parchomiuk, 'The Protection of Legitimate Expectations in Administrative Law: A Horizontal Perspective', p. 6.

335 The Tribunal in *Micula* concluded that "there must be a promise, assurance or representation attributable to a competent organ or representative of the state, which may be explicit or implicit. The crucial point is whether the state, through statements or conduct, has contributed to the creation of a reasonable expectation, in this case, a representation of regulatory stability", Ioan Micula, Viorel Micula, S.C. European Food S.A, S.C. Starmill S.R.L. and S.C. Multipack S.R.L. v. Romania, Award, 11 December 2013 ICSID Case No. ARB/05/20, para 669; also cited by Foresight and others v. Kingdom of Spain Final, Award, 14 November 2018 SCC Case No. V 2015/150, para. 353; Cavalum SGPS v. Kingdom of Spain, Decision on Jurisdiction, Liability and Directions on Quantum, 31 August 2020 ICSID Case No. ARB/15/34, para. 431.

336 Invesmart v. Czech Republic, Award, 26 June 2009 UNCITRAL, para. 252.

more general nature.[337] Specificity in this context means individualization, i.e. the promise or representation is addressed to the individual investor or a limited group of investors, and not to an undefined amount of potential investors.[338] Specific commitments, made explicitly or implicitly by the host states, are the strongest basis for legitimate expectations.[339] In contrast, general commitment is understood as the counterpart to specific commitments, i.e. any conduct of the state, which is not exclusively addressed to a specific investor or a limited group of investors, but any potential investor.[340] General commitments can be, inter alia, advertisements or the simple provision of information, without any link to a specific investor, as well as the legal framework of the host state.

How commitments on the part of the state are to be understood must be determined from the perspective of an objective recipient of the representation.[341] This gives the notion an objective scope and means that objective aspects are decisive. Hence, the understanding of the actual investor in the given case is supplementary at best. It can also be disregarded whether the state subjectively wished to commit itself. Rather, it must be assessed how an objective receiver in the position of the respective investor would have reasonably understood the host state's conduct.[342]

---

337 UNCTAD noted already in 2012 that "[a]rbitral decisions suggest in this regard that an investor may derive legitimate expectations either from (a) specific commitments addressed to it personally, for example, in the form of a stabilization clause, or (b) rules that are not specifically addressed to a particular investor but which are put in place with a specific aim to induce foreign investments and on which the foreign investor relied in making his investment", UNCTAD, 'Fair and Equitable Treatment', para. 69.

338 Potestà, 'Legitimate Expectations in Investment Treaty Law: Understanding the Roots and the Limits of a Controversial Concept', p. 105; El Paso Energy International Company v. The Argentine Republic, Award, 31 October 2011 ICSID Case No. ARB/03/15, para. 375–377.

339 Dolzer and Schreuer, *Principles of International Investment Law*, p. 145; Levashova, *The Right of States to Regulate in International Investment Law*, p. 139.

340 Potestà, 'Legitimate Expectations in Investment Treaty Law: Understanding the Roots and the Limits of a Controversial Concept', p. 110.

341 Maynard, 'Legitimate Expectations and the Interpretation of the 'Legal Stability Obligation'', p. 103; Garcia-Castrillon, *Spain and Investment Arbitration - The Renewable Energy Explosion*, p. 293; Invesmart v. Czech Republic, Award, 26 June 2009 UNCITRAL, para. 250.

342 Ioan Micula, Viorel Micula, S.C. European Food S.A, S.C. Starmill S.R.L. and S.C. Multipack S.R.L. v. Romania, Award, 11 December 2013 ICSID Case No. ARB/05/20, paa 669; also cited by Foresight and others v. Kingdom of Spain Final, Award, 14 November 2018 SCC Case No. V 2015/150, para. 353; Cavalum

The different types of commitments will be outlined in the following segment, in order to allow for proper categorization of the relevant conduct of the host states in the renewable energy cases.

a) Representatives of the State in International Investment Law

Before the different types of commitments can be examined, it must be clarified which authorities can act on behalf of the state, and thus issue commitments. It was highlighted that investors cannot base their expectations solely on hopes and assumptions. Rather, they must have relied on the commitment of a state to do or to omit to do something. In domestic law, a state is foremost represented by its government. The government again can be represented by lower-ranked state officials, as long as they act within their capacity. In international law, the same requirement applies that a representation, which may constitute a commitment, must be attributable to the government and hence the state.[343]

International Law Commission (ILC) has developed guiding principles on unilateral declarations in international law, in which it concludes that state authorities acting on behalf of the state must do so within their capacity.[344] It has been suggested that these public international law rules could be applied by analogy, within the investment law context.[345] However, it has not been accepted in international investment law that a state can challenge a representation on the grounds that a state official did

SGPS v. Kingdom of Spain, Decision on Jurisdiction, Liability and Directions on Quantum, 31 August 2020 ICSID Case No. ARB/15/34, para. 431.

343 *See* in regard to legitimate expectations created by constant jurisprudence of lower rank authorities ADF Group Inc. v. United States of America, Award, 9 January 2003 ICSID Case No. ARB (AF)/00/1, para. 189. *See also* with regard to representations made by state entities Ch. 4 I 2) a) (1).

344 Guiding Pinciple 4, International Law Commission, 'Guiding Principles Applicable to Unilateral Declarations of States Capable of Creating Legal Obligations, With Commentaries Thereto' (2006) <https://legal.un.org/ilc/texts/instruments/english/commentaries/9_9_2006.pdf> (accessed 3 May 2021).

345 Potestà, 'Legitimate Expectations in Investment Treaty Law: Understanding the Roots and the Limits of a Controversial Concept', p. 109; Total S.A. v. The Argentine Republic, Decision on Liability, 27 December 2010 ICSID Case No. ARB/04/01, para. 134; sceptical thereto Palombino, *Fair and Equitable Treatment and the Fabric of General Principles*, p. 107.

not act within its capacity.[346] The capacity of a state official is defined by national rules and internal administrative decisions which have no effect on the obligations of a state under international law.[347] In this regard, Article 27 VCLT provides that a state may not invoke the provisions of its internal law as justification for its failure to perform a treaty.[348] Similarly, a state cannot justify the breach of the obligation to provide FET to investors, if a state official acted *ultra vires*.[349] Hence, the state is generally perceived as one in international investment law, and may not rely on international regulations as a defence.[350]

It follows that states are generally responsible for any act or omission of any of their political subdivisions or agencies, which may constitute a violation of international obligations.[351] In terms of effectiveness, governmental representation has a greater impact on the legitimacy of investors' expectations, depending on the seniority of the rank of the official who acted on behalf of the state.[352] Furthermore, the representations become more convincing with each additional government official that is involved in the representation process.[353]

However, an investor may not blindly rely on each and every representation by a state official. Taking into account the due diligence requirement

---

346 Mairal, *Legitimate Expectations and Informal Administrative Representations*, p. 430; Metalclad Corporation v. The United Mexican States, Award, 30 August 2000 ICSID Case No. ARB(AF)/97/1, para. 87, 89.

347 Mairal, *Legitimate Expectations and Informal Administrative Representations*, p. 430; LG&E Energy Corp. LG&E Capital Corp. and LG&E International, Inc. v. The Argentine Republic, Decision on Liability, 3 October 2006 ICSID Case No. ARB/02/1, para. 94.

348 Dörr and Schmalenbach, *Vienna Convention on the Law of Treaties*, p. 493.

349 International Thunderbird Gaming Corporation v. The United Mexican States Separate Opinion of Thomas Wälde, 26 January 2006 UNCITRAL, para. 93. *See* Ch. 2 III 2) a).

350 Dolzer and Schreuer, *Principles of International Investment Law*, p. 219.

351 Mairal, *Legitimate Expectations and Informal Administrative Representations*, p. 428. *See also* Azurix Corp. v. The Argentine Republic, Award, 14 July 2006 ICSID Case No. ARB/01/12, para. 50.

352 MTD Equity Sdn. Bhd. and MTD Chile S.A. v. Republic of Chile, Award, 25 May 2004 ICSID Case No. ARB/01/7, para. 165; Metalclad Corporation v. The United Mexican States, Award, 30 August 2000 ICSID Case No. ARB(AF)/97/1, para. 32-34, 87; Azurix Corp. v. The Argentine Republic, Award, 14 July 2006 ICSID Case No. ARB/01/12, para. 176.

353 Metalclad Corporation v. The United Mexican States, Award, 30 August 2000 ICSID Case No. ARB(AF)/97/1, para. 32-34; MTD Equity Sdn. Bhd. and MTD Chile S.A. v. Republic of Chile, Award, 25 May 2004 ICSID Case No. ARB/01/7, para. 165.

of the investors, the representation must not constitute, at least from the horizon of the recipient, i.e. the individual investor, a manifest violation of the state's internal law.[354] Thus, despite the fact that an actual *ultra vires* action of a state official cannot, in general, hinder the attribution to the state, it must not be obvious that the state official acted outside its capacity.[355] Otherwise, there would be a risk that the excess of power of a lower-ranking state official could result in an investor being able to claim hundreds of millions of dollars in damages from states, without this being proportionate to the misconduct endured by the investor.[356]

These findings reveal the main differences between domestic law and international investment law: Whereas a state may under some jurisdictions in internal affairs rely on the fact that the state official making the representation acted *ultra vires*, states may, under international investment law, not raise such a defence.[357] Hence, it is not surprising that no issues regarding the representation of the state have arisen in the recent renewable energy cases.

b) Contractual Agreements

The host state can grant access to some form of support scheme under the relevant regulatory framework. This can be done either through an FIT provision in the law or through a long-term fixed-price power purchase agreement (PPA), which usually takes the form of a contractual agreement

354 International Thunderbird Gaming Corporation v. The United Mexican States Separate Opinion of Thomas Wälde, 26 January 2006 UNCITRAL, para. 93; Mairal, *Legitimate Expectations and Informal Administrative Representations*, p. 431.

355 The Tribunal in *Metaclad* held that the investor was entitled to rely on the representations of federal officials which made the investor believe that it was 'entitled to continue its construction' Metalclad Corporation v. The United Mexican States, Award, 30 August 2000 ICSID Case No. ARB(AF)/97/1, para. 86. *See also* Levashova, *The Right of States to Regulate in International Investment Law*, p. 125.

356 Dudas, 'A Sovereign's Broken Promise: the Golden Ticket to a Billion-Dollar Award?' (2016) <http://arbitrationblog.kluwerarbitration.com/2016/06/21/a-sovereigns-broken-promise-the-golden-ticket-to-a-billion-dollar-award/> (accessed 3 May 2021).

357 Dolzer and Schreuer, *Principles of International Investment Law*, p. 219.

with the local utility service company.[358] In general, the legal force of a commitment is stronger the more specific the commitment's legal form, content and wording are.[359] Thus, PPAs can regularly be considered the strongest type of commitment in the energy sector. Stemming from the principle of *pacta sunt servanda*, contractual agreements are the classical instruments that are acknowledged in almost all legal systems for the creation of legal stability and predictability.[360] Hence, they give rise to expectations that deserve a high level of protection.[361] While it is disputed whether contractual obligations themselves create rights, which can be subject to expropriation and are protected by investment treaties, tribunals have found that the non-observance of contractual agreements can amount to a violation of the FET standard.[362] However, the simple breach of a contract will not automatically be tantamount to a violation of the obligation to provide FET.[363] This follows from the distinction between domestic law on the one hand and international law on the other hand as two separate legal systems.[364] Another differentiation must be made regarding the question of whether the state entered into the contract in its capacity as a bearer of sovereign power or whether it concluded the contract as a regular commercial market participant.[365] Only if the state acted in its capacity as a sovereign, the contract has the potential to include a commitment that may raise legitimate expectations in the

---

358 Blackaby, 'Utilities, Government Regulations and Energy Investment Arbitrations' in Rowley, Bishop and Kaiser (eds), *The Guide to Energy Arbitrations* (Second Edition, Law Business Research Ltd 2017), p. 78, 79.

359 Levashova, *The Right of States to Regulate in International Investment Law*, p. 115, Secton 6.03. *See also* Total S.A. v. The Argentine Republic, Decision on Liability, 27 December 2010 ICSID Case No. ARB/04/01, para. 121.

360 Dolzer and Schreuer, *Principles of International Investment Law*, p. 152.

361 Potestà, 'Legitimate Expectations in Investment Treaty Law: Understanding the Roots and the Limits of a Controversial Concept', 101.

362 Mondev International Ltd. v United States of America, Award, 11 October 2002 ICSID Case No. ARB(AF)/99/2, para. 134; SGS Société Générale de Surveillance S.A. v. The Republic of Paraguay, Award, 10 February 2012 ICSID Case No. ARB/07/29, para. 146.

363 Levashova, *The Right of States to Regulate in International Investment Law*, p. 134.

364 Noble Ventures, Inc. v. Romania, Award, 12 October 2005 ICSID Case No. ARB/01/11, para. 53.

365 Impregilo S.p.A. v. The Argentine Republic, Award, 21 June 2011 ICSID Case No. ARB/07/17, para. 296; Bayindir Insaat Turizm Ticaret Ve Sanayi A.S. v. Islamic Republic of Pakistan, Award, 27 August 2009 ICSID Case No. ARB/03/29, para. 377.

investors which exceed the mere compliance with the contract.[366] Thus, the contractual agreement must entail, at least to some degree, a stabilising of the legal framework, by limiting the states' sovereignty, i.e. including a stabilisation clause.[367] Stabilization clauses are clauses, which are inserted into investor-state contracts, concluded between foreign investors and host states or state-entities, with the intended effect of exempting a specific investor from adverse future changes in the host state's legal framework.[368] It derives that the contractual agreement must bar the state from amending its legal framework, even without any discriminatory intent by the host state. Thus, a simple contractual claim to payment cannot create legitimate expectations.[369]

c) Unilateral Declarations and Specific Administrative Acts

States may create legitimate expectation through unilateral declarations, which are protected by the international obligation to provide FET under the respective investment treaties.[370] Unilateral declarations of state officials and administrative acts differ from the contractual agreements by the

366 Levashova, *The Right of States to Regulate in International Investment Law*, p. 138; *see also* Duke Energy Electroquil Partners & Electroquil S.A. v. Republic of Ecuador, Award, 18 August 2008 ICSID Case No. ARB/04/19, para. 348; Joy Mining Machinery Limited v. Arab Republic of Egypt Award on Jurisdiction, 6 August 2004 ICSID Case No. ARB/03/11, para. 79.

367 *See* MTD Equity Sdn. Bhd. and MTD Chile S.A. v. Republic of Chile, Award, 25 May 2004 ICSID Case No. ARB/01/7, para. 160-167; Waste Management, Inc. v. United Mexican States, Award, 30 April 2004 ICSID Case No. ARB(AF)/00/3, para. 108-117.

368 Potestà, 'Legitimate Expectations in Investment Treaty Law: Understanding the Roots and the Limits of a Controversial Concept', p. 114; Blackaby, *Utilities, Government Regulations and Energy Investment Arbitrations*, p. 79.

369 *See* Parkerings-Compagniet AS v. Republic of Lithuania, Award, 11 September 2007 ICSID Case No. ARB/05/8, para. 344; Duke Energy Electroquil Partners & Electroquil S.A. v. Republic of Ecuador, Award, 18 August 2008 ICSID Case No. ARB/04/19, para. 345.

370 The ILC's Guiding Principles state thereto that "[d]eclarations publicly made and manifesting the will to be bound may have the effect of creating legal obligations. When the conditions for this are met, the binding character of such declarations is based on good faith.", Guiding Principle 1, International Law Commission. International Law Commission 2006 – Guiding Principles Applicable to Unilateral.

lack of mutuality. They are usually directed at the individual investor, such as registrations, licenses and permits.[371]

There is no exhaustive list of governmental actions which might give rise to legitimate expectations.[372] The legal persuasiveness of a representation may, however, strongly depend on the state officials that acted and the intention that has been discernible for potential investors. Accordingly, a distinction can be made between acts of public authorities, which are intended to establish a promise, such as official statements addressing an issue of importance to induce the interest of investors, and the simple provision of information. The first type of acts is usually characterised by a demonstration of consideration conducted by the state authorities, which takes the interests at stake into account and aims to find a suitable solution.[373] The other type of acts lack such a demonstration of consideration and are simply characterised by a provision of certain information without prior evaluation of its impact.[374] These acts are usually not intended to establish a promise. However, depending on the manner of presentation of the information, investors may still rely on the information provided by the state, which is qualified to affect the interests of the investor.[375] This specific type of provision of information can take the form of a response to an investor's question or of an event of more general nature.[376] The potency of a state's conduct to create legitimate expectations is also linked to its specificity. Apart from the question of whether a promise or representation must be addressed to a single investor or to a group of potential investors, the act of the state must in itself be sufficiently specific, i.e. it must be precise as to its content and clear as to its form.[377]

---

371 Técnicas Medioambientales Tecmed, S.A. v. The United Mexican States, Award, 29 May 2003 ICSID Case No. ARB (AF)/00/2, para. 38-40; Alex Genin, Eastern Credit Limited, Inc. and A.S. Baltoil v. The Republic of Estonia, Award, 25 June 2001 ICSID Case No. ARB/99/2, para. 358; Ronald S. Lauder v. The Czech Republic, Award, 3 September 2001 UNCITRAL, para. 297; CME Czech Republic B.V. v. The Czech Republic Final, Award, 14 March 2013, para. 606.

372 Schreuer and Kriebaum, 'At What Time Must Legitimate Expectations Exist?', p. 273.

373 Palombino, *Fair and Equitable Treatment and the Fabric of General Principles*, p. 97.

374 ibid, p. 97.

375 ibid, p. 97.

376 ibid, p. 97.

377 Guiding Principle 7 International Law Commission. International Law Commission 2006 – Guiding Principles Applicable to Unilateral; Crystallex Interna-

In the recent cases subject to this research, unilateral declarations and administrative acts range from alleged administrative promises of state officials to administrative authorisation, and registration procedures. It is commonly argued that an administrative promise occurs where a state official guarantees that certain decisions will or will not be undertaken.[378] Additionally, it is undisputed that no compensation can be claimed under the FET standard, if the state has made no representation at all.[379] Once this bare minimum threshold of commitment on the side of the state has been reached, the specificity of the states' acts in regard to its intention and content must be considered in the assessment of the legitimate expectations.

d) Informal and General Administrative Acts

Apart from the administrative acts and unilateral declarations specifically addressed to an individual investor or a limited group of investors, the states' conduct can also take on a more informal and general form. Informal administrative representations are explicit or implicit administrative statements regarding fact, law, or intent, which do not constitute a regulation, a contract, or a proper and formal administrative act.[380] They can either be addressed to an individual investor or a group of investors or can simply constitute a provision of information.[381] Such a general type of provision of information can take the form of a declaration of intent or undertaking, an oral or written opinion on the construction of a piece of legislation, the announcement of a general policy, or administrative practice.[382] Recurring schemes of general and informal administrative rep-

---

tional Corporation v. Bolivarian Republic of Venezuela, Award, 4 April 2016 ICSID Case No. ARB(AF)/11/2, para. 547.

378 Palombino, *Fair and Equitable Treatment and the Fabric of General Principles*, p. 97.

379 *For example*, simply pursuing a license is not enough to legitimately expect any specific outcome before the investor received a certain confirmation, *see* Mairal, *Legitimate Expectations and Informal Administrative Representations*, p. 420; Snodgrass, 'Protecting Investors' Legitimate Expectations - Recognizing and Delimiting a General Principle', p. 45. *See also* William Nagel v. The Czech Republic Final, Award, 9 September 2003 SCC Case No. 049/2002, para. 297–329.

380 Mairal, *Legitimate Expectations and Informal Administrative Representations*, p. 425; Schønberg, *Legitimate Expectations in Administrative Law*, p. 107.

381 Mairal, *Legitimate Expectations and Informal Administrative Representations*, p. 414.

382 Ibid, p. 414.

resentations have also been advertisements by state authorities or state entities, such as memoranda that contained information to attract investors[383] or unofficial statements by authorities during official events, press conferences, and newspaper interviews[384]. Depending on the rank of the state official and the informality of the circumstances the memorandum or statement has been issued in, the commitment will have a different weight. Thereby, even informal statements, which contain explicit commitments, are capable of creating legitimate expectations.[385] In borderline cases, even informal representations of a more general nature can be given weight, if they are never publicly corrected.[386] Stemming from the duty to act in a transparent and consistent manner, even silence of the authorities, when confronted with a given course of conduct of other investors, may lead to self-commitment on the part of the state.[387]

However, acts in this category are generally only moderately capable of creating legitimate expectations. Their informality suggests that the state did not conduct considerations of balancing the rights at stake and did not want to give formal promises to investors that the rights will not be modified in due course.[388] There has not been any consensus among the tribunals, as to whether informal declarations of a general nature are suitable to constitute a commitment at all, if they are not directed at an individual investor. As those formal and informal administrative representations come in different varieties and show a different level of balancing considerations, a threshold must be defined, when a declaration entails a

383 BG Group Plc. v. The Argentine Republic, Award, 24 December 2007 UNCITRAL, para. 300, 305, 306; LG&E Energy Corp. LG&E Capital Corp. and LG&E International, Inc. v. The Argentine Republic, Decision on Liability, 3 October 2006 ICSID Case No. ARB/02/1, para. 175; National Grid P.L.C. v. The Argentine Republic, Award, 3 November 2008 UNCITRAL, para. 176.

384 MTD Equity Sdn. Bhd. and MTD Chile S.A. v. Republic of Chile, Award, 25 May 2004 ICSID Case No. ARB/01/7, para. 156,157; Eastern Sugar B.V. (Netherlands) v. The Czech Republic Partial, Award, 27 March 2007 SCC Case No. 088/2004, para. 244.

385 Crystallex International Corporation v. Bolivarian Republic of Venezuela, Award, 4 April 2016 ICSID Case No. ARB(AF)/11/2, para. 561.

386 Eastern Sugar B.V. (Netherlands) v. The Czech Republic Partial, Award, 27 March 2007 SCC Case No. 088/2004, para. 244.

387 Mairal, *Legitimate Expectations and Informal Administrative Representations*, p. 414.

388 Hydro Energy 1 S.A.R.L. and Hydroxana Sweden AB v. The Kingdom of Spain, Decision on Jurisdiction, Liability and Directions on Quantum, 9 March 2020 ICSID Case No. ARB/15/42, para. 594.

commitment, addressed to an investor that is eligible to create legitimate expectations.

Given the plethora of different state acts discussed in the renewable energy cases, the newly formed case law might help to further define the non-exhaustive list of government acts and determine what conduct of the state can be deemed sufficient to constitute a commitment, on which investors may base their legitimate expectations.

e) The Legal Regulatory Framework

It is undisputed that the expectations must be based on the host states' legal regulatory framework at the time of the investment.[389] However, it is strongly debated whether the law of the host state may, on its own, give rise to legitimate expectations. In general, the legal framework may include laws, policies and regulations of general application that existed at the time of the investment.[390]

Some scholars argue that active participation of the host state, as well as a certain level of specificity, precision and individualization, is required in order to create legitimate expectations.[391] A similar view was expressed by investment tribunals.[392] Hence, legislative acts, which are by definition binding on everyone falling within its scope of application, would lack such specificity. This view is further supplemented by the argument that the legitimate expectations doctrine could be misused for the purpose of safeguarding investors, who have not managed to bargain for a specific

---

389 Invesmart v. Czech Republic, Award, 26 June 2009 UNCITRAL, para. 257; International Thunderbird Gaming Corporation v. The United Mexican States, Award, 26 January 2006 UNCITRAL, para. 147. *See also* Dolzer and Schreuer, *Principles of International Investment Law*, p. 145; Potestà, 'Legitimate Expectations in Investment Treaty Law: Understanding the Roots and the Limits of a Controversial Concept', p. 110.

390 Levashova, *The Right of States to Regulate in International Investment Law*, p. 140.

391 Snodgrass, 'Protecting Investors' Legitimate Expectations - Recognizing and Delimiting a General Principle', p. 32; Campbell, 'House of Cards: The Relevance of Legitimate Expectations under Fair and Equitable Treatment Provisions in Investment Treaty Law', p. 369.

392 Sempra Energy International v. The Argentine Republic, Award, 28 September 2007 ICSID Case No. ARB/02/16, para. 298; Parkerings-Compagniet AS v. Republic of Lithuania, Award, 11 September 2007 ICSID Case No. ARB/05/8, para. 331; Continental Casualty Company v. The Argentine Republic, Award, 5 September 2008 ICSID Case No. ARB/03/9, para. 261.

commitment.[393] Thereby investors that actively engaged with the state would be treated equal to those who refrained from doing so. In such case, substantially unequal situations would be treated equally, which could violate the prohibition of discrimination. Additionally, the right of the states to regulate their legal framework freely is a key element of the states' sovereignty. The legal framework of a state is "by nature subject to subsequent modification, as well as to withdrawal and cancellation".[394] The right of the state to amend its legal framework is only limited by fundamental human rights and *ius cogens*.[395] Hence, investors cannot legitimately expect that the legal framework of a host state would be frozen in time, without any specific commitment of the state, especially in the context of international investments, for which the political risk is naturally high.[396]

According to opposing views among scholars[397] and tribunals[398], the legal framework can also form the basis of legitimate expectations, without

---

393 Potestà, 'Legitimate Expectations in Investment Treaty Law: Understanding the Roots and the Limits of a Controversial Concept', p. 114; Snodgrass, 'Protecting Investors' Legitimate Expectations - Recognizing and Delimiting a General Principle', p. 38; Maynard, 'Legitimate Expectations and the Interpretation of the 'Legal Stability Obligation'', p. 105; Vigotop Limited v. Hungary, Award, 1 October 2014 ICSID Case No. ARB/11/22, para. 625.

394 Continental Casualty Company v. The Argentine Republic, Award, 5 September 2008 ICSID Case No. ARB/03/9, para. 261.

395 ibid, para. 261.

396 Continental Casualty Company v. The Argentine Republic, Award, 5 September 2008 ICSID Case No. ARB/03/9, para. 261; Total S.A. v. The Argentine Republic, Decision on Liability, 27 December 2010 ICSID Case No. ARB/04/01, para. 122, 123; EDF (Services) Limited v. Romania, Award, 8 October 2009 ICSID Case No. ARB/05/13, para. 217.

397 Schreuer and Kriebaum, 'At What Time Must Legitimate Expectations Exist?', p. 273; Levashova, *The Right of States to Regulate in International Investment Law*, p. 114; Bücheler, *Proportionality in Investor-State Arbitration* (OUP 2015), p. 190; Kube, 'Tensions Between the International Investment Regime and Human Rights: A Regulatory Tilt?' in Kube (ed), *EU Human Rights, International Investment Law and Participation* (Interdisciplinary Studies in Human Rights. Springer International Publishing 2019), p. 165.

398 Electrabel S.A. v. Republic of Hungary, Award, 25 November 2015 ICSID Case No. ARB/07/19, para. 7.77; Enron Corporation and Ponderosa Assets, L.P. v. The Argentine Republic, Award, 22 May 2007 ICSID Case No. ARB/01/3, para. 265; MTD Equity Sdn. Bhd. and MTD Chile S.A. v. Republic of Chile, Award, 25 May 2004 ICSID Case No. ARB/01/7, para. 205; Parkerings-Compagniet AS v. Republic of Lithuania, Award, 11 September 2007 ICSID Case No. ARB/05/8, para. 331; Enron Corporation and Ponderosa Assets, L.P. v. The Argentine

the need for a specific commitment. If this was the case, the FET standard would be breached, if the host states alter their general legislative and regulatory framework in a way, which frustrates the legitimate expectations.[399] It is argued that legislation is a normative act specifically aimed to induce foreign investments, and on which foreign investors rely when making their investments.[400] From an economic perspective, one of the main contributions of law to any social system is to make economic life more calculable and thus establish a suitable investment environment.[401] Hence, investors will be more inclined to invest in a country with a legal framework promising stability.[402] Although not addressed to any investor specifically, the legal framework will substantially influence the business decisions of potential investors.[403] Therefore, the specificity of the commitment will simply make a difference in the assessment of the investors' information, and of the reasonability and legitimacy of their expectations, but will not be the exclusive basis for it.[404]

In comparison, the difference between the two approaches becomes evident: The first, more restrictive approach, demands specific commitment on the side of the state. Therefore, investors are obligated to get into contact with the host state and use their bargaining power, in order to

Republic, Award, 22 May 2007 ICSID Case No. ARB/01/3, para. 265; Total S.A. v. The Argentine Republic, Decision on Liability, 27 December 2010 ICSID Case No. ARB/04/01, para. 129, finding that "only exceptionally has the concept of legitimate expectations been the basis of redress when legislative actions by a state was at stake". *See also* recent developments in Ch. 4 I 2) b).

399 Potestà, 'Legitimate Expectations in Investment Treaty Law: Understanding the Roots and the Limits of a Controversial Concept', p. 110.

400 Palombino, *Fair and Equitable Treatment and the Fabric of General Principles*, p. 86.

401 Palombino, *Fair and Equitable Treatment and the Fabric of General Principles*, p. 86, p. 110. *See also* Suez, Sociedad General de Aguas de Barcelona, S.A. and Vivendi Universal, S.A. v. The Argentine RepublicRepublic, Decision on Liability, 30 July 2010 ICSID Case No. ARB/03/19, para. 226.

402 Simões, 'When Green Incentives Go Pale: Investment Arbitration and Renewable Energy Policymaking', p. 253; Palombino, *Fair and Equitable Treatment and the Fabric of General Principles*, p. 110; Tienhaara and Downie, 'Risky Business? The Energy Charter Treaty, Renewable Energy, and Investor-State Disputes', p. 458.

403 Investors have the obligation to assess the legal framework in their due diligence analysis preceding the business decision, Frontier Petroleum Services Ltd. v. The Czech Republic Final, Award, 12 November 2010, para 287. *See also* Ch. 2 III 3).

404 Electrabel S.A. v. Republic of Hungary, Award, 25 November 2015 ICSID Case No. ARB/07/19, para. 7.78.

obtain a secure environment for their investments. If they fail to do so, they should not benefit from a promise of a more general nature given through the legal framework.[405] In contrast, the second approach comes to the conclusion that a specific representation may make a difference to the assessment of the legitimacy of the investors' expectations, but is not necessary to create legitimate expectations in the first place. This approach is based on the fact that the state can already raise strong expectations through its legal framework, such that no further assurance through specific commitments is required.

Both approaches are comprehensible and bring forth valid arguments. The first approach rightly demands more active engagement with the state from the investor. The FET standard and the concept of legitimate expectations do not serve to protect investors from imprudent business decisions.[406] However, the legal framework is such an important component in investor decision-making that it can hardly be disregarded in the assessment of the legitimacy of the investors' expectations.[407] The superficial examination of this controversial topic does not reveal any apparent trend. Therefore, it remains to be seen whether the recent decisions in the renewable energy cases will lead the way to clearer jurisprudence on that topic.

3) The Due Diligence of the Investor

The overall role of the investors' conduct has gained importance over the course of the development of the notion of legitimate expectations.[408] Of

405 Potestà, 'Legitimate Expectations in Investment Treaty Law: Understanding the Roots and the Limits of a Controversial Concept', p. 114; Snodgrass, 'Protecting Investors' Legitimate Expectations - Recognizing and Delimiting a General Principle', p. 38; Maynard, 'Legitimate Expectations and the Interpretation of the 'Legal Stability Obligation'', p. 105; Vigotop Limited v. Hungary, Award, 1 October 2014 ICSID Case No. ARB/11/22, para 625.

406 Ortino, 'The Obligation of Regulatory Stability in the Fair and Equitable Treatment Standard: How Far Have We Come?' (2018) 21(4) Journal of International Economic Law 845, p. 855; EDF (Services) Limited v. Romania, Award, 8 October 2009 ICSID Case No. ARB/05/13, para. 217.

407 Palombino, *Fair and Equitable Treatment and the Fabric of General Principles*, p. 110; Kube, *Tensions Between the International Investment Regime and Human Rights: A Regulatory Tilt?*, p. 165.

408 The tribunal in *Biwater Gauff* concluded that "countervailing factors such as the responsibility of foreign investors, both in terms of prior due diligence, as well

the conduct prior and subsequent to the investment, the due diligence has been referenced frequently as the main element that should be considered in the overall evaluation of the legitimate expectations of the investor.[409]

In abstract, due diligence is characterised as the investigation or exercise of care that a reasonable business or person is expected to take before entering into an agreement or contract with another party, or an act with a certain standard of care.[410] Under international investment law, due diligence requires "a foreign investor has to make its business decisions and shape its expectations on the basis of the law and the factual situation prevailing in the country as it stands at the moment of the investment".[411] If the investor was, however, ill-informed or overly optimistic, the expectations are legitimate and will not give rise to claims for their frustration.[412] The investigation or the exercise of care is further defined by international soft law.[413] The fact that due diligence standards are developed by private entities and not by legislators and states show that it is not a legal obligation, but rather a voluntary investigation that the investors need to conduct, in order to receive or maintain certain benefits.[414]

The central purpose of the assessment, whether the investors' diligence was due, is to establish whether the investor relied on the representation

---

as subsequent conduct", must be taken into account in order to determine a violation of the FET standard, Biwater Gauff (Tanzania) Ltd. v. United Republic of Tanzania, Award, 24 July 2004 ICSID Case No. ARB/05/22, para. 601.

409 *See* Levashova, *The Right of States to Regulate in International Investment Law*, p. 29 and Section 6.

410 OECD, *Guidelines for Multinational Enterprises, 2011 Edition*, p. 23 <https://www.oecd.org/daf/inv/mne/oecdguidelinesformultinationalenterprises.html> (accessed 3 May 2021).

411 Frontier Petroleum Services Ltd. v. The Czech Republic Final, Award, 12 November 2010, UNCITRAL, para. 287. *See also* Joseph Charles Lemire v. Ukraine, Award, 28 March 2011 ICSID Case No. ARB/06/18, para. 285; Alasdair Ross Anderson et al v. Republic of Costa Rica, Award, 19 May 2010 ICSID Case No. ARB(AF)/07/3, para. 58.

412 Viñuales, 'Investor Diligence in Investment Arbitration: Sources and Arguments', p. 362; Invesmart v. Czech Republic, Award, 26 June 2009 UNCITRAL, para. 250.

413 *For example:* OECD, *Guidelines for Multinational Enterprises, 2011 Edition* and *IFC Performance Standard 1 - Assessment and Management of Environmental and Social Risks* (IFC 2012), <https://www.ifc.org/wps/wcm/connect/topics_ext_content/ifc_external_corporate_site/sustainability-at-ifc/policies-standards/performance-standards/ps1> (accessed 3 May 2021).

414 Viñuales, 'Investor Diligence in Investment Arbitration: Sources and Arguments', p. 346.

reasonably.[415] The reliance was reasonable if the investor in the given cases obtained all information necessary in order to reach a decision that corresponds with what an experienced business person would have done.[416] If a diligent investor, who had gathered and considered all relevant information, would have foreseen that the legal framework was going to change, the investor's expectations are not legitimate.[417] The due diligence requirement thereby adds another objective aspect to the assessment of the legitimate expectations.

In general, the due diligence requirement of legitimate expectations is treated only as a subsequent aspect in the assessment of legitimate expectations.[418] In some cases, however, the due diligence factor of the legitimate expectations becomes pivotal. Such a situation occurs in particular when the case turns on the question of whether the changes in the legal framework of the host state were foreseeable.[419] Thus, investors are be expected to exercise a certain level of due diligence concerning the legal framework of the host state, as well as all other relevant information regarding the

415 Viñuales, 'Investor Diligence in Investment Arbitration: Sources and Arguments', p. 362; UNCTAD, 'Fair and Equitable Treatment', p. 70.

416 International Thunderbird Gaming Corporation v. The United Mexican States Separate Opinion of Thomas Wälde, 26 January 2006 UNCITRAL, para. 47; Joseph Charles Lemire v. Ukraine Decision on Liability, 14 January 2010 ICSID Case No. ARB/06/18, para. 285; Alasdair Ross Anderson et al v. Republic of Costa Rica, Award, 19 May 2010 ICSID Case No. ARB(AF)/07/3, para. 58. *See also* OECD, *Guidelines for Multinational Enterprises, 2011 Edition*, p. 58.

417 Methanex Corporation v. United States of America Final, Award, 3 August 2005 UNCITRAL, Part IV, Ch. D, para. 9–10; Plama Consortium Limited v. Republic of Bulgaria, Award, 27 August 2008 ICSID Case No. ARB/03/24, para. 219-222.

418 *See* LG&E Energy Corp. LG&E Capital Corp. and LG&E International, Inc. v. The Argentine Republic, Decision on Liability, 3 October 2006 ICSID Case No. ARB/02/1, para. 130; Parkerings-Compagniet AS v. Republic of Lithuania, Award, 11 September 2007 ICSID Case No. ARB/05/8, para. 331; Duke Energy Electroquil Partners & Electroquil S.A. v. Republic of Ecuador, Award, 18 August 2008 ICSID Case No. ARB/04/19, para. 340.

419 *For example*, the Tribunal in *Methanex* found that certain new regulations in environmental law should have been foreseeable for the investor, since the topic had been heavily discussed in public before the investment was made, Methanex Corporation v. United States of America Final, Award, 3 August 2005 UNCITRAL, Part IV, Ch. D, para. 9–10.

investment environment.[420] If this is not done, investors can lose their right under the FET standard.[421]

Due diligence takes different forms, depending on its purpose. If investors want to legitimately rely on the stability of the legal framework, the due diligence report must encompass an analysis of the environment, in which the foreign investment takes place and which it affects.[422] Failure to do so may have an adverse impact on its claim at the stage of jurisdiction, admissibility, merits, and/or quantum, although it is usually discussed in the merits of the case.[423] The theory behind due diligence is that conducting business investigations will contribute significantly to a better risk assessment and thus to a more informed decision-making process by the investor.[424] Cross-border investments regularly involve transactions ranging from a few million to several hundred million Euros that—in the case of failure—investors oftentimes try to recover from the state that contributed to its demise.[425] Considering the sums at stake and following the standard of care of a reasonable business person, a diligent investor would obtain proper legal advice, if the amount of capital at stake is significant.[426]

This standard of care, however, is not a one-way street, but applies mutually to investors and states.[427] If investors are bound to observe a higher standard of due diligence, the opposite must apply to states as well. When dealing with investors making decisions about millions of

---

420 Viñuales, 'Investor Diligence in Investment Arbitration: Sources and Arguments', p. 362.

421 Viñuales, 'Investor Diligence in Investment Arbitration: Sources and Arguments', p. 362; Plama Consortium Limited v. Republic of Bulgaria, Award, 27 August 2008 ICSID Case No. ARB/03/24, para. 222.

422 Diehl, *The Core Standard of International Investment Protection*, p. 530.

423 Viñuales, 'Investor Diligence in Investment Arbitration: Sources and Arguments', p. 360.

424 Frontier Petroleum Services Ltd. v. The Czech Republic Final, Award, 12 November 2010, UNCITRAL, para. 287. The due diligence analysis is usually carried out by specialised consulting firms that increase the extent and quality of information available to decision-makers, and by ensuring that this information is systematically used to evaluate all costs, benefits, and risks of the investment project, Cavalum SGPS v. Kingdom of Spain, Decision on Jurisdiction, Liability and Directions on Quantum, 31 August 2020 ICSID Case No. ARB/15/34, para. 472.

425 Mairal, *Legitimate Expectations and Informal Administrative Representations*, p. 420.

426 ibid, p. 420.

427 *See* De Brabandere, 'Host States Due Diligence Obligations in International Investment Law'.

dollars of investment, government officials are also bound to exercise due diligence corresponding to the amount of capital at stake.[428] However, international investment treaties, like the Investment Agreement for the Common Market for Eastern and Southern Africa (COMESA), explicitly state that the interpretation of the FET standard must be flexible and based on the level of development of the respondent country.[429] Thereby, it is acknowledged that different Member States have different forms of administrative, legislative and judicial systems, and may not achieve the same standards depending on their development.[430] This provision illustrates that the standard of care strongly depends on the development of the legal system of the host state. Therefore, less developed states will not be burdened with an equally high standard of due diligence, as states with an advanced legal system.[431] In turn, this means for a reasonable business person to apply a higher standard of care, in order to counteract a possible lack of financial and personnel capabilities, educational standards, or experience and consistent practice of official authority in developing countries.[432] This extension of the investors' due diligence obligation is based on corporate social responsibility (CSR). The concept of CSR aims to oblige commercial companies to contribute to social goals and sustainable development of the host state, if the state cannot guarantee such on its own.[433] Thus, the FET standard does not establish a single international standard of care for investors investing in highly developed countries, and

428 Mairal, *Legitimate Expectations and Informal Administrative Representations*, p. 442.

429 Article 14(3) Investment Agreement for the Common Market for Eastern and Southern Africa (COMESA) (2007).

430 *See* FET provision in Article 14(3) COMESA. *See also* Potestà, 'Legitimate Expectations in Investment Treaty Law: Understanding the Roots and the Limits of a Controversial Concept', p. 118.

431 *See* Alex Genin, Eastern Credit Limited, Inc. and A.S. Baltoil v. The Republic of Estonia, Award, 25 June 2001 ICSID Case No. ARB/99/2, para. 370; Parkerings-Compagniet AS v. Republic of Lithuania, Award, 11 September 2007 ICSID Case No. ARB/05/8, para. 335; Mamidoil Jetoil Greek Petroleum Products Societe S.A. v. Republic of Albania, Award, 30 March 2015 ICSID Case No. ARB/11/24, para. 629.

432 Potestà, 'Legitimate Expectations in Investment Treaty Law: Understanding the Roots and the Limits of a Controversial Concept', p. 118; Saluka Investments B.V. v. The Czech Republic Partial, Award, 17 March 2006 UNCITRAL, para. 304.

433 Schill, *Sources of International Investment Law: Multilateralization, Arbitral Precedent, Comparativism, Soft Law*, p. 17.

developing or emerging economies alike.[434] The factor of special economic and socio-political circumstances in a host state needs to be considered by investors and tribunals assessing the reasonableness of their business decisions.[435] While some treaties[436] explicitly refer to CSR standards by incorporating a separate provision, the ECT remains silent on this topic.

Similarly, the ECT omits to explicitly provide for any due diligence requirement. However, arbitral tribunals have been considering the investors' diligence since the first investment disputes under the ECT.[437] Hence, the investors' expectations have to be analysed in detail to determine whether appropriate due diligence had been carried out under the relevant circumstances.[438] The following analysis of the renewable energy cases and their analysis shall help to determine to what extent investors need to perform due diligence.

4) Foundations for the Analysis of Recent Jurisprudence

Based on the aforesaid, states cannot be held liable based on an alleged violation of the FET standard, as long as there has not been any commitment. If, however, a public authority has induced an investor to rely upon its representations or conduct, the notion of legitimate expectations imposes the duty on public authorities to act in such a way that the reliance will

434 Duke Energy Electroquil Partners & Electroquil S.A. v. Republic of Ecuador, Award, 18 August 2008 ICSID Case No. ARB/04/19, para. 340; Alex Genin, Eastern Credit Limited, Inc. and A.S. Baltoil v. The Republic of Estonia, Award, 25 June 2001 ICSID Case No. ARB/99/2, para. 348, 370; Parkerings-Compagniet AS v. Republic of Lithuania, Award, 11 September 2007 ICSID Case No. ARB/05/8, para. 335-336; Bayindir Insaat Turizm Ticaret Ve Sanayi A.S. v. Islamic Republic of Pakistan, Award, 27 August 2009 ICSID Case No. ARB/03/29, para. 195; Toto Costruzioni Generali S.p.A. v. The Republic of Lebanon, Award, 7 June 2012 ICSID Case No. ARB/07/12, para. 245. *See also* Potestà, 'Legitimate Expectations in Investment Treaty Law: Understanding the Roots and the Limits of a Controversial Concept', p. 118. *See also* Ch. 4 II 3) a).

435 *See* Levashova, *The Right of States to Regulate in International Investment Law*, Section 6.05.

436 *See* Viñuales, 'Investor Diligence in Investment Arbitration: Sources and Arguments', p. 354, 355.

437 Such as Nykomb Synergetics Technology Holding AB v. The Republic of Latvia, SCC, Award, 16 December 2003 SCC, p. 34.

438 Potestà, 'Legitimate Expectations in Investment Treaty Law: Understanding the Roots and the Limits of a Controversial Concept', p. 119.

not be detrimental to the addressee of the representation.[439] Additionally, states seem to be able to commit to abiding by the investors' expectations through representations made by state officials or to some degree through the legal framework. It follows that investors might try to mitigate the risk of falling victim to regulatory changes by receiving a specific commitment from the host state, but this possibility is not without limits.[440] In order to legitimately rely on the commitment, investors must prove that they had good reason to believe that the host states were trustworthy.[441] Thereby, the basic rule has been outlined that the more specific and unambiguous state representations are, the more an investor may rely on them.[442] It can be argued that commitments can take any form, such as licence agreements, laws, letters, political statements, or simple advertisements.[443] If more general commitments are considered a valid basis for legitimate expectations, then the reliance of the investor may not be protected as strongly as under other more specific representations.[444] In order to determine the level of reliance an investor may place on them, depends—in addition to their legal form—on their content and their wording.[445]

If those representations are subsequently countermanded, it is a strong indication that the legitimate expectations of the investors were violated.[446] The notion of legitimate expectations, however, is much more complex than that, and does not allow for generalisations. Instead, the legitimacy of

---

439 Schønberg, *Legitimate Expectations in Administrative Law*, p. 10.

440 *For example*, the OECD, *Guidelines for Multinational Enterprises, 2011 Edition*, p. 21, 22, recommend investors to refrain from seeking or accepting exemptions not contemplated in the statutory or regulatory framework related to human rights, environmental, health, safety, labour, taxation, financial incentives, or other issues.

441 *See* in detail Ch. 4 II.

442 Duke Energy Electroquil Partners & Electroquil S.A. v. Republic of Ecuador, Award, 18 August 2008 ICSID Case No. ARB/04/19, para. 351; Total S.A. v. The Argentine Republic, Decision on Liability, 27 December 2010 ICSID Case No. ARB/04/01, para. 117-119; 9REN Holding S.a.r.l v. Kingdom of Spain, Award, 31 March 2019 ICSID Case No. ARB/15/15, para. 299. *See also* Levashova, *The Right of States to Regulate in International Investment Law*, Section 6.03; Kläger, *'Fair and Equitable Treatment' in International Investment Law*, p. 187.

443 Levashova, *The Right of States to Regulate in International Investment Law*, p. 126.

444 *See* Ch. 4 I 2).

445 Levashova, *The Right of States to Regulate in International Investment Law*, p. 126.

446 Dolzer and Schreuer, *Principles of International Investment Law*, p. 145; Levashova, *The Right of States to Regulate in International Investment Law*, p. 114.

the expectations must be assessed on a case-by-case basis, through an act of balancing.[447]

In the case-by-case assessment, investors must prove that: (1) a commitment attributable to the state forms the basis of their legitimate expectations, (2) the investor in the given case relied on that commitment, (3) the expectations raised by the host state were violated by actions or omissions taken by state authorities at a later stage, and (4) those actions or omissions caused harm to the investment—in order to successfully claim compensation for the frustration of legitimate expectations and subsequently the violation of the FET standard.[448]

IV. The Act of Balancing under International Investment Law

At the beginning of this Chapter, it has been demonstrated that the balancing of the rights at stake is the core purpose of the concept of legitimate expectations. A well-balanced act by the state interferes as little as possible with the investors' rights, in light of the objective pursued.[449] It must be determined, however, which factors are to be taken into account and how the balancing must be approached in practice.

---

447 Coop and Seif, *ECT and State's Right to Regulate*, para. 10.40; Apotex Holdings Inc. and Apotex Inc. v. United States of America, Award, 25 August 2014 ICSID Case No. ARB(AF)/12/1, para. 9.39, 9.48; AES Summit Generation Limited et. al. v. The Republic of Hungary, Award, 23 September 2010 ICSID Case No. ARB/07/22, para. 9.3.30.

448 Dolzer and Schreuer, *Principles of International Investment Law*, p. 145, 160; Max Baumgart and Sebastián Mantilla Blanco, 'Eneuerbare Energien und "legitime Erwartungen" in der neueren Schiedspraxis zum Vertrag über die Energiecharta: Die Entscheidungen im Verfahren Charanne, Isolux und Eiser' (2018) Recht der Energiewirtschaft 242, p. 243; Parkerings-Compagniet AS v. Republic of Lithuania, Award, 11 September 2007 ICSID Case No. ARB/05/8, para. 331; Mobil Investments Canada Inc. and Murphy Oil Corporation v. Canada Decision on Liability and on Principles of Quantum, 22 May 2012 ICSID Case No. ARB(AF)/07/4, para. 154.

449 The Tribunal in *RREEF* observed that "[t]he regulation must be closely adjusted to the attainment of its legitimate objective, interfering as little as possible with the effective exercise of the affected rights", RREEF Infrastructure (G.P.) Limited and RREEF Pan-European Infrastructure Two Lux S.à.r.l. v. Kingdom of Spain, Decision on Responsibility and on the Principles of Quantum, 30 November 2018 ICSID Case No. ARB/13/30, para. 465.

In the balancing act, the main countervailing interests of the state and the investor must be considered.[450] First, this includes the right of the state to regulate and act on the protection of the public interest. Second, the investors' interest in a stable and predictable investment environment, which they could legitimately expect in light of the conduct of the host state, and their due diligence analysis at the time of the investment. Third, the states' measures may not have a disproportionate impact on foreign investors. Proportionality in particular is a legal notion, which is crucial to strike a balance between impaired rights, but is often brushed over by tribunals. In order to achieve a proper balance between the countervailing rights, it is necessary to understand their legal significance and their correlations.

Accordingly, in the following Sections the right of the states to regulate and its relation to the concept of stability, as the core of investors' interests, are outlined. Finally, an attempt is made to work out the "right" application of the principle of proportionality.

1) The States' Right to Regulate

The right of the state to regulate is identified by some scholars as a freestanding concept of international law that has its legal basis in the international principle of state sovereignty.[451] References to the right to regulate can be found, inter alia, in investment agreements[452], arbitral

450 The Tribunal in *Lemire* analysed the prevailing case law and summarized that a tribunal "must also balance other legally relevant interests, and take into consideration a number of countervailing factors before it can establish that a violation of the FET standard [...]:

- the State's sovereign right to pass legislation and to adopt decisions for the protection of its public interests, especially if they do not provoke a disproportionate impact on foreign investors;
- the legitimate expectations of the investor, at the time he made his investment;
- the investor's duty to perform an investigation before effecting the investment;
- the investor's conduct in the host country.",

Joseph Charles Lemire v. Ukraine Decision on Liability, 14 January 2010 ICSID Case No. ARB/06/18, para. 285.

451 Levashova, *The Right of States to Regulate in International Investment Law*, p. 26.

452 *For example* Article 8.9 CETA (2016); Article 2.2. EU-Vietnam Investment Protection Agreement (IPA) (2019); Article 13.2 of the EU-Vietnam Free Trade Agreement (FTA) (2020); Article 2.2 of the EU-Singapore IPA (2018). For de-

decisions[453], and public authorities[454]. It can be defined as the "affirmation of the sovereign right for states to choose their political, social and economic priorities—within certain limits—through the adoption of legislation and administrative practices, without violating international rules protecting foreign investments".[455] Therefore, state sovereignty has, in addition to its external dimension, which grants states independence from other states in accordance with the *pares inter pares* principle, an international dimension.[456] The right to regulate is also frequently conceptualized as the "police powers"—inherent powers of the state derived from the states' sovereignty to protect the public interest.[457] Thereby, it is uniformly accepted that a state's legislation and regulation are dynamic and may, for the sake of the public interest, be amended, renewed, or overturned.[458]

---

tailed overview, *see* Levashova, *The Right of States to Regulate in International Investment Law*, Section 2.03.

453 *For example* Saluka Investments B.V. v. The Czech Republic Partial, Award, 17 March 2006 UNCITRAL, para. 305; International Thunderbird Gaming Corporation v. The United Mexican States, Award, 26 January 2006 UNCITRAL, para. 127; Parkerings-Compagniet AS v. Republic of Lithuania, Award, 11 September 2007 ICSID Case No. ARB/05/8, para. 332; El Paso Energy International Company v. The Argentine Republic, Award, 31 October 2011 ICSID Case No. ARB/03/15, para. 350; AWG Group Ltd. v. The Argentine Republic, Decision on Liability, 30 June 2010 ICSID Case No. ARB/03/19, para. 236.

454 Gaukrodger, 'The Balance Between Investor Protection and the Right to Regulate in Investment Treaties'; OECD, '"Indirect Expropriation" and the "Right to Regulate" in International Investment Law' (2004) <http://www.oecd.org/daf/inv/investment-policy/WP-2004_4.pdf> (accessed 3 May 2021).

455 Mouyal, *International Investment Law and the Right to Regulate: A Human Rights Perspective* (Routledge Research in International Economic Law, Routledge 2016), p. 8. In contrast, some scholars see the right to regulate as "the legal right exceptionally permitting the host state to regulate in derogation of international commitments it has undertaken by means of an investment agreement without incurring a duty to compensate", *see* Titi, *The Right to Regulate in International Investment Law*, p. 33. However, such a view is to reject as the right to regulate is the rule and its exeption are international law obligations and not the contrary.

456 Levashova, *The Right of States to Regulate in International Investment Law*, p. 238.

457 Zarra, 'Right to Regulate, Margin of Appreciation and Proportionality: Current Status in Investment Arbitration in Light of Philip Morris v. Uruguay' (2017) 14(2) RDI, p. 97; Kriebaum, 'Regulatory Takings: Balancing the Interests of the Investor and the State' (2007) 8(5) Journal of World Investment and Trade 717, p. 725, 726; Levashova, *The Right of States to Regulate in International Investment Law*, p. 35.

458 Rusoro Mining Ltd. v. Bolivarian Republic of Venezuela, Award, 22 August 2016 ICSID Case No. ARB(AF)/12/5, para. 525; El Paso Energy International Company v. The Argentine Republic, Award, 31 October 2011 ICSID Case

Of particular relevance for this research, this also includes the freedom of self-determination over political and socio-economic affairs.[459]

a) The EU's Reformation Efforts

Enforcing this generally held view, the EU has shown increasing effort to strengthen the right of the states to regulate in the ECT.[460] The negotiation directive issued by the EU sets out the aim that "[t]he Modernised ECT should explicitly reaffirm the right of ECT Contracting Parties to take measures to achieve legitimate public policy objectives, such as the protection of health, safety, the environment or public morals, social or consumer protection ('right to regulate')".[461] Although it will be demonstrated in this Section that a corresponding interpretation of the right to regulate under investment treaties is already accepted to some degree, this effort by the EU illustrates the movement among states to maintain or increase their flexibility in dealing with problems of importance to the protection of the public interest.

b) Limitations to the States' Sovereignty

In accordance with the general principles in international law, a state's sovereignty can only be limited, if the state has waived certain rights.[462] Such a waiver is, inter alia, the signing and ratification of investment treaties, in which a state obligates itself to comply with the rights granted

---

No. ARB/03/15, para. 365; International Thunderbird Gaming Corporation v. The United Mexican States, Award, 26 January 2006 UNCITRAL, para. 127; Mann, 'The Right of States to Regulate and International Investment Law' (International Institute for Sustainable Development 2002), p. 5.

459 Kläger, *'Fair and Equitable Treatment' in International Investment Law*, p 156.

460 Council of the EU, Press Release, 15 July 2019 <https://www.consilium.europa.eu/en/press/press-releases/2019/07/15/council-adopts-negotiation-directives-for-modernisation-of-energy-charter-treaty/> (accessed 3 May 2021).

461 Council of the EU, Negotiating Directives for the Modernisation of the Energy Charter Treaty, 2 July 2019, p. 3 <https://data.consilium.europa.eu/doc/document/ST-10745-2019-ADD-1/en/pdf> (accessed 3 May 2021).

462 Dolzer and Schreuer, *Principles of International Investment Law*, p. 20; ESPF Beteiligungs GmbH et. al. v. Italian Republic, Award, 14 September 2020 ICSID Case No. ARB/16/5, para. 418.

to the investors of the other signatory parties.[463] The basic principle of waiver of rights was introduced into public international law in the case of *The S.S. Lotus*[464]. In this case, the Permanent Court of International Justice (PCIJ) held that the scope for action of states under international law is limited only by positive prohibitions.[465] Earlier, the court had already explained that international obligations pose a limitation on the exercise of sovereign rights.[466] Accordingly, as the ECT is also an international treaty, the signatories limited their absolute sovereignty according to the principle laid out by the PCIJ to the scope of the investor protection rights offered by the ECT. With regard to investor protection, the states' right to regulate is in conflict with rights like non-expropriation, the FET standard, and national treatment.[467] A growing number of states show the tendency to safeguard their right to regulate by explicitly excluding specific regulatory concerns, such as the aforementioned, from the scope of investment treaties, thereby preserving regulatory flexibility in designated policy areas.[468] Nonetheless, such a far-sighted approach is not common among the IIAs that have been relevant in disputes involving FET issues in the past and present.[469] Given the open and vague nature of the FET standard, the limitations on the state's right to regulate can be fairly substantial.[470]

Hence, in the absence of a specific carve-out, the states' right to regulate must be balanced against the interests of the investors that are substantially

---

463 Coop and Seif, *ECT and State's Right to Regulate*, para. 10.02. *See also* ADC Affiliate Limited and ADC & ADMC Management Limited v. The Republic of Hungary, Award, 2 October 2016 ICSID Case No. ARB/03/16, para. 423.

464 The so-called Lotus Principle, PCIJ Judgment *The Case of the S.S. "Lotus" (France v. Turkey)*,7 September 1927 PCIJ Series A10.

465 ibid, para. 225.

466 In the decision of the *Wimbledon-Case*, the PCIJ found that Germany had limited its sovereign power over national waterways by entering into the Treaty of Versailles (1919), which obligated Germany to open the Kiel Canal in times of peace to vessels of all nations, PCIJ Judgment *The S.S. "Wimbledon", Britain et al. v. Germany,*17 August 1923 PCIJ Series A01, para. 34, 35.

467 Trujillo, 'Balancing Sustainability, the Right to Regulate, and the Need for Investor Protection: Lessons from the Trade Regime', p. 2739.

468 Titi, *The Right to Regulate in International Investment Law*, p. 300. *See also* Levashova, *The Right of States to Regulate in International Investment Law*, p. 27, 239; UNCTAD, 'Investment Policy Framework for Sustainable Development', UNCTAD Series on Issues in International Investment Agreements II (United Nations 2015), p. 103.

469 Titi, *The Right to Regulate in International Investment Law*, p. 300.

470 Levashova, *The Right of States to Regulate in International Investment Law*, p. 238-240.

protected by the respective investment treaty, in particular, the interests in stable legal conditions in the host state.[471] The restrictions or limitations upon the right to regulate must be construed as restrictively as possible, in order to comply with the absolute state sovereignty.[472] From a human rights perspective, some argue that the states have not only the right, but the duty to act for the protection of their people.[473] Although human rights and investment law are two separate systems of international law, the gravity of human rights cannot be ignored in assessing the states' right to regulate in terms of investment law.[474] Therefore, the objective of a state's measure must be taken into account, in order to determine whether the measure was covered by the right to regulate.[475] The closer an objective is linked to the public interest, the stronger the states' right to regulate, even in the presence of international obligations.[476] Thus, a state cannot be barred from dealing with situations and problems that may emerge

---

471 Coop and Seif, *ECT and State's Right to Regulate*, para. 10.05, 10.48; Dolzer and Schreuer, *Principles of International Investment Law*, p. 149; ADC Affiliate Limited and ADC & ADMC Management Limited v. The Republic of Hungary, Award, 2 October 2016 ICSID Case No. ARB/03/16, para. 423.

472 PCIJ Judgment *The S.S. "Wimbledon", Britain et al. v. Germany*, 17 August 1923 PCIJ Series A01, para. 34; Total S.A. v. The Argentine Republic, Decision on Liability, 27 December 2010 ICSID Case No. ARB/04/01, para. 130.

473 Mouyal, *International Investment Law and the Right to Regulate*, p. 158, refers, inter alia, to the International Covenant on Economic, Social and Cultural Rights of 16 December 1966 (ICESCR). The ICESCR obligates the signatory states to protect rights of paramount importance, such as labour rights and the right to health, the right to education, and the right to an adequate standard of living.

474 *See* Fanou and Tzevelekos, *Shared Territory of the ECHR and International Investment Law*, p. 123. Tribunals also drew guidance from the jurisprudence of the ECtHR, *see* Total S.A. v. The Argentine Republic, Decision on Liability, 27 December 2010 ICSID Case No. ARB/04/01, para. 128-130; Philip Morris Brands Sàrl et. al. v. Oriental Republic of Uruguay, Award, 8 July 2016 ICSID Case No. ARB/10/7, para. 399; Mondev International Ltd. v United States of America, Award, 11 October 2002 ICSID Case No. ARB(AF)/99/2, para. 138.

475 Henckels, *Proportionality and Deference in Investor-State Arbitration: Balancing Investment Protection and Regulatory Autonomy* (Cambridge Studies in International and Comparative Law vol. 122, CUP 2015), p. 126; Coop and Seif, *ECT and State's Right to Regulate*, para. 10.48; AES Summit Generation Limited et. al. v. The Republic of Hungary, Award, 23 September 2010 ICSID Case No. ARB/07/22, para. 10.3.7.

476 For elements that are pertinent to assessing the legitimacy of a state's objective *see* Levashova, *The Right of States to Regulate in International Investment Law*, Ch. 7.02, in particular Table 2, p. 201.

over time and were impossible to anticipate beforehand, conflicting with a public interest of paramount importance.[477] Public interest of paramount importance can be characterized as measures of a state that "have been taken in the interest of the welfare of the general public".[478] Such areas of importance to the public interests are, inter alia, renewable energy[479], waste management[480], public health[481], protection of the environment[482], and access to water[483].

Acknowledging the need for states to maintain their regulatory flexibility in those areas, a new generation of investment treaties is emerging, which explicitly incorporates those fields of public interest and creates carve-outs preserving the states' right to regulate.[484] Without such an explicit carve-out, however, there is no consensus among investment tri-

---

477 Palombino, *Fair and Equitable Treatment and the Fabric of General Principles*, p. 118; Titi, *The Right to Regulate in International Investment Law*, p. 33; Mann, 'The Right of States to Regulate and International Investment Law', p. 5. *See also* Levashova, *The Right of States to Regulate in International Investment Law*, Section 7.02 [C].

478 Levashova, *The Right of States to Regulate in International Investment Law*, p. 239.

479 *See* cases discussed in Ch. 3.

480 Técnicas Medioambientales Tecmed, S.A. v. The United Mexican States, Award, 29 May 2003 ICSID Case No. ARB (AF)/00/2; Metalclad Corporation v. The United Mexican States, Award, 30 August 2000 ICSID Case No. ARB(AF)/97/1; Waste Management, Inc. v. United Mexican States, Award, 30 April 2004 ICSID Case No. ARB(AF)/00/3.

481 Philip Morris Brands Sàrl et. al. v. Oriental Republic of Uruguay, Award, 8 July 2016 ICSID Case No. ARB/10/7; Apotex Holdings Inc. and Apotex Inc. v. United States of America, Award, 25 August 2014 ICSID Case No. ARB(AF)/12/1.

482 Chemtura Corporation v. Canada, Award, 2 August 2010 UNCITRAL.

483 AWG Group Ltd. v. The Argentine Republic, Award, 9 April 2015 ICSID Case No. ARB/03/19; Biwater Gauff (Tanzania) Ltd. v. United Republic of Tanzania, Award, 24 July 2004 ICSID Case No. ARB/05/22; Suez, Sociedad General de Aguas de Barcelona, S.A. and Vivendi Universal, S.A. v. The Argentine RepublicRepublic, Decision on Liability, 30 July 2010 ICSID Case No. ARB/03/19; Impregilo S.p.A. v. The Argentine Republic, Award, 21 June 2011 ICSID Case No. ARB/07/17; Azurix Corp. v. The Argentine Republic, Award, 14 July 2006 ICSID Case No. ARB/01/12; Urbaser SA and Consorcio de Aguas Bilbao Bizkaia, Bilbao Biskaia Ur Partzuergoa v The Argentine Republic, Award, 8 December 2016 ICSID Case No ARB/07/26. *See also* Panosch, *Das Menschenrecht auf Wasser im internationalen Investitionsrecht* (Nomos 2021).

484 *For example* Article 8.9 CETA (2016); Article 2.2. EU-Vietnam Investment Protection Agreement (IPA) (2019); Article 13.2 of the EU-Vietnam Free Trade Agreement (FTA) (2020); Article 2.2 of the EU-Singapore IPA (2018). For detailed overview, *see* Levashova, *The Right of States to Regulate in International Investment Law*, Section 2.03.

bunals, whether the possible impairment of paramount public interest is the only case in which states may fully exercise their right to regulate.[485] Nevertheless, the fact that the investors' rights stem from an international obligation, which the states entered into out of their free will, justifies the presumption that the states must pursue a profound purpose to fully exercise their right to regulate.[486] Such a profound purpose can be found in the promotion of a social, economic, or environmental aim.[487] This argument is supported by arbitral practice in investment law, which indicates that states are granted a wider margin of discretion, if they pursue a public interest of importance.[488]

Additionally, the right of the state to regulate in times of economic hardship to counteract sudden economic change has been addressed in a plethora of cases against the Argentine Republic in the early 2000s.[489]

---

485 The Tribunal in *AES Summit* concluded in the assessment of the states act, that it must demonstrate "the existence of a rational policy". A policy was deemed rational by the Tribunal if it "is taken by a state following a logical (good sense) explanation and with the aim of addressing a public interest matter", AES Summit Generation Limited et. al. v. The Republic of Hungary, Award, 23 September 2010 ICSID Case No. ARB/07/22, para. 10.3.7, 10.3.8. Other tribunals followed the same line of reasoning by requiring the state to act in the public interest, without demanding it to be of paramount importance, *For example* Philip Morris Brands Sàrl et. al. v. Oriental Republic of Uruguay, Award, 8 July 2016 ICSID Case No. ARB/10/7, para. 399, 418; Marvin Roy Feldman Karpa v. United Mexican States, Award, 16 December 2002 ICSID Case No. ARB(AF)/99/1, para. 103; Mobil Exploration and Development Inc. v. The Argentine Republic, Decision on Jurisdiction and Liability, 10 April 2013 ICSID Case No. ARB/04/16, para. 1028. *See also* Kriebaum, 'Regulatory Takings: Balancing the Interests of the Investor and the State', p. 726.

486 Trujillo, 'Balancing Sustainability, the Right to Regulate, and the Need for Investor Protection: Lessons from the Trade Regime', p. 2739, 2740.

487 Ibid, p. 2739, 2740.

488 *See* International Thunderbird Gaming Corporation v. The United Mexican States, Award, 26 January 2006 UNCITRAL, para. 127; Philip Morris Brands Sàrl et. al. v. Oriental Republic of Uruguay, Award, 8 July 2016 ICSID Case No. ARB/10/7, para. 399, 418; Apotex Holdings Inc. and Apotex Inc. v. United States of America, Award, 25 August 2014 ICSID Case No. ARB(AF)/12/1, para. 9.39, 9.48; Chemtura Corporation v. Canada, Award, 2 August 2010 UNCITRAL, para. 209.

489 *For example* LG&E Energy Corp. LG&E Capital Corp. and LG&E International, Inc. v. The Argentine Republic, Decision on Liability, 3 October 2006 ICSID Case No. ARB/02/1; CMS Gas Transmission Company v. The Argentine Republic, Award, 21 May 2005 ICSID Case No. ARB/01/8; BG Group Plc. v. The Argentine Republic, Award, 24 December 2007 UNCITRAL;Continental Casualty Company v. The Argentine Republic, Award, 5 September 2008 ICSID Case

The notion of public interest gained growing importance, in the context of the internal sovereignty of the state, when regulating the national market.[490] As an example, creating economic stability and sustainability was the main driver that eventually led to the regulatory changes disputed in the recent renewable energy cases. Therefore, regulations in the public interest, which also have an economic interest, are particularly important for the scope of this research and will be reflected upon in detail *infra*.[491] However, the states' acts must not be motivated solely by political activism in the face of an upcoming election and must demonstrate a certain degree of substantive tranquillity and coherence.[492] "Political activism" is characterized by the fact that it is usually one-sided and only follows the political agenda of certain state authorities.[493]

c) The States' Margin of Discretion

In general, sovereignty grants states the inherent right to freely choose their methods for achieving their regulatory objectives, within the restrictions laid down by international law.[494] Hence, states enjoy a wide margin of discretion in conducting their economic policy, to the extent that they are able to bring economic change for the public interest.[495] Tribunals

No. ARB/03/9; El Paso Energy International Company v. The Argentine Republic, Award, 31 October 2011 ICSID Case No. ARB/03/15; AWG Group Ltd. v. The Argentine Republic, Award, 9 April 2015 ICSID Case No. ARB/03/19.

490 Levashova, *The Right of States to Regulate in International Investment Law*, p. 116; Mouyal, *International Investment Law and the Right to Regulate*, p. 99.

491 *See* Section 4 III 1).

492 Kube, *Tensions Between the International Investment Regime and Human Rights: A Regulatory Tilt?*, p. 165; Bonnitcha, *Substantive Protection under Investment Treaties*, p. 177; Levashova, *The Right of States to Regulate in International Investment Law*, p. 195; Azurix Corp. v. The Argentine Republic, Award, 14 July 2006 ICSID Case No. ARB/01/12, para. 378.

493 *See* Bonnitcha, *Substantive Protection under Investment Treaties*, p. 173-180.

494 Mouyal, *International Investment Law and the Right to Regulate*, p. 32.

495 Saluka Investments B.V. v. The Czech Republic Partial, Award, 17 March 2006 UNCITRAL, para. 305; BG Group Plc. v. The Argentine Republic, Award, 24 December 2007 UNCITRAL, para. 344; Total S.A. v. The Argentine Republic, Decision on Liability, 27 December 2010 ICSID Case No. ARB/04/01, para. 115; Electrabel S.A. v. Republic of Hungary, Award, 25 November 2015 ICSID Case No. ARB/07/19, para. 165, 180; Cavalum SGPS v. Kingdom of Spain, Decision on Jurisdiction, Liability and Directions on Quantum, 31 August 2020 ICSID Case No. ARB/15/34, para. 424. The Tribunal in RREEF In-

went so far as to find the outer margin of the states' discretion is only overstepped in extreme cases. Such cases were found when regulations are unreasonable or inequitable, inconsistent with the public policy expressed by state representatives, or manifestly violating the requirements of transparency, even-handedness and non-discrimination.[496] Maintaining a certain degree of regulatory flexibility of states is important, as investments routinely last over the course of several elections. It follows that investors may be protected by their rights throughout the term of different governments, thereby hindering the ability of subsequent governments to introduce any substantial changes.[497]

This may also relate to the fact that states usually have specialist expertise, on which they built their measures, whereas the arbitrators deciding the dispute do not possess such expert knowledge.[498] It indicates that states are entitled to an assessment prerogative in regard to the adoption of measures addressing the public interest.[499] Therefore it is not surprising that investors have been relatively unsuccessful in claiming an imbalanced exercise of the right to regulate under the ECT in the past.[500] However, the margin of discretion cannot be unlimited. Otherwise, the states' deci-

---

frastructure (G.P.) Limited and RREEF Pan-European Infrastructure Two Lux S.à.r.l. v. Kingdom of Spain, Decision on Responsibility and on the Principles of Quantum, 30 November 2018 ICSID Case No. ARB/13/30, para. 468, even held that a tribunal must refrain from assessing the existence of other or more appropriate possible measures to face this situation. *See also* Palombino, *Fair and Equitable Treatment and the Fabric of General Principles*, p. 137.

496 Parkerings-Compagniet AS v. Republic of Lithuania, Award, 11 September 2007 ICSID Case No. ARB/05/8, para. 332; AES Summit Generation Limited et. al. v. The Republic of Hungary, Award, 23 September 2010 ICSID Case No. ARB/07/22, para. 10.3.36, 10.3.37; Saluka Investments B.V. v. The Czech Republic Partial, Award, 17 March 2006 UNCITRAL para. 303.

497 Gaukrodger, 'The Balance Between Investor Protection and the Right to Regulate in Investment Treaties', p. 18.

498 Levashova, *The Right of States to Regulate in International Investment Law*, p. 203, 204.

499 *See for example* Philip Morris Brands Sàrl et. al. v. Oriental Republic of Uruguay, Award, 8 July 2016 ICSID Case No. ARB/10/7, para. 399, 419; Chemtura Corporation v. Canada, Award, 2 August 2010 UNCITRAL, para. 134; Total S.A. v. The Argentine Republic, Decision on Liability, 27 December 2010 ICSID Case No. ARB/04/01, para. 115. *See also* Potestà, 'Legitimate Expectations in Investment Treaty Law: Understanding the Roots and the Limits of a Controversial Concept', p. 113.

500 Coop and Seif, *ECT and State's Right to Regulate*, para. 10.10. Although some commentators see a risk of "overshooting" in efforts to correct the balance in treaties towards allowing greater space for a right to regulate, *see* Gaukrodger,

sions would be unchallengeable under public international law.[501] States may have to take decisive action, when a public interest is at risk.[502] If their conduct, however, does not serve to mitigate the risk to the public interest or leads to a deepening of it, states cannot rely on their regulatory freedom.[503] Measures also exceed the margin of discretion, if they are manifestly unfounded, conducted in bad faith, or the state's authorities are unable to substantiate the underlying objectives.[504] Thus, acts of the state must at least be suitable to benefit the public interest, in order to be a legitimate exercise of the right to regulate.[505]

In recent renewable energy cases, the success rate of investors has been significantly higher.[506] This indicates that some of the states' measures exceeded the margin of discretion and thus overstepped the limitations of the right to regulate, thereby excessively infringing the interests of the investors protected by the ECT and subsequently the FET standard.

'The Balance Between Investor Protection and the Right to Regulate in Investment Treaties', p. 5.

501 RREEF Infrastructure (G.P.) Limited and RREEF Pan-European Infrastructure Two Lux S.à.r.l. v. Kingdom of Spain, Decision on Responsibility and on the Principles of Quantum, 30 November 2018 ICSID Case No. ARB/13/30, para. 468. Investor-friendly commentators even contend that the limitation of the states' right to regulate through international treaties can have a positive impact on the quality of government regulation, *see* Gaukrodger, 'The Balance Between Investor Protection and the Right to Regulate in Investment Treaties', p. 4.

502 The Tribunal in *Azurix* held that that governments "have to be vigilant and protect the public health of their citizens", but also concluded that statements and actions of the state may violated the FET standard, if they "contributed to the crisis rather than assisted in solving it", Azurix Corp. v. The Argentine Republic, Award, 14 July 2006 ICSID Case No. ARB/01/12, para. 144.

503 Ibid, para. 144.

504 Glamis Gold, Ltd. v. The United States of America, Award, 8 June 2009 UNCITRAL, para. 805; Philip Morris Brands Sàrl et. al. v. Oriental Republic of Uruguay, Award, 8 July 2016 ICSID Case No. ARB/10/7, para. 399. *See also* Levashova, *The Right of States to Regulate in International Investment Law*, p. 203.

505 This corresponds with the three-tiered proportionality test discussed *infra* Ch. 2 VI 3).

506 At the time of the writing, Spain lost 18 cases and won 4; Italy lost 4 cases, won 3 cases; the Czech Republic lost 1 case (confidential and not discussed in this research) and won 6 cases.

2) The Concept of Stability

The concept of stability is the major notion opposing the right of the state to regulate. As for investors, the regulatory change in the legal framework of the host state is one of the most potent political risks they have to face when conducting an investment.[507] According to a survey of the Multilateral Investment Guarantee Agency (MIGA), 58% of investors fear adverse regulatory changes within the next 3 years and 56% fear them within the next 6 months.[508] Therefore, stability and predictability of the investment environment are at the core of every investor's interest.[509] By waiving parts of their sovereignty, states use the FET standard as a tool for attracting investors and investments into providing legal guarantees against the state's regulatory risks.[510]

a) Protection of Stability in Arbitral Jurisprudence

Given the aforesaid, it is not surprising that a number of tribunals focused on the stability and predictability of the host state's regulatory framework.[511] It has been repeatedly expressed that a stable legal and business environment is, in general, an essential element of the FET standard.[512] Thus, investors can—leaving aside exceptional circum-

507 Hobér and Fellenbaum, 'Political Risk Insurance and Investment Treaty Protection' in Bungenberg and others (eds), *International Investment Law: A Handbook* (Nomos 2015), p. 1518.

508 MIGA, *World investment and political risk 2013* (The World Bank 2014), p. 21. *See also* Hobér and Fellenbaum, *Political Risk Insurance and Investment Treaty Protection*, p. 1520, 1521.

509 *See* Hobe, *The Development of the Law of Aliens and Emergence of General Principles of Protection under International Law*, p. 19.

510 Levashova, *The Right of States to Regulate in International Investment Law*, p. 238, 239; Gaukrodger, 'The Balance Between Investor Protection and the Right to Regulate in Investment Treaties', p. 5.

511 Occidental Exploration and Production Company v. The Republic of Ecuador Final, Award, 1 July 2004 LCIA Case No. UN3467, para. 190; CMS Gas Transmission Company v. The Argentine Republic, Award, 21 May 2005 ICSID Case No. ARB/01/8, para. 284; LG&E Energy Corp. LG&E Capital Corp. and LG&E International, Inc. v. The Argentine Republic, Decision on Liability, 3 October 2006 ICSID Case No. ARB/02/1, para. 124; Rupert Joseph Binder v. Czech Republic Final, Award, 15 July 2011 UNCITRAL, para. 446.

512 CMS Gas Transmission Company v. The Argentine Republic, Award, 21 May 2005 ICSID Case No. ARB/01/8, para. 274; LG&E Energy Corp. LG&E Capital Corp. and LG&E International, Inc. v. The Argentine Republic, Decision on

stances—expect states to act consistently, free from ambiguity, and with sufficient transparency in their relations with the foreign investor.[513] That way, reasonably diligent investors must gather all relevant information and familiarise themselves with all rules and regulations that will govern their investments. They must then plan their investment and comply with such regulations or alter their commercial strategy.[514] Investors can only make a well-informed business decision, if states communicate the goals of relevant policies, administrative practices and directives, as well as promise certainty that laws are not changed.[515] Clear communication also obligates states to provide clarity about the meaning and extent of its acts, and avoid any inconsistencies between previous practices and regulations and any subsequent changes.[516]

However, tribunals also noted that there are limits to the concept of stability. Concerns were raised that if the term "stability" was taken too literally, it would impose inappropriate and unrealistic obligations upon host states.[517] Therefore, the concept of stability is not to be understood in a way that the legal system would be frozen in time

Liability, 3 October 2006 ICSID Case No. ARB/02/1, para. 124; citing the aforementioned: Duke Energy Electroquil Partners & Electroquil S.A. v. Republic of Ecuador, Award, 18 August 2008 ICSID Case No. ARB/04/19, para. 339, 340.

513 Técnicas Medioambientales Tecmed, S.A. v. The United Mexican States, Award, 29 May 2003 ICSID Case No. ARB (AF)/00/2, para. 154; L.E.S.I. S.p.A. and ASTALDI S.p.A. v. République Algérienne, Award, 12 November 2008 ICSID Case No. ARB/05/3, para. 151.

514 Técnicas Medioambientales Tecmed, S.A. v. The United Mexican States, Award, 29 May 2003 ICSID Case No. ARB (AF)/00/2, para. 154; L.E.S.I. S.p.A. and ASTALDI S.p.A. v. République Algérienne, Award, 12 November 2008 ICSID Case No. ARB/05/3, para. 151.

515 Técnicas Medioambientales Tecmed, S.A. v. The United Mexican States, Award, 29 May 2003 ICSID Case No. ARB (AF)/00/2, para. 154; L.E.S.I. S.p.A. and ASTALDI S.p.A. v. République Algérienne, Award, 12 November 2008 ICSID Case No. ARB/05/3, para. 151; Occidental Exploration and Production Company v. The Republic of Ecuador Final, Award, 1 July 2004 LCIA Case No. UN3467, para. 184.

516 Técnicas Medioambientales Tecmed, S.A. v. The United Mexican States, Award, 29 May 2003 ICSID Case No. ARB (AF)/00/2, para. 154; L.E.S.I. S.p.A. and ASTALDI S.p.A. v. République Algérienne, Award, 12 November 2008 ICSID Case No. ARB/05/3, para. 151; Occidental Exploration and Production Company v. The Republic of Ecuador Final, Award, 1 July 2004 LCIA Case No. UN3467, para. 184.

517 Saluka Investments B.V. v. The Czech Republic Partial, Award, 17 March 2006 UNCITRAL, para. 304.

or that the regulatory power of the state would wholly disappear.[518] Furthermore, the stability of the legal and business framework does not guarantee the maintenance of the economic conditions for business, prevailing at the time of investment and economic health.[519] Neither does the stability of the legal order and business environment equate to the immutability of the legal framework and business environment.[520] Economic and legal life is by nature evolutionary and no experienced business person would reasonably expect that the legal framework in place, at the time of the investment, will maintain its exact features over the course of the investment.[521] This ties in with the role of the legal framework as a tool for the state to protect the public interest and foster economic and social development.[522] Given the volatile nature of domestic law, a reference to a stable legal framework in a preamble or such cannot be perceived as an unqualified guarantee that regulations will never change.[523] Such interpretation corresponds to the recently

---

518 CMS Gas Transmission Company v. The Argentine Republic, Award, 21 May 2005 ICSID Case No. ARB/01/8, para. 277; Enron Corporation and Ponderosa Assets, L.P. v. The Argentine Republic, Award, 22 May 2007 ICSID Case No. ARB/01/3, para. 261; Mobil Exploration and Development Inc. v. The Argentine Republic, Decision on Jurisdiction and Liability, 10 April 2013 ICSID Case No. ARB/04/16, para. 928.

519 El Paso Energy International Company v. The Argentine Republic, Award, 31 October 2011 ICSID Case No. ARB/03/15, para. 365; Mobil Exploration and Development Inc. v. The Argentine Republic, Decision on Jurisdiction and Liability, 10 April 2013 ICSID Case No. ARB/04/16, para. 928.

520 El Paso Energy International Company v. The Argentine Republic, Award, 31 October 2011 ICSID Case No. ARB/03/15, para. 365; Ioan Micula, Viorel Micula, S.C. European Food S.A, S.C. Starmill S.R.L. and S.C. Multipack S.R.L. v. Romania, Award, 11 December 2013 ICSID Case No. ARB/05/20, para. 673.

521 AES Summit Generation Limited et. al. v. The Republic of Hungary, Award, 23 September 2010 ICSID Case No. ARB/07/22, para. 9.3.29; El Paso Energy International Company v. The Argentine Republic, Award, 31 October 2011 ICSID Case No. ARB/03/15, para. 352. *See also* Potestà, 'Legitimate Expectations in Investment Treaty Law: Understanding the Roots and the Limits of a Controversial Concept', p. 113.

522 The Tribunal in *Lemire* rightly observed that "[e]conomic development is an objective which must benefit all, primarily national citizens and national companies, and secondarily foreign investors. Thus, the object and purpose of the Treaty are not to protect foreign investments per se, but as an aid to the development of the domestic economy", Joseph Charles Lemire v. Ukraine Decision on Liability, 14 January 2010 ICSID Case No. ARB/06/18, para. 272-273.

523 Notwithstanding that some tribunals attempted to interpret the FET standard in the light of the treaty's purpose, *see* Occidental Exploration and Production

expressed view of the EU in its negotiation directive for the modernisation of the ECT.[524]

b) The Tension between the Right to Regulate and Concept of Stability

Taking into account the states' sovereignty, investors may only rely on the stability with respect to specific aspects of the legal framework, if the host states limited their right to regulate through a commitment.[525] Therefore, there is nothing objectionable about amendments to the regulatory framework.[526] Investors must expect and anticipate that the legislation will change from time to time, in the absence of some degree of commitment by the host state giving rise to a legitimate expectation of stabilization.[527] If such a commitment exists, however, the turning point becomes the

---

Company v. The Republic of Ecuador Final, Award, 1 July 2004 LCIA Case No. UN3467, para. 183; CMS Gas Transmission Company v. The Argentine Republic, Award, 21 May 2005 ICSID Case No. ARB/01/8, para. 274; LG&E Energy Corp. LG&E Capital Corp. and LG&E International, Inc. v. The Argentine Republic, Decision on Liability, 3 October 2006 ICSID Case No. ARB/02/1, para. 124. Notwithstanding that the object and purpose are key tools for the interpretation of treaties according to Article 31(1) VCLT, it remains a redundant argument since investment treaties – in which the FET standard is most often applied in – always aims for the creation of a stable legal framework.

524 Council of the EU, Negotiating Directives for the Modernisation of the Energy Charter Treaty, 2. July 2019, p. 3 <https://data.consilium.europa.eu/doc/document/ST-10745-2019-ADD-1/en/pdf> (accessed 3 May 2021). *See also* Ch. 1 III.

525 Duke Energy Electroquil Partners & Electroquil S.A. v. Republic of Ecuador, Award, 18 August 2008 ICSID Case No. ARB/04/19, para. 340; Bayindir Insaat Turizm Ticaret Ve Sanayi A.S. v. Islamic Republic of Pakistan, Award, 27 August 2009 ICSID Case No. ARB/03/29, para. 179; Ioan Micula, Viorel Micula, S.C. European Food S.A, S.C. Starmill S.R.L. and S.C. Multipack S.R.L. v. Romania, Award, 11 December 2013 ICSID Case No. ARB/05/20, para. 669, 673.

526 Parkerings-Compagniet AS v. Republic of Lithuania, Award, 11 September 2007 ICSID Case No. ARB/05/8, para. 332; ADC Affiliate Limited and ADC & ADMC Management Limited v. The Republic of Hungary, Award, 2 October 2016 ICSID Case No. ARB/03/16, para. 423.

527 Ioan Micula, Viorel Micula, S.C. European Food S.A, S.C. Starmill S.R.L. and S.C. Multipack S.R.L. v. Romania, Award, 11 December 2013 ICSID Case No. ARB/05/20, para. 529; Saluka Investments B.V. v. The Czech Republic Partial, Award, 17 March 2006 UNCITRAL, para. 304, 305. *See also* Potestà, 'Legitimate Expectations in Investment Treaty Law: Understanding the Roots and the Limits of a Controversial Concept', p. 113.

question of whether the state struck the right balance between the interest in legal stability and legitimate expectations on the one hand, and the host state's right to amend the regulatory framework on the other hand.[528] In general, this requires that equilibrium must be found between the rights at stake by means of non-discriminatory measures.[529] The act of balancing in disputes including the challenge of legislation proves to be especially delicate. Such cases involve the interaction of investment treaties with democratic decision-making, hence intensifying the interference with the states' sovereignty.[530] Concerns have been raised that a broad interpretation of the FET standard may overly constrain the sovereignty of the states, in particular in the areas of paramount importance to the public interest.[531]

It follows from those observations that the legitimate expectations of investors protected by the international obligations a state has entered into must be measured against the same states' right to regulate through a balancing test.[532] This test must take into account the specific circumstances outlined in Section III of this Chapter.[533] How the balancing test should be applied will be examined in the next Chapter.

3) Application of the Proportionality Test in Balancing Legitimate Expectations

In the previous segments, it has been demonstrated that whenever an investor relies on the FET standard, the tribunal will have to balance the

528 Potestà, 'Legitimate Expectations in Investment Treaty Law: Understanding the Roots and the Limits of a Controversial Concept', p. 113.

529 Saluka Investments B.V. v. The Czech Republic Partial, Award, 17 March 2006 UNCITRAL, para. 306, 307; El Paso Energy International Company v. The Argentine Republic, Award, 31 October 2011 ICSID Case No. ARB/03/15, para. 358.

530 Gaukrodger, 'The Balance Between Investor Protection and the Right to Regulate in Investment Treaties', p. 14.

531 Kläger, *Revising Treatment Standards— Fair and Equitable Treatment in Light of Sustainable Development*, p. 67.

532 Levashova, *The Right of States to Regulate in International Investment Law*, p. 41; Kläger, *'Fair and Equitable Treatment' in International Investment Law*, p. 186, 187.

533 For the component of the legitimate expectations *see* Ch. 2 III.

competing interests of the rights at stake.[534] This act of balancing is frequently done through the application of the proportionality test. Proportionality in international investment law was first used in the assessment of expropriation claims, but it is particularly important in the context of the FET standard, as the tribunal has a broader margin of discretion here.[535] Applied to the notion of legitimate expectations, proportionality serves to establish whether the aim pursued by a state's action is excessive, in relation to the means employed to achieve this end.[536] Thus, the assessment of the proportionality of the state's acts will eventually determine what the investor and the state can legitimately expect from one another, and what is arbitrary or unfair.[537]

Whereas expropriation is an all-or-nothing situation, the assessment of proportionality provides a more refined tool to balance the interests of the host state and investors, when analysing the violation of the FET standard.[538] However, the tribunals' discretion is not without limits. The good faith aspect of the FET standard requires the arbitral tribunal to protect the host states' values, while balancing the rights at stake.[539]

An assessment of the investment practice shows that there is a growing number of arbitral tribunals that apply the principle of proportionality, in order to determine whether international investment obligations have been breached.[540] Especially the obligation to afford FET to investors has,

---

534 *See* Ch. 2 IV. *See also* Thomas Cottier and others, 'The Principle of Proportionality in International Law: Foundations and Variations' (2017) 18 The Journal of World Investment & Trade 628, p. 659.

535 Titi, *The Right to Regulate in International Investment Law*, stating that the FET standard requires by its "very nature" a balancing of interests, p. 277. *See also* Levashova, *The Right of States to Regulate in International Investment Law*, p. 104.

536 Kingsbury and Schill, 'Public Law Concepts to Balance Investors' Rights with State Regulatory Actions in the Public Interest—the Concept of Proportionality' in Schill (ed), *International Investment Law and Comparative Public Law* (OUP 2010), p. 85; Levashova, *The Right of States to Regulate in International Investment Law*, p. 99.

537 Stone Sweet, 'Investor-State Arbitration: Proportionality's New Frontier' (2010) 4(1) Law & Ethics of Human Rights, p. 62; Scheu, *Systematische Berücksichtigung von Menschenrechten in Investitionsschiedsverfahren* (Studies in International Investment Law vol. 23, Nomos 2017), p. 234.

538 Kriebaum, 'Regulatory Takings: Balancing the Interests of the Investor and the State', p. 719, 730.

539 Sipiorski, *Good Faith in International Investment Arbitration*, para. 10.03, 13.03.

540 *For example* Técnicas Medioambientales Tecmed, S.A. v. The United Mexican States, Award, 29 May 2003 ICSID Case No. ARB (AF)/00/2, para. 122; MTD Equity Sdn. Bhd. and MTD Chile S.A. v. Republic of Chile, Award, 25 May

on several occasions, been interpreted to entail the proportionality test to strike a balance between the rights and interests at stake.[541] This requires a thorough analysis of the facts and circumstances at hand, in order to determine, in accordance with the rule of law and the prohibition of arbi-

2004 ICSID Case No. ARB/01/7, para. 109; Azurix Corp. v. The Argentine Republic, Award, 14 July 2006 ICSID Case No. ARB/01/12, para. 311, 312; LG&E Energy Corp. LG&E Capital Corp. and LG&E International, Inc. v. The Argentine Republic, Decision on Liability, 3 October 2006 ICSID Case No. ARB/02/1, para. 195; Parkerings-Compagniet AS v. Republic of Lithuania, Award, 11 September 2007 ICSID Case No. ARB/05/8, para. 368; EDF (Services) Limited v. Romania, Award, 8 October 2009 ICSID Case No. ARB/05/13, para. 293; AES Summit Generation Limited et. al. v. The Republic of Hungary, Award, 23 September 2010 ICSID Case No. ARB/07/22, para. 10.3.36; Occidental Petroleum Corporation and Occidental Exploration and Production Company v. The Republic of Ecuador, Award, 5 October 2012 ICSID Case No. ARB/06/11, para. 404; Mobil Exploration and Development Inc. v. The Argentine Republic, Decision on Jurisdiction and Liability, 10 April 2013 ICSID Case No. ARB/04/16, para. 818; Charanne and Construction Investments v. Kingdom of Spain, Award, 21 January 2016 SCC Case No. V 062/2012, para. 514, 517; OperaFund Eco-Invest SICAV PLC and Schwab Holding AG v. Kingdom of Spain, Award, 6 September 2019 ICSID Case No. ARB/15/36, para. 555; RWE Innogy GmbH and RWE Innogy Aersa S.A.U. v. Kingdom of Spain, Decision on Jurisdicition, Liability, and certain Issues of Quantum, 6 January 2020 ICSID Case No. ARB/14/34, para. 600; Hydro Energy 1 S.A.R.L. and Hydroxana Sweden AB v. The Kingdom of Spain, Decision on Jurisdiction, Liability and Directions on Quantum, 9 March 2020 ICSID Case No. ARB/15/42, para. 676(4); Cavalum SGPS v. Kingdom of Spain, Decision on Jurisdiction, Liability and Directions on Quantum, 31 August 2020 ICSID Case No. ARB/15/34, para. 414, 415.

541 Occidental Petroleum Corporation and Occidental Exploration and Production Company v. The Republic of Ecuador, Award, 5 October 2012 ICSID Case No. ARB/06/11, para. 404; MTD Equity Sdn. Bhd. and MTD Chile S.A. v. Republic of Chile, Award, 25 May 2004 ICSID Case No. ARB/01/7, para. 109; Total S.A. v. The Argentine Republic, Decision on Liability, 27 December 2010 ICSID Case No. ARB/04/01 in footnote 232; Charanne and Construction Investments v. Kingdom of Spain, Award, 21 January 2016 SCC Case No. V 062/2012, para. 514, 517; OperaFund Eco-Invest SICAV PLC and Schwab Holding AG v. Kingdom of Spain, Award, 6 September 2019 ICSID Case No. ARB/15/36, para. 555; RWE Innogy GmbH and RWE Innogy Aersa S.A.U. v. Kingdom of Spain, Decision on Jurisdicition, Liability, and certain Issues of Quantum, 6 January 2020 ICSID Case No. ARB/14/34, para. 600; Hydro Energy 1 S.A.R.L. and Hydroxana Sweden AB v. The Kingdom of Spain, Decision on Jurisdiction, Liability and Directions on Quantum, 9 March 2020 ICSID Case No. ARB/15/42, para. 676(4); Cavalum SGPS v. Kingdom of Spain, Decision on Jurisdiction, Liability and Directions on Quantum, 31 August 2020 ICSID Case No. ARB/15/34, para. 414, 415. Thereby recurring back on the basic requirements afforded by the FET standard set up above in Ch. 1 III.

trariness, whether the state has acted moderately with the aim of ensuring justice in individual cases.[542] Undervaluing the states' right to regulate might hinder the states' ability to react in a proper manner to threats to the state itself or its people. Diminishing the concept of stability might bring economic ruin to the individual investor and could obstruct international investment in the region. FDI, in turn, is an essential component of sustainable development strategies at the national and global levels.[543]

Thus, in the assessment of the situation, a tribunal will be required to take into account the degree of economic impact created by the state's measures, as well as their context and purpose.[544] As the investors' rights stem from international obligations that the state has entered into out of free will, the state must pursue a profound purpose, such as the promotion of a paramount social, economic or environmental aim.[545] A counter consideration must be made as to the level of interference of the measure, with the reasonable investment-backed expectations of the investor.[546] The issue, which needs to be examined, is the question of how this proportionality test is conducted. As the FET standard, in particular the notion of legitimate expectations, is mostly developed by arbitral case law, the individual tribunal is vested with a wide margin of discretion as to how and in what depth it will conduct its balancing evaluation.[547]

In order to achieve a suitable understanding of proportionality under international law, the origins and systematics of the proportionality test, as well as its relation to the standard of reasonableness will be examined.

---

542 Scheu, *Systematische Berücksichtigung von Menschenrechten in Investitionsschiedsverfahren*, p. 234; Diehl, *The Core Standard of International Investment Protection*, p. 334.

543 Mann, 'The Right of States to Regulate and International Investment Law', p. 2.

544 Trujillo, 'Balancing Sustainability, the Right to Regulate, and the Need for Investor Protection: Lessons from the Trade Regime', p. 2739.

545 ibid, p. 2739.

546 Marvin Roy Feldman Karpa v. United Mexican States, Award, 16 December 2002 ICSID Case No. ARB(AF)/99/1, para. 112; Trujillo, 'Balancing Sustainability, the Right to Regulate, and the Need for Investor Protection: Lessons from the Trade Regime', p. 2740, 2741.

547 Levashova, *The Right of States to Regulate in International Investment Law*, p. 102, 103; Titi, *The Right to Regulate in International Investment Law*, p. 277.

a) The Origins of Proportionality in International Law

Proportionality is a frequently used concept in international law.[548] It can be found, inter alia, in EU law[549], the jurisprudence of the ECtHR[550], and international trade law[551]. Across all legal systems, the purpose of the proportionality test is to provide the basis for balancing different components and aspects at stake under the facts of a particular case, in the context of administrative action.[552] In its jurisprudence regarding the right to compensation for unlawful expropriation arising from Protocol 1 of the ECHR, the ECtHR adopted the test for proportionality and served thereby as a role model for constitutional courts and arbitral tribunals around the world.[553] Whereas the ECtHR prefers a broader balancing approach,

548 For an overview of the discussion whether proportionality is regarded as a free-standing principle in international law *see* Bücheler, *Proportionality in Investor-State Arbitration*, p. 79-82 and Cottier and others, 'The Principle of Proportionality in International Law: Foundations and Variations', p. 630.

549 Explicitly mentioned in Article 5(1)(4) and Articles 12(b) and 69 of the TEU; recognised by the CJEU as a general principle of EU law in CJEU Judgment *The Queen v Minister of Agriculture, Fisheries and Food and Secretary of State for Health,*13 November 1990 Case C-331/88, para. 13; CJEU Judgment *Rewe-Zentral AG v Bundesmonopolverwaltung für Branntwein,*20 February 1979 Case 120/78; CJEU Judgment *Commission of the European Communities v Federal Republic of Germany,*14 December 2004 Case C-463/01, para. 78.

550 ECtHR Judgment *Handyside v. United Kingdom,* 7 December 1976 Application No. 5493/72, para. 48, 49; ECtHR Judgment *Dudgeon v. United Kingdom,* 22 October 1981 Application No. 7525/76, para. 53; ECtHR Judgment *AD & OD v. United Kingdom,* 16 March 2010 Application No. 28680/06, para. 91.

551 Despite of using the name „necessity-test“ the WTO Appellate Body applies a similar three-tiered approach for balancing the interests at stake as in a classical proportionality test, *see* Korea — Measures Affecting Imports of Fresh, Chilled and Frozen Beef Report of the Appellate Body - *AB-2000-8* -,11 December 2000 WT/DS161/AB/R; WT/DS169/AB/R, para. 164, 166; Brazil - Measures Affecting Imports of Retreaded Tyres - AB-2007-4 Report of the Appellate Body, 3 December 2007 WT/DS332/AB/R, para. 152, 155, 156.

552 Occidental Petroleum Corporation and Occidental Exploration and Production Company v. The Republic of Ecuador, Award, 5 October 2012 ICSID Case No. ARB/06/11, para. 403; Cottier and others, 'The Principle of Proportionality in International Law: Foundations and Variations', p. 630.

553 Mathews, 'Reasonableness and Proportionality' (2016), p. 11 <https://papers.ssrn.com/sol3/papers.cfm?abstract_id=2836264> (accessed 3 May 2021); Stone Sweet, 'Investor-State Arbitration: Proportionality's New Frontier', p. 64.

which affords the states a "margin of appreciation"[554], the CJEU and the WTO appellate body follow a more systematic balancing test.[555] Through its recognition in most constitutional and international law systems, the proportionality test has developed to become an unwritten, general principle of law.[556]

Despite its early development in European administrative and constitutional systems[557], the proportionality test had not been used in international investment law before the 2000s, and therefore emerged at the same time as the notion of legitimate expectations.[558] This simultaneous emergence of both notions is not surprising, since proportionality opens the gates to the development of undefined legal concepts such as the notion of legitimate expectations and the FET standard.[559] This, again, allows for a comparative law analysis and to draw inspiration in the application of proportionality.[560] While the introduction of the proportionality test into investment law was controversial in the beginning, it is recognized as a

---

554 *See* ECtHR Judgment *Handyside v. United Kingdom,* 7 December 1976 Application No. 5493/72. *See also* Zarra, 'Right to Regulate, Margin of Appreciation and Proportionality: Current Status in Investment Arbitration in Light of Philip Morris v. Uruguay', p. 108.

555 Stone Sweet, 'Investor-State Arbitration: Proportionality's New Frontier', p. 71.

556 Stone Sweet and Mathews, 'Proportionality Balancing and Global Constitutionalism' (2008) 47(1) Columbia Journal of Transnational Law 73, p. 74, 75; Scheu, *Systematische Berücksichtigung von Menschenrechten in Investitionsschiedsverfahren*, p. 238.

557 The principle of proportionality has been used by German constitutional courts since the early 1900s and migrated into European law. *See* Kingsbury and Schill, *Public Law Concepts to Balance Investors' Rights with State Regulatory Actions in the Public Interest—the Concept of Proportionality*, p. 80-83; Scheu, *Systematische Berücksichtigung von Menschenrechten in Investitionsschiedsverfahren*, p. 234, 235; Stone Sweet and Mathews, 'Proportionality Balancing and Global Constitutionalism', p. 74, 75.

558 Vadi, 'The Migration of Constitutional Ideas: The Strange Case of Proportionality in International Investment Law and Arbitration' in Bjorklund (ed), *Yearbook on International Investment Law and Policy 2013-2014* (OUP 2015), p. 349; Stone Sweet, 'Investor-State Arbitration: Proportionality's New Frontier', p. 63, 64.

559 Bücheler, *Proportionality in Investor-State Arbitration*, p. 63.

560 *See* Kingsbury and Schill, *Public Law Concepts to Balance Investors' Rights with State Regulatory Actions in the Public Interest—the Concept of Proportionality*, p. 80-85; Henckels, *Proportionality and Deference in Investor-State Arbitration*, p. 45.

part of the FET standard today.[561] Such judicial law-making is necessary to restrict vague and overarching principles in international law, thus providing an outline for said legal concepts.[562] Nevertheless, judicial law-making raises concerns, with regard to the lack of authority of arbitral tribunals, particularly in investment arbitration.[563] Contrary to its purpose, proportionality also bears the risks of arbitrariness and an overly subjective exercise of discretion in the case by the adjudicative body.[564]

To counter the risk of arbitrariness in the evaluation of the facts and circumstances of a given case by tribunals, balancing through proportionality requires a uniform approach and a normative background.[565] In few areas of international law is this statement more important than in interpreting the FET standard. Although not considered a constitutional principle, a considerable number of elements of the FET standard can be found

561 *See* MTD Equity Sdn. Bhd. and MTD Chile S.A. v. Republic of Chile, Award, 25 May 2004 ICSID Case No. ARB/01/7, para. 109; Saluka Investments B.V. v. The Czech Republic Partial, Award, 17 March 2006 UNCITRAL, para. 306–308; Occidental Petroleum Corporation and Occidental Exploration and Production Company v. The Republic of Ecuador, Award, 5 October 2012 ICSID Case No. ARB/06/11, para. 404-409; Philip Morris Brands Sàrl et. al. v. Oriental Republic of Uruguay, Award, 8 July 2016 ICSID Case No. ARB/10/7, para. 409 Charanne and Construction Investments v. Kingdom of Spain, Award, 21 January 2016 SCC Case No. V 062/2012, para. 514, 517; OperaFund Eco-Invest SICAV PLC and Schwab Holding AG v. Kingdom of Spain, Award, 6 September 2019 ICSID Case No. ARB/15/36, para. 555; RWE Innogy GmbH and RWE Innogy Aersa S.A.U. v. Kingdom of Spain, Decision on Jurisdicition, Liability, and certain Issues of Quantum, 6 January 2020 ICSID Case No. ARB/14/34, para. 600; Hydro Energy 1 S.A.R.L. and Hydroxana Sweden AB v. The Kingdom of Spain, Decision on Jurisdiction, Liability and Directions on Quantum, 9 March 2020 ICSID Case No. ARB/15/42, para. 676(4); Cavalum SGPS v. Kingdom of Spain, Decision on Jurisdiction, Liability and Directions on Quantum, 31 August 2020 ICSID Case No. ARB/15/34, para. 414, 415.

562 Bücheler, *Proportionality in Investor-State Arbitration*, p. 63.

563 Vadi, *The Migration of Constitutional Ideas: The Strange Case of Proportionality in International Investment Law and Arbitration*, p. 353; Ortino, 'Investment Treaties, Sustainable Development and Reasonableness Review: A Case Against Strict Proportionality Balancing' (2017) 30(1) Leiden Journal of International Law 71, p. 91.

564 Bücheler, *Proportionality in Investor-State Arbitration*, p. 66; Ortino, 'Investment Treaties, Sustainable Development and Reasonableness Review: A Case Against Strict Proportionality Balancing', p. 91.

565 Bücheler, *Proportionality in Investor-State Arbitration*, p. 196; Scheu, *Systematische Berücksichtigung von Menschenrechten in Investitionsschiedsverfahren*, p. 244.

in international human rights charters.[566] Thus, a uniform application bears importance beyond the simple economic interests of an investor and affects the very essence of human rights in international law. Article 31(3)(c) VCLT includes the principle of systemic integration, which requires, in theory, that international legal principles are applied similarly by different judicial bodies in international law.[567] In practice, however, there is no consensus among arbitral tribunals regarding their approaches to balancing. While a number of arbitral tribunals took the jurisprudence of the ECtHR as guidelines[568], some only applied it in the context of expropriation[569]. A comprehensive comparison of the jurisprudence in international investment law shows that balancing is approached and carried out differently by bodies of law. While some tribunals follow the thorough three-step analysis of the "Continental European" approach, other tribunals take a rather superficial approach to proportionality.[570] Additionally, a test of

566 Fanou and Tzevelekos, *Shared Territory of the ECHR and International Investment Law*, p. 123. Compare also the decisions in Yukos Universal Ltd. (UK - Isle of Man) v. Russian Federation Final, Award, 18 July 2018 PCA Case No. AA 227 and ECtHR Judgment *Oao Neftyanaya Kompaniya Yukos v. Russia*, 8.3.2012 Application No. 14902/04 turning on the same facts and circumstances.

567 International Law Commission, 'Report on Fragmentation of International Law: Difficulties arising from the Diversification and Expansion of International Law' (2006) <https://legal.un.org/ilc/documentation/english/a_cn4_l682.pdf> (accessed 3 May 2021), para. 479, 480; Bücheler, *Proportionality in Investor-State Arbitration*, p. 194; Zarra, 'Right to Regulate, Margin of Appreciation and Proportionality: Current Status in Investment Arbitration in Light of Philip Morris v. Uruguay', p. 101.

568 *For example* Técnicas Medioambientales Tecmed, S.A. v. The United Mexican States, Award, 29 May 2003 ICSID Case No. ARB (AF)/00/2, para. 122 referencing to the ECtHR in the cases ECtHR Judgment *Matos e Silva, Lda. and Others v. Portugal,* 16 September 1996 Application No. 15777/89, para. 92 and ECtHR Judgment *James and others v. United Kingdom,* 21 February 1986 Application No. 8793/79, para. 50. *See also* with general reference to the jurisprudence of the EctHR and CJEU, Occidental Petroleum Corporation and Occidental Exploration and Production Company v. The Republic of Ecuador, Award, 5 October 2012 ICSID Case No. ARB/06/11, para. 403.

569 LG&E Energy Corp. LG&E Capital Corp. and LG&E International, Inc. v. The Argentine Republic, Decision on Liability, 3 October 2006 ICSID Case No. ARB/02/1, para. 195; Técnicas Medioambientales Tecmed, S.A. v. The United Mexican States, Award, 29 May 2003 ICSID Case No. ARB (AF)/00/2, para. 122, Azurix Corp. v. The Argentine Republic, Award, 14 July 2006 ICSID Case No. ARB/01/12, para. 311; Mobil Exploration and Development Inc. v. The Argentine Republic, Decision on Jurisdiction and Liability, 10 April 2013 ICSID Case No. ARB/04/16, para. 818-821.

570 *See below* Ch. 2 IV 3) b).

reasonableness is a common occurrence in the balancing process, either instead of, or accompanied by, an assessment of the proportionality of a measure.[571] This raises the question of what the "right" approach to the balancing demanded by the notion of legitimate expectations is.

b) The "Continental European" Approach to Proportionality

TecMed v. Mexico was the first tribunal introducing the test of proportionality into investment law.[572] In its assessment, the Tribunal continuously referred to the jurisprudence of the ECtHR, thereby hinting at the systematic approach used in the assessment. The ECtHR, as well as the CJEU, have adopted a three-step analysis, which will be referred to in the following as the "Continental European" approach. This approach to proportionality stems, inter alia, from German legal tradition in constitutional and administrative law, and includes the three components of suitability, necessity, and proportionality *stricto sensu*.[573]

Suitability establishes whether a specific measure taken by the state is suitable to achieve a legitimate purpose.[574] This step is usually identified as an assessment of the legitimacy of a states' objective and the suitability of the measure to achieve this objective.[575] If measures are not suitable to achieve the objective, i.e. no rational relationship exists between a measure adopted by the government and the alleged purpose or goal of that mea-

---

571 *See below* Ch. 2 IV 3) c).

572 The tribunal in *TecMed* held that it must be assessed "whether such actions or measures are proportional to the public interest, presumably protected thereby and to the protection legally granted to investments, taking into account that the significance of such impact has a key role upon deciding the proportionality", Técnicas Medioambientales Tecmed, S.A. v. The United Mexican States, Award, 29 May 2003 ICSID Case No. ARB (AF)/00/2, para. 122. *See also* Scheu, *Systematische Berücksichtigung von Menschenrechten in Investitionsschiedsverfahren*, p. 253, 254.

573 Scheu, *Systematische Berücksichtigung von Menschenrechten in Investitionsschiedsverfahren*, p. 234-243. *See also* Cavalum SGPS v. Kingdom of Spain, Decision on Jurisdiction, Liability and Directions on Quantum, 31 August 2020 ICSID Case No. ARB/15/34, para. 415.

574 Kingsbury and Schill, *Public Law Concepts to Balance Investors' Rights with State Regulatory Actions in the Public Interest—the Concept of Proportionality*, p. 86; Henckels, *Proportionality and Deference in Investor-State Arbitration*, p. 48-53.

575 Scheu, *Systematische Berücksichtigung von Menschenrechten in Investitionsschiedsverfahren*, p. 239, 240; Levashova, *The Right of States to Regulate in International Investment Law*, p. 100.

sure, they can be deemed arbitrary from the beginning, thereby manifestly violating the FET standard.[576]

Necessity establishes whether there are measures available to the state to achieve the purpose of the measure which are less infringing, but equally effective.[577] This stage of the test narrows down the range of measures a state has. The state must have availed itself of the most effective, yet least burdensome one.[578] In the case of public interests of paramount importance, tribunals tend to afford the states some assessment prerogative, with regard to the adoption of measures.[579]

Proportionality *stricto sensu* evaluates whether a measure is overall excessive.[580] While the first two steps evaluate the measures chosen, with a view to achieving a certain objective, proportionality *strico sensu* involves assessing the objective and its legal weight in comparison to the opposing

---

576 Levashova, *The Right of States to Regulate in International Investment Law*, p. 206.

577 Kingsbury and Schill, *Public Law Concepts to Balance Investors' Rights with State Regulatory Actions in the Public Interest—the Concept of Proportionality*, p. 86-87; Henckels, *Proportionality and Deference in Investor-State Arbitration*, p. 57.

578 Henckels, *Proportionality and Deference in Investor-State Arbitration: Balancing Investment Protection and Regulatory Autonomy*, p. 154; Scheu, *Systematische Berücksichtigung von Menschenrechten in Investitionsschiedsverfahren*, p. 241.

579 As an example, the Tribunal in *TecMed* doubted that, in order to protect the environment, the state had no choice, but to immediately withdraw the investor's permit to operate a hazardous landfill, without contacting the investor beforehand, and thereby giving it the opportunity to adapt its business model to the amended conditions, Técnicas Medioambientales Tecmed, S.A. v. The United Mexican States, Award, 29 May 2003 ICSID Case No. ARB (AF)/00/2, para. 173, 174. Had the Tribunal applied the three-step proportionality test according to the Continental European approach, it might have reached the conclusion that allowing the investor some transition time to relocate is less infringing on the investor's rights and equally effective to achieve the aim of environmental protection. Thereby, it would making the abrupt revocation of the license not necessary. *See also* Philip Morris Brands Sàrl et. al. v. Oriental Republic of Uruguay, Award, 8 July 2016 ICSID Case No. ARB/10/7, para. 399, 419; Chemtura Corporation v. Canada, Award, 2 August 2010 UNCITRAL, para. 134; Total S.A. v. The Argentine Republic, Decision on Liability, 27 December 2010 ICSID Case No. ARB/04/01, para. 115.

580 Palombino, *Fair and Equitable Treatment and the Fabric of General Principles*, p. 127-128; Cottier and others, 'The Principle of Proportionality in International Law: Foundations and Variations', p. 666; Kingsbury and Schill, *Public Law Concepts to Balance Investors' Rights with State Regulatory Actions in the Public Interest—the Concept of Proportionality*, p. 87, 88; Henckels, *Proportionality and Deference in Investor-State Arbitration*, p. 106.

rights.[581] Thereby, a judicial body assessing the situation must balance the value of the protected right against the value of the impaired right, and has to take into account the intensity of the measure.[582] Imbalance is found, if the weighing exercise reveals that the state measures were excessive in light of the objective pursued and the rights affected.[583]

Although the three-tiered proportionality test has traditionally been applied by international courts and investment tribunals in issues of indirect expropriation, the jurisprudence has also influenced the assessment of the FET standard.[584] The Tribunal in *Occidental v. Ecuador* was the first tribunal to apply a full-fledged three-step analysis with a general reference to European jurisprudence.[585] The majority of the tribunals assessing proportionality under the FET standard, however, did not delve into a thorough

581 Scheu, *Systematische Berücksichtigung von Menschenrechten in Investitionsschiedsverfahren*, p. 242, 243; Palombino, *Fair and Equitable Treatment and the Fabric of General Principles*, p. 128.

582 Kingsbury and Schill, *Public Law Concepts to Balance Investors' Rights with State Regulatory Actions in the Public Interest—the Concept of Proportionality*, p. 87; Scheu, *Systematische Berücksichtigung von Menschenrechten in Investitionsschiedsverfahren*, p. 242, 243.

583 Cavalum SGPS v. Kingdom of Spain, Decision on Jurisdiction, Liability and Directions on Quantum, 31 August 2020 ICSID Case No. ARB/15/34, para. 415; RREEF Infrastructure (G.P.) Limited and RREEF Pan-European Infrastructure Two Lux S.à.r.l. v. Kingdom of Spain, Decision on Responsibility and on the Principles of Quantum, 30 November 2018 ICSID Case No. ARB/13/30, para. 465; Novenergia II - Energy & Environment (SCA), SICAR v. The Kingdom of Spain, Award, 15 February 2018 SCC Case No. V 2015/063, para. 657; Electrabel S.A. v. Republic of Hungary, Award, 25 November 2015 ICSID Case No. ARB/07/19, para. 165, 180.

584 This migration of the proportionality test can be seen, inter alia, in the case of *EDF v. Romania*, in which the Tribunal adopted the proportionality approach taken by the *Azurix v. Argentina* Tribunal in its indirect expropriation analysis, EDF (Services) Limited v. Romania, Award, 8 October 2009 ICSID Case No. ARB/05/13, para. 293, citing Azurix Corp. v. The Argentine Republic, Award, 14 July 2006 ICSID Case No. ARB/01/12, para. 311. *See also* Leonhardsen, 'Looking for Legitimacy: Exploring Proportionality Analysis in Investment Treaty Arbitration' (2012) 3(1) Journal of International Dispute Settlement 95, p. 135.

585 Occidental Petroleum Corporation and Occidental Exploration and Production Company v. The Republic of Ecuador, Award, 5 October 2012 ICSID Case No. ARB/06/11, para. 403, 410-452.

analysis.[586] Rather, tribunals assess either only the necessity requirement[587] or the *strico sensu* part of the European approach[588]. Notwithstanding the insufficient provision of reasoning, this application of the proportionality analysis *stricto sensu* considerably aids in balancing the expectations of the investor against the conduct of the state and the general context.[589] The balancing act will then reveal whether the state measure was fair and equitable based on the facts of the given case.[590] Nonetheless, only a few of the tribunals, which applied the "Continental European Approach" to proportionality, used the full spectrum for the analysis.[591]

c) Reasonableness and Proportionality

Another approach to the balancing issue is the "Anglo-American" approach which, in contrast, uses the "standard of reasonableness", in order to determine whether a measure was appropriate.[592] The standard

586 Coming to the same conclusion based on earlier arbitral jurisprudence: Scheu, *Systematische Berücksichtigung von Menschenrechten in Investitionsschiedsverfahren*, 252.

587 *For example*, the Tribunal in AWG simply concluded that there would have been other measures addressing the economic crisis that were allegedly less adverse to the investor's rights, AWG Group Ltd. v. The Argentine Republic, Decision on Liability, 30 June 2010 ICSID Case No. ARB/03/19, para. 235.

588 *For example* AES Corporation and Tau Power B.V. v. Republic of Kazakhstan, Award, 1 November 2013 ICSID Case No. ARB/10/16, para. 408-412; Electrabel S.A. v. Republic of Hungary, Award, 25 November 2015 ICSID Case No. ARB/07/19, para. 180-186.

589 Leonhardsen, 'Looking for Legitimacy: Exploring Proportionality Analysis in Investment Treaty Arbitration', p. 134.

590 Ibid, p. 134.

591 Recently RWE Innogy GmbH and RWE Innogy Aersa S.A.U. v. Kingdom of Spain, Decision on Jurisdicition, Liability, and certain Issues of Quantum, 6 January 2020 ICSID Case No. ARB/14/34, para. 550-600; Watkins Holdings S.à.r.l. and others v. Kingdom of Spain, Award, 21 January 2020 ICSID Case No. ARB/15/44, para. 601-603; Hydro Energy 1 S.A.R.L. and Hydroxana Sweden AB v. The Kingdom of Spain, Decision on Jurisdiction, Liability and Directions on Quantum, 9 March 2020 ICSID Case No. ARB/15/42, para. 573, 574, 676(6). Coming to the same conclusion based on earlier arbitral jurisprudence: Scheu, *Systematische Berücksichtigung von Menschenrechten in Investitionsschiedsverfahren*, p. 254.

592 Scheu, *Systematische Berücksichtigung von Menschenrechten in Investitionsschiedsverfahren*, p. 246, 247; Langfeldt, 'Proportionality in Investment Treaty Arbitration and the Necessity for Tribunals to Adopt a Clear Methodology' (2019), p. 26.

of reasonableness has been applied alongside the proportionality test in the assessment of an alleged violation of the obligation to afford FET.[593] Stemming from the United Kingdom's domestic law, the standard advanced into other common law jurisdictions and investment law.[594] The requirement of reasonableness is also enshrined in sentence 3 of Article 10(1) ECT, which explicitly prohibits unreasonable conduct of the states, as part of the obligation to provide FET.[595] However, the meaning of the standard of reasonableness has been controversial from the very beginning.[596] The migration of the notion into other domestic jurisdictions and international law has only intensified the uncertainties about the content of reasonableness.[597] Investment tribunals concurred that "reasonableness means that the State's conduct bears a reasonable relationship to some rational policy".[598]

Superficially, it is not surprising that reasonableness and proportionality are sometimes used synonymously or at least closely coupled.[599] Both notions share the specific feature that they serve as a benchmark for the compliance of a state's measure against an investor with international

593 Vadi, 'Proportionality, Reasonableness, and Standards of Review in Investment Treaty Arbitration' in Bjorklund (ed), *Yearbook on International Investment Law and Policy 2013-2014* (OUP 2015), p. 211-213.

594 The Standard can be traced back to the case of Associated Provincial Picture Houses Ltd. v. Wednesbury Corporation Judgment, 10 November 1947 [1948] 1 KB 223.

595 Benson, Yim and Orlowski, *The Energy Charter Treaty*, p. 41; AES Summit Generation Limited et. al. v. The Republic of Hungary, Award, 23 September 2010 ICSID Case No. ARB/07/22, para. 10.3.7-10.3.9.

596 Several attempts at definition were already made in the original judgment, such as opining that an act of the state is only unreasonable if it is "so absurd that no sensible person could ever dream that it lay within the powers of the authority", or that "it might almost be described as being done in bad faith", Associated Provincial Picture Houses Ltd. v. Wednesbury Corporation Judgment, 10 November 1947 [1948] 1 KB 223, para. 5.

597 Mathews, *Reasonableness and Proportionality*, p. 2, 3.

598 Saluka Investments B.V. v. The Czech Republic Partial, Award, 17 March 2006 UNCITRAL, para. 179; Hydro Energy 1 S.A.R.L. and Hydroxana Sweden AB v. The Kingdom of Spain, Decision on Jurisdiction, Liability and Directions on Quantum, 9 March 2020 ICSID Case No. ARB/15/42, para. 569. *See also* Ioan Micula, Viorel Micula, S.C. European Food S.A, S.C. Starmill S.R.L. and S.C. Multipack S.R.L. v. Romania, Award, 11 December 2013 ICSID Case No. ARB/05/20, para. 525.

599 Ortino, 'Investment Treaties, Sustainable Development and Reasonableness Review: A Case Against Strict Proportionality Balancing', p. 87; Levashova, *The Right of States to Regulate in International Investment Law*, p. 205.

obligations, and seek for a rational connection between a measure and its objective.[600] Their shared purpose is to strike balance between two rights, which points to their mutual origins in the principle of good faith. Therefore, it is not surprising that the notion of reasonableness and proportionality overlap on a large scale and have influenced each other's development over time.[601] Despite their similarities, the test of reasonableness is not equal to the proportionality test.[602] As an example, the ECtHR opted against a mere test of reasonableness, and repeatedly held that the states' measures must be proportionate to the aim sought-after objective.[603] The review of reasonableness is typically used as an open-ended justification requirement.[604] Because of its open and undefined nature, the test for reasonableness tends to get out of hand and lose its contour, whereas the analysis under the proportionality test is more focused.[605] Therefore, a simple test of reasonableness fosters the risk of arbitrary law-making by tribunals, which undermines the legitimacy of investment arbitration as a whole.

Recent tribunals have further intertwined proportionality and reasonableness. It was held that there needs to be an appropriate correlation between the state's rational public policy objective and the measure adopted

600 Vadi, *Proportionality, Reasonableness, and Standards of Review in Investment Treaty Arbitration*, p. 208; Ortino, 'Investment Treaties, Sustainable Development and Reasonableness Review: A Case Against Strict Proportionality Balancing', p. 87, 88.

601 Mathews, *Reasonableness and Proportionality*, p. 17; Ortino, 'Investment Treaties, Sustainable Development and Reasonableness Review: A Case Against Strict Proportionality Balancing', p. 87.

602 *See* Scheu, *Systematische Berücksichtigung von Menschenrechten in Investitionsschiedsverfahren*, p. 246, 247; Vadi, *Proportionality, Reasonableness, and Standards of Review in Investment Treaty Arbitration*, p. 208-210; Langfeldt, *Proportionality in Investment Treaty Arbitration and the Necessity for Tribunals to Adopt a Clear Methodology*, p. 28.

603 Bücheler, *Proportionality in Investor-State Arbitration*, p. 75. *See* ECtHR Judgment *Handyside v. United Kingdom,* 7 December 1976 Application No. 5493/72, para. 49; ECtHR Judgment *James and others v. United Kingdom,* 21 February 1986 Application No. 8793/79, para. 50; ECtHR Judgment *Oao Neftyanaya Kompaniya Yukos v. Russia,* 8.3.2012 Application No. 14902/04, para. 556.

604 Mathews, *Reasonableness and Proportionality*, p. 10; Vadi, *Proportionality, Reasonableness, and Standards of Review in Investment Treaty Arbitration*, p. 210.

605 Mathews, *Reasonableness and Proportionality*, p. 10; Scheu, *Systematische Berücksichtigung von Menschenrechten in Investitionsschiedsverfahren*, p. 247.

to achieve the objective, under the standard of reasonableness.[606] Tribunals thereby use a test of "proportionality and reasonableness", in order to evaluate the lawfulness of the disputed measures. This is no uncommon occurrence. Tribunals regularly apply both notions in conjunction.[607] What remains unclear, however, is the exact hierarchy between reasonableness and proportionality. In some cases, reasonableness seems to be a criterion for the proportionality test.[608] In other cases, reasonableness and proportionality are used in parallel, thereby indicating that both notions have an independent meaning.[609] A third approach to interpretation finds a measure to be reasonable, if it abides by criteria common to the proportionality test.[610] Following this approach, proportionality is used as "a weighting mechanism that seeks a fair balance between competing

606 AES Summit Generation Limited et. al. v. The Republic of Hungary, Award, 23 September 2010 ICSID Case No. ARB/07/22, para. 10.3.7-10.3.9; Electrabel S.A. v. Republic of Hungary, Award, 25 November 2015 ICSID Case No. ARB/07/19, para. 179; Ioan Micula, Viorel Micula, S.C. European Food S.A, S.C. Starmill S.R.L. and S.C. Multipack S.R.L. v. Romania, Award, 11 December 2013 ICSID Case No. ARB/05/20, para. 525; Watkins Holdings S.à.r.l. and others v. Kingdom of Spain, Award, 21 January 2020 ICSID Case No. ARB/15/44, para. 596.

607 Total S.A. v. The Argentine Republic, Decision on Liability, 27 December 2010 ICSID Case No. ARB/04/01, para. 162; Philip Morris Brands Sàrl et. al. v. Oriental Republic of Uruguay, Award, 8 July 2016 ICSID Case No. ARB/10/7, p. 410; Stadtwerke München GmbH and others v. Kingdom of Spain, Award, 2 December 2019 ICSID Case No. ARB/15/1, para. 325-327.

608 The Tribunal in *Blusun* held that "if [the subsidies] are lawfully granted, and if it becomes necessary to modify them, this should be done in a manner which is not disproportionate to the aim of the legislative amendment and should have due regard to the reasonable reliance interests of recipients who may have committed substantial resources on the basis of the earlier regime.", Blusun S.A., Jean-Pierre Lecorcier and Michael Stein v. Italian Republic, ICSID Case No. ARB/14/3, para. 319(5).

609 The Tribunal in *Charanne* held that "the legitimate expectations of an investor are frustrated, even in the absence of specific commitments, when the receiving State performs acts incompatible with a criterion of economic reasonableness, with public interest or with the principle of proportionality.", Charanne and Construction Investments v. Kingdom of Spain, Award, 21 January 2016 SCC Case No. V 062/2012, para. 513, 514.

610 The Tribunal in *RREEF* engaged in a more thorough balancing analysis and defined the requirements for "reasonableness" as follows:
"(1) *Legitimacy of purpose*, inasmuch as it represents interests of the society as a whole and does not alter the substance of the rights affected by the regulation.
(2) *Necessity*, which implies the existence of a pressing social need. The threshold for 'necessary' is more demanding than the one for 'useful' or 'desirable'.

interests and/or principles affected by the regulation, taking into account all relevant circumstances".[611] Given the close relation of both notions, the latter approach seems to be the most comprehensible one. The notion of reasonableness affords a tribunal a wider margin of discretion regarding the balancing. However, a specific balancing procedure is applied with the notion of legitimate expectations, to counter arbitrariness and restrict the wide margin of discretion.[612] Therefore, it does not seem effective to use yet another undefined test. This notwithstanding, a uniform hierarchy is not established, even in recent case law.

In conclusion, it is evident that both notions are dogmatically different, but share great similarities, as both concepts require that states provide substantive justification for their taken measures.[613] Therefore, it can be argued that tribunals should observe the three-step analysis provided by the traditional proportionality test, regardless of whether they use the notion of reasonableness as a benchmark or skip ahead to the proportionality test immediately.

---

(3) *Suitability*, in that it must make it possible to achieve the legitimate objective pursued.",
RREEF Infrastructure (G.P.) Limited and RREEF Pan-European Infrastructure Two Lux S.à.r.l. v. Kingdom of Spain, Decision on Responsibility and on the Principles of Quantum, 30 November 2018 ICSID Case No. ARB/13/30, para 464. *See also* Hydro Energy 1 S.A.R.L. and Hydroxana Sweden AB v. The Kingdom of Spain, Decision on Jurisdiction, Liability and Directions on Quantum, 9 March 2020 ICSID Case No. ARB/15/42, para. 573 and Cavalum SGPS v. Kingdom of Spain, Decision on Jurisdiction, Liability and Directions on Quantum, 31 August 2020 ICSID Case No. ARB/15/34, para. 414.

611 RREEF Infrastructure (G.P.) Limited and RREEF Pan-European Infrastructure Two Lux S.à.r.l. v. Kingdom of Spain, Decision on Responsibility and on the Principles of Quantum, 30 November 2018 ICSID Case No. ARB/13/30, para. 465.

612 Leonhardsen, 'Looking for Legitimacy: Exploring Proportionality Analysis in Investment Treaty Arbitration', p. 134.

613 Langfeldt, *Proportionality in Investment Treaty Arbitration and the Necessity for Tribunals to Adopt a Clear Methodology*, p. 28; Scheu, *Systematische Berücksichtigung von Menschenrechten in Investitionsschiedsverfahren*, p. 246; RREEF Infrastructure (G.P.) Limited and RREEF Pan-European Infrastructure Two Lux S.à.r.l. v. Kingdom of Spain, Decision on Responsibility and on the Principles of Quantum, 30 November 2018 ICSID Case No. ARB/13/30, para. 463.

d) The Importance of a Systematic Approach to the Balancing Issue

Having examined both the conventional approach to traditional proportionality and the related, yet different notion of reasonableness, it can be said that the proportionality test has found its way into international investment law practice in one way or another. The recognition of this principle in national and international legal systems indicates that it has developed into a general principle of international law.[614] Hence, according to Article 38 ICJ Statute, any judicial body must take this general principle of law into account when deciding a dispute.

What remains unclear, however, is the exact approach, when conducting the proportionality test. While superficially using the same wording, tribunals tend to have a vastly different understanding of the respective meanings. The use of "proportionality" and "reasonableness" as synonyms or as requirements for one another is unsatisfactory from a systematic point of view, as both notions are not interchangeable. Rather, their different origins and the different systematic approaches defining them must be taken into consideration by arbitral jurisprudence. However, since almost none of the tribunals carry out a detailed analysis of the principle of proportionality, no uniform schematics have developed so far.[615] The lack of understanding of the differences in terminology has been observed by scholars analysing the prevailing jurisprudence as well.[616] Among other things, this shows a misunderstanding regarding the importance of a systematic analysis. Given the origins of the notions of legitimate expectations and proportionality stemming from domestic legal systems, the user has to be aware that the systematic approach developed under domestic law should not be disregarded. Such a systematic approach can be used as a guideline, if the user has a clear and detailed understanding of relevant legal concepts, which a tribunal seeks to import into international invest-

---

614 Bücheler, *Proportionality in Investor-State Arbitration*, p. 62; Henckels, *Proportionality and Deference in Investor-State Arbitration*, p. 19; Levashova, *The Right of States to Regulate in International Investment Law*, p. 98.

615 *Leonhardsen* expresses his concerns regarding the application of the proportianlity test, "because its introduction has sometimes seemed less solid than over-eager", Leonhardsen, 'Looking for Legitimacy: Exploring Proportionality Analysis in Investment Treaty Arbitration', p. 136.

616 Henckels, *Proportionality and Deference in Investor-State Arbitration*, p. 71; Scheu, *Systematische Berücksichtigung von Menschenrechten in Investitionsschiedsverfahren*, p. 255, 256; Kläger, *'Fair and Equitable Treatment' in International Investment Law*, p. 289; Kriebaum, *Arbitrary/Unreasonable or Discriminatory Measures*, p. 792.

ment law.[617] However, in case the tribunals import a certain principle, such as proportionality, without following a systematic legal approach, the principle will erode over time and lose its definition.[618]

Additionally, when talking about the investors' interests, one has to keep in mind that those interests are only relevant in international law because the states waived their sovereignty in that regard.[619] As demonstrated, a restriction of the states' sovereignty and their right to regulate must be well justified.[620] Such a severe encroachment on the core of every state's sovereignty requires a thorough and systematic analysis of the facts and circumstances in order to meet the high threshold of justification. This is further supplemented by the fact that some of the new investment treaties concluded seem to be more adapt for the application of the proportionality test.[621]

As the proportionality test becomes more dominant in investment practice, it follows that it is crucial to develop a uniform approach in order to decrease the fragmentation of international law and not to overly interfere with the states' sovereignty. A solid proportionality framework and its consolidation in international law have the potential to establish a global, best-practice standard for dealing with normative conflicts of a particular structure.[622]

However, the analysis revealed that tribunals have not yet taken the last step to elevate the proportionality test to a level of sophistication worthy of the rights it is balancing, and fulfilling the requirement of systemic integration set out in Article 31(3)(c) VCLT. The principle of proportionality entails considerable potential to counteract arbitrariness and overly subjective decisions on the side of the investment tribunals, but also can foster the sustainable development dimension of the FET standard.[623] This

---

617 Potestà, 'Legitimate Expectations in Investment Treaty Law: Understanding the Roots and the Limits of a Controversial Concept', p. 93; Scheu, *Systematische Berücksichtigung von Menschenrechten in Investitionsschiedsverfahren*, p. 243, 244.

618 Potestà, 'Legitimate Expectations in Investment Treaty Law: Understanding the Roots and the Limits of a Controversial Concept', p. 93.

619 *See* Ch. 2 IV 1).

620 PCIJ Judgment *The S.S. "Wimbledon", Britain et al. v. Germany,* 17 August 1923 PCIJ Series A01, para. 34; Total S.A. v. The Argentine Republic, Decision on Liability, 27 December 2010 ICSID Case No. ARB/04/01, para. 129.

621 Leonhardsen, 'Looking for Legitimacy: Exploring Proportionality Analysis in Investment Treaty Arbitration', p. 136.

622 Stone Sweet, 'Investor-State Arbitration: Proportionality's New Frontier', p. 49.

623 Kläger, *Revising Treatment Standards— Fair and Equitable Treatment in Light of Sustainable Development*, p. 80.

may also mitigate the negative impact of judicial law-making on the legitimacy discussion concerning investment arbitration.[624] At the same time, proportionality allows tribunals to express that they might have decided otherwise, if the facts had been different.[625]

In conclusion, one must be mindful of the different understandings, when assessing the legal reasoning of the tribunals in regard to the legitimate expectations of the investors, until investment practice has adopted a uniform approach.

624 Leonhardsen, 'Looking for Legitimacy: Exploring Proportionality Analysis in Investment Treaty Arbitration', p. 136; Scheu, *Systematische Berücksichtigung von Menschenrechten in Investitionsschiedsverfahren*, p. 250, 251.

625 Stone Sweet, 'Investor-State Arbitration: Proportionality's New Frontier', p. 50.

Chapter 3: The Renewable Energy Cases

The previous Chapter demonstrated that the legitimate expectations are influenced by both parties to a dispute: The investors as well as the host states. While the states can create legitimate expectations by their acts and measures, the investors have to assert a certain amount of due diligence, on which they can base their expectations. In order to find case groups and specific requirements for the commitment of the states and the investors' due diligence, the historical, technological, and factual backgrounds of the recent cases in the renewable energy sector need to be reviewed and analysed.

I. Historical Background

To understand the reasoning of the tribunals, it is crucial to know the chain of events that led to the regulatory changes in dispute. The beginning of the transition to renewable energy sources was marked by the signing of the Kyoto Protocol in 1992.[626] The aims set out in the Kyoto Protocol compelled the EU to introduce Directive 2001/77/EC[627] and Directive 2009/28/EC[628], which stipulated certain quotas of electricity generated from renewable energy sources.[629] To comply with the directives, the Member States introduced different support and subsidy mechanism, of which FITs and FIPs above the wholesale market price, as well as tax in-

---

626 *See* Part III of the Introduction.

627 Directive 2001/77/EC of the European Parliament and of the Council of 27 September 2001 on the promotion of electricity produced from renewable energy sources in the internal electricity market, <https://eur-lex.europa.eu/legal-content/EN/TXT/?uri=CELEX%3A32001L0077> (accessed 3 May 2021).

628 Directive 2009/28/EC of the European Parliament and of the Council of 23 April 2009 on the promotion of the use of energy from renewable sources and amending and subsequently repealing Directives 2001/77/EC and 2003/30/EC, <https://eur-lex.europa.eu/legal-content/EN/ALL/?uri=CELEX%3A32009L0028> (accessed 3 May 2021).

629 Recital No. 1 in the Preamble to Directive 2001/77/EC and Recital No. 1 in the Preamble to Directive 2009/28/EC.

centives, are the most frequently used.[630] Although these support schemes were initially implemented to reduce financial and regulatory risk, all three respondent states in this research have later repealed or altered their regulatory framework to the detriment of the investors.[631]

II. Technological Background

In addition to the historical context, a minimum of technical understanding is needed, in order to fully grasp why the impact of the regulatory changes on certain technologies justified a different legal evaluation, with regard to the impact the measures had on the investments.

The most common renewable energy sources in the cases at hand are Photovoltaik (PV) and Concentrated Solar Power (CSP). PV technology is used to transfer solar power directly into electricity. Single PV-cells are combined into a solar panel system, which is at the core of the PV power plant.[632] In contrast, CSP is an indirect way of electricity generation. CSP systems utilise mirrors, in order to concentrate the sun's energy on a single spot.[633] The immense temperature created in that process heats up heat-absorbent oil, which will eventually evaporate water and drive steam power generators. Excess heat is stored in storages of molten salts and can be used to generate electricity 24 hours a day, independent from the sun.[634] The different mechanics illustrate why CSP plants require, due to their complexity of the technology, a much higher upfront investment and are more costly to operate. The total costs of different energy technologies can be compared by the levelized costs of electricity, which takes into

630 Restrepo, 'Modification of Renewable Energy Support Schemes Under the Energy Charter Treaty: Modification of Renewable Energy Support Schemes Under the Energy Charter Treaty: Eiser and Charanne in the Context of Climate Change', p. 102. *See also* Espa, 'Promoting Renewables in the Energy Union: Current Strategies and the Challenges Ahead', p. 232-235.

631 Tienhaara and Downie, 'Risky Business? The Energy Charter Treaty, Renewable Energy, and Investor-State Disputes', p. 457; Patrizia and others, *Investment Disputes Involving the Renewable Energy Industry Under the Energy Charter Treaty*, p. 47, 48.

632 Azad, *Advances in Clean Energy Technologies* (Academic Press 2021), p. 4, 5.

633 ibid, p. 4, 5.

634 Stadtwerke München GmbH and others v. Kingdom of Spain, Award, 2 December 2019 ICSID Case No. ARB/15/1, para. 81.

account the capital expense and the operating expenses.[635] A comparison between the CSP and the PV technologies show, that the levelized costs of electricity of PV plants are lower than those of CSP plants.[636] Thus, CSP power plants need to generate higher revenue in order to recoup their construction costs, and cuts in subsidies will affect the economic efficiency of a CSP plant more drastically.[637]

The third category of renewable energy power plants is hydro-electric plants, which is a versatile technology that generates electrical energy from a wide variety of water flow levels and head heights.[638] They are particularly efficient in terms of environmental and energy costs, and have a long asset life of up to 50 years.[639] The fourth renewable energy technology is wind farms, which consist of several wind turbines that use the kinetic energy of the wind and transform it into electricity.[640] The wind power sector was generally subject to fewer amendments and hence played only a minor role in the recent renewable energy sector.

As a consequence, this imbalance in cost intensity results in the need for a differentiated evaluation, regarding the appropriateness of measures to regulate the four technologies.

III. Factual Background and Arbitral Jurisprudence

In the factual background, the different regulatory frameworks of Spain, Italy, and the Czech Republic and their development over the period of the first promotion of renewable energies, the economic crisis, and the final change of the respective support schemes are presented. It is not intended to portray the different legislative frameworks in-depth and in full detail. Instead, the overview is intended to provide a basic understanding of the particularities of the individual legal systems. This approach offers the opportunity to identify similarities and differences in the legal frameworks which lead the tribunals to particular conclusions regarding

635 Hernández-Moro and Martínez-Duart, 'Analytical model for solar PV and CSP electricity costs: Present LCOE values and their future evolution', p. 121.

636 ibid, p. 130.

637 ibid, p. 123.

638 Azad, *Advances in Clean Energy Technologies*, p. 295, 296.

639 Hydro Energy 1 S.A.R.L. and Hydroxana Sweden AB v. The Kingdom of Spain, Decision on Jurisdiction, Liability and Directions on Quantum, 9 March 2020 ICSID Case No. ARB/15/42, para. 432, 433.

640 Azad, *Advances in Clean Energy Technologies*, p. 209.

the FET standard. Moreover, the cases concluded to date will be examined and set in relation to the timeframe in which the investment was made, and give an overview of the specific features of each case. Subsequently, possible trends are identified.

1) The Spanish Renewable Energy Saga

During the last decades, Spain has become a world leader in promoting the use of solar power.[641] It has done so by implementing a generous support scheme for the promotion of renewable energies. The incentive programme implemented through 2005-2010 boosted the investment in Spanish renewable energies and Spain as a country, along with a number of Spanish companies, became leaders in the field.[642]

a) Disputed Measures

In 1997, during the time of the Kyoto Convention, Spain had introduced the Energy Law (EL) 54/1997[643] on the electricity sector, as the first step towards the promotion of renewable energies. The EL divided the legal framework into an *Ordinary* and a *Special Regime*. While the *Ordinary Regime* covered electricity obtained from fossil energy sources, the *Special Regime* sought to promote the production of electricity from renewable energies. Since some of the renewable energy technologies were subject to a plethora of special regulations, the focus of the forthcoming overview will be on the laws and decrees setting out the main body of the *Special Regime* and those concerning PV and CSP technologies.

The Spanish regulatory framework uses in a hierarchical order "Laws", "Royal Decree Laws" (RDL), "Royal Decrees" (RD), and "Ministerial Orders". Laws are directly enacted by the parliament, whereas RDLs are adopted by the government and have an immediate effect, but require

641 Patrizia and others, *Investment Disputes Involving the Renewable Energy Industry Under the Energy Charter Treaty*, p. 48.

642 Hendel and Pérez, 'The Past, Present and Possible Future of the Spanish Remewable Energy Arbitration Saga' (2018) 31(1) International Law Practicum 96, p. 96.

643 Law 54/1997, 27 November 1997, on the Electricity Sector.

parliamentary approval.[644] RDs constitute the exercise of regulatory powers created through laws or RDLs approved by parliament and are implemented by Ministerial Orders and Resolutions.[645] Hence, the higher the hierarchy of the regulation, the more authoritative a measure is.

(1) The Rise of the Special Regime

The *Special Regime* under the EL 54/1997 was initially set out by RD 2818/1998[646] and later RD 436/2004[647], which were then abrogated by RD 661/2007[648]. In order to be eligible for the *Special Regime*, EL 54/1997 required registration of the renewable energy plants with the Administrative Registry for Electrical Power Generating Units (RAIPRE).[649] The new *Special Regime* under RD 661/2007 introduced an increasingly rewarding incentive regime for the production of electricity from renewable energies. While the remuneration under the *Ordinary Regime* derived solely from the wholesale market price of electricity, the generators under the *Special Regime* could choose between two kinds of subsidies: The fixed FITs or FIPs. This premium was set by the Spanish Government to guarantee cost coverage and a certain return.[650] The legal framework set out by RD 661/2007 fostered national and foreign investments, in particular in the solar PV and CSP sectors. In addition, the Spanish State advertised investments in the solar energy sector with its advertising campaign "The sun can be yours", which promised a return of up to 15%.[651] In 2008,

---

644 Stadtwerke München GmbH and others v. Kingdom of Spain, Award, 2 December 2019 ICSID Case No. ARB/15/1, para. 58.

645 ibid, para. 58.

646 Royal Decree 2818/1998, 23 December 1998, on the Production of Electricity in Facilities supplied by Renewable Energy Sources, Waste and Cogeneration.

647 Royal Decree 436/2004, 12 March 2004, on the Methodology to Actualize and Systematize the Economic and Legal Regime of Electricity Production Activity under the Special Regime.

648 Royal Decree 661/2007, 25 May 2007, on the Regulation of the Electricity Production under the Special Regime.

649 *See* Novenergia II - Energy & Environment (SCA), SICAR v. The Kingdom of Spain, Award, 15 February 2018 SCC Case No. V 2015/063, para. 79.

650 Garcia-Castrillon, *Spain and Investment Arbitration - The Renewable Energy Explosion*, p. 287.

651 IDAE, "El Sol puede ser suyo", 6 June 2007 and 24 May 2005. *See also* Novenergia II - Energy & Environment (SCA), SICAR v. The Kingdom of Spain, Award, 15 February 2018 SCC Case No. V 2015/063, para. 112-118.

the initial limitations on the energy production volumes were extended by RD 1578/2008[652] and at the same time limited the period for the FIT to 25 years, which was expected to be the lifetime of an average PV plant.

(2) The Amendment of the Special Regime in 2010

While the incentive programme was successful in attracting many investors, it also caused a gap between the regulated tariff collection and the associated real costs (tariff deficit).[653] Spain's annual tariff deficit first materialized in 2000, and was accepted and deemed necessary to comply with the EU regulations. However, the tariff deficit continued to grow and subsequently peaked in a loss of 6 billion Euros for the year 2008.[654] In the context and aftermath of the economic crisis, the Spanish Government decided that the resources are needed in other sectors.[655]

In the following events, RDL 6/2009[656] was adopted as the first measure in 2009 addressing the tariff deficit. In the law, the legislator explained its motives by stating that the *Special Regime* had led to a deficit in the Spanish State budget, which imposed a risk not only to the financial situation of electricity companies, but also to the sustainability of the whole sector.[657] In its preamble, it stated that the rights and expectations of the owners of the facilities are respected, with the necessary caution being exercised, in any event.[658] However, in Article 4.2. it obligated the operator to register in the so-called Pre-Assignment Registry, as a necessary

652 Royal Decree 1578/2008, 26 September 2008, on the Payment of the Production of Electricity by Photovoltaic Solar Technology in Facilities established after the Final Date for Payment given by RD 661/2007.

653 Garcia-Castrillon, *Spain and Investment Arbitration - The Renewable Energy Explosion*, p. 288.

654 *See* Foresight and others v. Kingdom of Spain Final, Award, 14 November 2018 SCC Case No. V 2015/150, Figure 7-1 para. 116.

655 Hendel and Pérez, 'The Past, Present and Possible Future of the Spanish Remewable Energy Arbitration Saga'. p. 96, 97.

656 Royal Decree Law 6/2009, 30 April 2009, on the adoption of certain measures in the energy sector and the approval of the social bond.

657 Garcia-Castrillon, *Spain and Investment Arbitration - The Renewable Energy Explosion*, para. 288.

658 "It is therefore necessary to adopt emergency measures that guarantees the necessary legal certainty for all those who have made investments, and lays the foundations for the establishment of new economic regimes that promote compliance with the intended objectives [...]" (unofficial translation).

condition to being awarded the right to the economic regime established in RD 661/2007. In addition to this, RD 1003/2010[659] established that no new facilities could access the *Special Regime* and its benefits after 29 September 2008.

From the beginning of 2010 onwards, further cutbacks to the incentive system were introduced by a set of measures (2010 Amendments): RD 1565/2010[660] eliminated regulated tariffs from the twenty-sixth year of the plant's operation, and added further technical requirements. This measure applied to all plants regardless of whether they already registered with the RAIPRE.[661] RD 1614/2010[662] introduced, inter alia, a limit on annual operation hours with a right to receive premiums or premium equivalents.[663] However, it only applied to CSP, thermal and wind technologies, therefore having no effect on PV plants. Nonetheless were PV plants equally affected by caps on annual operating hours introduced by RDL 14/2010[664]. If the energy output of a plant exceeded its caps, the additional electricity could only be sold at market prices.

In summary, the amendments of RD 661/2007 starting in 2010 provided, inter alia, for a limitation of the annual operation hours, as well as a reduction of certain revenues and cost consignments so that all stakeholders in the sector contribute an additional and shared effort to the reduction of the deficit in the electricity system.[665]

In 2011 a new government was elected, and the president openly declared that the massive gap in the household due to the tariff deficit

---

659 Royal Decree 1003/2010, 5 August 2010, on the Liquidation of the Equivalent Premium to the Facilities Producing Electricity from Photovoltaic Technology under the Special Regime.

660 Royal Decree 1565/2010, 19 November 2010, on amending Certain Aspects of the Special Regime for Electricity Production.

661 *See* Novenergia II - Energy & Environment (SCA), SICAR v. The Kingdom of Spain, Award, 15 February 2018 SCC Case No. V 2015/063, para. 121.

662 Royal Decree 1614/2010, 7 December 2010, on the Regulation and Modification of Certain Aspects of the Production of Electricity from Solar Thermoelectric and Wind Technologies.

663 *See* Charanne and Construction Investments v. Kingdom of Spain, Award, 21 January 2016 SCC Case No. V 062/2012, para. 155.

664 Royal Decree Law 14/2010, 23 December 2010, on Urgent Measures to Correct the tariff deficit in the Electricity Sector.

665 *See* Charanne and Construction Investments v. Kingdom of Spain, Award, 21 January 2016 SCC Case No. V 062/2012, para. 156.

has to be filled.[666] Thus, the previous measures were further reinforced by RDL 1/2012[667] suspending pre-allocation payment procedures and abolishing economic incentives for new electricity production facilities, by means of co-generation, renewable energy and waste. Additionally, Law 15/2012[668] reintroduced a hydrocarbons levy on the supply and import of natural gas, if it is used for any purposes other than engine fuel and heating fuel, and created a tax on the value of the production of electrical energy (TVPEE).[669]

(3) The Abrogation and the Replacement of the Special Regime in 2013

However, the most drastic changes were introduced in 2013. The starting point of the new support scheme framework was marked by

666 Mir-Artigues, Cerdá and del Río, 'Analysing the Economic Impact of the New Renewable Electricity Support Scheme on Solar PV Plants in Spain' (2018) 114 Energy Policy 323, p. 323.

667 Royal Decree Law 1/2012, 27 March 2012, on the Suspension of the Pre-Allocation Payment Procedures and the Abolition of the Economic Incentives for New Electricity Production Facilities from Cogeneration, Renewable Energies and Waste.

668 Royal Decree Law 15/2012, 21 April 2012, on Fiscal Measures for Energy Sustainability.

669 Although the majority of the investors challenged the TVPEE, its compliance with the FET standard has not been considered by the tribunals due to the tax carve-out in Article 21(1) ECT, *see* NextEra Energy Global Holdings B.V. and NextEra Energy Spain Holdings B.V. v. Kingdom of Spain, Decision on Jurisdiction, Liability and Quantum Principles, 12 March 2019 ICSID Case No. ARB/14/11, para. 383; Antin Infrastructure Services Luxembourg S.à.r.l. and Antin Energia Termosolar B.V. v. Kingdom of Spain, Award, 15 June 2018 ICSID Case No. ARB/13/31, para. 320, 323; Eiser Infrastructure Limited and Energía Solar Luxembourg S.à.r.l. v. Kingdom of Spain, Award, 4 May 2017 ICSID Case No. ARB/13/36, para. 269-271; Cube Infrastructure Fund SICAV and others v. Kingdom of Spain, Decision on Jurisdiction, Liability and Partial Decision on Quantum, 19 February 2019 ICSID Case No. ARB/15/20, para. 231, 233; 9REN Holding S.a.r.l v. Kingdom of Spain, Award, 31 March 2019 ICSID Case No. ARB/15/15, para. 207; Watkins Holdings S.à.r.l. and others v. Kingdom of Spain, Award, 21 January 2020 ICSID Case No. ARB/15/44, para. 274; Hydro Energy 1 S.A.R.L. and Hydroxana Sweden AB v. The Kingdom of Spain, Decision on Jurisdiction, Liability and Directions on Quantum, 9 March 2020 ICSID Case No. ARB/15/42, para. 273, 274.

RDL 2/2013[670], which abolished the FIP option altogether and left the power generators with only the option for the market price, according to a newly calculated Consumer Price Index (CPI) or a FIT lower than the CPI.[671]

Despite all efforts, the Spanish State still faced a tariff deficit and accumulated further debts in the renewable energy sector. This factor led to the enactment of RDL 9/2013[672], which eventually phased out the remainders of the *Special Regime* while—according to its preamble—maintaining a support system that allows "renewable, co-generation and waste energy installations to cover the costs needed to compete in the market on an equal level with other technologies and to obtain a reasonable return".[673]

Finally, the New Energy Law (NEL) 24/2013[674] superseded the EL 54/1997 and set out the basis for the new regulatory regime (2013 Regime). It established the principle of "economic and financial sustainability of the electricity system", by abandoning the distinction between the *Ordinary* and the *Special Regime*.[675] Moreover, the NEL provided the legal basis for the introduction of RD 413/2014[676], which set out a new regulatory regime intended to attain a prescribed reasonable return, calculated on the basis of a hypothetical "efficient" plant.[677] Crucial details of the new regime, however, were left to the government regulators.[678] It was specified by the Ministerial Order IET/1045/2014[679]. A main feature of the new scheme was that it applied to already established plants, which were

---

670 Royal Decree Law 2/2013, 1 February 2013, on Urgent Measures for the National Electricity and Financial Systems.

671 *See* Stadtwerke München GmbH and others v. Kingdom of Spain, Award, 2 December 2019 ICSID Case No. ARB/15/1, para. 91.

672 RDL 9/2013, 12 July 2013, on the Adoption of Urgent Measures to Guarantee the Financial Stability of the Electricity System.

673 *See* Stadtwerke München GmbH and others v. Kingdom of Spain, Award, 2 December 2019 ICSID Case No. ARB/15/1, para. 92.

674 Law 24/2013, 26 December 2013, on the Electricity Sector.

675 *See* Novenergia II - Energy & Environment (SCA), SICAR v. The Kingdom of Spain, Award, 15 February 2018 SCC Case No. V 2015/063, para. 145.

676 Royal Decree Law 413/2014, 6 June 2014, on Electrical Generation by Means of Renewable, Cogeneration and Waste Facilities.

677 *See* Foresight and others v. Kingdom of Spain Final, Award, 14 November 2018 SCC Case No. V 2015/150, para. 57.

678 Eiser Infrastructure Limited and Energía Solar Luxembourg S.à.r.l. v. Kingdom of Spain, Award, 4 May 2017 ICSID Case No. ARB/13/36, para. 147.

679 Ministerial Order IET/1045/2014, 16 June 2014, adopting the Remuneration Parameters for the Facility Type applicable to certain Energy Production Facilities from Renewable Energies, Cogeneration and Waste.

subject to the previous regulation, giving the changes retroactive effect.[680] The measures proved to be effective enough to compensate for the tariff deficit in total and even turn the revenue from the renewable energy market into a surplus in 2014.[681]

b) The Spanish Cases

Discussing all cases in detail would exceed the scope of this research and would not contribute to the quality of the analysis. Hence, the following analysis is therefore limited to a chronological categorization and a summary of the specific characteristics.

The investments can roughly be grouped into three types: First, investments conducted under the original 2007 *Special Regime* or prior. Second, investments under the 2010 Amendments to the *Special Regime*. Third, investments under the support scheme after 2012, when the reformation of the regulatory framework for renewable energy producers was in full force. The awards will be reviewed with regard to the chronology of the underlying facts, in order to illustrate the influence of the time of the investment and the already implemented changes on the legitimacy of the expectations.

(1) Investments under the 2007 Special Regime

The investments under the *Special Regime*, as established by RD 661/2007 and its predecessors, is characterised by a high degree of stability. Power plants eligible for support pursuant to the *Special Regime* were granted fixed remuneration for 25 years and additional electricity offtake starting from the 26th year of operation.

---

680 Mir-Artigues, Cerdá and del Río, 'Analysing the Economic Impact of the New Renewable Electricity Support Scheme on Solar PV Plants in Spain', p. 323. Whether or not the measures actually had retroactive effect is controversial among the tribunals, *see* Ch. 4 III 2).

681 Foresight and others v. Kingdom of Spain Final, Award, 14 November 2018 SCC Case No. V 2015/150, *see* para. 116, in particular figure 7-1.

(a) Charanne and Construction Investments S.a.r.l. v. Spain

Charanne and Construction Investments S.a.r.l. (Charanne) v. Spain [682] was the first renewable energy award to be decided on the alleged breach of the FET standard under the ECT. The scope of the dispute was limited to the 2010 measures and did not concern the changes under the 2013 Regime, which were more severe for investors in the renewable energy sector.[683] The investor in the case acquired stakes in an established enterprise owning 34 PV plants, in February and December 2009.[684] While the operators, who duly registered under RD 661/2007 and RD 1578/2008, continued receiving the FIT or FIP provided by these laws, the remuneration of the renewable energy plants in question followed the regulations set out in the 2010 laws. Furthermore, the payment was made on account of the liquidation resulting from the application of the new methodology, adopted on the basis of RDL 9/2013.

The investor asserted that the legislative amendments in 2010 by Spain reduced the profitability of the plants subject to RD 1578/2008 by 10% and plants subjected to RD 661/2007 by 8,5%.[685] The Tribunal concluded that the 2010 Amendments had not altered the regulatory framework without eliminating its essential characteristics.[686] Additionally, the Tribunal stated that it does not intend to "prejudge in any way the conclusions that could be reached by another arbitration tribunal based on the analysis of all the regulations enacted to date, including the 2013 regulations".[687] However, it did not find that the legal framework can be the basis for legitimate expectations.

Guido Santiago Tawil dissented from this conclusion by expressing the view that RD 661/2007 and RD 1578/2008 were capable of inducing legiti-

682 Charanne and Construction Investments v. Kingdom of Spain, Award, 21 January 2016 SCC Case No. V 062/2012.

683 The Tribunal in *Charanne* indicates that the Claimant did not challenge the 2013 Regime because it already filed a claim with regard to the later changes in the proceedings of *Isolux v. Spain*, Charanne and Construction Investments v. Kingdom of Spain, Award, 21 January 2016 SCC Case No. V 062/2012, para. 191, 395.

684 ibid, para. 143.

685 ibid, para. 284.

686 ibid, para. 539.

687 ibid, para. 542 (unofficial translation).

mate expectations, as their intent was clear enough and they declared the purpose of attracting investments in a specific sector of the economy.[688]

(b) Eiser Infrastructure Ltd and Energía Solar Luxembourg S.à.r.l. v. Spain

The investments in *Eiser Infrastructure Ltd and Energía Solar Luxembourg S.à.r.l. (Eiser) v. Spain*[689] concerned the construction of a CSP plant under the *Special Regime* laid out in RD 661/2007 between 2008 and 2012. As explained, the building of a CSP plant requires a heavily front-loaded investment.[690] For acquiring the funds, the investors relied heavily on debt capital. After changes to the remuneration of CSP substitutions, the revenue of the investors' power plant dropped by 66%.[691] According to the investors, this massive decrease in income rendered the investment effectively worthless since it did not even cover the maintenance costs, let alone the instalment payments for the debt capital.

The Tribunal compared the 2010 Amendments with the 2013 Regime, and concluded that the last set of measures constituted a drastic and abrupt change, which could not have been expected by the investor and eventually violated the FET standard, in light of assurance given by the *Special Regime* under RD 661/2007.[692]

(c) Novenergia II - Energy & Environment (SCA), SICAR v. Spain

The investor in *Novenergia II - Energy & Environment (SCA), SICAR (Novenergia) v. Spain* had acquired indirectly through a holding structure various

---

688 Charanne and Construction Investments v. Kingdom of Spain, Dissenting Opinion Guido Santiago Tawil, 21 January 2016 SCC Case No. V 062/2012, para. 6.

689 The award was annulled by the decision in Eiser Infrastructure Limited and Energía Solar Luxembourg S.à.r.l. v. Kingdom of Spain Decision of Annullment, 11 June 2020 ICSID Case No. ARB/13/36 on the grounds of nondisclosure of existence of a relationship between one of the claimants' damages expert and one arbitrator. Since this annulment ground does not relate to matters of liability, the Tribunal's findings will be considered as valid guidance in the forthcoming analysis.

690 *See* Ch. 3 II.

691 Eiser Infrastructure Limited and Energía Solar Luxembourg S.à.r.l. v. Kingdom of Spain, Award, 4 May 2017 ICSID Case No. ARB/13/36, para. 389.

692 ibid, para. 412, 413, 419.

project companies for the erection of new PV power plants in July 2007.[693] The power plant was duly registered under RD 661/2007. The Tribunal took into consideration a number of statements and assurances made by the Spanish State with regard to the stability of the *Special Regime* and concluded that they were aimed at inducing investments, and hence formed part of the investor's legitimate expectations.[694] Based thereon, the Tribunal agreed with *Eiser v. Spain* that the *Special Regime* contained a stabilization promise and the 2013 Regime drastically altered the support scheme in a way that violated the legitimate expectations of the investor.[695]

(d) Cavalum SGPS v. Spain

The investor *Cavalum SGPS (Cavalum) v. Spain* developed several PV plants between August 2007 and October 2009.[696] Most plants were registered duly with the RAIPRE or the Pre-Assignment Registry.[697] Those plants that did not receive registration confirmation were abandoned.[698] The Tribunal took into consideration the legislative framework at the time of the investment, as well as the decisions of the Spanish Supreme Court, and concluded by majority that investors could only have expected that the *Special Regime* would not be changed radically and fundamentally without notice.[699] The majority found that the legitimate expectations of the investors are not violated, as long as they still receive a reasonable return, by reference to the cost of money in the capital markets.[700]

David R. Haigh dissented from this holding by opining that the legal framework had contained a broader stability commitment, under which investors were entitled to the originally prescribed remuneration under

---

693 Novenergia II - Energy & Environment (SCA), SICAR v. The Kingdom of Spain, Award, 15 February 2018 SCC Case No. V 2015/063, para. 2, 3.

694 ibid, para. 666-669.

695 ibid, para. 697.

696 Cavalum SGPS v. Kingdom of Spain, Decision on Jurisdiction, Liability and Directions on Quantum, 31 August 2020 ICSID Case No. ARB/15/34, para. 92, 93.

697 ibid, para. 453, 454.

698 ibid, para. 455.

699 ibid, para. 538, 556.

700 ibid, para. 601, 612, 666.

RD 661/2007 and RD 1578/2008, which was ultimately violated when the 2013 Regime was introduced.[701]

(e) Masdar Solar & Wind Cooperatief U.A. v. Spain

The investors in *Masdar Solar & Wind Cooperatief U.A. (Masdar) v Spain* commissioned the construction of several CSP projects in 2008 and developed the projects over the course of several years.[702] The investment suffered heavily under the reduction in revenue, subsequent to the alteration of RD 661/2007 and RD 1578/2008. The Tribunal found that the changes were neither unreasonable, nor unjustified. However, it agreed with the previous tribunals insofar as Spain had given the specific commitment in regard to the application of the *Special Regime* under RD 661/2007, which was breached by retroactively applying the 2013 Regime.[703] Noteworthy is that the Tribunal considered that the specific commitment—at least partly—resulted from the constant engagement of the investor with the state.[704] Moreover, the decision is of particular interest, as it elaborates on the due diligence standard in international investment law[705] and the schools of thought in regard to the creation of legitimate expectations by the regulatory framework[706].

(f) Foresight v. Spain

The investments in *Foresight Luxembourg Solar, Greentech Energy Systems A/S, GWM Renewable Energy S.P.A. (Foresight) v. Spain* were comprised of three PV plants, acquired between May 2009 and May 2010.[707] After the investments were affected by the transition from the 2007 *Special Regime* to the 2013 Regime, the investors sold the PV plants over the course of 2015

701 Cavalum SGPS v. Kingdom of Spain, Dissenting Opinion of David R. Haigh, 31 August 2020 ICSID Case No. ARB/15/34, para. 27, 77.

702 Masdar Solar & Wind Cooperatief U.A. v. Kingdom of Spain, Award, 16 May 2018 ICSID Case No. ARB/14/1, para. 92-99.

703 ibid, para. 512, 521, 522.

704 ibid, para. 515-521.

705 ibid, in particular para. 497.

706 ibid, para. 490-493.

707 Foresight and others v. Kingdom of Spain Final, Award, 14 November 2018 SCC Case No. V 2015/150, para. 94.

to 2016.[708] Although the power plants were still profitable under the 2013 Regime, the Tribunal concluded that the investor did not only have the legitimate expectations to receive a "reasonable return", but the specific return promised by RD 661/2007.[709]

Raúl Emilio Vinuesa dissented from this decision by finding that EU law was applicable to the dispute.[710] On this premise and in light of the jurisprudence of the CJEU, the dissenter concurs that the investor could only legitimately rely on receiving a reasonable return and not a fixed rate.[711] Additionally, *Vinuesa* criticized that the investor did not commission due diligence on Spanish as well as on EU law, so that no legitimate expectations could exist.[712]

(g) Cube Infrastructure v. Spain

Cube Infrastructure Fund SICAV and others (Cube) acquired interests in three Spanish PV plants in April-June 2008 and further broadened their investment by investing in 16 hydro-plants in June 2011 and June 2012.[713] The Tribunal considered that support regimes in highly regulated areas, such as the energy sector, are plainly intended to create expectations upon which investors will rely.[714] Based thereon, it is not necessary to specifically commit to each individual investor, to create the legitimate expectation that a certain support system would stay in force. The changes brought by the 2013 Regime therefore, breached those expectations.[715] However, this reasoning was only considered to apply to the first set of investments. The hydro-plants were acquired at a time in which the regulatory framework was already undergoing change. Therefore, investors could only have legit-

708 ibid, para. 142-144.

709 ibid, para. 533.

710 Foresight and others v. Kingdom of Spain, Dissenting Opinion Raúl Emilio Vinuesa, 14 November 2018 SCC Case No. V 2015/150, para. 12.

711 ibid, para. 33.

712 ibid, para. 44.

713 Cube Infrastructure Fund SICAV and others v. Kingdom of Spain, Decision on Jurisdiction, Liability and Partial Decision on Quantum, 19 February 2019 ICSID Case No. ARB/15/20, para. 238, 239.

714 ibid, para. 388.

715 ibid, para. 428, 429, 434.

imately relied on that there was no “dramatic” or “fundamental” incoming change in the *Special Regime*.[716]

Christian Tomuschat disagreed with the finding of the majority, in regard to the hydro-plants. Whereas the PV plants were acquired at a time in which the *Special Regime* was newly introduced, the hydro-plant investment was made at a stage when a change was imminent.[717] Moreover, the dissenter did not find the legal framework at the time of the investment to give rise to legitimate expectations in regard to specific remuneration, but only “reasonable profitability”.[718]

(h) NextEra v. Spain

The investors *NextEra Energy Global Holdings B.V. and NextEra Energy Spain Holdings B.V. (NextEra) v. Spain* developed two CSP projects between 2008 and 2009 and entered into a loan agreement for the construction of the plants of 589 Million in 2011.[719] When the two projects were finally registered in 2013, Spanish authorities confirmed that the plants will be eligible to receive remuneration in accordance with RD 661/2007.[720] The Tribunal held the view that neither the regulatory framework nor communication by Spanish authorities were persuasive enough to justify legitimate expectations on their own.[721] However, in conjunction, the investor could legitimately rely on the stability of the support scheme set out by RD 661/2007.[722]

---

716 ibid, para. 440, 442.

717 Cube Infrastructure Fund SICAV and others v. Kingdom of Spain, Separate and Partial Dissenting Opinion Christian Tomuschat, 19 February 2019 ICSID Case No. ARB/15/20, para. 14, 15.

718 ibid, para. 23.

719 NextEra Energy Global Holdings B.V. and NextEra Energy Spain Holdings B.V. v. Kingdom of Spain, Decision on Jurisdiction, Liability and Quantum Principles, 12 March 2019 ICSID Case No. ARB/14/11, para. 168-176.

720 ibid, para. 178.

721 ibid, para. 587.

722 ibid, para. 596.

(i) 9Ren Holding S.a.r.l v. Spain

9REN Holding S.a.r.l (9Ren) began investing in a company developing solar projects at various stages in Spain from 2008 to 2011.[723] The Tribunal concluded that the investor could have reasonably relied upon a legitimate expectation that the benefits of RD 661/2007 would apply to all facilities registered before the amendment of the *Special Regime* by RD 1578/2008, which contemplated future revision of the regime.[724] Under the new amendments, the *Special Regime* was not equally clear in regard to the stability of the regulatory framework, and was therefore not deemed to include a stabilisation promise.[725] Hence, the investors could only legitimately expect that the *Special Regime* would continue to apply to those investments made in early 2008.[726]

(j) SolEs Badajoz GmbH v. Spain

SolEs Badajoz GmbH (SolEs) acquired shares of the company operating PV power plants in March 2010.[727] In its assessment of the legitimate expectations of the investor, the Tribunal took into account the specific wording of the *Special Regime*, as amended by RD 1578/2008, and the communication of the *National Energy Commission* (CNE) prior to the investment.[728] Albeit acknowledging that the amended regime and the communication indicated a change to the regulatory framework, it considered that the drastic abolition and replacement of the *Special Regime* in its entirety was not foreseeable for a prudent investor.[729] The Tribunal's interpretation thereby differs from the findings of the Tribunal in *9Ren*, in regard to the expectations induced by RD 1578/2008.

723 9REN Holding S.a.r.l v. Kingdom of Spain, Award, 31 March 2019 ICSID Case No. ARB/15/15, para. 5, 103-105.
724 ibid, para. 297.
725 ibid, para. 298.
726 ibid, para. 310.
727 SolEs Badajoz GmbH v. Kingdom of Spain, Award, 31 July 2019 ICSID Case No. ARB/15/38, para. 418.
728 ibid, para. 423-425.
729 ibid, para. 439.

(k) OperaFund v. Spain

OperaFund Eco-Invest and Schwab Holding (OperaFund) made their investments in Spain in July 2008 and April 2009.[730] The Tribunal opined that the regulatory framework included a specific commitment, which allowed investors to expect the remuneration promised by RD 661/2007.[731] In contrast to the prior arbitral decisions, the Tribunal considered all amendments since the introduction of the RD 1565/2010 onwards, as violations of the investor's legitimate expectations.[732]

Phillippe Sands challenged the findings of the majority that the investor had an expectation that the tariff regime established by RD 661/2007 was immutable, during the reasonable life of their investments, relied on that expectation in making their investments, and carried out the necessary exercise in the due diligence required by the ECT.[733]

(l) Stadtwerke München v. Spain

Stadtwerke München GmbH, RWE Innogy GmbH, and others (Stadtwerke München) made their investment in one of the largest CSP plants worldwide, in October 2009.[734] The commissioning and the registration with the RAIPRE, however, did not occur until April 2012.[735] In contrast to most renewable energy projects, the investment included almost no debt capital.[736] Nonetheless, the majority of the Tribunal came to the conclusion that there was no commitment on the side of Spain to refrain from modification of the regulatory framework governing renewable energy.[737] Rather, the regulatory history of RD 661/2007 and the circumstances surrounding the changes in the regulatory system for solar energy should have made

730 OperaFund Eco-Invest SICAV PLC and Schwab Holding AG v. Kingdom of Spain, Award, 6 September 2019 ICSID Case No. ARB/15/36, para. 173.

731 ibid, para. 485.

732 ibid, para. 490.

733 OperaFund Eco-Invest SICAV PLC and Schwab Holding AG v. Kingdom of Spain, Dissenting Opinion Philippe Sands, 6 September 2019 ICSID Case No. ARB/15/36, para. 2.

734 Stadtwerke München GmbH and others v. Kingdom of Spain, Award, 2 December 2019 ICSID Case No. ARB/15/1, para. 84.

735 ibid, para. 266.

736 ibid, para. 82.

737 ibid, para. 261.

the investors aware that changes were possible.[738] The only threshold was a reasonable return, which the investors still received.[739]

Opposing the majority's decision, *Kaj Hobér* reasoned that the RD 661/2007 regime itself and the statements of and conduct by representatives of Spain were sufficient to legitimately be relied on by investors.[740] Therefore, the investors could have expected not only a reasonable return, but the return promised under the *Special Regime* established by RD 661/2007, whose characteristic features had been drastically altered.[741]

(m) BayWa r.e. v. Spain

The investors in *BayWa r.e. Renewable Energy GmbH and BayWa r.e. Asset Holding GmbH (BayWa) v. Spain* acquired shares in two wind farms in Spain, the first in 2009 and the second in 2011.[742] The facts underlying the case differ from the other PV and CSP investments. Wind farms were nonetheless subject to the *Special Regime* under RD 661/2007 and were affected by the amendment and the abolishment of the support scheme regardless. The Tribunal reached by majority the conclusion that the investors could not have legitimately expected that the initial remuneration set out by the *Special Regime* would be paid during the lifetime of the wind farms, but eventually opined that the retroactive clawback by Spain introduced through the 2013 Regime constituted a breach of the stability obligation included in the FET standard.[743] However, the majority found that the investors could have foreseen amendments due to the possible conflicts with EU state aid laws, if they had conducted proper due diligence and thus rejected any further claims concerning compensation for the changed remuneration method.[744]

Horacio A. Grigera Naón agreed in his dissent with the liability of Spain for the abolishment of the *Special Regime*, but further elaborated that

738 ibid, para. 261, 262.

739 ibid, para. 354.

740 Stadtwerke München GmbH and others v. Kingdom of Spain, Dissenting Opinion Kaj Hobér, 2 December 2019 ICSID Case No. ARB/15/1, para. 14.

741 ibid, para. 20, 21.

742 BayWa r.e. Renewable Energy GmbH and BayWa r.e. Asset Holding GmbH v. Kingdom of Spain, Decision on Jurisdiction, Liability and Directions on Quantum, 2 December 2019 ICSID Case No. ARB/15/16, para. 75-81.

743 ibid, para. 591.

744 ibid, para. 589, 590.

investors cannot be required to conduct a higher level of due diligence regarding the compatibility of the *Special Regime* and EU state aid law than the respondent state.[745] Hence, the investors are not only entitled to compensation for the retroactive changes, but also for all past and future damages resulting from the 2013 Regime.[746]

(n) RWE Innogy GmbH and RWE Innogy Aersa S.A.U. v. Spain

The investors in *RWE Innogy GmbH and RWE Innogy Aersa S.A.U. (RWE) v. Spain* developed in several stages a number of hydro-electric and wind power plants between 2001 and 2011.[747] The first set of investments was conducted between May 2002 and December 2003 under the *Special Regime* of RD 2818/1998 and under RD 436/2004.[748] The second set of investments consisted of the acquisition of shares in further project companies in June 2008 and May 2009, while RD 661/2007 was effective.[749] The last significant investments were made between October 2010 and December 2011, after the implementation of the 2010 Amendments.[750] The Tribunal concurred that the regulatory regime before the adoption of RD 661/2007 did not contain any type of stability commitment and therefore could not serve as a basis for legitimate expectations.[751] In regard to RD 661/2007, the Tribunal opined that nothing in the law, nor in the representations by state authorities justified the view that the *Special Regime* would remain unaltered and grant a specific tariff for the lifetime of the plants.[752] In determining the violation of the legitimate expectations, the Tribunal conducted a detailed three-tiered proportionality analysis and concluded that the burden borne by the investor exceeded what can reasonably be expected in light of the background context of general

745 BayWa r.e. Renewable Energy GmbH and BayWa r.e. Asset Holding GmbH v. Kingdom of Spain, Dissenting Opinion Horacio A. Grigera Naón, 2 December 2019 ICSID Case No. ARB/15/16, para. 41.

746 ibid, para. 43.

747 RWE Innogy GmbH and RWE Innogy Aersa S.A.U. v. Kingdom of Spain, Decision on Jurisdicition, Liability, and certain Issues of Quantum, 6 January 2020 ICSID Case No. ARB/14/34, para. 190.

748 ibid, para. 196-198.

749 ibid, para. 205-207.

750 ibid, para. 208, 209.

751 ibid, para. 488, 489.

752 ibid, para. 542.

invitation and encouragement by the host state to invest in a particular sector by reference to benefits including a very favourable remuneration scheme.[753] Hence, the treatment of power plants, which returns dropped below 7% after the implementation of the 2013 Regime, was deemed disproportionate. In contrast to prior decisions, the Tribunal did not find any retroactive effect of the 2013 Regime.[754] However, it is to be noted that none of the investments were made in the solar and photovoltaic sector, and thus, the investors could not rely on representations like "The sun can be yours" advertising campaign.

(o) The PV Investors v. Spain

The various claimants in *The PV Investors v. Spain* began investing in the Spanish PV plants under RD 661/2007.[755] The Tribunal considered that EL 54/1997 had established in the *Special Regime* the "cardinal principle" of reasonable profitability or a reasonable rate of return, leaving it to the implementing regulation to determine which remuneration is reasonable at the given time.[756] In light of this cardinal principle, the majority of the tribunal found that RD 661/2007 could not be construed to entail a specific commitment that guaranteed investors an immutable tariff for the operational lifetime of their plants.[757] Instead, investors could only claim compensation on the basis of the violation of legitimate expectations, if their return rate fell below a reasonable return of around 7% after tax per year.[758]

Charles N. Brower assessed the previous cases in length and considered that the allegation of an overriding "cardinal principle" in the *Special Regime* is neither conforming with consistent arbitral case law nor does it reflect the factual circumstances of the case.[759] Hence, the regulations and the compliance with RAIPRE registration deadline gave rise to legitimate

753 ibid, para. 598, 600.

754 ibid, para. 617.

755 The PV Investors v. Kingdom of Spain Final, Award, 28 February 2020 PCA Case No. 2012-14, para. 195.

756 ibid, para. 596.

757 ibid, para. 600.

758 ibid, para. 754, 847.

759 The PV Investors v. Kingdom of Spain, Concurring and Dissenting Opinion of Charles N. Brower, 28 February 2020 PCA Case No. 2012-14, para. 16.

expectations with regard to the specific remuneration prescribed in RD 661/2007.[760]

(p) Hydro Energy 1 S.À R.L. and Hydroxana Sweden AB v. Spain

Hydro Energy 1 S.À R.L. and Hydroxana Sweden AB (Hydro) invested in two PV power plants in 2009 and 2010 and in a number of hydro-power plants in May 2011 and December 2011.[761] Each of the hydro-power plants has been commissioned and was in full operation at the time of the investment.[762] The Tribunal criticized that the claimants did not disclose that they were already challenging the amendments made to the PV sector as part of the *PV Investor v. Spain* proceedings at the time of the hydro-investments in 2011, and concluded that the investors could not legitimately rely on the immutability of the *Special Regime* under RD 661/2007.[763] However, the Tribunal considered that the previous amendments and conduct of state officials did not give an indication of the scale of the changes and the stability obligation in Article 10(1) ECT prohibited the state to make radical changes to the regime.[764] Thus, the Tribunal explicitly agreed with the findings in *RREEF v. Spain* and observed that investors under the *Special Regime* could expect a reasonable rate of return, but no specific remuneration.[765]

(2) Investments under the 2010 Amendments

Investments conducted under the 2010 Amendments differ from previous investments in regard to the stronger evidence of upcoming changes. Not only have the amendments shown that the *Special Regime* under RD 661/2007 is subject to changes during the lifetime of the investment, but also was the tariff deficit in the Spanish household specifically ad-

---

760 ibid, para. 17.

761 Hydro Energy 1 S.A.R.L. and Hydroxana Sweden AB v. The Kingdom of Spain, Decision on Jurisdiction, Liability and Directions on Quantum, 9 March 2020 ICSID Case No. ARB/15/42, para. 62, 63.

762 ibid, para. 436.

763 ibid, para. 628, 629.

764 ibid, para. 673-676.

765 ibid, para. 695.

dressed in the preambles and the accompanying legislative material of the royal decrees.

(a) Antin Infrastructure Services and Antin Energia Termosolar v. Spain

In *Infrastructure Services Luxembourg S.à.r.l. and Energia Termosolar B.V. (Antin) v Spain,* the investment consisted of the acquisition of a shareholding in two CSP power plants in 2011.[766] The power plants were duly registered under the *Special Regime* in accordance with RD 661/2007, but still suffered severe losses. The Tribunal took into account the preamble of RD 1614/2010 and the accompanying reports, as well as press releases of state authorities, and concluded that regardless of the upcoming changes, the *leitmotiv* of Spain's measures was still the stability of the regulatory regime at the time of the investments in 2011.[767] In particular, the registration with RAIPRE was deemed the type of state conduct that was intended to create legitimate expectations in investors that the treatment prescribed in the *Special Regime* would be accorded for a defined period of time.[768] Those expectations were eventually defeated by the introduction of the 2013 Regime.[769]

Thereby, the Tribunal contrasted the findings in *9Ren v. Spain*, in which the Tribunal opined that the stabilisation promise was not upheld in the 2010 Amendments.[770]

(b) RREEF Infrastructure (GP) Ltd et al v. Spain

The investors in *RREEF Infrastructure (G.P.) Limited and RREEF Pan-European Infrastructure Two Lux S.à r.l. (RREEF) v. Spain* first invested in Spain in February 2011 by indirectly acquiring an equity interest in three project companies with activities in the wind power sector, and further broadened their investment by attaining shares in three CSP power plants in June

766 Antin Infrastructure Services Luxembourg S.à.r.l. and Antin Energia Termosolar B.V. v. Kingdom of Spain, Award, 15 June 2018 ICSID Case No. ARB/13/31, para. 70.

767 ibid, para. 548.

768 ibid, para. 552.

769 ibid, para. 572, 573.

770 *See* 9REN Holding S.a.r.l v. Kingdom of Spain, Award, 31 March 2019 ICSID Case No. ARB/15/15, para. 298.

and July 2011.[771] In line with the holding in *Antin v. Spain*, Tribunal in the present case observed that RD 1614/2010 acknowledged a clear possibility of modification, which could not have been disregarded by a diligent investor.[772] However, the retroactive application of the 2013 Regime was qualified as a violation of the FET standard.[773] Moreover, the Tribunal considered that the investors could legitimately expect to receive a reasonable return on their investments, which does not imply that the regulatory framework would remain unchanged but obligates the host state to keep all modifications reasonable and equitable.[774] Only by majority, the Tribunal concluded that the remuneration of the CSP plant under the 2013 Regime was under certain circumstances not reasonable anymore.[775]

In his partially dissenting opinion, *Robert Volterra* concurred that the calculations on whether the return of the investments fell below a reasonable rate must be conducted on the basis of a global assessment, which has to take into consideration the financial structure of the whole of the investments.[776]

(c) InfraRed Environmental Infrastructure GP Limited and others v. Spain

The investors in *InfraRed Environmental Infrastructure GP Limited and others (InfraRed) v. Spain* acquired shares in two CSP plants in July 2011.[777] At this time, the plants were registered in the Pre-Allocation Registry, but did not receive final registration on the RAIPRE yet.[778] The Tribunal considered various legislative, official, as well as unofficial representations, and concluded that Spain had made a commitment to the CSP sector that CSP

771 RREEF Infrastructure (G.P.) Limited and RREEF Pan-European Infrastructure Two Lux S.à.r.l. v. Kingdom of Spain, Decision on Responsibility and on the Principles of Quantum, 30 November 2018 ICSID Case No. ARB/13/30, para. 142.

772 ibid, para. 321.

773 ibid, para. 330.

774 ibid, para. 399.

775 ibid, para. 589.

776 RREEF Infrastructure (G.P.) Limited and RREEF Pan-European Infrastructure Two Lux S.à.r.l. v. Kingdom of Spain, Partially Dissenting Opinion of Robert Volterra, 30 November 2018 ICSID Case No. ARB/13/30, para. 46-49.

777 InfraRed Environmental Infrastructure GP Limited and others v. Kingdom of Spain, Award, 2 August 2019 ICSID Case No. ARB/14/12 para. 57.

778 ibid para. 57.

plants registered in the Pre-allocation Register, which was more specific than those received by PV investors under the 2010 Amendments.[779]

(d) Watkins Holdings S.à.r.l. and others v. Kingdom of Spain

The investors in *Watkins Holdings S.à.r.l. and others (Watkins) v. Spain* entered into a purchase agreement in regard to seven wind farms in August 2011.[780] Despite the late stage of investment, the Tribunal concluded in its majority decision that Spain had altered the *Special Regime*, with the introduction of the 2013 Regime, in a drastic and radical manner, which violated the legitimate expectations of the investor.[781] The majority found that "any undertakings and representations made explicitly or implicitly by the host State" may be seen as a source for legitimate expectations.[782] Through its legal framework—including the 2010 Amendments—and its overall investment-friendly policy, Spain made a commitment to attract investments by offering stability, without any obligation to do so.[783]

Hélène Ruiz Fabri dissented on the grounds that the majority did not consider clearly enough the fact that the greater number of the claimants' investments were made in the wind energy and not in the solar energy sector, as in most of the previous cases against Spain.[784] In the dissenter's view, the legal framework covering the wind energy sector did not convey any legitimate expectations regarding the stability of the *Special Regime*.[785] Moreover, it was stated that the late stage, in which the investment was made, was not taken into account properly. Even if there had been a stabilisation promise in 2007, the probability of regulatory change was evident and hence the intensity of the investors' legitimate expectations weaker at the time of the investment in August 2011, thereby referring

779 ibid, para. 448, 449.

780 Watkins Holdings S.à.r.l. and others v. Kingdom of Spain, Award, 21 January 2020 ICSID Case No. ARB/15/44, para. 134, 139.

781 ibid, para. 599.

782 Watkins Holdings S.à.r.l. and others v. Kingdom of Spain, Award, 21 January 2020 ICSID Case No. ARB/15/44, para. 518. These holdings are in line with the arguments expressed, inter alia, by *Guido Tawil* in his dissents or the Tribunal in *Masdar v. Spain*.

783 Watkins Holdings S.à.r.l. and others v. Kingdom of Spain, Award, 21 January 2020 ICSID Case No. ARB/15/44, para. 527, 528, 532.

784 Watkins Holdings S.à.r.l. and others v. Kingdom of Spain, Dissenting Opinion Helene Ruiz Fabri, 21 January 2020 ICSID Case No. ARB/15/44, para. 4.

785 ibid, para. 11.

to the decision in *Isolux v. Spain*.[786] Lastly, the dissenter criticised that the majority limited Spain's margin of discretion, by concluding that the new regime was not an "appropriate solution" to the tariff deficit, without exercising a proper act of balancing.[787]

(e) STEAG GmbH v. Spain

The investor in *STEAG GmbH (STEAG) v. Spain* acquired shares in a Spanish CSP plant in June 2012.[788] The plant had already successfully registered under the Pre-Assignment Registry.[789] The investor was thereby granted the right to enjoy the benefits under RD 661/2007 and RD 1614/2010, if the final registration with RAIPRE was accomplished before 1 January 2014.[790] The majority qualified the registration confirmation, in conjunction with the legislative framework, as a specific commitment. The commitment was deemed to include a promise to the stability of FITs for a prescribed period of time, the availability of FIPs, as well as pre-determined upper and lower limits for future modifications to FIPs.[791] Accordingly, the majority found that Spain violated this specific commitment with the introduction of the 2013 Regime, which abolished the option to FIPs and introduced the new method for calculation of remuneration.[792]

Pierre-Marie Dupuys dissented from this holding on the grounds that the superseding legislative promise included in EL 1997 provided only for a reasonable and not a specific return, which the investors continued to receive.[793]

786 ibid, para. 12, 13.

787 ibid, para. 14.

788 STEAG GmbH v. Kingdom of Spain, Decision on Jurisdiction, Liability and Directions on Quantum, 8 October 2020 ICSID Case No. ARB/15/4, para. 150, 151.

789 ibid, para. 137, 138, 626.

790 ibid, para. 137, 138, 626.

791 ibid para. 509, 537, 594.

792 ibid, para. 639.

793 STEAG GmbH v. Kingdom of Spain, Dissenting Opinion Dupuy, 8 October 2020 ICSID Case No. ARB/15/4, para. 9. The dissenter thereby aligned with the interpretation of the hierarchy of Spain's regulatory framework in *Stadtwerke v. Spain* and *PV Investors v. Spain*.

(f) Isolux Netherlands B.V. v. Spain

The dispute in *Isolux Netherlands B.V. (Isolux) v. Spain* covered an investment into PV power plants in October 2012.[794] From a chronological point of view, this is the latest investment subject to an investment dispute to date. Therefore, it is not surprising that the majority of the Tribunal concluded that, at a time when the transition to the 2013 Regime, through the introduction of RDL 1/2012 and Law 15/2012, was already in full swing, a diligent investor could have foreseen the critical changes in the legal framework.[795] Hence, the investor could not have legitimately relied on the expectations that the support scheme will remain in place unaltered.

Similar to his holdings in *Charanne v. Spain*, *Guido Santiago Tawil* dissented from the majority's decision in regard to the creation of legitimate expectations by the regulatory framework.[796] However, contrary to what the dissent may suggest, the members of the Tribunal did not disagree on the fact that the legal framework is in abstract capable of inducing legitimate expectations. Rather, their subsumption differs in regard to the particular provisions of the *Special Regime* in the given case.

2) The Italian Renewable Energy Saga

The Italian Republic implemented the Directive 2001/77/EC through Legislative Decree (LD) 387/2003[797] on the promotion of electricity from renewable energy sources in the EU internal electricity market. LD 387/2003 established a simplified authorisation procedure for the construction of renewable energy plants with a capacity above 20 KW, according to which renewable energy projects needed to obtain authorisation granted by a joint conference, in which all relevant authorities participated to assess the application (the *Autorizzazione Unica* - AU).[798] Renewable energy plants with less than 20 KW were subject to the Decree of the President of the

794 Isolux Netherlands, BV v. Kingdom of Spain Final, Award, 17 July 2016 SCC Case V2013/153, para. 141, 147.

795 ibid, para. 784, 785, 787.

796 Isolux Netherlands, BV v. Kingdom of Spain, Dissenting Opinion Guido Santiago Tawil, 17 July 2016 SCC Case V2013/153, para. 4.

797 Law Decree, 29 December 2003, No. 387.

798 Blusun S.A. Jean-Pierre Lecorcier and Michael Stein v. Italian Republic, Award, 27 December 2016 ICSID Case No. ARB/14/3, para. 66.

Republic No. 380[799], which only required the presentation of a declaration and supporting documentation by the applicant *(Denuncia di Inizio Attivitci* - DIA). If the authorities did not object within 30 days, the application was deemed to be granted.

The support scheme laid out by LD 387/2003 promoted renewable energy sources through several kinds of FITs and FIPs, implemented by the Italian Ministry of Economic Development through a series of so-called *Conto Energia* (Energy Account) ministerial decrees.[800] Each of the Energy Account decrees expressly provided that the tariff premiums, once granted, would be paid over a twenty-year period, commencing from the date of a PV plant's entry into operation.[801] Additionally, smaller PV installations were promoted through an "off-take regime", whereby the *Gestore dei Servizi Energetici* (GSE), the state-owned energy regulatory agency directly purchased electricity, at minimum guaranteed prices, in order to make up for the higher relative operating costs.[802] The *Autorità per l'energia elettrica e il gas* (AEEG) was in charge of the determination of the remuneration was, and amended the minimum price through resolutions.[803]

The support scheme for an equitable recovery of investment and operating costs by PV energy producers was introduced by Energy Account I, which entered into force between July 2005 and February 2006.[804] To maintain control over the maximum spending on subsidies, an annual cap of 500 MW was implemented for the support scheme.[805] Any investors registering after the annual cap was exceeded, were not eligible for future FITs. The exact remuneration of the 20-year FIT was then set out by private contracts concluded between renewable energy producers and the GSE

799 Decree of the President of the Republic, 6 June 2001, No. 380.

800 Patrizia and others, *Investment Disputes Involving the Renewable Energy Industry Under the Energy Charter Treaty*, p. 51.

801 Greentech Energy Systems A/S, NovEnergia II Energy & Environment (SCA) SICAR, and NovEnergia II Italian Portfolio SA v. Italian Republic, Award, 23 December 2018 SCC Arbitration V (2015/095), para. 109.

802 ibid, para. 129.

803 Such as AEEG Resolution No. 34/2005 and AEEG Resolution No. 280/2007 on Minimum Prices.

804 Ministerial Decree No. 18908 of 28 July 2005 of the Ministry of Productive Activities, as integrated and amended by Ministerial Decree No. 20998 of 6 February 2006 of the Ministry of Productive Activities (Energy Account I).

805 Belenergia S.A. v. Italian Republic, Award, 6 August 2019 ICSID Case No. ARB/15/40, para. 397.

(GSE Conventions).[806] In these Conventions, the GSE confirmed the right to a specific tariff rate, by means of a letter to the person or company holding the project rights to a PV facility, as well as by a contract entered into with the person or company.[807] Contracts between the GSE and the owners of PV facilities became effective on the date when the PV facility entered into operation.[808] The GSE Conventions, private contracts between investors and Italy through the GSE, set out, inter alia, the remuneration of the FITs. They also established that the FITs are subject to annual renewal on an inflation index basis, which became a concern in terms of foreseeability of the amendment of the FITs.[809]

In February 2007, Energy Account II was implemented in order to encourage the efficiency of PV plants.[810] The new regime did not affect acquired rights under Energy Account I and confirmed the 20-year FITs. Additionally, it established a new threshold of 1200 MW without annual caps.[811] The first progressive reduction of FITs was introduced by Energy Account III in August 2010.[812] Again, the new Energy Account did not affect the rights acquired under the previous Energy Accounts.[813] However, the criticism of PV plant owners against the unclear application of Energy Account II lead to the postponement of the application of Energy Account III decree until June 2011.[814]

806 Greentech Energy Systems A/S, NovEnergia II Energy & Environment (SCA) SICAR, and NovEnergia II Italian Portfolio SA v. Italian Republic, Award, 23 December 2018 SCC Arbitration V (2015/095), para. 128.

807 ibid, para. 111.

808 ibid, para. 111.

809 Belenergia S.A. v. Italian Republic, Award, 6 August 2019 ICSID Case No. ARB/15/40, para. 154, 394.

810 Ministerial Decree of 19 February 2007 from the Ministry of Economic Development (Energy Account II).

811 Belenergia S.A. v. Italian Republic, Award, 6 August 2019 ICSID Case No. ARB/15/40, para. 397.

812 Ministerial Decree of 6 August 2010 from the Ministry of Economic Development (Energy Account III).

813 Article 1(3) of Ministerial Decree of 6 August 2010.

814 Belenergia S.A. v. Italian Republic, Award, 6 August 2019 ICSID Case No. ARB/15/40, para. 397.

a) Disputed Measures

The first disputed measure was implemented in March 2011, when the Italian Government enacted LD 28/2011 (*Romani Decree*) in the implementation of Directive 2009/28/EC, which entered into force on 29 March 2011.[815] The *Romani Decree* introduced a set of reforms, the most significant of which was the modification of the FITs granted by Energy Account III. First, the qualification period of Energy Account III was significantly shortened, requiring plants to enter into operation by May 2011, instead of December 2013.[816] Second, the *Romani Decree* excluded PV plants that were built on agricultural land, had a capacity exceeding 1 MW and occupied more than 10% of the parcel from the scope of the support scheme.[817]

The trend of further reducing the FITs for larger plants continued with the adoption of Energy Account IV in May 2011 after the enactment of the *Romani Decree*.[818] Energy Account IV applied to plants commissioned after August 2011 and related to the overall nominal installed capacity of PV plant owners.[819] The purpose of the new regulation was to review the FITs, when annual costs of the support scheme reached 6 billion Euro for the Italian State.[820]

When the annual costs continued to grow, Energy Account V was enacted in July 2012.[821] It set up a new set of technical requirements for PV plants commissioned after August 2012, which made them eligible for an "all-inclusive tariff".[822] Moreover, Energy Account V introduced an administrative fee to cover the GSE's costs, which was directly offset

815 Legislative Decree No. 28/2011 of 3 March 2011 (Romani Decree).

816 Greentech Energy Systems A/S, NovEnergia II Energy & Environment (SCA) SICAR, and NovEnergia II Italian Portfolio SA v. Italian Republic, Award, 23 December 2018 SCC Arbitration V (2015/095), para. 122.

817 Eskosol S.p.A. in liquidazione v. Italian Republic, Award, 4 September 2020 ICSID Case No. ARB/15/50, para. 157.

818 Ministerial Decree of 5 May 2011 from the Ministry of Economic Development and the Ministry of Environment, Land and Sea (Energy Account IV).

819 Belenergia S.A. v. Italian Republic, Award, 6 August 2019 ICSID Case No. ARB/15/40, para. 397.

820 ibid, para. 397.

821 Ministerial Decree of 5 July 2012 from the Ministry of Economic Development and the Ministry of Environment, Land and Sea (Energy Account V).

822 Greentech Energy Systems A/S, NovEnergia II Energy & Environment (SCA) SICAR, and NovEnergia II Italian Portfolio SA v. Italian Republic, Award, 23 December 2018 SCC Arbitration V (2015/095), para. 126.

against the tariff paid to the energy producers.[823] At the same time, the AEEG laid the legal groundwork for charging renewable energy producers with imbalance fees, who were exempted before.[824] Renewable energy producers were thereby burdened with additional costs.

Up to this point, the regulatory changes had only an effect on renewable energy producers, who were new to the market. None of the previous Energy Accounts was designed to affect rights already acquired, under previous Energy Accounts. However, the policy of non-retroactivity was ended with the enactment of the LD 145/2013 (*Destinazione Italia Decree*)[825]. The new decree provided PV plant owners, inter alia, with the option to continue to receive the Energy Account incentives at the same rate for the remainder of the twenty-year period, but also foreclosed the possibility of receiving additional incentives thereafter.[826] Alternatively, renewable energy producers could accept reductions to the Energy Account incentives in exchange for an extension of the tariff period of seven additional years.[827] The final modification to the support scheme was introduced by the LD 91/2014[828], pursuant to which the FITs previously granted under the five Energy Accounts, were altered as of 1 January 2015. LD 91/2014 was converted into law by Law 116/2014 (*Spalma Incentivi Decree*)[829]. The *Spalma Incentivi Decree* left the operators of large power plants basically with only three options: (1) extending the duration of incentives from 20 to 24 years, while reducing incentives proportionally to the PV plant's lifetime, (2) keeping the 20-year duration, but varying the quantum of incentives throughout time, or (3) reducing 6-8% of incentives altogether, in

823 ibid, pras 156, 157.

824 CEF Energia B.V. v. Italian Republic, Award, 16 January 2019 SCC Arbitration No. 2015/158, para. 168.

825 Legislative Decree No. 145/2013 of 23 December 2013 (Destinazione Italia Decree).

826 Greentech Energy Systems A/S, NovEnergia II Energy & Environment (SCA) SICAR, and NovEnergia II Italian Portfolio SA v. Italian Republic, Award, 23 December 2018 SCC Arbitration V (2015/095), para. 143; Belenergia S.A. v. Italian Republic, Award, 6 August 2019 ICSID Case No. ARB/15/40, para. 122.

827 Greentech Energy Systems A/S, NovEnergia II Energy & Environment (SCA) SICAR, and NovEnergia II Italian Portfolio SA v. Italian Republic, Award, 23 December 2018 SCC Arbitration V (2015/095), para. 143; Belenergia S.A. v. Italian Republic, Award, 6 August 2019 ICSID Case No. ARB/15/40, para. 122.

828 Legislative Decree No. 91/2014 of 24 June 2014.

829 Law No. 116/2014 of 11 August 2014 (Spalma Incentivi Decree).

proportion to the PV plant's annual production capacity.[830] Although the GSE Conventions generally included a clause that prohibited unilateral alteration, the legislative changes affected power plant operators regardless of the rights granted under the agreements with the GSE.[831]

Considering the characteristics of the changes, the support scheme shows similar development as Spain's regulatory framework, including tariff reductions that were introduced from 2010 onwards and the final abolishment of the then existing regime in 2014.

b) The Italian Cases

In contrast to the Spanish renewable energy support system, the Italian Energy Accounts were gradually altered. Additionally, the Italian cases are characterised by the fact that the investments were generally made over a long period of time.

(1) Blusun SA, Jean-Pierre Lecorcier and Michael Stein v. Italy

The case of *Blusun SA, Jean-Pierre Lecorcier and Michael Stein (Blusun) v Italy*[832] is exceptional in regard to the measures challenged and the stage at which the investment was abandoned. The investors had planned the construction of PV plants in the Region of Puglia, but never finished the project due to administrative restrictions.[833] Based on the legal framework of the Italian Government, the Puglia region had also adopted laws and regulations regarding the construction of PV plants. These included Puglia Regional Law 1/2008[834], and Puglia Regional Law 31/2008[835]. Both regional laws allowed the use of the DIA procedure under LD 387/2003, for solar plants with a capacity of up to 1 MW. The Puglia project was split up into 120 smaller projects, with a capacity of 1 MW each, thus

---

830 Patrizia and others, *Investment Disputes Involving the Renewable Energy Industry Under the Energy Charter Treaty*, p. 51.

831 ibid, p. 51.

832 Blusun S.A. Jean-Pierre Lecorcier and Michael Stein v. Italian Republic, Award, 27 December 2016 ICSID Case No. ARB/14/3.

833 Simões, 'Blusun S.A. and others v Italy : Legal (in)stability and renewable energy investments' (2017) 26(3) RECIEL 298, p. 299.

834 Puglia Regional Law No. 1/2008 of 19 February 2008.

835 Puglia Regional Law No. 31/2008 of 21 October 2008.

falling under the accelerated declaratory procedure.[836] The smaller projects were initially supervised and developed by 12 project companies. Between 2008 and 2009, the local project companies had acquired certain rights and permits for the development of the plants, inter alia, under the DIA procedure.[837] In July 2010, the investors acquired shares in project companies through its subsidiary Eskosol.[838] Earlier, in March 2010, the Italian Constitutional Court ruled that the extension of the DIA procedure to 1 MW power plants, in Regional Law 31/2008, was unconstitutional.[839] However, already registered PV plants were still eligible. Nonetheless, the local authorities argued that the 120 PV plants belonged to a single owner or were part of a unitary project and tried to revoke the permission granted to the individual 1 MW projects, under the DIA procedure in January 2012.[840] Due to the lack of permission, the construction of the 120 PV plants never finished. Although the revocation was overruled on the basis of the excess of power by the local authorities, the construction was further delayed and eventually abandoned after new requirements for the support scheme were introduced by LD 1/2012[841] and the *Spalma Incentivi Decree*.[842]

The investors claimed that Italy had violated its stability obligation by introducing the *Spalma Incentivi Decree*, thereby rendering the PV investment economically unviable.[843] The Tribunal rejected the investors' contention that the delay due to the unlawful revocation of the permission and the amendment of the regulatory framework had caused the eventual abandonment of the project.[844] Rather, the Tribunal concluded that the lack of project financing and the justified concerns about the scope of DIA authorisation played an essential role in the loss of the investment.[845] Hence, the investors failed to prove a causal connection between the prac-

---

836 Blusun S.A. Jean-Pierre Lecorcier and Michael Stein v. Italian Republic, Award, 27 December 2016 ICSID Case No. ARB/14/3, para. 55.

837 ibid, para. 81.

838 ibid, para. 62, 83.

839 Italian Consitutional Court, Decision No. 119 of 26 March 2010.

840 Blusun S.A. Jean-Pierre Lecorcier and Michael Stein v. Italian Republic, Award, 27 December 2016 ICSID Case No. ARB/14/3, para. 69.

841 Law Decree No. 1/2012 of 24 January 2012.

842 Simões, 'Blusun S.A. and others v Italy : Legal (in)stability and renewable energy investments', p. 299.

843 Blusun S.A. Jean-Pierre Lecorcier and Michael Stein v. Italian Republic, Award, 27 December 2016 ICSID Case No. ARB/14/3, para. 162, 313.

844 ibid, para. 394.

845 ibid, para. 394.

tice acts of the Italian State and the damage incurred. In its decision, the Tribunal particularly put emphasis on the state's right to regulate.[846]

(2) Eskosol S.P.A. v. Italy

The dispute in *Eskosol S.P.A. (Eskosol) v. Italy* revolves around the same facts as in *Blusun v. Italy*. Eskosol was established by Blusun to acquire the 120 PV projects in Puglia in 2010.[847] As in the decision by the Tribunal in *Blusun v. Italy*, the *Eskosol* Tribunal considered unofficial statements by the GSE addressed directly to Eskosol, public statements from state officials describing the future of the regulatory regime, as well as Energy Account III itself, and concluded that the investors could not have had legitimate expectations that the legal framework would be maintained unaltered.[848] In particular, the Tribunal observed that the investors could not have derived any legitimate expectations from the regulatory framework before its PV plants even qualified for the support scheme.[849]

The Tribunal emphasised that it considered the decision by the *Blusun* Tribunal, but eventually reached its conclusion based on "on its own independent analysis, and not on the basis of the decisions of other tribunals".[850]

(3) ESPF Beteiligungs GmbH et. al. v. Italy

The investors in *ESPF Beteiligungs GmbH et. al. (ESPF) v. Italy* acquired shares in several PV plants over the course of late 2009 until the end of 2012.[851] All PV plants were eligible under Energy Accounts I-IV depending on their date of entering into operation.[852] The Tribunal found by majority that the Energy Accounts provided for clear and specific commit-

846 ibid, para. 319(4). *See also* Simões, 'Blusun S.A. and others v Italy : Legal (in)stability and renewable energy investments', p. 300.

847 Eskosol S.p.A. in liquidazione v. Italian Republic, Award, 4 September 2020 ICSID Case No. ARB/15/50, para. 121, 122, 130.

848 ibid, para. 425-449.

849 ibid, para. 449.

850 ibid, para. 278.

851 ESPF Beteiligungs GmbH et. al. v. Italian Republic, Award, 14 September 2020 ICSID Case No. ARB/16/5, para. 132-147.

852 ibid, para. 132-147

ments, which were violated with the introduction of the *Spalma Incentivi Decree*.[853] In particular, the Tribunal qualified the express language of the Energy Accounts and the subsequent communication by the GSE, which stated that duly registered PV plants were entitled to FITs for a fixed period of time as a specific guarantee.[854] This left authorities without any discretion with regard to the eligibility of plant owners for the FITs.[855]

Laurence Boisson de Chazournes disagreed with the majority's interpretation of the Energy Accounts and opined that the legal framework did not contain any assurance of stability and immutability.[856] The dissenter specifically criticised that the majority had not conducted the weighing and balancing exercise in light of the specific circumstances and facts of the present case.[857]

(4) Greentech Energy Systems A/S et. al. v Italy

The investors in *Greentech Energy Systems A/S, et. al. (Greentech) v. Italy* had invested in eighty-two PV projects in Italy over the course of 2009 to 2013.[858] All PV plants were eligible under the respective Energy Account applicable at the time of their commencement in operation.[859] When the *Spalma Incentivi Decree* was enacted, the PV plants suffered severe losses under all three options provided by the new support scheme. The Tribunal found that "[t]he repeated and precise assurances to specific investors amounted to guarantees that the tariffs would remain fixed for two decades".[860] The Italian State thereby effectively waived its right to regulate, as long as there is no state of necessity that amounts to *force majeur*.[861] Facing "a situation of economic difficulty" was not deemed sufficient to excuse mistreatment by the state.[862]

---

853 ibid, para. 578, 579, 639, 645.
854 ibid, para. 515-517, 529.
855 ibid, para. 515-517, 529.
856 ibid, para. 645, 709.
857 ibid, para. 645.
858 Greentech Energy Systems A/S, NovEnergia II Energy & Environment (SCA) SICAR, and NovEnergia II Italian Portfolio SA v. Italian Republic, Award, 23 December 2018 SCC Arbitration V (2015/095), para. 133, 140, 141.
859 ibid, para. 134, 141.
860 ibid, para. 450.
861 ibid, para. 450.
862 ibid, para. 451.

Giorgio Sacerdoti criticised in his dissent, inter alia, the majority's methodical approach to the notion of legitimate expectations.[863] Based thereon, the dissenter found that the balancing of the rights of the state to regulate and the magnitude of the negative impact of the measures on the investment was not disproportionate in light of Italy's economic hardship.[864]

(5) CEF Energia B.V. v. Italy

The investor in *CEF Energia B.V. (CEF) v. Italy* had acquired an interest in three PV projects in Italy. The first investment was made in December 2010, the second in October 2011 and the third in March 2012.[865] The first two projects concerned the construction of two PV plants, whereas the third investment simply consisted of the acquisition of shares of an already commissioned and grid-connected plant. All projects were eligible under the Energy Accounts and received tariffs at various levels, and were subsequently affected by the regulatory changes implemented by the *Spalma Incentivi Decree*. The Tribunal refers largely to the holding of the Tribunal in *Antaris Solar v. Czech Republic*[866] and concluded, in regard to the first two projects, that the investor had still multiple practical and administrative hurdles ahead, at the time of the investment.[867] Therefore, the investment's economic success chances had not crystallised and the investor could not have had specific expectations yet.[868] On the contrary, the third project had, at the time of the acquisition by the claimant, already concluded

863 Greentech Energy Systems A/S, NovEnergia II Energy & Environment (SCA) SICAR, and NovEnergia II Italian Portfolio SA v. Italian Republic, Dissenting Opinion of Giorgio Sacerdoti, 23 December 2018 SCC Arbitration V (2015/095), para. 5, 6. The Dissenter finds that legitimate expectations require an belancing act between the rights infringed and the exercise of the state's right to regulate. In the view of *Sacerdoti*, this also includes an subjective due diligence part on the side of the investor, thereby closely following the approach set out in Ch. 2 IV.

864 ibid, para. 12.

865 CEF Energia B.V. v. Italian Republic, Award, 16 January 2019 SCC Arbitration No. 2015/158, para. 151-161.

866 Antaris Solar and Dr. Michael Göde v. Czech Republic, Award, 2 May 2018 PCA Case No. 2014-01. *See below* Ch. 3 III 3) b) (1).

867 CEF Energia B.V. v. Italian Republic, Award, 16 January 2019 SCC Arbitration No. 2015/158, para. 185, 188.

868 ibid, para. 188, 189.

agreements with the GSE.[869] These agreements stipulated that the power plant would continue to receive an incentive tariff for the next 20 years.[870] Therefore, the investor had legitimate expectations (at least in regard to the third project) that the regulatory framework would not undergo major changes, which were eventually frustrated by the implementation of the *Spalma Incentivi Decree*.[871]

As in *Greentech v. Italy*, Giorgio Sacerdoti dissented on the basis of improper balancing between the rights at stake.[872]

(6) SunReserve Holdings v. Italy

The claimants in *SunReserve Luxco Holdings S.A.R.L, SunReserve Luxco Holdings II S.A.R.L, SunReserve Luxco Holdings III S.A.R.L (SunReserve) v. Italy* invested in a total of nine PV plants between 2010 and 2011.[873] All plants were eligible for a FIT under Energy Account II or III for a period of 20 years.[874] However, only the first of the nine PV plants concluded a GSE Convention before the acquisition by the investors.[875] The Tribunal set a high threshold for the violation of the FET obligation, requiring the state conduct to fall far below international standards.[876] It emphasised that not every breach of the investors' legitimate expectations may qualify as a violation of the FET standard under Article 10(1) ECT.[877] Accordingly, the investors could, on the basis of the legislative framework and the statements of government officials and agencies, not expect to receive a fixed tariff for a period of 20 years.[878] In the view of the Tribunal, the Energy Account regulations did not automatically convey a specific right on any particular investor, but set out various technical and construction criteria which had to be met, in order to be eligible for the support scheme.[879]

869 ibid, para. 217.
870 ibid, para. 217.
871 ibid, para. 244.
872 ibid, para. 247.
873 SunReserve Luxco Holdings v. Italian Republic Final, Award, 25 March 2020 SCC Arbitration V (2016/32), para. 183.
874 ibid, para. 189-210.
875 ibid, para. 209.
876 ibid, para. 727, 728.
877 ibid, para. 727, 728.
878 ibid, para. 788, 789.
879 ibid, para. 792.

Moreover, LD 387/2003, which was the legal basis for the regulations and was hierarchically superior to any Energy Account, provided only the right to "fair remuneration".[880] For the eight plants that received the GSE Conventions after their acquisition by the investors, the Tribunal observed that the claimants could not have objective certainty that they would receive any remuneration for a fixed period of time.[881] They, hence, lacked legitimacy with regard to their expectations. The Tribunal acknowledged that the investors had legitimate expectations in relation to the first PV plant that had already received the GSE Convention.[882] However, it rejected any alleged breaches of the protected expectations, as the reduction left the PV plant still with a "fair remuneration".[883]

(7) Belenergia S.A. v. Italy

Belenergia S.A (Belenergia) invested in 20 PV plants in the south of Italy between September 2011 and December 2013. Nineteen of these plants had a capacity of just under 1 MW.[884] The investment was conducted in three waves, taking place in September 2011, July 2013 and December 2013.[885] The PV plants of the first wave were all granted feed-in tariffs under Energy Account IV pursuant to Ministerial Decree of 5 May 2011.[886] The second and third investment wave took place when Energy Account V was effective. Although Energy Account V was already at its cap at the time of the investment, the acquired PV power plants continued to receive tariffs under previous Energy Accounts (Energy Account I, II, IV).[887] Each companies operating the power plants concluded agreements with the GSE, which stipulated the application of the incentive tariff for a period of 20 years and the level of minimum prices.[888] Nine of ten of Belenergia's PV companies benefited from minimum prices extending through different periods, starting with the conclusion of the respective GSE Con-

880 ibid, para. 801.
881 ibid, para. 836.
882 ibid, para. 871.
883 ibid, para. 871.
884 Belenergia S.A. v. Italian Republic, Award, 6 August 2019 ICSID Case No. ARB/15/40, para. 145.
885 ibid, para. 149.
886 *See* overview ibid, para. 152, 158.
887 *See* overview ibid, para. 152, 158.
888 For the wording of the GSE Conventions *see* ibid para. 154.

vention.[889] The companies were then adversely affected by the minimum price reduction by AEEG Resolution 618/2013 and the final cut by the *Destinazione Italia Decree*, by the end of the same year.[890]

In contrast to the holding in *CEF v. Italy*, the Tribunal found that the GSE Conventions simply reflected the legal framework and did not grant any additional rights.[891] Additionally, the Tribunal analysed the due diligence of the investors and observed that no prudent investor could have believed in the stability of the legal framework, as the investors invested at a very late stage when new incentives were subject to reduction and annual cost caps set by the Italian legislator were being reached.[892]

3) The Czech Renewable Energy Saga

Upon accession to the EU in 2004, the Czech Republic strived to harmonize its legal system with EU law. As a result of following the Directive 2001/77/EC, the Act 180/2005 on the Promotion of the Use of Renewable Sources[893] was introduced. The act obligated power grid operators to pay either a fixed FIT depending on the source of energy used or an FIP ("Green Bonus") on top of the regular market price of electricity. Power plant operators were initially eligible to the support scheme for 15 years from the date of commissioning the respective plants, with a minimum annual return of 7%.[894] The Czech Energy Regulatory Office (ERO) later extended this to 20 years.[895] The annual rate of FITs and Green Bonuses for plants connected to the grid was determined by the ERO in the following year. The law also provided for a "brake rule". This "brake rule" stipulated that the tariff rate could only be decreased by 5% each year, thereby effectively precluding any drastic decrease in remuneration.[896]

---

889 ibid, para. 160.

890 ibid, para. 160.

891 ibid, para. 580.

892 ibid, para. 594, 595.

893 Act No. 180/2005 Coll. on the Promotion of Electricity Production from Renewable Energy Sources.

894 I.C.W. Europe Investments Limited v. The Czech Republic, Award, 15 May 2019 PCA CASE No 2014-22, para. 640.

895 ERO Regulation No. 364/2007 Coll.; C-30, ERO Regulation No. 409/2009 Coll.

896 Patrizia and others, *Investment Disputes Involving the Renewable Energy Industry Under the Energy Charter Treaty*, p. 50.

a) Disputed Measures

This generous support scheme attracted more investors than initially expected and led to a "solar boom" between 2008 and 2009, in which the number of power plants eligible for the support system rapidly increased.[897] However, the popularity of the program coupled with decreasing costs of renewable energy production facilities made an increase in electricity prices for households and industrial consumers likely.[898] To counter this effect and to adapt the legal system to the rapidly decreasing prices of solar energy, the Czech Republic ended the 5% "brake rule" in 2010[899] and limited the support scheme to small PV plants, with a capacity of up to 30 kWh in 2011[900]. Additionally, the Czech Republic eliminated tax incentives[901] and effectively applied a solar levy of 26% on FITs and 28% on Green Bonuses, in December 2010[902].

Act 180/2005 was then repealed and replaced by Act 165/2012[903] in May 2012. The new support scheme was amended again in October 2013, to extend the Solar Levy at a rate of 10% of the FIT for the plants commissioned in 2010 for the entire period of time during which these plants would have a right to electricity support.[904]

Similar to the Spanish renewable energy support system, the EC classified the new Czech support scheme as EU law compatible state aid.[905] Additionally, the Czech Constitutional Court decided in May 2012 that the Solar Levy and the abolishment of the tax exemption were constitu-

897 Jürgen Wirtgen, Stefan Wirtgen, Gisela Wirtgen and JSW Solar (zwei) GmbH & Co. KG v. Czech Republic, Award, 11 October 2017 PCA Case No. 2014-03, *see* figure para. 382.

898 Antaris Solar and Dr. Michael Göde v. Czech Republic, Award, 2 May 2018 PCA Case No. 2014-01, para. 120; Jürgen Wirtgen, Stefan Wirtgen, Gisela Wirtgen and JSW Solar (zwei) GmbH & Co. KG v. Czech Republic, Award, 11 October 2017 PCA Case No. 2014-03, *see* figure para. 377.

899 Amendment Act No. 137/2010 Coll.

900 Amendment Act No. 330/2010 Coll.

901 Amendment Act No. 346/2010 Coll.

902 Amendment Act No. 402/2010 Coll.

903 Act 165/2012 Coll., on Promotion of Sources of Energy and Amending Certain Acts.

904 Amendment Act No. 310/2013 Coll.

905 Press Relase "State aid: Commission approves Czech scheme supporting renewable energy", 11 June 2014, <https://ec.europa.eu/commission/presscorner/detail/en/IP_14_664> (accessed 3 May 2021).

tional.[906] The Court held that producers were at most entitled to expect that their investment would be paid back in 15 years, which time was maintained despite the Solar Levy and the tax exemption.[907]

b) The Czech Cases

Notably, the majority of the claimants in the investment cases against the Czech Republic originated from Germany. Hence, it is not surprising that most of the claims were raised under the ECT and also/or exclusively under the Germany-Czech Republic BIT.[908] This could cast doubt on whether the decisions of the tribunals based on the FET standard in the BIT could be used for the analysis. However, due to the high degree of correspondence between the FET standard in the ECT and other BITs[909], it is to be assumed that the holdings of the respective tribunals can be included in the comparison, without distorting the results of the analysis.

(1) Antaris Solar GmbH and Dr. Michael Göde v. Czech Republic

The investors in *Antaris Solar GmbH and Dr. Michael Göde (Antaris) v. Czech Republic* had invested in five PV power plants, of which the first was acquired in 2008, the second in 2009 and the other three over the course of 2010.[910] Only the first power plant remained unaffected by the implementation of the Solar Levy and the elimination of the tax incentive.[911]

The Tribunal took into account the political and economic landscape at the time of the investment. It concluded that the countermeasures prepared by the Czech Republic, during the investments in 2010, should have been a warning sign to all investors that change of the support scheme

906 Czech Supreme Court, Decision of 15 May 2012, Case No. Pl. ÚS 17/11, para. 71-73.

907 Jürgen Wirtgen, Stefan Wirtgen, Gisela Wirtgen and JSW Solar (zwei) GmbH & Co. KG v. Czech Republic, Award, 11 October 2017 PCA Case No. 2014-03, para. 58

908 Patrizia and others, *Investment Disputes Involving the Renewable Energy Industry Under the Energy Charter Treaty*, p. 50.

909 *See* Chapter 1 IV.

910 Antaris Solar and Dr. Michael Göde v. Czech Republic, Award, 2 May 2018 PCA Case No. 2014-01, para. 401-409.

911 ibid, para. 401.

was coming.[912] Instead, the claimant "was essentially an opportunistic investor, who saw a window of opportunity and who was aware, or should have been aware, that dealing with the solar boom was a fast-moving and controversial political issue".[913] Hence, no prudent investor could have legitimately expected that the legal framework would remain unchanged. Moreover, the Tribunal found that the legitimate expectations in regard to the earlier investments have not been frustrated either, as there was no promise that the return would exceed 7% annually, which was received despite the changes.[914]

Gary Born dissented on the grounds that the legal framework in place at the time of the investment was "crystal clear", so that any prudent investor could have expected a certain level of return without conducting any extensive due diligence.[915]

(2) Jürgen Wirtgen, Stefan Wirtgen, Gisela Wirtgen et. al. v Czech Republic

The investors in *Jürgen Wirtgen, Stefan Wirtgen, Gisela Wirtgen et. al. (Wirtgen) v Czech Republic* first initiated the construction of a PV power plant at the end of 2009.[916] Two more PV power plants were commissioned and put into service in 2010.[917] The investments were subject to the abolishment of tax incentives and the Solar Levy, by Act 346/2010 and Act 402/2010. The Tribunal reviewed the expectations investors could have legitimately had under Act 180/2005 and concluded that there was no promise of a specific revenue. Rather, investors could have only expected that the "FIT would be set at a level ensuring a 15-year payback of capital expenses and a return on investment or profit of at least 7% per year over 15 years".[918] The Tribunal, thereby, corresponded with the findings of the Czech Supreme Court Since neither the abrogation of the tax incentives

912 ibid, para. 401.

913 ibid, para. 431.

914 ibid, para. 440.

915 Antaris Solar and Dr. Michael Göde v. Czech Republic Dissenting Opinion, 2 May 2018 PCA Case No. 2014-01, para. 12.

916 Jürgen Wirtgen, Stefan Wirtgen, Gisela Wirtgen and JSW Solar (zwei) GmbH & Co. KG v. Czech Republic, Award, 11 October 2017 PCA Case No. 2014-03, para. 31.

917 ibid, para. 34, 36, 40.

918 ibid, para. 369, 416.

nor the Solar Levy decreased the return on the investment beneath 7%, the legitimate expectations of the investor at the time of the investment were not frustrated.[919]

Again, *Gary Born* dissented forcefully from the majority's decision regarding the specificity of the Czech Republic's commitment through its legal framework.[920]

(3) Voltaic Network, Knopf, I.C.W. Investments, WA Investment v. Czech Republic

The four investors *Photovoltaic Knopf Betriebs GMBH (Knopf), Voltaic Network GMBH (Voltaic), I.C.W. Europe Investments Ltd. (ICW Europe) and WA Investments Europa Nova Ltd. (WA Investments)* invested in the Czech Republic between September 2009 and April 2010[921] as well as in May[922], July[923], and August 2010[924].

Although there are strictly speaking four different awards, the Tribunal consisted of the same members, after the Czech Republic rejected the consolidation of the proceedings. Moreover, the Tribunal essentially applied the same reasoning on similar facts. Hence, the awards do not bear any additional legal persuasiveness and are to be handled as "one" decision, so as to not distort the outcome of this research with the objective of finding a stable system of soft precedent.[925]

The Tribunal followed the line of argument presented by the previous decisions and concluded that the legal framework in place at the time of the investment did not contain any specific commitment in regard to certain revenue, since the original support scheme only gave rise to expec-

---

919 ibid, para. 425, 437.

920 Jürgen Wirtgen, Stefan Wirtgen, Gisela Wirtgen and JSW Solar (zwei) GmbH & Co. KG v. Czech Republic, Dissenting Opinion, 11 October 2017 PCA Case No. 2014-03, para. 25.

921 WA Investments-Europa Nova Limited v. The Czech Republic, Award, 15 May 2019 PCA CASE No 2014-19, para. 154, 155.

922 Voltaic Network GmbH v. Czech Republic, Award, 15 September 2019 PCA CASE No 2014-20, para. 151, 152.

923 I.C.W. Europe Investments Limited v. The Czech Republic, Award, 15 May 2019 PCA CASE No 2014-22, para. 151, 152.

924 Photovoltaik Knopf Betriebs-GmbH v. The Czech Republic, Award, 15 May 2019 PCA CASE No 2014-21, para. 151.

925 Due to the almost identical wording of legal findings, each citation can be regarded as representative for all four awards if not expressed differently.

tations that the recuperation time of the investment would be 15 years, with a minimum annual return of 7%.[926] However, all investors continued to receive revenue that exceeded the 7% mark. Thus, the Tribunal did not find any violation of the obligation to stability, any legitimate expectations, or any other aspect of the FET standard in any of the cases.[927] The Tribunal also assessed whether the investors considered EU law and concluded that, if they had done so, they would have been aware that the lack of EU state aid approval could have resulted in a subsequent change of the Czech support scheme.[928]

IV. Summary of the Tendency in Arbitral Jurisprudence

At first glance, some trends can be identified in arbitral jurisprudence. In particular, the direct comparison between the different regulatory changes demonstrates that arbitral tribunals do not have a clear tendency in favour of either investors or states. While the Czech Republic was able to fend off most claims so far, Spain lost the majority of its cases. The success rate against Italy is equally distributed. However, it is to be noted that in the cases against Italy, which remained futile, extraordinary circumstances prevailed.[929] This diverse evaluation of the different legal frameworks by the various tribunals allows for a comparison of the promises provided by the support schemes and their subsequent amendments. The comparison

926 WA Investments-Europa Nova Limited v. The Czech Republic, Award, 15 May 2019 PCA CASE No 2014-19, para. 548, 549.

927 I.C.W. Europe Investments Limited v. The Czech Republic, Award, 15 May 2019 PCA CASE No 2014-22, para. 536; WA Investments-Europa Nova Limited v. The Czech Republic, Award, 15 May 2019 PCA CASE No 2014-19, para. 577; Photovoltaik Knopf Betriebs-GmbH v. The Czech Republic, Award, 15 May 2019 PCA CASE No 2014-21, para. 490; Voltaic Network GmbH v. Czech Republic, Award, 15 September 2019 PCA CASE No 2014-20, para. 494.

928 Voltaic Network GmbH v. Czech Republic, Award, 15 September 2019 PCA CASE No 2014-20, para. 537.

929 *For example*, in *Blusun*, the plant was never finished, Blusun S.A. Jean-Pierre Lecorcier and Michael Stein v. Italian Republic, Award, 27 December 2016 ICSID Case No. ARB/14/3, para. 394, in *Belenergia*, the individual due diligence of the investor was not sufficient, Belenergia S.A. v. Italian Republic, Award, 6 August 2019 ICSID Case No. ARB/15/40, para. 594, 595, and in *SunReserve*, the investors acquired the plants before they received confirmation of specific remuneration, SunReserve Luxco Holdings v. Italian Republic Final, Award, 25 March 2020 SCC Arbitration V (2016/32), para. 792.

will aid in pinpointing which measures are within the states' margin of discretion, when exercising their right to regulate, and which were deemed a violation of the FET standard. For example, the success of the Czech Republic in the renewable energy cases greatly depended on the tribunals finding that the investors had legitimate expectations but were not frustrated by the changes.[930] In contrast, a number of tribunals assessing the changes in the Spanish regime concluded that the changes were so "drastic and radical", in a way that violated the legitimate expectations of the investors.[931]

In general, investors in the renewable energy cases considered the risk of change of the regulatory framework applicable to financed projects to be low, since all of the support schemes expressed to some degree that the eligible plants would receive FITs or FIPs for a certain period of time.[932] Against this background, investors, who invested during the first stage of the regulatory framework, made their projections with the assumption that the projects would receive fixed FITs for the entire life of the plants.[933] This lead investors to believe that their investments faced

930 Antaris Solar and Dr. Michael Göde v. Czech Republic, Award, 2 May 2018 PCA Case No. 2014-01, para. 440; Jürgen Wirtgen, Stefan Wirtgen, Gisela Wirtgen and JSW Solar (zwei) GmbH & Co. KG v. Czech Republic, Award, 11 October 2017 PCA Case No. 2014-03, para. 425, 437; I.C.W. Europe Investments Limited v. The Czech Republic, Award, 15 May 2019 PCA CASE No 2014-22, para. 536; WA Investments-Europa Nova Limited v. The Czech Republic, Award, 15 May 2019 PCA CASE No 2014-19, para. 577; Photovoltaik Knopf Betriebs-GmbH v. The Czech Republic, Award, 15 May 2019 PCA CASE No 2014-21, para. 490; Voltaic Network GmbH v. Czech Republic, Award, 15 September 2019 PCA CASE No 2014-20, para. 494. *See also* Ch. 4 III 3) b).

931 Eiser Infrastructure Limited and Energía Solar Luxembourg S.à.r.l. v. Kingdom of Spain, Award, 4 May 2017 ICSID Case No. ARB/13/36, para. 363, 387; Novenergia II - Energy & Environment (SCA), SICAR v. The Kingdom of Spain, Award, 15 February 2018 SCC Case No. V 2015/063, para. 697; Foresight and others v. Kingdom of Spain Final, Award, 14 November 2018 SCC Case No. V 2015/150, para. 397-398; OperaFund Eco-Invest SICAV PLC and Schwab Holding AG v. Kingdom of Spain, Award, 6 September 2019 ICSID Case No. ARB/15/36, para. 513; Hydro Energy 1 S.A.R.L. and Hydroxana Sweden AB v. The Kingdom of Spain, Decision on Jurisdiction, Liability and Directions on Quantum, 9 March 2020 ICSID Case No. ARB/15/42, para. 673-676.

932 Eiser Infrastructure Limited and Energía Solar Luxembourg S.à.r.l. v. Kingdom of Spain, Award, 4 May 2017 ICSID Case No. ARB/13/36, para. 118; ESPF Beteiligungs GmbH et. al. v. Italian Republic, Award, 14 September 2020 ICSID Case No. ARB/16/5, para. 543.

933 Eiser Infrastructure Limited and Energía Solar Luxembourg S.à.r.l. v. Kingdom of Spain, Award, 4 May 2017 ICSID Case No. ARB/13/36, para. 118;

none or at least a very low regulatory risk. This notwithstanding, none of the tribunals accepted that the support scheme, no matter how crystal clear, gave rise to "immutable economic rights that could not be altered by changes in the regulatory regime".[934] Thus, the states' right to regulate has been uniformly acknowledged and taken into consideration by arbitral tribunals assessing the legitimacy of expectations.

1) Types of Commitments by the States

With regard to the investors' legitimate expectations, the tribunals demonstrated three different approaches: Some tribunals interpreted the regulatory framework itself to include a commitment that gave rise to legitimate expectations to some degree of stability.[935] The second group of tribunals considered individual representations, which had been made towards a given investor alongside the regulatory framework, as a basis for legitimate

---

Blusun S.A. Jean-Pierre Lecorcier and Michael Stein v. Italian Republic, Award, 27 December 2016 ICSID Case No. ARB/14/3, para. 384 (although assumption was unfounded); Cube Infrastructure Fund SICAV and others v. Kingdom of Spain, Decision on Jurisdiction, Liability and Partial Decision on Quantum, 19 February 2019 ICSID Case No. ARB/15/20, para. 301; Masdar Solar & Wind Cooperatief U.A. v. Kingdom of Spain, Award, 16 May 2018 ICSID Case No. ARB/14/1, para. 359; Cavalum SGPS v. Kingdom of Spain, Decision on Jurisdiction, Liability and Directions on Quantum, 31 August 2020 ICSID Case No. ARB/15/34, para. 521; ESPF Beteiligungs GmbH et. al. v. Italian Republic, Award, 14 September 2020 ICSID Case No. ARB/16/5, para. 543.

934 Eiser Infrastructure Limited and Energía Solar Luxembourg S.à.r.l. v. Kingdom of Spain, Award, 4 May 2017 ICSID Case No. ARB/13/36, para. 363; Novenergia II - Energy & Environment (SCA), SICAR v. The Kingdom of Spain, Award, 15 February 2018 SCC Case No. V 2015/063, para. 654; Foresight and others v. Kingdom of Spain, Dissenting Opinion Raúl Emilio Vinuesa, 14 November 2018 SCC Case No. V 2015/150, para. 366, 388.

935 Eiser Infrastructure Limited and Energía Solar Luxembourg S.à.r.l. v. Kingdom of Spain, Award, 4 May 2017 ICSID Case No. ARB/13/36, para. 362, 363; Foresight and others v. Kingdom of Spain Final, Award, 14 November 2018 SCC Case No. V 2015/150, para. 386, 388; Cube Infrastructure Fund SICAV and others v. Kingdom of Spain, Decision on Jurisdiction, Liability and Partial Decision on Quantum, 19 February 2019 ICSID Case No. ARB/15/20, para. 388; OperaFund Eco-Invest SICAV PLC and Schwab Holding AG v. Kingdom of Spain, Award, 6 September 2019 ICSID Case No. ARB/15/36, para. 485; Cavalum SGPS v. Kingdom of Spain, Decision on Jurisdiction, Liability and Directions on Quantum, 31 August 2020 ICSID Case No. ARB/15/34, para. 538, 556, 601, 612.

expectations.[936] The third type of tribunals struggled in construing the underlying regulatory framework to include a commitment due to its general nature.[937] Generally, the more expressly the language of the regulatory framework indicated the stability of the support scheme, the more likely a tribunal was to find it inducing legitimate expectations.

Since the registration with certain state authorities is a common theme in any support system, all tribunals assessed the question of whether the approval of power plants conveyed a specific commitment or whether they are simply a requirement stipulated by law, which cannot grant any rights exceeding those already established by the regulatory framework. However, the expressed views have been conflicting, with numerous tri-

936 Novenergia II - Energy & Environment (SCA), SICAR v. The Kingdom of Spain, Award, 15 February 2018 SCC Case No. V 2015/063, para. 656, 681; Masdar Solar & Wind Cooperatief U.A. v. Kingdom of Spain, Award, 16 May 2018 ICSID Case No. ARB/14/1, para. 521, 522; NextEra Energy Global Holdings B.V. and NextEra Energy Spain Holdings B.V. v. Kingdom of Spain, Decision on Jurisdiction, Liability and Quantum Principles, 12 March 2019 ICSID Case No. ARB/14/11, para. 596; SolEs Badajoz GmbH v. Kingdom of Spain, Award, 31 July 2019 ICSID Case No. ARB/15/38, para. 423-425, 462; 9REN Holding S.a.r.l v. Kingdom of Spain, Award, 31 March 2019 ICSID Case No. ARB/15/15, para. 299; Antin Infrastructure Services Luxembourg S.à.r.l. and Antin Energia Termosolar B.V. v. Kingdom of Spain, Award, 15 June 2018 ICSID Case No. ARB/13/31, para. 548; InfraRed Environmental Infrastructure GP Limited and others v. Kingdom of Spain, Award, 2 August 2019 ICSID Case No. ARB/14/12, para. 449; Watkins Holdings S.à.r.l. and others v. Kingdom of Spain, Award, 21 January 2020 ICSID Case No. ARB/15/44, para. 527, 528, 532; STEAG GmbH v. Kingdom of Spain, Decision on Jurisdiction, Liability and Directions on Quantum, 8 October 2020 ICSID Case No. ARB/15/4 para. 509, 537, 594; Greentech Energy Systems A/S, NovEnergia II Energy & Environment (SCA) SICAR, and NovEnergia II Italian Portfolio SA v. Italian Republic, Award, 23 December 2018 SCC Arbitration V (2015/095), para. 447; CEF Energia B.V. v. Italian Republic, Award, 16 January 2019 SCC Arbitration No. 2015/158, para. 242; ESPF Beteiligungs GmbH et. al. v. Italian Republic, Award, 14 September 2020 ICSID Case No. ARB/16/5, para. 515-517, 529.

937 Belenergia S.A. v. Italian Republic, Award, 6 August 2019 ICSID Case No. ARB/15/40, para. 580, 583; RWE Innogy GmbH and RWE Innogy Aersa S.A.U. v. Kingdom of Spain, Decision on Jurisdicition, Liability, and certain Issues of Quantum, 6 January 2020 ICSID Case No. ARB/14/34, para. 486-489, 542. However, the Tribunal in *RWE* compensated the rejection of legitimate expectations on the side of the investor by resorting to a separate proportionality analysis, thereby arriving at a similar result, para. 598, 600.

bunals accepting[938] and rejecting[939] their role in the creation of legitimate expectations. Similarly, more general representations like press releases or police reports were given different weight.[940]

Nonetheless, investors who sought constant contact and reassurance with state representatives or suffered huge losses had a higher success rate in general.[941] In the same vein, investments that were conducted before the effects of the economic crisis and the boom of the renewable energy investments became evident, i.e. before 2009 and 2010, are likely to be protected by the FET standard.[942] In contrast, claims have been unsuccess-

938 Antin Infrastructure Services Luxembourg S.à.r.l. and Antin Energia Termosolar B.V. v. Kingdom of Spain, Award, 15 June 2018 ICSID Case No. ARB/13/31, para. 552; OperaFund Eco-Invest SICAV PLC and Schwab Holding AG v. Kingdom of Spain, Award, 6 September 2019 ICSID Case No. ARB/15/36, para. 483; Masdar Solar & Wind Cooperatief U.A. v. Kingdom of Spain, Award, 16 May 2018 ICSID Case No. ARB/14/1, para. 512-520; Novenergia II - Energy & Environment (SCA), SICAR v. The Kingdom of Spain, Award, 15 February 2018 SCC Case No. V 2015/063, para. 665-667; Cavalum SGPS v. Kingdom of Spain, Dissenting Opinion of David R. Haigh, 31 August 2020 ICSID Case No. ARB/15/34, para. 9, 10; STEAG GmbH v. Kingdom of Spain, Decision on Jurisdiction, Liability and Directions on Quantum, 8 October 2020 ICSID Case No. ARB/15/4, para. 516, 520.

939 Belenergia S.A. v. Italian Republic, Award, 6 August 2019 ICSID Case No. ARB/15/40, para. 580; Charanne and Construction Investments v. Kingdom of Spain, Award, 21 January 2016 SCC Case No. V 062/2012, para. 510; NextEra Energy Global Holdings B.V. and NextEra Energy Spain Holdings B.V. v. Kingdom of Spain, Decision on Jurisdiction, Liability and Quantum Principles, 12 March 2019 ICSID Case No. ARB/14/11, para. 585; Stadtwerke München GmbH and others v. Kingdom of Spain, Award, 2 December 2019 ICSID Case No. ARB/15/1, para. 306; RWE Innogy GmbH and RWE Innogy Aersa S.A.U. v. Kingdom of Spain, Decision on Jurisdicition, Liability, and certain Issues of Quantum, 6 January 2020 ICSID Case No. ARB/14/34, para. 544; RREEF Infrastructure (G.P.) Limited and RREEF Pan-European Infrastructure Two Lux S.à.r.l. v. Kingdom of Spain, Decision on Responsibility and on the Principles of Quantum, 30 November 2018 ICSID Case No. ARB/13/30, para. 285; Cube Infrastructure Fund SICAV and others v. Kingdom of Spain, Decision on Jurisdiction, Liability and Partial Decision on Quantum, 19 February 2019 ICSID Case No. ARB/15/20, para. 453; 9REN Holding S.a.r.l v. Kingdom of Spain, Award, 31 March 2019 ICSID Case No. ARB/15/15, para. 346

940 *See* Ch. 4 I 2) a).

941 *For example* Masdar Solar & Wind Cooperatief U.A. v. Kingdom of Spain, Award, 16 May 2018 ICSID Case No. ARB/14/1, para. 512-522; Eiser Infrastructure Limited and Energía Solar Luxembourg S.à.r.l. v. Kingdom of Spain, Award, 4 May 2017 ICSID Case No. ARB/13/36, para. 368, 418.

942 *See* Foresight and others v. Kingdom of Spain Final, Award, 14 November 2018 SCC Case No. V 2015/150, para. 374; Cube Infrastructure Fund SICAV and

ful, if the investment was conducted at a stage in which the changes were already indicated by representatives of the host state or prior amendments, and were therefore considered imminent and predictable at the time of the investment.[943] Also, as a matter of due diligence, tribunals tended to give fair consideration to the domestic case law of the host state, in order to assess whether the investors' expectations that the regulatory framework would not be altered was protected under international law.[944]

2) Limitations to the Investors' Expectations

Even if the existence of legitimate expectations were established, not every claim remained successful. A second reason why claims remained futile concerned the fact that the commitment conveyed by the states' conduct did only give rise to expectations regarding the reception of a reasonable and/or minimum return. Tribunals found that the investors continued to receive this reasonable return even after the changes became effective.[945]

---

others v. Kingdom of Spain, Separate and Partial Dissenting Opinion Christian Tomuschat, 19 February 2019 ICSID Case No. ARB/15/20, para. 14.

943 Isolux Netherlands, BV v. Kingdom of Spain Final, Award, 17 July 2016 SCC Case V2013/153, para. 784, 785, 787; Antaris Solar and Dr. Michael Göde v. Czech Republic, Award, 2 May 2018 PCA Case No. 2014-01, para. 431; Belenergia S.A. v. Italian Republic, Award, 6 August 2019 ICSID Case No. ARB/15/40, para. 594, 595; Foresight and others v. Kingdom of Spain Final, Award, 14 November 2018 SCC Case No. V 2015/150, para. 369, 378; Watkins Holdings S.à.r.l. and others v. Kingdom of Spain, Dissenting Opinion Helene Ruiz Fabri, 21 January 2020 ICSID Case No. ARB/15/44, para. 14; Cube Infrastructure Fund SICAV and others v. Kingdom of Spain, Separate and Partial Dissenting Opinion Christian Tomuschat, 19 February 2019 ICSID Case No. ARB/15/20, para. 14.

944 *For example* Foresight and others v. Kingdom of Spain Final, Award, 14 November 2018 SCC Case No. V 2015/150, para. 370-372; SolEs Badajoz GmbH v. Kingdom of Spain, Award, 31 July 2019 ICSID Case No. ARB/15/38, para. 429-432; RWE Innogy GmbH and RWE Innogy Aersa S.A.U. v. Kingdom of Spain, Decision on Jurisdicition, Liability, and certain Issues of Quantum, 6 January 2020 ICSID Case No. ARB/14/34, para. 517, 518, 525; Cube Infrastructure Fund SICAV and others v. Kingdom of Spain, Decision on Jurisdiction, Liability and Partial Decision on Quantum, 19 February 2019 ICSID Case No. ARB/15/20, para. 300. *See* Ch. 4 II 2) c).

945 The prime examples thereof are the cases against the Czech Republic, which almost uniformly remained unsuccessful because the investors could only expect a reasonable return, Antaris Solar and Dr. Michael Göde v. Czech Republic, Award, 2 May 2018 PCA Case No. 2014-01, para. 440; Jürgen Wirtgen, Stefan

Moreover, different types of investments, i.e. investments with a different cost/return policy, had a varying success rate, depending on the cost intensity and the impact of the measures implemented by the host states. CSP plants due to their high upfront investments have been shown to enjoy a higher degree of protection, whereas PV investments seemed to have suffered less under the regulatory changes.

3) Key Considerations for the Forthcoming Analysis

Despite the different outcomes, it must still be examined whether the tribunals only subsumed the facts of the case differently, but actually applied uniform legal principles. Thereby, some key questions can be identified which need to be answered in a more thorough analysis of the arbitral jurisprudence:

The main issue in most cases related to the question of how specific and clear the conduct of the state must be, in order to give rise to legitimate expectations. Does the registration with a state authority suffice to secure rights protected by the notion of legitimate expectations or must the state's conduct demonstrate a higher degree of consideration? Moreover, have the tribunals demonstrated different levels of acceptance of the legal framework serving as grounds for legitimate expectations?

Subsequently, the connection between the level of due diligence and the specificity of the state's conduct needs to be examined: How much due diligence must an investor carry out under the backdrop of the legal framework prevailing at the time of the investment and the specific commitments of the host state?

Wirtgen, Gisela Wirtgen and JSW Solar (zwei) GmbH & Co. KG v. Czech Republic, Award, 11 October 2017 PCA Case No. 2014-03, para. 425, 437; I.C.W. Europe Investments Limited v. The Czech Republic, Award, 15 May 2019 PCA CASE No 2014-22, para. 536; WA Investments-Europa Nova Limited v. The Czech Republic, Award, 15 May 2019 PCA CASE No 2014-19, para. 577; Photovoltaik Knopf Betriebs-GmbH v. The Czech Republic, Award, 15 May 2019 PCA CASE No 2014-21, para. 490; Voltaic Network GmbH v. Czech Republic, Award, 15 September 2019 PCA CASE No 2014-20, para. 494. Also, the Spanish cases show a similar tendency, in which the tribunals found that the state's commitment guaranteed only a reasonable and not the specific return under the original support scheme, Stadtwerke München GmbH and others v. Kingdom of Spain, Award, 2 December 2019 ICSID Case No. ARB/15/1, para. 275, 354; The PV Investors v. Kingdom of Spain Final, Award, 28 February 2020 PCA Case No. 2012-14, para. 754, 847. *See also* Ch. 3 III 3) b).

Another major aspect becoming evident is the impact of the regulatory changes on the revenue of the investment overall. In cases in which the investors still received a "reasonable" or a "fair" return, tribunals were reluctant to find legitimate expectations have been violated.[946] This raises the questions of how severe the impact on the economic viability of the investment and how drastic the changes implemented by the host state have to be.

Thus, the different forms of commitment, the due diligence requirement under international law, and the degree of allowed changes need to be examined in detail, in the following in-depth analysis of the present and the prior case law.

---

946 Antaris Solar and Dr. Michael Göde v. Czech Republic, Award, 2 May 2018 PCA Case No. 2014-01, para. 440; Jürgen Wirtgen, Stefan Wirtgen, Gisela Wirtgen and JSW Solar (zwei) GmbH & Co. KG v. Czech Republic, Award, 11 October 2017 PCA Case No. 2014-03, para. 425, 437; I.C.W. Europe Investments Limited v. The Czech Republic, Award, 15 May 2019 PCA CASE No 2014-22, para. 536; WA Investments-Europa Nova Limited v. The Czech Republic, Award, 15 May 2019 PCA CASE No 2014-19, para. 577; Photovoltaik Knopf Betriebs-GmbH v. The Czech Republic, Award, 15 May 2019 PCA CASE No 2014-21, para. 490; Voltaic Network GmbH v. Czech Republic, Award, 15 September 2019 PCA CASE No 2014-20, para. 494; Stadtwerke München GmbH and others v. Kingdom of Spain, Award, 2 December 2019 ICSID Case No. ARB/15/1, para. 354; The PV Investors v. Kingdom of Spain Final, Award, 28 February 2020 PCA Case No. 2012-14, para. 754, 847; SunReserve Luxco Holdings v. Italian Republic Final, Award, 25 March 2020 SCC Arbitration V (2016/32), para. 871.

Chapter 4: Analysis of the Case Law Involving Legitimate Expectations

In Chapter 2 it was made clear that the right to regulate results from state sovereignty. Regulatory flexibility can therefore only be limited, if the state voluntarily restricts itself through international treaties.[947] Such self-imposed restrictions can be placed by making a commitment that the state will not exercise its right to regulate in a way, which is detrimental to the investment.[948] However, investors can only rely on the state's commitment, if they have themselves applied an appropriate level of due diligence.[949] In order to find a violation of the FET standard, those legitimate expectations of the investor must then have been breached.

Hence, based on the open questions identified in Chapter 3[950], the approach to the analysis of the case law must be an assessment of (1) the commitments that are able to limit the state's right to regulate, (2) the level of due diligence an investor is required to conduct under international investment law, and (3) the impact regulatory changes are allowed to have on the investments in light of the assurances given through commitments. The objective of the analysis is to identify abstract rules and not to evaluate the findings of the individual tribunals in the context of the respective state conduct.

I. Restrictions of the Right to Regulate through Commitments

The commitment on the part of states is the most fundamental factor when it comes to self-imposed restrictions of the right to regulate.[951] It is accepted that the state can always modify its legislative regime, particu-

947 *See* Ch. 2 IV 1).

948 Coop and Seif, *ECT and State's Right to Regulate*, para. 10.02; ADC Affiliate Limited and ADC & ADMC Management Limited v. The Republic of Hungary, Award, 2 October 2016 ICSID Case No. ARB/03/16, para. 423.

949 Dolzer and Schreuer, *Principles of International Investment Law*, p. 145; Kläger, 'Fair and Equitable Treatment A Look at the Theoretical Underpinnings of Legitimacy and Fairness', p. 441.

950 *See* Ch. 3 IV.

951 *See* Ch. 2 IV 1 b).

larly if in the public interest.[952] However, if the state committed itself to maintain a certain legal situation or refrain from implementing adverse changes, the legitimate expectations of the investors will generally restrict the right to regulate.[953] In general, commitments bar states from enacting any measures which infringe upon the investors' rights within the scope of the expectations.[954] This notwithstanding, not every act of the state or representation by its officials constitutes a commitment sufficient to create legitimate expectations. When assessing whether the state commitment was capable of creating legitimate expectations, the benchmark for the host state's actions is international law, i.e. investment law, and not domestic rules and obligations.[955] Contractual agreements, specific administrative measures, unilateral official declarations, informal and general representations, and the regulatory framework can be identified as the principal sources of expectations.[956]

However, not all of those sources are equally accepted by the jurisprudence in investment law. Additionally, even if the sources are deemed sufficient to create legitimate expectations, different tribunals have given different weight to them in their analyses. Thus, it remains to be examined what threshold the states' conduct must meet or surpass, in order to be reasonably relied on by investors, and what legal effect the different sources are given.

---

952 Rusoro Mining Ltd. v. Bolivarian Republic of Venezuela, Award, 22 August 2016 ICSID Case No. ARB(AF)/12/5, para. 525; El Paso Energy International Company v. The Argentine Republic, Award, 31 October 2011 ICSID Case No. ARB/03/15, para. 365; International Thunderbird Gaming Corporation v. The United Mexican States, Award, 26 January 2006 UNCITRAL, para. 127; Mann, 'The Right of States to Regulate and International Investment Law', p. 5.

953 Dolzer and Schreuer, *Principles of International Investment Law*, p. 145; Isolux Netherlands, BV v. Kingdom of Spain, Dissenting Opinion Guido Santiago Tawil, 17 July 2016 SCC Case V2013/153, para. 9.

954 Dolzer and Schreuer, *Principles of International Investment Law*, p. 145; Isolux Netherlands, BV v. Kingdom of Spain, Dissenting Opinion Guido Santiago Tawil, 17 July 2016 SCC Case V2013/153, para. 9.

955 Charanne and Construction Investments v. Kingdom of Spain, Award, 21 January 2016 SCC Case No. V 062/2012, para. 510.

956 *See* Ch. 2 III 2). *See also* NextEra Energy Global Holdings B.V. and NextEra Energy Spain Holdings B.V. v. Kingdom of Spain, Decision on Jurisdiction, Liability and Quantum Principles, 12 March 2019 ICSID Case No. ARB/14/11, para. 588.

1) Specific Commitments by the Host State

In general, undertakings and representations made explicitly or implicitly by the host state are the strongest basis for legitimate expectations.[957] Although there is no general definition of what constitutes a specific commitment, there can be two types of specificity identified: With regard to the addressee of the commitment, as well as its object and purpose.[958] The basic rule has been outlined that the more specific and unambiguous state representations are, the more an investor may rely on them.[959] Investors are entitled to legitimately rely on representations by the host state that assume a specific legal obligation for the future.[960] However, only a few of the investors in the renewable energy cases were able to rely on contractual or semi-contractual agreements, such as the GSE Conventions. The vast majority relied on confirmation letters received upon completion of a required registration process, resolutions issued by a ministry or an agency, or different types of informal administrative acts. In theory, such specific formal assurances are capable of creating legitimate expectations, if they were issued to induce investment.[961] The question, therefore, is whether those formal and also informal representations in question were sufficient to induce investment in the host states, and constitute specific commitments.

---

957 Dolzer and Schreuer, *Principles of International Investment Law*, p. 145; Levashova, *The Right of States to Regulate in International Investment Law*, p. 123; Mamidoil Jetoil Greek Petroleum Products Societe S.A. v. Republic of Albania, Award, 30 March 2015 ICSID Case No. ARB/11/24, para. 642.

958 El Paso Energy International Company v. The Argentine Republic, Award, 31 October 2011 ICSID Case No. ARB/03/15, para. 375; Mobil Exploration and Development Inc. v. The Argentine Republic, Decision on Jurisdiction and Liability, 10 April 2013 ICSID Case No. ARB/04/16, para. 957.

959 *See* Levashova, *The Right of States to Regulate in International Investment Law*, Section 6.03; Kläger, *'Fair and Equitable Treatment' in International Investment Law*, p. 187; Total S.A. v. The Argentine Republic, Decision on Liability, 27 December 2010 ICSID Case No. ARB/04/01, para. 117; Duke Energy Electroquil Partners & Electroquil S.A. v. Republic of Ecuador, Award, 18 August 2008 ICSID Case No. ARB/04/19, para. 351. *See also* Ch. 2 III 2).

960 The Tribunal in *Total* held that those commitments can be concession agreements or stabilisation clauses, Total S.A. v. The Argentine Republic, Decision on Liability, 27 December 2010 ICSID Case No. ARB/04/01, para. 117.

961 The Tribunal in *Venezuela Holdings* observed with regard thereto that "[l]egitimate expectations may result from specific formal assurances given by the host state in order to induce investment", Venezuela Holdings et. al. v. Venezuela,, Award, 9 October 2014 ICSID Case No. ARB/07/27, para. 256.

a) Registration with Administrative Authority

Registration proceedings are a common requirement in the energy sector. They allow states to monitor the number of new energy producers and to calculate the need for subsidies on this basis.[962] After going through the registration, investors usually receive confirmation about their registration and the conditions under which they will receive their FITs and FIPs, over a certain period of time. This procedure is usually supplementary or alternative to the conclusion of PPAs with each individual power plant.[963]

However, registration proceedings are relevant for the creation of legitimate expectations from an international law perspective, with regard to two particular aspects: First, it is unclear whether the simple confirmation of a successful registration constitutes a promise that the power plant is going to receive certain remuneration for a given duration or whether the actual right is derived from the underlying law.[964] If the latter were to be the case, it would make the registration confirmation simply a repetition of the law without any individual legal value. Second, the registration only takes place after the construction of the power plant is sufficiently certain.[965] Hence, in the event that the investors are constructing plants on their own, the registration confirmation will most likely be dated after the investors have already committed significant funds, i.e. the date of the investment. If so, they will not have relevance for the creation of legitimate expectations.[966]

(1) Pre-Assignment Registry and RAIPRE

Under the Spanish *Special Regime*, the Pre-Assignment Registry was a mandatory procedure power plant operators had to undergo to receive

962 RWE Innogy GmbH and RWE Innogy Aersa S.A.U. v. Kingdom of Spain, Decision on Jurisdicition, Liability, and certain Issues of Quantum, 6 January 2020 ICSID Case No. ARB/14/34, para. 544.

963 Blackaby, *Utilities, Government Regulations and Energy Investment Arbitrations*, p. 78, 79.

964 *See* Ch. 4 I 1) a) (1).

965 *See* CEF Energia B.V. v. Italian Republic, Award, 16 January 2019 SCC Arbitration No. 2015/158, para. 186, 187; SunReserve Luxco Holdings v. Italian Republic Final, Award, 25 March 2020 SCC Arbitration V (2016/32), para. 778.

966 *See* Ch. 2 II.

FITs or FIPs, introduced by RDL 6/2009.[967] The registration with the RAIPRE was then the final step that completed the registration proceeding under the Spanish *Special Regime*.[968]

With regard to the Pre-Assignment Registry, it was concluded that its sole aim was to create a further obstacle for access to the remuneration provisions of the *Special Regime* and to enable the Spanish Government to take steps to reduce the tariff deficit based on the registered plant capacities.[969] Thus, the Pre-Assignment Registry was deemed simply an administrative hurdle, which did not have the result of conferring more extensive rights than the investors already had.[970] Only one tribunal found that the registration in an official register was a "concrete and particular administrative act", which, read in conjunction with the legislative framework, incorporated specific commitments.[971]

Whereas the view of tribunals with regard to the Pre-Assignment Registry was mostly uniform, different approaches emerged when assessing the legal value of the registration confirmation with RAIPRE. A large portion of tribunals held that the final registration was simply an administrative requirement to gain grid access and sell electricity from renewable energy sources.[972] Hence, the registration did not purport any right to a

967 Article 4.2. Royal Decree Law 6/2009, 30 April 2009, on the adoption of certain measures in the energy sector and the approval of the social bond.

968 *See* Novenergia II - Energy & Environment (SCA), SICAR v. The Kingdom of Spain, Award, 15 February 2018 SCC Case No. V 2015/063, para. 79.

969 *See* Stadtwerke München GmbH and others v. Kingdom of Spain, Award, 2 December 2019 ICSID Case No. ARB/15/1, para. 300.

970 Stadtwerke München GmbH and others v. Kingdom of Spain, Award, 2 December 2019 ICSID Case No. ARB/15/1, para. 306. *See also* NextEra Energy Global Holdings B.V. and NextEra Energy Spain Holdings B.V. v. Kingdom of Spain, Decision on Jurisdiction, Liability and Quantum Principles, 12 March 2019 ICSID Case No. ARB/14/11, para. 585.

971 STEAG GmbH v. Kingdom of Spain, Decision on Jurisdiction, Liability and Directions on Quantum, 8 October 2020 ICSID Case No. ARB/15/4, para. 509, 516 (unofficial translation).

972 Charanne and Construction Investments v. Kingdom of Spain, Award, 21 January 2016 SCC Case No. V 062/2012, para. 510; NextEra Energy Global Holdings B.V. and NextEra Energy Spain Holdings B.V. v. Kingdom of Spain, Decision on Jurisdiction, Liability and Quantum Principles, 12 March 2019 ICSID Case No. ARB/14/11, para. 585; Stadtwerke München GmbH and others v. Kingdom of Spain, Award, 2 December 2019 ICSID Case No. ARB/15/1, para. 306; RWE Innogy GmbH and RWE Innogy Aersa S.A.U. v. Kingdom of Spain, Decision on Jurisdicition, Liability, and certain Issues of Quantum, 6 January 2020 ICSID Case No. ARB/14/34, para. 544; RREEF Infrastructure (G.P.) Limited and RREEF Pan-European Infrastructure Two Lux S.à.r.l. v.

pre-determined compensation. A requirement, however, is not equal to a commitment establishing rights under international investment law.[973] Thus, the registration in administrative registries, such as the Pre-Assignment Registry or the RAIPRE, would not grant any rights on its own but rather constitutes a simple condition to receive FITs or FIPs. The right to remuneration would derive directly from the legal framework underlying the support scheme and is not expanded in any way by the registration.[974] This view is supported by the purpose of the registration procedure, which is to ensure appropriate monitoring of the FITs and FIPs due to be paid under the support scheme, as well as the swift management and control of the reception of the remuneration.[975]

On the contrary, this view was considered inconsistent with Spain's contemporary representations, which assured that any future changes in the support scheme will not affect facilities that are duly registered with the RAIPRE and finished construction within the prescribed period of time.[976] Thus, a number of tribunals opined that the RAIPRE registration is an important additional element to assess the legitimate expectations of the

---

Kingdom of Spain, Decision on Responsibility and on the Principles of Quantum, 30 November 2018 ICSID Case No. ARB/13/30, para. 285; Cube Infrastructure Fund SICAV and others v. Kingdom of Spain, Decision on Jurisdiction, Liability and Partial Decision on Quantum, 19 February 2019 ICSID Case No. ARB/15/20, para. 453; 9REN Holding S.a.r.l v. Kingdom of Spain, Award, 31 March 2019 ICSID Case No. ARB/15/15, para. 346; Cavalum SGPS v. Kingdom of Spain, Decision on Jurisdiction, Liability and Directions on Quantum, 31 August 2020 ICSID Case No. ARB/15/34, para. 550.

973 RREEF Infrastructure (G.P.) Limited and RREEF Pan-European Infrastructure Two Lux S.à.r.l. v. Kingdom of Spain, Decision on Responsibility and on the Principles of Quantum, 30 November 2018 ICSID Case No. ARB/13/30, para. 285.

974 Charanne and Construction Investments v. Kingdom of Spain, Award, 21 January 2016 SCC Case No. V 062/2012, para. 509, 510; NextEra Energy Global Holdings B.V. and NextEra Energy Spain Holdings B.V. v. Kingdom of Spain, Decision on Jurisdiction, Liability and Quantum Principles, 12 March 2019 ICSID Case No. ARB/14/11, para. 584, 585.

975 RWE Innogy GmbH and RWE Innogy Aersa S.A.U. v. Kingdom of Spain, Decision on Jurisdicition, Liability, and certain Issues of Quantum, 6 January 2020 ICSID Case No. ARB/14/34, para. 544.

976 Antin Infrastructure Services Luxembourg S.à.r.l. and Antin Energia Termosolar B.V. v. Kingdom of Spain, Award, 15 June 2018 ICSID Case No. ARB/13/31, para. 552; The PV Investors v. Kingdom of Spain, Concurring and Dissenting Opinion of Charles N. Brower, 28 February 2020 PCA Case No. 2012-14, para. 16, 17.

investors.[977] The registration perfected the stabilization promise already included in the legislative framework, which guaranteed that renewable energy plants duly registered would receive the remuneration prescribed in the legal framework.[978] While it can be argued that the registration requirement is then deprived of any legal content—apart from proving that the registration proceeding was concluded successfully—it can nonetheless serve as a clarification of the legislator's intent when introducing the support scheme.[979]

(2) Ministerial Resolutions and Registration Letters

In some cases, resolutions from regional governments or ministries were sent to the plant operators alongside the Pre-Assignment or RAIPRE confirmation. These resolutions from Spanish authorities included express language that the legal framework in place at the time of the registration

977 OperaFund Eco-Invest SICAV PLC and Schwab Holding AG v. Kingdom of Spain, Award, 6 September 2019 ICSID Case No. ARB/15/36, para. 483, 484; Antin Infrastructure Services Luxembourg S.à.r.l. and Antin Energia Termosolar B.V. v. Kingdom of Spain, Award, 15 June 2018 ICSID Case No. ARB/13/31, para. 552; Masdar Solar & Wind Cooperatief U.A. v. Kingdom of Spain, Award, 16 May 2018 ICSID Case No. ARB/14/1, para. 512-520; Novenergia II - Energy & Environment (SCA), SICAR v. The Kingdom of Spain, Award, 15 February 2018 SCC Case No. V 2015/063, para. 665-667; The PV Investors v. Kingdom of Spain, Concurring and Dissenting Opinion of Charles N. Brower, 28 February 2020 PCA Case No. 2012-14, para. 16, 17; Cavalum SGPS v. Kingdom of Spain, Dissenting Opinion of David R. Haigh, 31 August 2020 ICSID Case No. ARB/15/34, para. 52.

978 OperaFund Eco-Invest SICAV PLC and Schwab Holding AG v. Kingdom of Spain, Award, 6 September 2019 ICSID Case No. ARB/15/36, para. 483, 484; Antin Infrastructure Services Luxembourg S.à.r.l. and Antin Energia Termosolar B.V. v. Kingdom of Spain, Award, 15 June 2018 ICSID Case No. ARB/13/31, para. 552; Masdar Solar & Wind Cooperatief U.A. v. Kingdom of Spain, Award, 16 May 2018 ICSID Case No. ARB/14/1, para. 512-520; Novenergia II - Energy & Environment (SCA), SICAR v. The Kingdom of Spain, Award, 15 February 2018 SCC Case No. V 2015/063, para. 665-667; The PV Investors v. Kingdom of Spain, Concurring and Dissenting Opinion of Charles N. Brower, 28 February 2020 PCA Case No. 2012-14, para. 16, 17; Cavalum SGPS v. Kingdom of Spain, Dissenting Opinion of David R. Haigh, 31 August 2020 ICSID Case No. ARB/15/34, para. 52.

979 OperaFund Eco-Invest SICAV PLC and Schwab Holding AG v. Kingdom of Spain, Award, 6 September 2019 ICSID Case No. ARB/15/36, para. 484, 485.

would apply to the respective plant.[980] They were directly addressed to the investors and included an express guarantee with regard to the FIT and the duration of the application period. Therefore, some tribunals took into consideration the uniqueness and the specificity of the letter in the context of other representations and qualified it as a specific commitment.[981]

However, this approach was not followed consistently by later tribunals. In 2010, a Ministerial Resolution was sent to plant operators upon registration, which had confirmed that all energy producers participating in the Pre-Assignment Registry are eligible to remuneration under RD 661/2007.[982] This resolution was considered not to include a commitment with individual value and was simply an informative repetition of

980 The resolution sent to the investors in *NextEra* stated, for example, that "the economic regime applicable for invoicing the power and energy fed to the grid shall be the one established by RD 661/2007", NextEra Energy Global Holdings B.V. and NextEra Energy Spain Holdings B.V. v. Kingdom of Spain, Decision on Jurisdiction, Liability and Quantum Principles, 12 March 2019 ICSID Case No. ARB/14/11, para. 178. *See also* Masdar Solar & Wind Cooperatief U.A. v. Kingdom of Spain, Award, 16 May 2018 ICSID Case No. ARB/14/1, para. 516, 517.

981 Masdar Solar & Wind Cooperatief U.A. v. Kingdom of Spain, Award, 16 May 2018 ICSID Case No. ARB/14/1, para. 520; InfraRed Environmental Infrastructure GP Limited and others v. Kingdom of Spain, Award, 2 August 2019 ICSID Case No. ARB/14/12, para. 433, 434.

982 NextEra Energy Global Holdings B.V. and NextEra Energy Spain Holdings B.V. v. Kingdom of Spain, Decision on Jurisdiction, Liability and Quantum Principles, 12 March 2019 ICSID Case No. ARB/14/11, para. 586.

the law.[983] Nonetheless, statements in writing by state officials may be regarded as proof of an underlying specific commitment.[984]

Therefore, it cannot be said with certainty that the confirmation of a successful registration already constitutes a specific commitment. However, such administrative acts can concretise and give specificity to a promise of the state, which it has given through other types of representations.

(3) The GSE Conventions and the "Tariff Recognition Letters"

The GSE Conventions were private contracts concluded between the power plant operators and the state-owned GSE, which laid down the terms of the business relationship and set out the remuneration over a certain period of time.[985] Under certain Energy Accounts, additional "Tariff Recognition Letters" were sent out by the GSE to the individual plant operators alongside the GSE Conventions, which confirmed that the right to a specific tariff would remain constant for a twenty-year period.[986]

A number of tribunals assessed the specificity of the GSE Conventions in connection with the Energy Accounts and other representations of the

983 The Tribunal in *NextEra* held that ministerial resolutions cannot guarantee the terms of the regulatory framework, if the framework itself does not contain a specific commitment, NextEra Energy Global Holdings B.V. and NextEra Energy Spain Holdings B.V. v. Kingdom of Spain, Decision on Jurisdiction, Liability and Quantum Principles, 12 March 2019 ICSID Case No. ARB/14/11, para. 586. Similarly, the Tribunal in *RREEF* out the requirement that resolutions must not be "merely an informative", i.e. repetition of the legislative framework in place or a simple collection of the applicable laws and regulation, without a promise that said framework would be maintained, RREEF Infrastructure (G.P.) Limited and RREEF Pan-European Infrastructure Two Lux S.à.r.l. v. Kingdom of Spain, Decision on Responsibility and on the Principles of Quantum, 30 November 2018 ICSID Case No. ARB/13/30, para. 396. *See also* 9REN Holding S.a.r.l v. Kingdom of Spain, Award, 31 March 2019 ICSID Case No. ARB/15/15, para. 299.

984 NextEra Energy Global Holdings B.V. and NextEra Energy Spain Holdings B.V. v. Kingdom of Spain, Decision on Jurisdiction, Liability and Quantum Principles, 12 March 2019 ICSID Case No. ARB/14/11, para. 590.

985 *See* Belenergia S.A. v. Italian Republic, Award, 6 August 2019 ICSID Case No. ARB/15/40, para. 154, 394.

986 Greentech Energy Systems A/S, NovEnergia II Energy & Environment (SCA) SICAR, and NovEnergia II Italian Portfolio SA v. Italian Republic, Award, 23 December 2018 SCC Arbitration V (2015/095), para. 127.

state and observed that they bore the hallmarks of an agreement.[987] It was found that the conclusion of the GSE Convention was characterised by a greater level of engagement between the investors and Italy through the GSE.[988] The GSE Conventions did not simply state that the FITs were recognized, but expressively required the signature of the plant operators to secure the prescribed tariffs.[989] Additionally, the fact that the GSE Conventions set forth specific tariff rates for a fixed duration of 20 years, was qualified as a "stabilisation clause or otherwise".[990] By doing so, the tribunals attributed to the GSE Conventions the character of PPAs. Even though the GSE Conventions did not bar the state from unilaterally modifying the conventions through legislation, they were considered by a number of tribunals as a binding obligation under international law.[991]

However, a portion of tribunals did not assess the GSE Conventions as single and self-standing guarantees, but viewed them in conjunction with the Energy Accounts and the GSE letters.[992] Again, the argument is raised that the promises given in the contracts simply derived from the

---

987 Greentech Energy Systems A/S, NovEnergia II Energy & Environment (SCA) SICAR, and NovEnergia II Italian Portfolio SA v. Italian Republic, Award, 23 December 2018 SCC Arbitration V (2015/095), para. 453, citing Parkerings-Compagniet AS v. Republic of Lithuania, Award, 11 September 2007 ICSID Case No. ARB/05/8, para. 332; CEF Energia B.V. v. Italian Republic, Award, 16 January 2019 SCC Arbitration No. 2015/158, para. 243.

988 CEF Energia B.V. v. Italian Republic, Award, 16 January 2019 SCC Arbitration No. 2015/158, para. 243.

989 ibid, para. 212.

990 Greentech Energy Systems A/S, NovEnergia II Energy & Environment (SCA) SICAR, and NovEnergia II Italian Portfolio SA v. Italian Republic, Award, 23 December 2018 SCC Arbitration V (2015/095), para. 466.

991 The Tribunal in *Greentech* explicitly stated that this reasoning would not change, if the GSE Conventions were to be considered simply "accessory contracts" that only reflect the underlying regulations. Even as accessory contracts, the GSE Conventions would also be specific enough for investors to form legitimate expectations, Greentech Energy Systems A/S, NovEnergia II Energy & Environment (SCA) SICAR, and NovEnergia II Italian Portfolio SA v. Italian Republic, Award, 23 December 2018 SCC Arbitration V (2015/095), para. 465. Similar, the Tribunal in *ESPF* saw the registration letters sent out by the GSE as a confirmation of the legitimacy of the investors' expectations, ESPF Beteiligungs GmbH et. al. v. Italian Republic, Award, 14 September 2020 ICSID Case No. ARB/16/5, para. 517, 527.

992 The Tribunal in *Belenergia* held that neither the 20-year term set out in the GSE Conventions nor the prohibition on unilateral changes could be qualified as an explicit promise to stability, Belenergia S.A. v. Italian Republic, Award, 6 August 2019 ICSID Case No. ARB/15/40, para. 580. SunReserve Luxco Holdings

legislative framework that automatically applied to the plants.[993] The legal framework did not need an administrative act declaring the eligibility of the support scheme to the plants.[994] The hierarchically superior LD No. 387/2003, however, only granted the right to "fair remuneration" and therefore limited what the GSE Conventions could assure.[995] Additionally, it was observed that the contractual prohibition on unilateral changes concerned the GSE and not the Italian legislator, and it could not legitimately induce expectations that the law will not be altered.[996]

Hence, there was no uniform view on whether the GSE Convention constituted a specific commitment. Nonetheless, it is worth noting that the GSE Conventions differ from the RAIPRE registration in such a way that they did not simply restate what the law already stipulated. They required the investors to print and sign the agreements in order to be eligible for the incentive tariffs for a period of twenty years.[997] Thereby, they bore the characteristics of a contractual stability obligation of the state, which is the strongest type of specific commitment. Accordingly, tribunals observed that the GSE letters and agreements left the investors in no doubt that they would not receive incentives for a period of twenty years, pursuant to private law contracts, which could not be amended unilaterally.[998]

Moreover, it is notable that some of the tribunals took into consideration the time of the investment, the issuance date of the GSE Conventions

---

v. Italian Republic Final, Award, 25 March 2020 SCC Arbitration V (2016/32), para. 641, 816.

993 SunReserve Luxco Holdings v. Italian Republic Final, Award, 25 March 2020 SCC Arbitration V (2016/32), para. 641, 816.

994 The Tribunal in *SunReserve* found that the GSE Conventions and letters, due to their simple "accessory" nature, are not capable of creating "any commitments or expectations above and beyond the administrative or public acts that they are sourced in", SunReserve Luxco Holdings v. Italian Republic Final, Award, 25 March 2020 SCC Arbitration V (2016/32), para. 641, 816, 821, 823.

995 ibid, para. 801, 803.

996 Belenergia S.A. v. Italian Republic, Award, 6 August 2019 ICSID Case No. ARB/15/40, para. 579, 580.

997 CEF Energia B.V. v. Italian Republic, Award, 16 January 2019 SCC Arbitration No. 2015/158, para. 211, 212.

998 CEF Energia B.V. v. Italian Republic, Award, 16 January 2019 SCC Arbitration No. 2015/158, para. 217; ESPF Beteiligungs GmbH et. al. v. Italian Republic, Award, 14 September 2020 ICSID Case No. ARB/16/5, para. 516, 517.

and letters.[999] They opined that the GSE Conventions and letters cannot contribute to the expectations of the investor, since the renewable energy plants still had to undergo several steps, until the right to certain remuneration crystallized.[1000] Thus, none of the communication by the GSE was able to create legitimate expectations, if the time of the investment predates the grid connection.[1001] However, communication by the GSE post-dating the investment may confirm the legitimacy of expectations based on the legal framework.[1002]

Following this line of reasoning, these types of representations may create legitimate expectations, if they resemble contractual agreements. The issuance of the letters and agreements must also pre-date the investment, i.e. must be made before investors acquire shares in a project. If they post-date the investment, they may still be considered as confirmation of the legitimacy of certain expectations conveyed by the legal framework.

(4) ERO Regulations

In contrast to the other support systems, the purchase price in the Czech Republic for electricity from renewable energy sources was determined annually by the ERO in its regulations.[1003] The regulations set out the purchase price, in accordance with a pre-determined methodology.[1004] In the case of the ERO, it becomes evident that it simply set out the FITs pursuant to the law and did not contain any independent promise of specific or even general nature. Therefore, it was concluded that the price

999 CEF Energia B.V. v. Italian Republic, Award, 16 January 2019 SCC Arbitration No. 2015/158, para. 187, 188; SunReserve Luxco Holdings v. Italian Republic Final, Award, 25 March 2020 SCC Arbitration V (2016/32), para. 777, 781.

1000 CEF Energia B.V. v. Italian Republic, Award, 16 January 2019 SCC Arbitration No. 2015/158, para. 187, 188; SunReserve Luxco Holdings v. Italian Republic Final, Award, 25 March 2020 SCC Arbitration V (2016/32), para. 777, 781.

1001 CEF Energia B.V. v. Italian Republic, Award, 16 January 2019 SCC Arbitration No. 2015/158, para. 186, 187; SunReserve Luxco Holdings v. Italian Republic Final, Award, 25 March 2020 SCC Arbitration V (2016/32), para. 778.

1002 ESPF Beteiligungs GmbH et. al. v. Italian Republic, Award, 14 September 2020 ICSID Case No. ARB/16/5, para. 516, 517.

1003 *See* Jürgen Wirtgen, Stefan Wirtgen, Gisela Wirtgen and JSW Solar (zwei) GmbH & Co. KG v. Czech Republic, Award, 11 October 2017 PCA Case No. 2014-03, para. 364, 365.

1004 *See* ibid, para. 364, 365.

decisions by the ERO are not evidence of any independent commitment by the state.[1005]

(5) Legal Value of Registration Proceedings

The examination of the different types of registration confirmations demonstrated that these acts will have greater legal value the more they bear the features of an individual agreement. If the legal framework sets out the requirements, under which an investor is eligible for remuneration and the confirmation is simply a formalistic act, such acts will most likely not have significant relevance for the determination of the investors' legitimate expectations. If they constitute more than a repetition of the law and are characterised by a greater detail of individualisation, they can nonetheless be considered a basis for the investors' reliance.

b) Informal Administrative Acts

Informal administrative acts can be informal notices or comments by state agencies and officials on a given topic.[1006] They can cover a wide variety of agency activity that is not regulated by a formal act. Similar to registration confirmations, it is unclear to what extent informal administrative acts might convey specific commitments. This is mainly due to their informal nature, which may indicate a lack of balancing considerations and intent of the state to bind itself.

The majority of the informal acts in the renewable energy cases, for example informal letters or other representations, have already been addressed in the Sections above. Such representations regularly occur in connection with formal administrative acts. Hence, current jurisprudence in the renewable energy cases does not allow for a differentiated analysis. However, it was held that informal statements made in writing by state

---

1005 Jürgen Wirtgen, Stefan Wirtgen, Gisela Wirtgen and JSW Solar (zwei) GmbH & Co. KG v. Czech Republic, Award, 11 October 2017 PCA Case No. 2014-03, para. 424; Voltaic Network GmbH v. Czech Republic, Award, 15 September 2019 PCA CASE No 2014-20, para. 463; Antaris Solar and Dr. Michael Göde v. Czech Republic, Award, 2 May 2018 PCA Case No. 2014-01, para. 438.

1006 *See* Ch. 2 III 2) d).

officials constitute evidence for state commitments.[1007] Similarly, unofficial agreements between the investors and authorities of the host state can establish legitimate expectations, when found in conjunction with legislative and official representations.[1008] Such unofficial representations do not need to be binding under domestic law. Rather, they form legally cognisable facts, which can be qualified as evidence of a representation by the host state to maintain a certain degree of stability.[1009] Nonetheless, investors must at least be able to produce written records of unofficial representations by state authorities.[1010] Moreover, a distinction must be made between written statements, which were made autonomously by the state or those which were only an answer to a query posed by the investor.[1011] An assurance, which is given autonomously, demonstrates a stronger will by the host state to bind itself, as opposed to a simple reply, which may not have grasped the full scope of the promise given. Thus, the latter type of informal act must be given less legal weight in the assessment of a specific commitment.

In the past, tribunals have elaborated on similar informal acts. For example, an *Information Memorandum*, which was circulated by Argentinian authorities when promoting the privatization of a state company, was regarded as additional evidence that the host state had induced the investment.[1012] Hence, expectations built on this *Informal Memorandum* were considered legitimate. Particular focus has been set in the assessment on the fact that the memorandum was handed out prior to the bidding process and explained the guarantees contained in the regulatory frame-

1007 NextEra Energy Global Holdings B.V. and NextEra Energy Spain Holdings B.V. v. Kingdom of Spain, Decision on Jurisdiction, Liability and Quantum Principles, 12 March 2019 ICSID Case No. ARB/14/11, para. 590.

1008 InfraRed Environmental Infrastructure GP Limited and others v. Kingdom of Spain, Award, 2 August 2019 ICSID Case No. ARB/14/12, para. 413, 423, 427.

1009 ibid, para. 427.

1010 Eskosol S.p.A. in liquidazione v. Italian Republic, Award, 4 September 2020 ICSID Case No. ARB/15/50, para. 426.

1011 NextEra Energy Global Holdings B.V. and NextEra Energy Spain Holdings B.V. v. Kingdom of Spain, Decision on Jurisdiction, Liability and Quantum Principles, 12 March 2019 ICSID Case No. ARB/14/11, para. 589.

1012 LG&E Energy Corp. LG&E Capital Corp. and LG&E International, Inc. v. The Argentine Republic, Decision on Liability, 3 October 2006 ICSID Case No. ARB/02/1, para. 50, 175; BG Group Plc. v. The Argentine Republic, Award, 24 December 2007 UNCITRAL, para. 305, 306; Sempra Energy International v. The Argentine Republic, Award, 28 September 2007 ICSID Case No. ARB/02/16, para. 110, 113.

work as part of an advertising campaign.[1013] Additionally, the host state's objection that the *Information Memorandum* was erroneous and did not reflect the intentions of the government was rejected. It was observed that it would have been the duty of the state in such a situation to clarify the erroneous misrepresentation to avoid the creation of false legitimate expectations.[1014]

A decisive factor for the legal quality of informal representations is also their clarity. Legitimate expectations can be based on informal representations, which are "definitive, unambiguous and repeated".[1015] Investors cannot, however, rely on representations that are "at best ambiguous and largely informal".[1016] This again alludes to the conclusion that the assurances of the host state must be analysed in conjunction with one another, in order to get a "full picture" of on what promises the investors based their expectations. However, representations of a more general nature made by state authorities or general investment-friendly policies announced by the host state may not be sufficiently clear and too vague to constitute a specific commitment.

To decide whether general representations can constitute a commitment, it was required that the promise of the state must be made with regard to a "substantive benefit", and that it must be "precise as to its content and clear as to its form".[1017] Legitimate expectations require, by definition, "a promise of the administration on which the [investors] rely

---

1013 Sempra Energy International v. The Argentine Republic, Award, 28 September 2007 ICSID Case No. ARB/02/16, para. 110, 113; BG Group Plc. v. The Argentine Republic, Award, 24 December 2007 UNCITRAL, para. 305, 306; LG&E Energy Corp. LG&E Capital Corp. and LG&E International, Inc. v. The Argentine Republic, Decision on Liability, 3 October 2006 ICSID Case No. ARB/02/1, para. 175.

1014 Sempra Energy International v. The Argentine Republic, Award, 28 September 2007 ICSID Case No. ARB/02/16, para. 113.

1015 Marvin Roy Feldman Karpa v. United Mexican States, Award, 16 December 2002 ICSID Case No. ARB(AF)/99/1, para. 149, with reference to Metalclad Corporation v. The United Mexican States, Award, 30 August 2000 ICSID Case No. ARB(AF)/97/1, para. 28-41.

1016 Marvin Roy Feldman Karpa v. United Mexican States, Award, 16 December 2002 ICSID Case No. ARB(AF)/99/1, para. 149, with reference to Metalclad Corporation v. The United Mexican States, Award, 30 August 2000 ICSID Case No. ARB(AF)/97/1, para. 28-41.

1017 Crystallex International Corporation v. Bolivarian Republic of Venezuela, Award, 4 April 2016 ICSID Case No. ARB(AF)/11/2, para. 547.

to assert a right that needs to be observed".[1018] Thus, the administrative acts of the state must be clearly directed at the inducement of investors by giving a certain promise.[1019]

In general, political statements have been considered to have the least legal value.[1020] Although this statement may seem counter-intuitive, two arguments can be made in favour of it. First, political statements of an individual may lack a sufficient level of consideration. Second, by their very nature, simple political statements are still susceptible to later modification or withdrawal.[1021] If the political statements are given too much weight in the assessment of the FET standard, the state's right would probably vastly be diminished.[1022] Hence, they may only contribute to the overall *leitmotiv* of the proclaimed policy of the host state, but cannot create legitimate expectations individually.

1018 PSEG Global Inc and others v. Republic of Turkey, Award, 9 January 2007 ICSID Case No. ARB/02/5, para. 241.

1019 As an example, a declaration of intent to negotiate investment contracts or statements advertising the investment-friendliness of the host state by state officials lack the specificity necessary to create any express expectations, Frontier Petroleum Services Ltd. v. The Czech Republic Final, Award, 12 November 2010, para. 468; Continental Casualty Company v. The Argentine Republic, Award, 5 September 2008 ICSID Case No. ARB/03/9, para. 252, 261. The simple policy statement of the host state to encourage and welcome investment is also insufficient to create legitimate expectations, as it lacks a promise made specifically to certain investors about the success of their project, PSEG Global Inc and others v. Republic of Turkey, Award, 9 January 2007 ICSID Case No. ARB/02/5, para. 243.

1020 El Paso Energy International Company v. The Argentine Republic, Award, 31 October 2011 ICSID Case No. ARB/03/15, para. 392; Continental Casualty Company v. The Argentine Republic, Award, 5 September 2008 ICSID Case No. ARB/03/9, para. 261(i), adding „regrettably but notoriously so".

1021 El Paso Energy International Company v. The Argentine Republic, Award, 31 October 2011 ICSID Case No. ARB/03/15, para. 395; Eskosol S.p.A. in liquidazione v. Italian Republic, Award, 4 September 2020 ICSID Case No. ARB/15/50, para. 433.

1022 The Tribunal in *El Paso* conceded that—although political statements may induce investors to invest in the host state—they did not amount to "a specific commitment to foreign investors not to modify the existing framework, which was designed to attract them" as general statements in treaties or legislation of general regulations which are due to their nature likely to evolve, El Paso Energy International Company v. The Argentine Republic, Award, 31 October 2011 ICSID Case No. ARB/03/15, para. 396.

c) Requirements for Administrative Acts to Constitute Specific Commitments

In summary of the previous Sections, the states' specific conduct can be categorised into (1) representations made in writing to the investors by state officials, (2) statements made in writing by investors to state officials that were not contradicted or disagreed with by state officials, although responded to, (3) oral statements by state officials addressed to the investor, and (4) general statements made to industry, such as advertisements.[1023]

(1) Administrative Acts and their Relation to the Legal Framework

Recent arbitral jurisprudence has demonstrated that administrative acts may only have individual legal value, if they either specify legislative promises or convey commitments that go above and beyond what can already be found in the law.

In the Italian cases, the argument was made that the prohibition of unilateral modification of the GSE Conventions simply bound the GSE itself and not the legislator.[1024] Therefore, the investors were not protected against modifications of the law, which then affected the GSE Conventions. However, prior arbitral jurisprudence already indicated that unilateral modifications of contractual undertakings by the host state require a higher degree of scrutiny, in light of the context, reasons, effects.[1025] As a rule, contractual undertakings generate legal rights.[1026] Hence expectations of the host state's compliance with these rights can be regarded as legitimate. This statement holds particularly true when the contractual agreement was issued in conformity with a legislative framework, in order to induce investment.[1027] Following this line of argument, it is comprehensible

---

1023 *See* list of representations presented by the investors in NextEra Energy Global Holdings B.V. and NextEra Energy Spain Holdings B.V. v. Kingdom of Spain, Decision on Jurisdiction, Liability and Quantum Principles, 12 March 2019 ICSID Case No. ARB/14/11, para. 588.

1024 Belenergia S.A. v. Italian Republic, Award, 6 August 2019 ICSID Case No. ARB/15/40, para. 579.

1025 Continental Casualty Company v. The Argentine Republic, Award, 5 September 2008 ICSID Case No. ARB/03/9, para. 261(iii).

1026 ibid, para. 261(iii).

1027 ibid, para. 261(iii).

that—in contrast to the repeated critique of arbitrator *Giorgio Sacerdoti*[1028] —tribunals in the Italian cases have shown a tendency to give less weight to the state's right to regulate.[1029] It was held that those amendments were simply implemented to reduce the costs of the renewable energy support scheme, without having to deal with a financial crisis that would amount to a state of necessity or *force majeure*.[1030]

In the analysis is has been shown to be most controversial whether investors may have legitimate expectations based on administrative representations once a registration process was successfully concluded. Under all reviewed jurisdictions, the renewable energy power plants must be registered with state agencies, in order to be eligible for renewable energy subsidies. Again, early arbitral jurisprudence observed that state conduct contrary to representations given in good faith to investors to induce investment can be regarded as unreasonable, and hence a violation of the investors' rights.[1031] These observations were also adopted in recent jurisprudence.[1032] Representations were considered specific commitments not only when they were addressed to a particular investor or group of investors, but also when they were "specific regarding their object and

---

1028 Greentech Energy Systems A/S, NovEnergia II Energy & Environment (SCA) SICAR, and NovEnergia II Italian Portfolio SA v. Italian Republic, Dissenting Opinion of Giorgio Sacerdoti, 23 December 2018 SCC Arbitration V (2015/095), para. 12; CEF Energia B.V. v. Italian Republic, Award, 16 January 2019 SCC Arbitration No. 2015/158, para. 247.

1029 Greentech Energy Systems A/S, NovEnergia II Energy & Environment (SCA) SICAR, and NovEnergia II Italian Portfolio SA v. Italian Republic, Award, 23 December 2018 SCC Arbitration V (2015/095), para. 451, 454; CEF Energia B.V. v. Italian Republic, Award, 16 January 2019 SCC Arbitration No. 2015/158, para. 245. The Tribunal in ESPF Beteiligungs GmbH et. al. v. Italian Republic, Award, 14 September 2020 ICSID Case No. ARB/16/5, para. 421, did not conduct a balancing act but simply assessed the extent of the host state's commitment.

1030 Greentech Energy Systems A/S, NovEnergia II Energy & Environment (SCA) SICAR, and NovEnergia II Italian Portfolio SA v. Italian Republic, Award, 23 December 2018 SCC Arbitration V (2015/095), para. 451, 454; CEF Energia B.V. v. Italian Republic, Award, 16 January 2019 SCC Arbitration No. 2015/158, para. 245.

1031 BG Group Plc. v. The Argentine Republic, Award, 24 December 2007 UNCITRAL, para. 343.

1032 Watkins Holdings S.à.r.l. and others v. Kingdom of Spain, Award, 21 January 2020 ICSID Case No. ARB/15/44, para. 598; Novenergia II - Energy & Environment (SCA), SICAR v. The Kingdom of Spain, Award, 15 February 2018 SCC Case No. V 2015/063, para. 705; Antaris Solar and Dr. Michael Göde v. Czech Republic, Dissenting Opinion, 2 May 2018 PCA Case No. 2014-01, para. 53.

purpose".[1033] Even if the qualification of administrative representations as primary sources of legitimate expectations is rejected, contemporaneous statements and actions of government officials and major stakeholders at least confirm the general understanding of the legal framework.[1034] Applying this reasoning on registration confirmations, one may conclude that they at least foster the legitimacy of the investors' expectations that renewable energy plants duly registered will not be affected by retroactive detrimental adjustments.[1035]

However, despite the above-said, the analysis revealed that recent awards demonstrate divergences in the jurisprudence as to the question of whether administrative acts accompanying the registration process bear any legal significance in the determination of the legitimate expectations of the investors.[1036] So far, tribunals have not developed a common approach as to whether registration proceedings are simply an administrative requirement to sell energy, without any further legal consequence, or whether they create legitimate expectations within the applicants, upon the conclusion of the registration process. In general, the analysis of the awards shows two main approaches: On the one hand, it is assumed that the agreements and administrative acts following the registration procedures confirm that the legal framework applies to the respective renewable energy project of the individual investor.[1037] Hence, they would constitute specific commitments. On the other hand, it is assumed that the actual promise, if there is any, derives directly from the legal framework.[1038]

1033 OperaFund Eco-Invest SICAV PLC and Schwab Holding AG v. Kingdom of Spain, Award, 6 September 2019 ICSID Case No. ARB/15/36, para. 431, citing El Paso Energy International Company v. The Argentine Republic, Award, 31 October 2011 ICSID Case No. ARB/03/15, para. 375.

1034 OperaFund Eco-Invest SICAV PLC and Schwab Holding AG v. Kingdom of Spain, Award, 6 September 2019 ICSID Case No. ARB/15/36, para. 431.

1035 ibid, para. 431.

1036 *See* Ch. 4 I 1) a) (5).

1037 Antin Infrastructure Services Luxembourg S.à.r.l. and Antin Energia Termosolar B.V. v. Kingdom of Spain, Award, 15 June 2018 ICSID Case No. ARB/13/31, para. 552; OperaFund Eco-Invest SICAV PLC and Schwab Holding AG v. Kingdom of Spain, Award, 6 September 2019 ICSID Case No. ARB/15/36, para. 483; Masdar Solar & Wind Cooperatief U.A. v. Kingdom of Spain, Award, 16 May 2018 ICSID Case No. ARB/14/1, para. 512-521; Greentech Energy Systems A/S, NovEnergia II Energy & Environment (SCA) SICAR, and NovEnergia II Italian Portfolio SA v. Italian Republic, Award, 23 December 2018 SCC Arbitration V (2015/095), para. 465, 466.

1038 Charanne and Construction Investments v. Kingdom of Spain, Award, 21 January 2016 SCC Case No. V 062/2012, para. 509, 510; NextEra Energy Global

Subsequent administrative acts would therefore only be of a clarifying nature and would not contain an independent promise. They rather confirm the intention of the legislator and may concretise the general promise of stability given in the law to the individual investor.[1039] Therefore, if a tribunal finds that the underlying legal framework does not contain a specific stabilisation commitment, certain agreements and administrative acts may also compensate for this fundamental flaw.

The answer as to which approach is more convincing is closely linked to the understanding of the legal framework of the host state, as a source for legitimate expectations. Only if tribunals hold the view that a state can commit itself by a legislative promise, may they find that auxiliary administrative acts simply clarify the scope of the promise. In contrast, tribunals that reject the view that legislative promises may constitute legitimate expectations, must engage more closely in the examination of auxiliary acts, or else investors in the energy sector would not have a realistic chance to gain protection under the FET standard.

(2) Time of the Administrative Acts

With regard to administrative registration procedures, it is persuasive that investors should not have legitimate expectations before the registration process is concluded. If a plant is built from scratch, there are a number of practical and administrative hurdles to overcome. At the time when an investor advances a large part of the funds, the investor bears a whole range of risks that may negatively influence the profitability of the investment. And it is precisely at this point that legitimate expectations are determined. No investor can legitimately expect that the respective support scheme applies with certainty, unless the construction is completed and the plant underwent a successful registration process.[1040] This is also illustrated by due diligence reports obtained by investors, which primarily spotted the risk that the plants would not be connected to the grid in time to be

Holdings B.V. and NextEra Energy Spain Holdings B.V. v. Kingdom of Spain, Decision on Jurisdiction, Liability and Quantum Principles, 12 March 2019 ICSID Case No. ARB/14/11, para. 585.

1039 ESPF Beteiligungs GmbH et. al. v. Italian Republic, Award, 14 September 2020 ICSID Case No. ARB/16/5, para. 527, 529.

1040 Blusun S.A. Jean-Pierre Lecorcier and Michael Stein v. Italian Republic, Award, 27 December 2016 ICSID Case No. ARB/14/3, para. 385, 386, 394.

eligible for the support schemes.[1041] Hence, the differentiated approach by some of the tribunals, which distinguished the value of the representations in light of the time of the investment, is particularly persuasive.[1042]

(3) Influence of the Formality of an Administrative Act

Arbitral jurisprudence attributes different legal weight to each type of state conduct. It has been shown that acts from the host state were more likely to be qualified as a specific commitment, if they were more formal and they demonstrated increased signs of consideration by the host state of the investor's circumstances.[1043] Informal administrative acts were generally perceived as supplementary to the investor's case, either by contributing to the overall picture of a specific commitment or by constituting evidence of such commitment.[1044] Although such low requirements to the formality of a commitment may raise doubts with regard to an excessive restraint of the states' right to regulate, the arbitral case law is, in general, in line with the jurisprudence of the CJEU. The CJEU has acknowledged informal statements, including sufficiently precise oral representations and by government conduct, either by itself or in combination with written assurances, as a source for the creation of legitimate expectations.[1045]

1041 *See for example* Blusun S.A. Jean-Pierre Lecorcier and Michael Stein v. Italian Republic, Award, 27 December 2016 ICSID Case No. ARB/14/3, para. 384; Eiser Infrastructure Limited and Energía Solar Luxembourg S.à.r.l. v. Kingdom of Spain, Award, 4 May 2017 ICSID Case No. ARB/13/36, para. 118; Masdar Solar & Wind Cooperatief U.A. v. Kingdom of Spain, Award, 16 May 2018 ICSID Case No. ARB/14/1, para. 359, 497.

1042 CEF Energia B.V. v. Italian Republic, Award, 16 January 2019 SCC Arbitration No. 2015/158, para. 186-189; Belenergia S.A. v. Italian Republic, Award, 6 August 2019 ICSID Case No. ARB/15/40, para. 590-593; SunReserve Luxco Holdings v. Italian Republic Final, Award, 25 March 2020 SCC Arbitration V (2016/32), para. 747, 751 779; 9REN Holding S.a.r.l v. Kingdom of Spain, Award, 31 March 2019 ICSID Case No. ARB/15/15, para. 299.

1043 *See above* Section 1 a).

1044 *See above* Section 1 b).

1045 *See* International Thunderbird Gaming Corporation v. The United Mexican States Separate Opinion of Thomas Wälde, 26 January 2006 UNCITRAL, para. 28; P. P Craig, 'Substantive Legitimate Expectations in Domestic and Community Law' (1996) 55(2) Cambridge Law Journal 289, p. 304-310.

d) Interim Conclusion on the Requirements for Administrative Acts

The analysis revealed that host states can make specific commitments both through (1) formal administrative representations or (2) informal administrative acts, which must (3) be given prior to the investment and (4) be precise to their object and purpose. With regard to informal representations, investors must demonstrate that these representations were definitive, unambiguous and repeated and they must produce at least some sort of written evidence. Purely political proclamations may attribute to the overall *leitmotiv* of the host states' conduct but may not give rise to legitimate expectations individually.

2) General Commitment by the Host State

It has been addressed above that general commitment, i.e. commitments not addressed to an individual, but rather to an unknown number of potential investors, do not fulfil the requirement of specificity.[1046] Specificity is the core aspect that gives legitimacy to the protection of certain expectations.[1047] However, it will be demonstrated in the following Sections that, in certain cases, laws or administrative acts may contain commitments, in particular, when they are specifically directed at foreign investors. The issue with general commitments is that—despite their general nature—they are usually given by state authorities and entities to induce investment. Such commitments can take the form of communication by the state of a certain investment-friendly policy to foreign investors or of implementation of a legal framework explicitly designed to attract foreign direct investment in the host state.

a) Advertisements, Reports and Authoritative Statements

States rely on foreign direct investment, in order to acquire the funds necessary to accelerate the transmission from fossil fuels to renewable

1046 *See* Ch. 2 III 2).

1047 Potestà, 'Legitimate Expectations in Investment Treaty Law: Understanding the Roots and the Limits of a Controversial Concept', p. 105; El Paso Energy International Company v. The Argentine Republic, Award, 31 October 2011 ICSID Case No. ARB/03/15, para. 375–377.

energy sources.[1048] Therefore, host states have developed an investment-friendly policy plan and communicated this policy to foreign investors. These communications may take the form of advertising campaigns or reports released by state entities elaborating on the favourable investment environment in the host state. Those measures were not addressed to specific investors, but to all potential investors in the renewable energy sector. Notwithstanding that there is—in theory—an infinite number of addressees of the representations, the actual number of potential investors in the renewable energy sector is rather limited.[1049]

(1) The Spanish "The sun can be yours" Campaign

In the Spanish renewable energy cases, an advertising campaign was the subject of repeated references from investors. In 2005, the Institute for Energy Diversification and Savings (IDAE) started the worldwide advertising campaign "The sun can be yours", through its wholly-owned private entity "InvestInSpain".[1050] From the perspective of state organisation, the IDAE is an agency of the Ministry of Energy, Tourism and Digital Agenda on which it is organically dependent.[1051] The campaign was aimed at enticing international investors. It consisted of documents and presentations, which, inter alia, emphasised that the tariffs set in RD 661/2007 would

1048 *See* Part III of the Introduction.

1049 Isolux Netherlands, BV v. Kingdom of Spain, Dissenting Opinion Guido Santiago Tawil, 17 July 2016 SCC Case V2013/153, para. 4; Charanne and Construction Investments v. Kingdom of Spain, Dissenting Opinion Guido Santiago Tawil, 21 January 2016 SCC Case No. V 062/2012, para. 8.

1050 IDAE, "El Sol puede ser suyo", 6 June 2007 and 24 May 2005. *See* InfraRed Environmental Infrastructure GP Limited and others v. Kingdom of Spain, Award, 2 August 2019 ICSID Case No. ARB/14/12, para. 24; OperaFund Eco-Invest SICAV PLC and Schwab Holding AG v. Kingdom of Spain, Award, 6 September 2019 ICSID Case No. ARB/15/36, para. 117; Novenergia II - Energy & Environment (SCA), SICAR v. The Kingdom of Spain, Award, 15 February 2018 SCC Case No. V 2015/063, para. 113; Charanne and Construction Investments v. Kingdom of Spain, Award, 21 January 2016 SCC Case No. V 062/2012, para. 102.

1051 OperaFund Eco-Invest SICAV PLC and Schwab Holding AG v. Kingdom of Spain, Award, 6 September 2019 ICSID Case No. ARB/15/36, para. 115.

remain stable for the lifetime of the power plants, and suggested returns of up to 15%.[1052]

Notwithstanding the seemingly favourable conditions promised in the advertising campaign, tribunals assessed the competence of the IDEA and observed that its authority is restricted to attracting foreign investment projects to Spain.[1053] The role of IDEA was simply technical and advisory, and hence, it did not hold any regulatory power.[1054] Therefore, it was concluded that diligent investors could have only based their expectations legitimately on the law and not "upon promotional literature about what the law says".[1055] Tribunals also considered the advertising campaign to consist of "very informal documents which can hardly be considered as commitments of the State", and "too general as to engender legitimate expectations that the legal framework would not be modified".[1056] Additionally, it was opined that the campaign, which was addressed to a general audience, lacked the specificity required.[1057]

On the other side of the spectrum, tribunals assessed the object and purpose, as well as the effect of the advertising campaign, and found it sufficient to constitute a commitment.[1058] By doing so, the advertising

1052 *See* Novenergia II - Energy & Environment (SCA), SICAR v. The Kingdom of Spain, Award, 15 February 2018 SCC Case No. V 2015/063, para. 112-118.

1053 Stadtwerke München GmbH and others v. Kingdom of Spain, Award, 2 December 2019 ICSID Case No. ARB/15/1, para. 286; Hydro Energy 1 S.A.R.L. and Hydroxana Sweden AB v. The Kingdom of Spain, Decision on Jurisdiction, Liability and Directions on Quantum, 9 March 2020 ICSID Case No. ARB/15/42, para. 663.

1054 Hydro Energy 1 S.A.R.L. and Hydroxana Sweden AB v. The Kingdom of Spain, Decision on Jurisdiction, Liability and Directions on Quantum, 9 March 2020 ICSID Case No. ARB/15/42, para. 663.

1055 Stadtwerke München GmbH and others v. Kingdom of Spain, Award, 2 December 2019 ICSID Case No. ARB/15/1, para. 287.

1056 RREEF Infrastructure (G.P.) Limited and RREEF Pan-European Infrastructure Two Lux S.à.r.l. v. Kingdom of Spain, Decision on Responsibility and on the Principles of Quantum, 30 November 2018 ICSID Case No. ARB/13/30, para. 396; Charanne and Construction Investments v. Kingdom of Spain, Award, 21 January 2016 SCC Case No. V 062/2012, para. 496, 497; The PV Investors v. Kingdom of Spain Final, Award, 28 February 2020 PCA Case No. 2012-14, para. 615.

1057 Charanne and Construction Investments v. Kingdom of Spain, Award, 21 January 2016 SCC Case No. V 062/2012, para. 496, 497.

1058 Watkins Holdings S.à.r.l. and others v. Kingdom of Spain, Award, 21 January 2020 ICSID Case No. ARB/15/44, para. 532, 553; Novenergia II - Energy & Environment (SCA), SICAR v. The Kingdom of Spain, Award, 15 February 2018 SCC Case No. V 2015/063, para. 668, 669.

campaign was taken into consideration in conjunction with other state representations. It was reasoned that the "The Sun can be all yours"-campaign, alongside policy reports, was "aimed at incentivising companies to invest heavily in the Spanish electricity sector".[1059] The campaign, therefore, contributed to the formation of legitimate expectations.[1060] The combined representations set out the *leitmotiv* of the Spanish renewable energy policy, on which the investors could rely, when interpreting the underlying regulatory regime.[1061]

In conclusion, it can be said that advertising campaigns are in principle too general to represent an independent commitment. Nevertheless, they may, under certain circumstances, be suitable for contributing to the overall picture of an existing commitment on the part of the state.[1062] In this respect, however, it must be taken into consideration which competence the advertising body holds, from the perspective of domestic law.

(2) Policy Plans Issued by the Host State

Parallel to the advertising campaigns, the IDAE published action plans for the development of renewable energies in Spain. The first of these was the Plan for Renewable Energies (PER) 2005–2010.[1063] In this publication, it

1059 Novenergia II - Energy & Environment (SCA), SICAR v. The Kingdom of Spain, Award, 15 February 2018 SCC Case No. V 2015/063, para. 668, 669.

1060 Ibid, para. 668, 669.

1061 Antin Infrastructure Services Luxembourg S.à.r.l. and Antin Energia Termosolar B.V. v. Kingdom of Spain, Award, 15 June 2018 ICSID Case No. ARB/13/31, para. 548; Novenergia II - Energy & Environment (SCA), SICAR v. The Kingdom of Spain, Award, 15 February 2018 SCC Case No. V 2015/063, para. 674; NextEra Energy Global Holdings B.V. and NextEra Energy Spain Holdings B.V. v. Kingdom of Spain, Decision on Jurisdiction, Liability and Quantum Principles, 12 March 2019 ICSID Case No. ARB/14/11, para. 587.

1062 The Tribunal in *Wirtgen* considered an advertisement presentation assessed the Czech renewable energy sector as a potential source of legitimate expectations but ultimately rejected it as the content of the presentation was too vague, Jürgen Wirtgen, Stefan Wirtgen, Gisela Wirtgen and JSW Solar (zwei) GmbH & Co. KG v. Czech Republic, Award, 11 October 2017 PCA Case No. 2014-03, para. 434.

1063 IDAE, "Plan de Energías Renovables en España (PER) 2005-2010", <https://www.idae.es/uploads/documentos/documentos_PER_2005-2010_8_de_gosto-2005_Completo.(modificacionpag_63)_Copia_2_301254a0.pdf> (accessed 3 May 2021).

was explained that the host state intended to maintain stability to induce investment.[1064] In contrast to the previous version of the policy plan, the term for the expected returns changed from "minimum rate of return" to "around 7%".[1065] Additionally, the PER 2005-2010 was explicitly referred to in RD 661/2007.[1066] The PER 2005-2010 was followed by the National Action Plan for Renewable Energy in Spain (PANER) 2011-2020.[1067] The new action plan alluded to future cost reductions to minimise the socio-economic effect of the energy transition.[1068] However, the express aim was to always guarantee a reasonable return for investors.[1069]

Based on the texts of the publications, tribunals deduced that "reasonable return" or "reasonable profitability" was the main specific commitment conveyed by the legislative framework and clarified by auxiliary

1064 The IDAE explained that the *Special Regime* should maintain "investor's confidence [...] through a stable and predictable support scheme", IDEA, PER 2005-2010, p. 17-18 (unofficial translation). *See also* Novenergia II - Energy & Environment (SCA), SICAR v. The Kingdom of Spain, Award, 15 February 2018 SCC Case No. V 2015/063, para. 105.

1065 IDEA, PER 2005–2010, p. 274. *See* OperaFund Eco-Invest SICAV PLC and Schwab Holding AG v. Kingdom of Spain, Award, 6 September 2019 ICSID Case No. ARB/15/36, para. 136.

1066 *See* Novenergia II - Energy & Environment (SCA), SICAR v. The Kingdom of Spain, Award, 15 February 2018 SCC Case No. V 2015/063, para. 103.

1067 IDAE, "Plan de Acción Nacional de Energías Renovables (PANER) 2011-2020", <https://www.acta.es/medios/leyes/PANER_2011_2020.pdf> (accessed 3 May 2021).

1068 The PANER provided that the *Special Regime* will be revised and that the reviews should "take account of cost trends associated with each technology with three objectives in mind: to see that renewable technologies become as competitive as possible with *Ordinary Regime* generation, to foster a technological development balance and to see that the remunerative scheme moves in the direction of minimising socio-economic and environmental costs", IDAE, PANER, p. 115 (unofficial translations). *See* RREEF Infrastructure (G.P.) Limited and RREEF Pan-European Infrastructure Two Lux S.à.r.l. v. Kingdom of Spain, Decision on Responsibility and on the Principles of Quantum, 30 November 2018 ICSID Case No. ARB/13/30, para. 385.

1069 In particular, the PANER stated that "remuneration amounts [...] may be modified on the basis of technological developments within the sectors, market behaviour, [...], **while always guaranteeing reasonable rates of return**", IDAE, PANER, p. 115 (unofficial translation; emphasis added). *See* RREEF Infrastructure (G.P.) Limited and RREEF Pan-European Infrastructure Two Lux S.à.r.l. v. Kingdom of Spain, Decision on Responsibility and on the Principles of Quantum, 30 November 2018 ICSID Case No. ARB/13/30, para. 383.

representations.[1070] While not all tribunals followed the reasoning that only a reasonable return was promised[1071], the plans were qualified as part of a wider scheme to "heavily incentivise" the necessary investments in the renewable energy sector of the host, on which investors could legitimately rely.[1072]

Hence, tribunals attributed them some, but not overly extensive, legal weight in the assessment of whether a commitment was made on the side of the state. This is unsurprising as these representations were specific to their object and purpose, but not specifically addressed to an individual investor. Again, the analysis shows that policy plans, as general representations, may give rise to expectations in conjunction with other assurances, but are not capable of constituting a specific commitment on their own.

(3) The CNE Reports & Statements

The CNE existed between 1999 and 2013 and was established as the regulator of the energy sector under EL 54/1997.[1073] The CNE repeatedly issued public reports (CNE Reports), which commented on the legislative development of the *Special Regime*, indicated a certain degree of stability and that adjustments to the FITs would apply only to newly commissioned facilities.[1074] Additionally, representatives of the CNE had consistently stat-

---

1070 RREEF Infrastructure (G.P.) Limited and RREEF Pan-European Infrastructure Two Lux S.à.r.l. v. Kingdom of Spain, Decision on Responsibility and on the Principles of Quantum, 30 November 2018 ICSID Case No. ARB/13/30, para. 384-386; Stadtwerke München GmbH and others v. Kingdom of Spain, Award, 2 December 2019 ICSID Case No. ARB/15/1, para. 275; Watkins Holdings S.à.r.l. and others v. Kingdom of Spain, Award, 21 January 2020 ICSID Case No. ARB/15/44, para. 498; The PV Investors v. Kingdom of Spain Final, Award, 28 February 2020 PCA Case No. 2012-14, para. 596.

1071 *See* Ch. 4 III 3) c) (1).

1072 Antin Infrastructure Services Luxembourg S.à.r.l. and Antin Energia Termosolar B.V. v. Kingdom of Spain, Award, 15 June 2018 ICSID Case No. ARB/13/31, para. 545, 548; Novenergia II - Energy & Environment (SCA), SICAR v. The Kingdom of Spain, Award, 15 February 2018 SCC Case No. V 2015/063, para. 668, 669.

1073 *See* SolEs Badajoz GmbH v. Kingdom of Spain, Award, 31 July 2019 ICSID Case No. ARB/15/38, para. 102, footnote 20.

1074 *For example*, in its 3/2007 Report, the CNE observed that the *Special Regime* under RD 661/2007 "must offer sufficient guarantees to ensure that the economic incentives are stable and predictable throughout the service life of the facility", CNE, Report 3/2007 of 14 February 2007 (unoffical translation). *See*

ed in presentations that the aim of the *Special Regime* under RD 661/2007 was to ensure reasonable profitability of investments in the renewable energy sector.[1075]

Despite the favourable statements, Spain repeatedly objected that the CNE exceeded its authority by promoting the Spanish renewable energy support system to Spanish or foreign investors.[1076] Partly, it was agreed with this contention on the grounds that a reasonable investor would have understood the limited authority of the CNE.[1077] Diligent investors would not have relied upon the presentations, to the extent that it would justify any specific expectations regarding the reception of a specific remuneration.[1078] However, such a view contrasts with the already established principle in international law that the state is generally perceived as one and may not rely on international regulations as a defence.[1079] Thus, the CNE Reports were considered as a factor relevant for the determination of legitimate expectations.[1080]

In general, it was accepted that the CNE spoke in its reports and its representation in an advisory role to the government, rather than as a body that could make determinations on the relevant law.[1081] However, this role was not held to necessarily preclude the capability of the CNE to make a binding representation vis à vis investors. Those tribunals that

---

Novenergia II - Energy & Environment (SCA), SICAR v. The Kingdom of Spain, Award, 15 February 2018 SCC Case No. V 2015/063, para. 109. *See also* SolEs Badajoz GmbH v. Kingdom of Spain, Award, 31 July 2019 ICSID Case No. ARB/15/38, para. 423-425.

1075 *See* OperaFund Eco-Invest SICAV PLC and Schwab Holding AG v. Kingdom of Spain, Award, 6 September 2019 ICSID Case No. ARB/15/36, para. 118.

1076 OperaFund Eco-Invest SICAV PLC and Schwab Holding AG v. Kingdom of Spain, Award, 6 September 2019 ICSID Case No. ARB/15/36, para. 118, para. 118; RREEF Infrastructure (G.P.) Limited and RREEF Pan-European Infrastructure Two Lux S.à.r.l. v. Kingdom of Spain, Decision on Responsibility and on the Principles of Quantum, 30 November 2018 ICSID Case No. ARB/13/30, para. 367.

1077 Stadtwerke München GmbH and others v. Kingdom of Spain, Award, 2 December 2019 ICSID Case No. ARB/15/1, para. 285.

1078 ibid, para. 285.

1079 Dolzer and Schreuer, *Principles of International Investment Law*, p. 219. *See also* 2 III 2) a).

1080 Watkins Holdings S.à.r.l. and others v. Kingdom of Spain, Award, 21 January 2020 ICSID Case No. ARB/15/44, para. 527.

1081 RWE Innogy GmbH and RWE Innogy Aersa S.A.U. v. Kingdom of Spain, Decision on Jurisdicition, Liability, and certain Issues of Quantum, 6 January 2020 ICSID Case No. ARB/14/34, para. 541.

engaged in the evaluation of the reports expressed the opinion that, in the overall assessment of the legitimate expectations, the CNE's publicly stated views could not be left disregarded.[1082] Additionally, the CNE Reports and its other public statements were taken into account in the assessment of appropriate due diligence, when determining the reasonableness of the investors' reliance.[1083]

(4) The ERO Reports and Presentations

The ERO was not only in charge of setting the annual rate for FITs and Green Bonuses, but also issued explanatory reports and gave presentations.[1084] Those reports, inter alia, stated that the forthcoming Czech renewable energy support system was aimed at a stable promotion of investments and hinted at a guaranteed long-term and stable support.[1085] A number of tribunals found that official statements by government officials and from ERO bear legal weight or at least considered them as a source of legitimate expectations.[1086] This notwithstanding, they were unable to

1082 Watkins Holdings S.à.r.l. and others v. Kingdom of Spain, Award, 21 January 2020 ICSID Case No. ARB/15/44, para. 527, 551-553; RWE Innogy GmbH and RWE Innogy Aersa S.A.U. v. Kingdom of Spain, Decision on Jurisdicition, Liability, and certain Issues of Quantum, 6 January 2020 ICSID Case No. ARB/14/34, para. 533, 541, 549; Antin Infrastructure Services Luxembourg S.à.r.l. and Antin Energia Termosolar B.V. v. Kingdom of Spain, Award, 15 June 2018 ICSID Case No. ARB/13/31, para. 548; Novenergia II - Energy & Environment (SCA), SICAR v. The Kingdom of Spain, Award, 15 February 2018 SCC Case No. V 2015/063, para. 663, 667; Stadtwerke München GmbH and others v. Kingdom of Spain, Dissenting Opinion Kaj Hobér, 2 December 2019 ICSID Case No. ARB/15/1, para. 12, 14.

1083 Masdar Solar & Wind Cooperatief U.A. v. Kingdom of Spain, Award, 16 May 2018 ICSID Case No. ARB/14/1, para. 496, 498.

1084 *See* Antaris Solar and Dr. Michael Göde v. Czech Republic, Award, 2 May 2018 PCA Case No. 2014-010, para. 84-88.

1085 For a summary *see* Antaris Solar and Dr. Michael Göde v. Czech Republic, Award, 2 May 2018 PCA Case No. 2014-010, para. 123, 124; Photovoltaik Knopf Betriebs-GmbH v. The Czech Republic, Award, 15 May 2019 PCA CASE No 2014-21, para. 498.

1086 Antaris Solar and Dr. Michael Göde v. Czech Republic, Award, 2 May 2018 PCA Case No. 2014-01, para. 366, 440; Jürgen Wirtgen, Stefan Wirtgen, Gisela Wirtgen and JSW Solar (zwei) GmbH & Co. KG v. Czech Republic, Award, 11 October 2017 PCA Case No. 2014-03, para. 424, 422; I.C.W. Europe Investments Limited v. The Czech Republic, Award, 15 May 2019 PCA CASE No 2014-22, para. 554.

find any specific promise in the reports, as they were either too general or simply reiterating the content of the underlying regulatory framework.[1087] In contrast, *Gary Born* took the sum of the representations made by the ERO and other state agencies into account and concluded that they qualified due to their uniformity and continuity, as a valid basis for specific commitments.[1088]

In comparison with the CNE Reports, it can be deduced from the holdings that the creation of legitimate expectations failed primarily because of the vague content of the explanatory reports, rather than the legal classification of the reports as representations of administrative authorities. Nonetheless, they also were considered to add to the host state's policy *leitmotiv*, which was in the given case only a policy of reasonable return.

(5) Other Press Releases and Political Statements

Aside from the explanatory reports discussed above, novel legislation is often accompanied by press releases or other types of statements directly issued by state authorities to clarify the novel law's content.[1089] Tribunals assessed these press releases and concluded that they included guarantees by the Spanish State to refrain from any adjustment of tariffs, thereby

---

1087 Antaris Solar and Dr. Michael Göde v. Czech Republic, Award, 2 May 2018 PCA Case No. 2014-01, para. 366, 440; Jürgen Wirtgen, Stefan Wirtgen, Gisela Wirtgen and JSW Solar (zwei) GmbH & Co. KG v. Czech Republic, Award, 11 October 2017 PCA Case No. 2014-03, para. 424; I.C.W. Europe Investments Limited v. The Czech Republic, Award, 15 May 2019 PCA CASE No 2014-22, para. 554.

1088 Jürgen Wirtgen, Stefan Wirtgen, Gisela Wirtgen and JSW Solar (zwei) GmbH & Co. KG v. Czech Republic, Dissenting Opinion, 11 October 2017 PCA Case No. 2014-03, para. 50, 51.

1089 As an example, the enactment of RD 661/2007 was accompanied by press releases from Spanish ministries, i.e. Ministry of Industry, Tourism and Commerce, announcement of 25 May 2007 regarding RD 661/2007, "The Government prioritises profitability and stability in the new Royal Decree on renewable energy and combined heat and power" and Ministry of Energy, Official Press Release of 25 May 2007 regarding RD 661/2007, *see* RWE Innogy GmbH and RWE Innogy Aersa S.A.U. v. Kingdom of Spain, Decision on Jurisdicition, Liability, and certain Issues of Quantum, 6 January 2020 ICSID Case No. ARB/14/34, para. 174; OperaFund Eco-Invest SICAV PLC and Schwab Holding AG v. Kingdom of Spain, Award, 6 September 2019 ICSID Case No. ARB/15/36, para. 431.

qualifying them as stability commitment.[1090] A central requirement for a commitment was that these press releases must have had included representations in specific terms, and promised legal safety for investors.[1091] Statements from state authorities regarding general regulatory stability of the support scheme were not qualified as specific commitments.[1092] Additionally, the press releases must not be a simple reiteration of the underlying law but must have self-standing content.[1093] However, even if the representation did not exceed the scope of the law, some ministerial press releases were seen at least as a support for a certain understanding of the legal framework.[1094] The Tribunal in *SunReserve v. Italy* assessed various public statements made by Italian State officials and considered such general representations in theory as capable of creating legitimate expectations.[1095] Nonetheless, the Tribunal also emphasised that such state-

1090 OperaFund Eco-Invest SICAV PLC and Schwab Holding AG v. Kingdom of Spain, Award, 6 September 2019 ICSID Case No. ARB/15/36, para. 431; RWE Innogy GmbH and RWE Innogy Aersa S.A.U. v. Kingdom of Spain, Decision on Jurisdicition, Liability, and certain Issues of Quantum, 6 January 2020 ICSID Case No. ARB/14/34, para. 532, 533.

1091 *For example*, the Tribunal in *Cube* held that "a specific commitment can be found in words such as '[t]he revisions carried out in the future of the tariffs will not affect those Installations already in operation. This guarantee provides legal safety for the producer, affording stability to the sector and fostering its development'", Cube Infrastructure Fund SICAV and others v. Kingdom of Spain, Decision on Jurisdiction, Liability and Partial Decision on Quantum, 19 February 2019 ICSID Case No. ARB/15/20, para. 273, 277, 401. *See also* RREEF Infrastructure (G.P.) Limited and RREEF Pan-European Infrastructure Two Lux S.à.r.l. v. Kingdom of Spain, Decision on Responsibility and on the Principles of Quantum, 30 November 2018 ICSID Case No. ARB/13/30, para. 396.

1092 Cavalum SGPS v. Kingdom of Spain, Decision on Jurisdiction, Liability and Directions on Quantum, 31 August 2020 ICSID Case No. ARB/15/34, para. 556.

1093 RREEF Infrastructure (G.P.) Limited and RREEF Pan-European Infrastructure Two Lux S.à.r.l. v. Kingdom of Spain, Decision on Responsibility and on the Principles of Quantum, 30 November 2018 ICSID Case No. ARB/13/30, para. 396.

1094 RWE Innogy GmbH and RWE Innogy Aersa S.A.U. v. Kingdom of Spain, Decision on Jurisdicition, Liability, and certain Issues of Quantum, 6 January 2020 ICSID Case No. ARB/14/34, para. 537; BayWa r.e. Renewable Energy GmbH and BayWa r.e. Asset Holding GmbH v. Kingdom of Spain, Decision on Jurisdiction, Liability and Directions on Quantum, 2 December 2019 ICSID Case No. ARB/15/16, para. 476.

1095 SunReserve Luxco Holdings v. Italian Republic Final, Award, 25 March 2020 SCC Arbitration V (2016/32), para. 776.

ments cannot promise anything "above and beyond" the commitments conveyed in the legal framework.[1096] Therefore, the content of the general representations must build on the law and further specify its content, but may not go beyond its scope. They can, thus, only further specify a general promise, but not establish a new commitment. Last, it is required that the statements relied on by the investors must be attributable to the state, which was, inter alia, accepted when the press release was published on the competent ministry's website.[1097]

Hence, it can be deduced from the case law that press releases issued by a competent authority are generally capable of creating legitimate expectations for the investor. However, it is required that the press releases do not only reiterate the legislative's acts wording, but must serve as an explanatory tool that further defines a general promise, which is already embedded in the law.

(6) Interim Conclusion on the Potential of General Representations to Create Legitimate Expectations

The jurisprudence has demonstrated that the representations of state agencies and officials, such as policy plans, reports and press releases, play a significant role in the assessment of the legitimate expectations despite their general nature. Those representations gain importance as they provide public information on the interpretation of the general legal framework.[1098]

Taking general (political) representations into consideration, when assessing whether a commitment exists on the side of the host state, can be traced back to a series of cases.[1099] Recent tribunals aimed to base

1096 ibid, para. 699-703, 817.

1097 Cube Infrastructure Fund SICAV and others v. Kingdom of Spain, Decision on Jurisdiction, Liability and Partial Decision on Quantum, 19 February 2019 ICSID Case No. ARB/15/20, para. 277.

1098 Jürgen Wirtgen, Stefan Wirtgen, Gisela Wirtgen and JSW Solar (zwei) GmbH & Co. KG v. Czech Republic, Dissenting Opinion, 11 October 2017 PCA Case No. 2014-03, para. 62.

1099 *For example*, the Tribunal in *MTD* even assessed an informal speech of the Chilean President at an evening event, but did not give it any distinct evidential weight due to the existence of other, more specific assurances, MTD Equity Sdn. Bhd. and MTD Chile S.A. v. Republic of Chile, Award, 25 May 2004 ICSID Case No. ARB/01/7, para. 63, 166. The Tribunal in *Eastern Sugar* gave credence to newspaper interviews and statements of government officers

their decision on former jurisprudence. In particular, the qualification of political statements to have "least legal value"[1100] was construed to reject that stabilisation provisions offered in general legislation, or by informal representations, such as political announcements, may create legitimate expectations.[1101] However, such a view misinterprets the meaning of "least legal value". Political statements, albeit bearing less weight, tipped the scale in favour of the investor in several decisions.[1102]

Following the reasoning revealed in the previous Sections, it can be deduced that representations of a general nature may not be able to constitute legitimate expectations individually, but they are capable of further defining an already existing commitment on the side of the host state. More important than their categorization in "general" and "specific" or "formal" and "informal", is the question of whether a commitment was issued with the clear object of giving "a real guarantee of stability to the investor".[1103] Considering these arguments, it can be concluded that clear commitments by state officials are—as a matter of principle—capable of generating legitimate expectations.[1104] They do not need to address individual investors but can be given to a defined group of possible addressees.[1105] However, it is not the norm that general statements engender clear stability commitments. Rather, there must be a continuous and precise reiteration of the same type of commitment in different types of general statements.[1106]

---

because the contents thereof were never publicly corrected by the government, Eastern Sugar B.V. (Netherlands) v. The Czech Republic Partial, Award, 27 March 2007 SCC Case No. 088/2004, para. 244.

1100 Continental Casualty Company v. The Argentine Republic, Award, 5 September 2008 ICSID Case No. ARB/03/9, para. 261(i).

1101 Masdar Solar & Wind Cooperatief U.A. v. Kingdom of Spain, Award, 16 May 2018 ICSID Case No. ARB/14/1, para. 506, 507.

1102 *See* SolEs Badajoz GmbH v. Kingdom of Spain, Award, 31 July 2019 ICSID Case No. ARB/15/38, para. 439; InfraRed Environmental Infrastructure GP Limited and others v. Kingdom of Spain, Award, 2 August 2019 ICSID Case No. ARB/14/12, para. 428, 430.

1103 El Paso Energy International Company v. The Argentine Republic, Award, 31 October 2011 ICSID Case No. ARB/03/15, para. 375, 377.

1104 Eskosol S.p.A. in liquidazione v. Italian Republic, Award, 4 September 2020 ICSID Case No. ARB/15/50, para. 432.

1105 ibid, para. 432.

1106 El Paso Energy International Company v. The Argentine Republic, Award, 31 October 2011 ICSID Case No. ARB/03/15, para. 377; Novenergia II - Energy & Environment (SCA), SICAR v. The Kingdom of Spain, Award, 15 February 2018 SCC Case No. V 2015/063, para. 668; Cavalum SGPS v. Kingdom

This still requires that, in light of the circumstances, the object and purpose to give the investors a guarantee of stability to legitimately rely on, must be sufficiently clear. Jurisprudence demands that the stability of the regulatory regime must be the *leitmotiv* of the state's actions.[1107] As states are usually no economic participants from whom it can be expected to do advertisements, it can be argued that such statements have some weight because of their official character. However, general representations, such as advertisements and reports, must concretise the content of the underlying legal framework, without going "above and beyond" its scope.[1108] Thus, general statements, in particular advertising campaigns and explanatory reports, are in theory capable of creating legitimate expectations.[1109]

These findings illustrate the significance of the overall conduct of the state to the creation of legitimate expectations. Although one might argue that those representations were not specific enough, they nonetheless contribute heavily to the creation of expectations, if they reaffirm or further specify a commitment conveyed by the legal framework, without exceeding or contradicting said commitment.

---

of Spain, Decision on Jurisdiction, Liability and Directions on Quantum, 31 August 2020 ICSID Case No. ARB/15/34, para. 433; Eskosol S.p.A. in liquidazione v. Italian Republic, Award, 4 September 2020 ICSID Case No. ARB/15/50, para. 432; ESPF Beteiligungs GmbH et. al. v. Italian Republic, Award, 14 September 2020 ICSID Case No. ARB/16/5, para. 535.

1107 Most notably, the *Antin* Tribunal took the CNE Reports, the press releases from the competent ministry, as well as the advertisement materials into consideration and concluded that "[t]he stability of the regulatory regime for investments in the renewable energy sector was thus the *leitmotiv* of Spain's acts at the time of the Claimants' investment", Antin Infrastructure Services Luxembourg S.à.r.l. and Antin Energia Termosolar B.V. v. Kingdom of Spain, Award, 15 June 2018 ICSID Case No. ARB/13/31, para. 548. *See also* Novenergia II - Energy & Environment (SCA), SICAR v. The Kingdom of Spain, Award, 15 February 2018 SCC Case No. V 2015/063, para. 674 and Cavalum SGPS v. Kingdom of Spain, Dissenting Opinion of David R. Haigh, 31 August 2020 ICSID Case No. ARB/15/34, para. 56.

1108 SunReserve Luxco Holdings v. Italian Republic Final, Award, 25 March 2020 SCC Arbitration V (2016/32), para. 817; Jürgen Wirtgen, Stefan Wirtgen, Gisela Wirtgen and JSW Solar (zwei) GmbH & Co. KG v. Czech Republic, Award, 11 October 2017 PCA Case No. 2014-03, para. 422.

1109 *See above* Section 4 I 2) a) (2)-(4).

b) Legitimate Expectations through the Legal Framework

The legal framework is one of the most important factors in the investment question. This is particularly true for investments in the renewable energy sector, which are characterized by the long lifetime of the power plants.[1110] For such investments, a stable and predictably legal framework is necessary to recoup the high upfront costs.[1111] Accordingly, it is essential for investors that the legal framework offers sufficient stability and certainty. Consequently, investors place certain expectations on the regulatory framework. However, whether or not those expectations can be regarded as legitimate is disputed between prior and recent tribunals.

Although the argument is more complex in detail, generally two schools of thought can be identified.[1112] On the one hand, proponents of the first view are of the opinion that the legal framework is by definition designed for an indefinite number of addressees and is therefore too general to be a promise of the host state. On the other hand, proponents of the second view argue that legislative promises are nonetheless naturally capable of creating legitimate expectations. This issue first gained prominence for the first time in the cases against the Argentine Republic, in the aftermath of its financial crisis. As recent tribunals had to decide their cases on the basis of domestic support systems, the questions of whether the legal framework can create legitimate expectations moved heavily into focus again.

(1) Development during the Argentine Cases

The Argentine cases revolve around measures of the Argentine State to counter the effects of its financial crisis between 1998–2002. Most of the first generation Argentine cases have turned on the issue of stability of the regulatory framework.[1113] The Argentine government introduced

1110 Patrizia and others, *Investment Disputes Involving the Renewable Energy Industry Under the Energy Charter Treaty*, p. 47.

1111 ibid, p. 47.

1112 For an overview *see* Masdar Solar & Wind Cooperatief U.A. v. Kingdom of Spain, Award, 16 May 2018 ICSID Case No. ARB/14/1, para. 490-495.

1113 Potestà, 'Legitimate Expectations in Investment Treaty Law: Understanding the Roots and the Limits of a Controversial Concept', p. 111-112. *See* CMS Gas Transmission Company v. The Argentine Republic, Award, 21 May 2005 ICSID Case No. ARB/01/8; LG&E Energy Corp. LG&E Capital Corp. and LG&E International, Inc. v. The Argentine Republic, Decision on Liability,

a number of regulatory changes to the energy sector, in order to cope with its financial crisis. The changes abolished the automatic annual tariff adjustments of FITs with the inflation rate and set aside the tariff regime while establishing a binding renegotiation process.[1114] This adversely affected investments in the energy sector as FITs were not adjusted to the high inflation rate of the Argentine Pesos.[1115] Under the former regulatory regime, the key feature had been the establishment of a 1-to-1 fixed parity between the Pesos and the US-Dollar.[1116] Aside from the regulatory framework, investors in the Argentine energy sector also relied on licences, which were granted to them by the government by decree.[1117] Like the GSE Conventions in the recent Italian cases, the licenses could—in theory—not be unilaterally altered. Although they were qualified as part of the legislative framework, they were addressed to specific investors and were characterized by a higher degree of individualization than regular legislation.[1118]

---

3 October 2006 ICSID Case No. ARB/02/1; Enron Corporation and Ponderosa Assets, L.P. v. The Argentine Republic, Award, 22 May 2007 ICSID Case No. ARB/01/3; Metalpar S.A. and Buen Aire S.A. v. The Argentine Republic, Award, 6 June 2008 ICSID Case No. ARB/03/5, para. 186; Suez, Sociedad General de Aguas de Barcelona, S.A. and Vivendi Universal, S.A. v. The Argentine RepublicRepublic, Decision on Liability, 30 July 2010 ICSID Case No. ARB/03/19; AWG Group Ltd. v. The Argentine Republic, Decision on Liability, 30 June 2010 ICSID Case No. ARB/03/19; El Paso Energy International Company v. The Argentine Republic, Award, 31 October 2011 ICSID Case No. ARB/03/15; Mobil Exploration and Development Inc. v. The Argentine Republic, Decision on Jurisdiction and Liability, 10 April 2013 ICSID Case No. ARB/04/16.

1114 AWG Group Ltd. v. The Argentine Republic, Decision on Liability, 30 June 2010 ICSID Case No. ARB/03/19, para. 192.

1115 BG Group Plc. v. The Argentine Republic, Award, 24 December 2007 UNCITRAL, para. 17, 345.

1116 ibid, para. 17, 345.

1117 *For example* CMS Gas Transmission Company v. The Argentine Republic, Award, 21 May 2005 ICSID Case No. ARB/01/8; LG&E Energy Corp. LG&E Capital Corp. and LG&E International, Inc. v. The Argentine Republic, Decision on Liability, 3 October 2006 ICSID Case No. ARB/02/1; Enron Corporation and Ponderosa Assets, L.P. v. The Argentine Republic, Award, 22 May 2007 ICSID Case No. ARB/01/3. *See also* Potestà, 'Legitimate Expectations in Investment Treaty Law: Understanding the Roots and the Limits of a Controversial Concept', p. 112.

1118 Potestà, 'Legitimate Expectations in Investment Treaty Law: Understanding the Roots and the Limits of a Controversial Concept', p. 112.

After examining earlier arbitral jurisprudence, the Tribunal in *Metalpar v. Argentina* found that in the absence of a "bid, license, permit or contract of any kind", the investors could not have entertained legitimate expectations.[1119] This view, however, was not followed by later tribunals, which observed that the investor's expectations are legitimate, if they originated from the laws and regulations adopted by the host state.[1120] The key consideration was that the investors acted in reliance upon the legislation to a degree in which they changed their economic position as a result.[1121] Additionally, tribunals focused on the fact that the regulatory framework applicable in the Argentine cases was sector-specific and therefore less general than regular legislation.[1122] Eventually, it was observed that there are no general requirements to the specificity of a commitment, as long as they are either specifically addressed to a limited group of investors or specific regarding their object and purpose.[1123] Thus, the legal framework is not barred from becoming the basis for legitimate expectations per se.

1119 Metalpar S.A. and Buen Aire S.A. v. The Argentine Republic, Award, 6 June 2008 ICSID Case No. ARB/03/5, para. 186 (unofficial translation).

1120 Suez, Sociedad General de Aguas de Barcelona, S.A. and Vivendi Universal, S.A. v. The Argentine RepublicRepublic, Decision on Liability, 30 July 2010 ICSID Case No. ARB/03/19, para. 226; AWG Group Ltd. v. The Argentine Republic, Decision on Liability, 30 June 2010 ICSID Case No. ARB/03/19, para°226; Enron Corporation and Ponderosa Assets, L.P. v. The Argentine Republic, Award, 22 May 2007 ICSID Case No. ARB/01/3, para. 264-266; LG&E Energy Corp. LG&E Capital Corp. and LG&E International, Inc. v. The Argentine Republic, Decision on Liability, 3 October 2006 ICSID Case No. ARB/02/1, para. 162, 163. *See also* Palombino, *Fair and Equitable Treatment and the Fabric of General Principles*, p. 113-115.

1121 Suez, Sociedad General de Aguas de Barcelona, S.A. and Vivendi Universal, S.A. v. The Argentine RepublicRepublic, Decision on Liability, 30 July 2010 ICSID Case No. ARB/03/19, para. 226; AWG Group Ltd. v. The Argentine Republic, Decision on Liability, 30 June 2010 ICSID Case No. ARB/03/19, para°226.

1122 Enron Corporation and Ponderosa Assets, L.P. v. The Argentine Republic, Award, 22 May 2007 ICSID Case No. ARB/01/3, para. 264, 265; LG&E Energy Corp. LG&E Capital Corp. and LG&E International, Inc. v. The Argentine Republic, Decision on Liability, 3 October 2006 ICSID Case No. ARB/02/1, para. 175; BG Group Plc. v. The Argentine Republic, Award, 24 December 2007 UNCITRAL, para. 304-307, 310.

1123 El Paso Energy International Company v. The Argentine Republic, Award, 31 October 2011 ICSID Case No. ARB/03/15, para. 375; Mobil Exploration and Development Inc. v. The Argentine Republic, Decision on Jurisdiction and Liability, 10 April 2013 ICSID Case No. ARB/04/16, para. 955, 957.

In the assessment of the specificity of promises included in the legal framework, some of the tribunals considered the preambles of the applicable BITs.[1124] It was concluded by some tribunals that the preambles included the promise of a certain degree of stability.[1125] The legitimate expectations of the investors were then violated when the Argentine Republic completely dismantled "the very legal framework constructed to attract investors".[1126] However, not all tribunals accepted that a representation in the preamble was specific enough and expectations based thereon were misplaced.[1127] Notwithstanding, this does not imply that general laws engender any commitment at all. Rather, tribunals emphasised that legislative promises only convey reduced expectations and can only be a basis for redress in exceptional cases.[1128] Hence, the regulatory framework granting rights is not generally shielding investors from subsequent changes.[1129] Nonetheless, even in the absence of specific promises by the host state, investors may legitimately expect that the regulatory framework

---

1124 CMS Gas Transmission Company v. The Argentine Republic, Award, 21 May 2005 ICSID Case No. ARB/01/8, para. 266–284, in particular 274; Occidental Exploration and Production Company v. The Republic of Ecuador Final, Award, 1 July 2004 LCIA Case No. UN3467, para. 183, 191. *See also* Kläger, 'Fair and Equitable Treatment A Look at the Theoretical Underpinnings of Legitimacy and Fairness', p. 441.

1125 CMS Gas Transmission Company v. The Argentine Republic, Award, 21 May 2005 ICSID Case No. ARB/01/8, para. 266–284, in particular 274; Occidental Exploration and Production Company v. The Republic of Ecuador Final, Award, 1 July 2004 LCIA Case No. UN3467, para. 183, 191. *See also* Kläger, 'Fair and Equitable Treatment A Look at the Theoretical Underpinnings of Legitimacy and Fairness', p. 441.

1126 LG&E Energy Corp. LG&E Capital Corp. and LG&E International, Inc. v. The Argentine Republic, Decision on Liability, 3 October 2006 ICSID Case No. ARB/02/1, para. 132-139. *See also* Total S.A. v. The Argentine Republic, Decision on Liability, 27 December 2010 ICSID Case No. ARB/04/01, para. 168, and CMS Gas Transmission Company v. The Argentine Republic, Award, 21 May 2005 ICSID Case No. ARB/01/8, para. 274.

1127 Continental Casualty Company v. The Argentine Republic, Award, 5 September 2008 ICSID Case No. ARB/03/9, para. 258.

1128 Continental Casualty Company v. The Argentine Republic, Award, 5 September 2008 ICSID Case No. ARB/03/9, para. 261(ii); Total S.A. v. The Argentine Republic, Decision on Liability, 27 December 2010 ICSID Case No. ARB/04/01, para. 122, 129.

1129 Total S.A. v. The Argentine Republic, Decision on Liability, 27 December 2010 ICSID Case No. ARB/04/01, para. 122, 129.

will only be amended in accordance with the basic principle of economic rationality, public interest, reasonableness and proportionality.[1130]

(2) Subsequent Development

Although the jurisprudence developed in the Argentine cases was used as guidance by subsequent tribunals, the approach to the question of whether investors may base their expectations on the legal framework has not been uniform. In general, it was held that the investors' reliance can be based on various types of promises and guarantees made by the host state, including legislation, treaties, decrees, licenses, and contracts, forming legitimate expectations protected under international investment law.[1131] The violation of legitimate expectations can then be claimed if the investor demonstrates that the state acted unfairly, unreasonably or inequitably in the exercise of its legislative power.[1132]

Nonetheless, this investor-friendly view was not shared univocally in the past. With regard to amendments of the legal framework regulating the advertisement on tobacco products, the Tribunal in *Philip Morris v. Uruguay* observed that "provisions of general legislation applicable to a plurality of persons or to a category of persons do not create legitimate expectations that there will be no change in the law".[1133] However, a distinction must

1130 ibid, para. 333.

1131 *For example*, the Tribunal in *Electrabel* observed that a specific commitment, in general, is needed in order to form legitimate expectations. However, the Tribunal also noted that such specific commitment "is not always indispensable", thereby acknowledging that legitimate expectations can also stem from other, more general sources, Electrabel S.A. v. Republic of Hungary, Award, 25 November 2015 ICSID Case No. ARB/07/19, para. 7.78. Similarly, the Tribunal in *Micula* accepted that the "promise, assurance or representation may have been issued generally or specifically, but it must have created a specific and reasonable expectation in the investor", thereby shifting the focus to the individual investor, which must have been addressed by the commitment, regardless of its legal form, Ioan Micula, Viorel Micula, S.C. European Food S.A, S.C. Starmill S.R.L. and S.C. Multipack S.R.L. v. Romania, Award, 11 December 2013 ICSID Case No. ARB/05/20, para. 671. *See also* Frontier Petroleum Services Ltd. v. The Czech Republic Final, Award, 12 November 2010, para. 285

1132 Parkerings-Compagniet AS v. Republic of Lithuania, Award, 11 September 2007 ICSID Case No. ARB/05/8, para. 334, 337.

1133 Philip Morris Brands Sàrl et. al. v. Oriental Republic of Uruguay, Award, 8 July 2016 ICSID Case No. ARB/10/7, para. 426.

be drawn between a general promise of legislative stability conveyed by the legal framework and a specific guarantee made in the law of the host state. Laws, given their "general and impersonal in nature", usually leave a wide margin of discretion to the state.[1134] Thus, the legal framework may purport only vague undetermined legitimate expectations, but as long as the state does not specifically commit to guarantee a certain right, investors may not rely on receiving any specific right or treatment.[1135] Specific commitment is particularly necessary, when the measures infringing the investors' rights take the form of "commonly-used regulatory mechanisms, in pursuit of goals that had been clearly announced at the time when the investment was contemplated and made".[1136]

In sum, arbitral jurisprudence demonstrated greater reluctance to accept legitimate expectations in cases, in which investors relied on a broader and more general legal framework.

(3) Current State of Discussion

In advanced legal systems, the regulatory regime in the renewable energy sector outlines clear requirements under which a renewable energy production plant is eligible for remuneration. Usually, the regulatory framework also lays out the calculation method for remuneration.[1137] Hence, the renewable energy support system is generally highly regulated and is a central aspect of any investment decision for investors.

In the recent renewable energy cases, those tribunals, which rejected the creation of legitimate expectations based on the regulatory framework, advanced their argument mostly on the lack of specificity a promise in the law.[1138] The criticism was raised that regulatory frameworks only in-

---

1134 Crystallex International Corporation v. Bolivarian Republic of Venezuela, Award, 4 April 2016 ICSID Case No. ARB(AF)/11/2, para. 552.

1135 The Tribunal in *AES Corporation and Tau Power* considered that investments made in the context of general legislation "would require the very clearest of commitments on the part of the State to refrain from adjusting that regulatory framework in some specified manner to give rise to any expectation that an investment would be insulated from the effects of normal legal and regulatory evolution", AES Corporation and Tau Power B.V. v. Republic of Kazakhstan, Award, 1 November 2013 ICSID Case No. ARB/10/16, para. 289.

1136 ibid, para. 289.

1137 *See* Ch. 3 III 1) a), 2) a), and 3) a).

1138 *See* Blusun S.A. Jean-Pierre Lecorcier and Michael Stein v. Italian Republic, Award, 27 December 2016 ICSID Case No. ARB/14/3, para. 367, 371; Cha-

clude *erga omnes* promises, which, due to the framework's general nature, apply to every other renewable energy plant falling within its scope and therefore lacks any specificity.[1139] This criticism is further supported when comparing laws, i.e. norms of greater or lesser generality, with commitments of clear specific nature, such as promises or contractual obligations, that are individually addressed to the respective investor.[1140] Additionally, the argument is raised that legislation cannot be sufficient to create legitimate expectations to its own stability as it is subject to constant development and modification, in order to adapt to the present's challenges and can thus be changed at any time during the investment period.[1141]

Hence, in the absence of a specific commitment, the state is not bound by international law to grant certain subsidies, such as FITs and FIPs, or to maintain them unchanged once granted.[1142] The creation of legitimate expectations through the legal framework could be seen as an "excessive limitation" on the states' right to regulate their economy in accordance with the public interest.[1143] However, it is noteworthy that none of the tribunals per se rejected the idea that legitimate expectations may derive

---

ranne and Construction Investments v. Kingdom of Spain, Award, 21 January 2016 SCC Case No. V 062/2012, para. 493, 510; Jürgen Wirtgen, Stefan Wirtgen, Gisela Wirtgen and JSW Solar (zwei) GmbH & Co. KG v. Czech Republic, Award, 11 October 2017 PCA Case No. 2014-03, para. 417; Belenergia S.A. v. Italian Republic, Award, 6 August 2019 ICSID Case No. ARB/15/40, para. 580-583; WA Investments-Europa Nova Limited v. The Czech Republic, Award, 15 May 2019 PCA CASE No 2014-19, para. 548, 549.

1139 CEF Energia B.V. v. Italian Republic, Award, 16 January 2019 SCC Arbitration No. 2015/158, para. 222; Belenergia S.A. v. Italian Republic, Award, 6 August 2019 ICSID Case No. ARB/15/40, para. 580.

1140 Blusun S.A. Jean-Pierre Lecorcier and Michael Stein v. Italian Republic, Award, 27 December 2016 ICSID Case No. ARB/14/3, para. 367, 371.

1141 NextEra Energy Global Holdings B.V. and NextEra Energy Spain Holdings B.V. v. Kingdom of Spain, Decision on Jurisdiction, Liability and Quantum Principles, 12 March 2019 ICSID Case No. ARB/14/11, para. 584; RREEF Infrastructure (G.P.) Limited and RREEF Pan-European Infrastructure Two Lux S.à.r.l. v. Kingdom of Spain, Decision on Responsibility and on the Principles of Quantum, 30 November 2018 ICSID Case No. ARB/13/30, para. 245, 246.

1142 Blusun S.A. Jean-Pierre Lecorcier and Michael Stein v. Italian Republic, Award, 27 December 2016 ICSID Case No. ARB/14/3, para. 319(5); Cavalum SGPS v. Kingdom of Spain, Dissenting Opinion of David R. Haigh, 31 August 2020 ICSID Case No. ARB/15/34, para. 24.

1143 Charanne and Construction Investments v. Kingdom of Spain, Award, 21 January 2016 SCC Case No. V 062/2012, para. 493 (unofficial translation).

from the legal framework.[1144] Rather, their rejection of the investors' contention of legitimate expectations was based on the interpretation of the legislative framework, which was considered to be too general to create specific and legitimate expectations.

Numerous other tribunals and dissenters, however, held that legitimate expectations can also be based on legislative representations and do not necessarily require a specific commitment to protect specific expectations.[1145] *Gary Born* in his dissents observed that "a State may, under international law, make a binding commitment to foreign investors in its legislation, rather than in individual contracts or specific representations to individual investors".[1146] This standpoint is supplemented by political and economic arguments. Foremost, it can be argued that the purpose of a legislative framework on the promotion of a specific sector includes a commitment to stability, because otherwise investors would not be induced to invest.[1147] The stability of the legal framework is one of the major concerns of investors.[1148] Additionally, the basic principles expressed in the FET standard, such as procedural fairness, justice, and the rule of law, apply no less to democratically-enacted laws than to a state's contractual commit-

---

1144 *See for example* the caveats explicitly made in Blusun S.A. Jean-Pierre Lecorcier and Michael Stein v. Italian Republic, Award, 27 December 2016 ICSID Case No. ARB/14/3, para. 371 and Isolux Netherlands, BV v. Kingdom of Spain Final, Award, 17 July 2016 SCC Case V2013/153, para. 775.

1145 *See* Charanne and Construction Investments v. Kingdom of Spain, Dissenting Opinion Guido Santiago Tawil, 21 January 2016 SCC Case No. V 062/2012, para. 5; 9REN Holding S.a.r.l v. Kingdom of Spain, Award, 31 March 2019 ICSID Case No. ARB/15/15, para. 299; SunReserve Luxco Holdings v. Italian Republic Final, Award, 25 March 2020 SCC Arbitration V (2016/32), para. 699-703, 817; Cavalum SGPS v. Kingdom of Spain, Decision on Jurisdiction, Liability and Directions on Quantum, 31 August 2020 ICSID Case No. ARB/15/34, para. 432; ESPF Beteiligungs GmbH et. al. v. Italian Republic, Award, 14 September 2020 ICSID Case No. ARB/16/5, para. 512.

1146 Jürgen Wirtgen, Stefan Wirtgen, Gisela Wirtgen and JSW Solar (zwei) GmbH & Co. KG v. Czech Republic, Dissenting Opinion, 11 October 2017 PCA Case No. 2014-03, para. 11; Antaris Solar and Dr. Michael Göde v. Czech Republic, Dissenting Opinion, 2 May 2018 PCA Case No. 2014-01, para. 42.

1147 Jürgen Wirtgen, Stefan Wirtgen, Gisela Wirtgen and JSW Solar (zwei) GmbH & Co. KG v. Czech Republic, Dissenting Opinion, 11 October 2017 PCA Case No. 2014-03, para. 43-45.

1148 MIGA, *World investment and political risk 2013*, p. 21. *See also* Hobér and Fellenbaum, *Political Risk Insurance and Investment Treaty Protection*, p. 1520, 1521.

ments or administrative declarations.[1149] In fact, the very function of rules of law is to create areas of predictability and security and thereby allow an objective evaluation of the legislators' intent.[1150] Thus, "the distinctions between 'statutory' and 'contractual' undertakings or 'general legislation' and 'specific assurances'" would be artificial and arbitrary, regardless of whether the state's actions and statements have actually contributed to the creation of legitimate expectations.[1151] Following this line of argument, tribunals have taken into consideration the clear and detailed language included in the *Special Regime* under RD 661/2007, with particular focus set on the promise of its application for a certain period of time.[1152] It was concluded that the regulatory regime satisfied the requirements to be viewed as a commitment, which is—despite its general nature—specific enough to create legitimate expectations in investors.[1153] In a highly regulated industry, such as the renewable energy sector, and in the absence of any unclear or contradictory state representations, it can be regarded as sufficient that a regulatory regime is established "with the overt aim of attracting investments".[1154] By doing so, the host state gives potential investors "the prospect that the investments will be subject to a set of

1149 Antaris Solar and Dr. Michael Göde v. Czech Republic, Dissenting Opinion, 2 May 2018 PCA Case No. 2014-01, para. 44.

1150 BayWa r.e. Renewable Energy GmbH and BayWa r.e. Asset Holding GmbH v. Kingdom of Spain, Dissenting Opinion Horacio A. Grigera Naón, 2 December 2019 ICSID Case No. ARB/15/16, para. 6.

1151 Antaris Solar and Dr. Michael Göde v. Czech Republic, Dissenting Opinion, 2 May 2018 PCA Case No. 2014-01, para. 44.

1152 Antin Infrastructure Services Luxembourg S.à.r.l. and Antin Energia Termosolar B.V. v. Kingdom of Spain, Award, 15 June 2018 ICSID Case No. ARB/13/31, para. 552; 9REN Holding S.a.r.l v. Kingdom of Spain, Award, 31 March 2019 ICSID Case No. ARB/15/15, para. 229; Watkins Holdings S.à.r.l. and others v. Kingdom of Spain, Award, 21 January 2020 ICSID Case No. ARB/15/44, para. 527.

1153 Antin Infrastructure Services Luxembourg S.à.r.l. and Antin Energia Termosolar B.V. v. Kingdom of Spain, Award, 15 June 2018 ICSID Case No. ARB/13/31, para. 552; 9REN Holding S.a.r.l v. Kingdom of Spain, Award, 31 March 2019 ICSID Case No. ARB/15/15, para. 229; Watkins Holdings S.à.r.l. and others v. Kingdom of Spain, Award, 21 January 2020 ICSID Case No. ARB/15/44, para. 527.

1154 Cube Infrastructure Fund SICAV and others v. Kingdom of Spain, Decision on Jurisdiction, Liability and Partial Decision on Quantum, 19 February 2019 ICSID Case No. ARB/15/20, para. 388. *See also* Isolux Netherlands, BV v. Kingdom of Spain Final, Award, 17 July 2016 SCC Case V2013/153, para. 775 and ESPF Beteiligungs GmbH et. al. v. Italian Republic, Award, 14 September 2020 ICSID Case No. ARB/16/5, para. 535.

specific regulatory principles that will, as a matter of deliberate policy, be maintained in force for a finite length of time".[1155] Similar, the specificity of the context of a promise can also be relevant. If the legal framework is designed to attract investment by setting out specific requirements, which investors had to meet within a certain period of time to be eligible for certain benefits, these promises can be regarded as sufficient to create legitimate expectations.[1156] Such findings, however, are closely tied to the special role of support schemes to induce international investment. Support schemes are directed at a specific category of investors, as opposed to the indeterminate "generality", to attract investment to a specific sector of the economy.[1157] Hence, the reliance of the investors on the regulatory framework is not just a simple by-product, but the declared aim of such support schemes and are—generally—objectively reasonable.[1158] Although specific commitment gives rise to stronger and more precise expectations, legislative promises cannot be disregarded.[1159]

Nonetheless, if investors intend to rely on such general representations, they must demonstrate that they have exercised appropriate due diligence by familiarising themselves with the regulatory framework.[1160] Scepticism

1155 Cube Infrastructure Fund SICAV and others v. Kingdom of Spain, Decision on Jurisdiction, Liability and Partial Decision on Quantum, 19 February 2019 ICSID Case No. ARB/15/20, para. 388. *See also* Isolux Netherlands, BV v. Kingdom of Spain Final, Award, 17 July 2016 SCC Case V2013/153, para. 775 and ESPF Beteiligungs GmbH et. al. v. Italian Republic, Award, 14 September 2020 ICSID Case No. ARB/16/5, para. 535.

1156 The Tribunal in *ESPF* concurred that it was a sufficiently specific commitment, if the legal framework was "designed to attract investment and [was] directed at investors who made investments that met specific requirements on the relevant timeline", ESPF Beteiligungs GmbH et. al. v. Italian Republic, Award, 14 September 2020 ICSID Case No. ARB/16/5, para. 518.

1157 Isolux Netherlands, BV v. Kingdom of Spain, Dissenting Opinion Guido Santiago Tawil, 17 July 2016 SCC Case V2013/153, para. 4.

1158 Cube Infrastructure Fund SICAV and others v. Kingdom of Spain, Decision on Jurisdiction, Liability and Partial Decision on Quantum, 19 February 2019 ICSID Case No. ARB/15/20, para. 388; 9REN Holding S.a.r.l v. Kingdom of Spain, Award, 31 March 2019 ICSID Case No. ARB/15/15, para. 292-296; ESPF Beteiligungs GmbH et. al. v. Italian Republic, Award, 14 September 2020 ICSID Case No. ARB/16/5, para. 512.

1159 9REN Holding S.a.r.l v. Kingdom of Spain, Award, 31 March 2019 ICSID Case No. ARB/15/15, para. 299.

1160 The Tribunal in *Masdar* observed that "[i]f the general legislation is to be regarded as a source of an investor's legitimate expectations, the investor must demonstrate that it has exercised appropriate due diligence and that it has familiarised itself with the existing laws", Masdar Solar & Wind Cooperatief

was expressed that it may be an undue restriction of the states' right to regulate if investors could rely solely on the regulatory framework, in a manner that is protected under the FET standard.[1161] Therefore, a larger number of tribunals concluded that the legal framework may contain a general promise only in conjunction with additional affirmative acts.[1162] Hence, in order to grant investors legitimate reliance on a legislative promise, the law must be sufficiently specified through advertising or political declarations of intent or administrative statements.[1163] While registration requirements and general representations are on their own not sufficient to create legitimate expectations, they are capable of perfecting the general promise purported by the legal framework.[1164] Therefore, the

U.A. v. Kingdom of Spain, Award, 16 May 2018 ICSID Case No. ARB/14/1, para. 494.

1161 ibid, para. 494.

1162 Charanne and Construction Investments v. Kingdom of Spain, Dissenting Opinion Guido Santiago Tawil, 21 January 2016 SCC Case No. V 062/2012, para. 6; Novenergia II - Energy & Environment (SCA), SICAR v. The Kingdom of Spain, Award, 15 February 2018 SCC Case No. V 2015/063, para. 665-669; Masdar Solar & Wind Cooperatief U.A. v. Kingdom of Spain, Award, 16 May 2018 ICSID Case No. ARB/14/1, para. 512-520; OperaFund Eco-Invest SICAV PLC and Schwab Holding AG v. Kingdom of Spain, Award, 6 September 2019 ICSID Case No. ARB/15/36, para. 483; Foresight and others v. Kingdom of Spain Final, Award, 14 November 2018 SCC Case No. V 2015/150, para. 378; CEF Energia B.V. v. Italian Republic, Award, 16 January 2019 SCC Arbitration No. 2015/158, para. 222, 234; STEAG GmbH v. Kingdom of Spain, Decision on Jurisdiction, Liability and Directions on Quantum, 8 October 2020 ICSID Case No. ARB/15/4, para. 508, 520.

1163 Charanne and Construction Investments v. Kingdom of Spain, Dissenting Opinion Guido Santiago Tawil, 21 January 2016 SCC Case No. V 062/2012, para. 6; Novenergia II - Energy & Environment (SCA), SICAR v. The Kingdom of Spain, Award, 15 February 2018 SCC Case No. V 2015/063, para. 665-669; Masdar Solar & Wind Cooperatief U.A. v. Kingdom of Spain, Award, 16 May 2018 ICSID Case No. ARB/14/1, para. 512-520; OperaFund Eco-Invest SICAV PLC and Schwab Holding AG v. Kingdom of Spain, Award, 6 September 2019 ICSID Case No. ARB/15/36, para. 483; Foresight and others v. Kingdom of Spain Final, Award, 14 November 2018 SCC Case No. V 2015/150, para. 378; CEF Energia B.V. v. Italian Republic, Award, 16 January 2019 SCC Arbitration No. 2015/158, para. 222, 234; STEAG GmbH v. Kingdom of Spain, Decision on Jurisdiction, Liability and Directions on Quantum, 8 October 2020 ICSID Case No. ARB/15/4, para. 508, 520.

1164 OperaFund Eco-Invest SICAV PLC and Schwab Holding AG v. Kingdom of Spain, Award, 6 September 2019 ICSID Case No. ARB/15/36, para. 483; Antin Infrastructure Services Luxembourg S.à.r.l. and Antin Energia Termosolar B.V. v. Kingdom of Spain, Award, 15 June 2018 ICSID Case No. ARB/13/31,

question of whether domestic legislation may give rise to legitimate expectations must always be assessed by taking into account the context of the legal framework and its background.[1165] This includes official statements or other representations, which may confirm the legislator's intentions to commit to a certain conduct.[1166]

(4) Interim Conclusion on the Legal Framework's Status as Source of Legitimate Expectations in Arbitral Jurisprudence

The evaluation of case law has shown that tribunals were initially reluctant to accept the legal framework as a basis for legitimate expectations. Just like the notion of legitimate expectations, no uniform concept was developed to limit the far-reaching effect of the newly accepted trend.[1167] However, during the recent decisions, arbitral tribunals demonstrated attempts to gradually contour the concept of legislative promises.

First of all, it is to be noted that no tribunals in recently rendered decisions took the view that the legal framework may, due to its theoretically unlimited addressees, under no circumstances be the basis for legitimate expectations.[1168] While there is a broad consensus that the specificity of a commitment gives the reliance of an investor on a certain representations greater effect, it has been restated that there is no objective requirement in international law that the commitment must be specific, as opposed to a more general promise of the state.[1169] Rather, the expectations must derive from some affirmative action of the state, regardless of its form, and

---

para. 552, 554; Masdar Solar & Wind Cooperatief U.A. v. Kingdom of Spain, Award, 16 May 2018 ICSID Case No. ARB/14/1, para. 512-520; Novenergia II - Energy & Environment (SCA), SICAR v. The Kingdom of Spain, Award, 15 February 2018 SCC Case No. V 2015/063, para. 665-669.

1165 InfraRed Environmental Infrastructure GP Limited and others v. Kingdom of Spain, Award, 2 August 2019 ICSID Case No. ARB/14/12, para. 418, 430.

1166 ibid, para. 418, 430.

1167 With regard to the development of the legal framework as the basis for legitimate expecations in the "Argentine Cases", *see* Potestà, 'Legitimate Expectations in Investment Treaty Law: Understanding the Roots and the Limits of a Controversial Concept', p. 113.

1168 *See above* Ch. 4 I 2 b) (3).

1169 Antaris Solar and Dr. Michael Göde v. Czech Republic, Dissenting Opinion, 2 May 2018 PCA Case No. 2014-01, para. 45, citing Electrabel S.A. v. Republic of Hungary, Award, 25 November 2015 ICSID Case No. ARB/07/19, para. 7.78.

not from subjective considerations of the investor.[1170] As long as a legislative act is clear to its intent and purpose, there is no striking argument, that would bar an investor from placing legitimate reliance on the act. Tribunals that eventually rejected the violation of legitimate expectations based on the legislative framework did so because of reasons lying in the individual case at hand and not because of the general incapacity of the legislative promises to create expectations.[1171]

When assessing the value of the legal framework as a source of legitimate expectations, it must be borne in mind that the greater number of decisions in favour of investors have been taken in the energy sector. The energy sector is highly regulated and investors rely on the stability of the legal framework due to the structuring of their investments. Moreover, the legal framework in the energy sector typically targets only a small group of investors, who have a background in such a field of investment. This is particularly the case when the legal framework is explicitly addressed to international investors and aims at attracting FDI because the domestic market could otherwise not provide sufficient financial resources.[1172]

1170 Antin Infrastructure Services Luxembourg S.à.r.l. and Antin Energia Termosolar B.V. v. Kingdom of Spain, Award, 15 June 2018 ICSID Case No. ARB/13/31, para. 538.

1171 Some tribunals concluded that the framework in the given case was not specific enough or has been modified before, and therefore could not convey any promise to stability, *see* Belenergia S.A. v. Italian Republic, Award, 6 August 2019 ICSID Case No. ARB/15/40, para. 594, 595; Blusun S.A. Jean-Pierre Lecorcier and Michael Stein v. Italian Republic, Award, 27 December 2016 ICSID Case No. ARB/14/3, para. 371; Isolux Netherlands, BV v. Kingdom of Spain Final, Award, 17 July 2016 SCC Case V2013/153, para. 784-787. Other tribunals accepted that the legal framework may purport commitment on the side of the state, but said commitment has not been breached, *see* Jürgen Wirtgen, Stefan Wirtgen, Gisela Wirtgen and JSW Solar (zwei) GmbH & Co. KG v. Czech Republic, Award, 11 October 2017 PCA Case No. 2014-03, para. 422, 425; Antaris Solar and Dr. Michael Göde v. Czech Republic, Award, 2 May 2018 PCA Case No. 2014-01, para. 444-446; WA Investments-Europa Nova Limited v. The Czech Republic, Award, 15 May 2019 PCA CASE No 2014-19, para. 687; SunReserve Luxco Holdings v. Italian Republic Final, Award, 25 March 2020 SCC Arbitration V (2016/32), para. 871; The PV Investors v. Kingdom of Spain Final, Award, 28 February 2020 PCA Case No. 2012-14, para. 596, 638, 754; Stadtwerke München GmbH and others v. Kingdom of Spain, Award, 2 December 2019 ICSID Case No. ARB/15/1, para. 275, 282.

1172 Isolux Netherlands, BV v. Kingdom of Spain Final, Award, 17 July 2016 SCC Case V2013/153, para. 771, citing Liman Caspian Oil BV and NCL Dutch In-

Considering the narrowed scope of addressees, this gives the legislative guarantees a certain specificity.

In general, even in economic sectors in which it is apparent that the investment projects need governmental support in order to be economically viable, there is an inherent risk that successive governments will change their policy.[1173] In cases, in which the investors could have negotiated specific stability promises, they are not in need of protection by international law.[1174] If, however, the sector invested in is highly regulated and investors have no freedom for negotiations, the host states must conduct modifications of the legislative support system in "a manner which is not disproportionate to the aim of the legislative amendment".[1175] The host state must also consider the level of reliance on the side of the investors, who may have invested substantial resources on the basis of the earlier regulatory regime.[1176] This notwithstanding, general legislation only conveys reduced expectations in a context where the political risk is high.[1177] While the legislative framework and the promises entailed in it are by nature evolutionary and subject to subsequent modification, they may be the basis for legitimate expectations nonetheless. The analysis of the recent case law revealed that this holds particularly true in cases in which the legislative promises are further refined by subsequent administrative acts.[1178] Tribunals regularly assessed the legal framework in conjunction with representations of state authorities, which have added assurance in regard to the commitment of the state. It is noteworthy that most tribunals found that the auxiliary representations did not convey an individual commitment, but rather specified the legislative promise already included in the legal framework.[1179]

The distinction between a purely legislative promise and a legislative promise, further clarified by auxiliary representations, lies within the dis-

vestment BV v. Kazakhstan, Award, 22 June 2010 ICSID Case No. ARB/07/14, para. 448.

1173 Vigotop Limited v. Hungary, Award, 1 October 2014 ICSID Case No. ARB/11/22, para. 625.

1174 ibid, para. 625.

1175 Blusun S.A. Jean-Pierre Lecorcier and Michael Stein v. Italian Republic, Award, 27 December 2016 ICSID Case No. ARB/14/3, para. 319(5).

1176 ibid, para. 319(5).

1177 Continental Casualty Company v. The Argentine Republic, Award, 5 September 2008 ICSID Case No. ARB/03/9, para. 261(ii).

1178 *See* Ch. 4 I 1) c).

1179 *See* Ch. 4 I 1) c).

cretion of the authority issuing the assurance. In principle, the legislator can anticipate a discretionary decision of the administration by formulating precise criteria in advance. However, if the legislator grants the administration discretionary powers, the administration can balance the conflicting interests within the legal framework and decide on the basis of this weighting. One could consider that such a decision represents a more specific commitment than the simple application of the law. However, such a view would disregard the fact that the legislator already prejudges the balancing of interests.[1180] Thus, the legislator has already weighed the consequences and considered them to be appropriate. From this perspective, a legal commitment is not inferior to a discretionary decision by the administration.

Although the question of whether the legal framework itself can create legitimate expectations is highly controversial, the case law demonstrates that the majority of tribunals accepts the creation of expectations with concretising representations or without any specific commitment on the side of the state. Most tribunals did not focus on the form in which the commitment was given, but rather on whether the guarantee or promise was sufficiently precise in content and clear to its object, to legitimately raise expectations in investors in light of the overall circumstances.

Based on the foregoing, it can be deduced that a regulatory framework can be legitimately relied on by investors if it (1) provides very specific provisions that would apply only to certain investors, (2) contained a stability commitment, (3) is part of a wider international and domestic policy, (4) is accompanied by representations of state authorities confirming the interpretation, and (5) is aimed at attracting investments by guaranteeing a necessary benefit.[1181]

1180 This, at least, applies in cases in which the legislative framework foresees a "bound decision", i.e. sets out certain requirements and leaves no discretion to the administration whether or not the legal consequences apply to the investor's case, *see* ESPF Beteiligungs GmbH et. al. v. Italian Republic, Award, 14 September 2020 ICSID Case No. ARB/16/5, para. 518.

1181 This abstract view can also be deduced from Watkins Holdings S.à.r.l. and others v. Kingdom of Spain, Award, 21 January 2020 ICSID Case No. ARB/15/44, para. 527 and ESPF Beteiligungs GmbH et. al. v. Italian Republic, Award, 14 September 2020 ICSID Case No. ARB/16/5, para. 518-520.

3) Interim Conclusion on the Restrictions on the Right to Regulate

A number of state representations were deemed sufficient to restrict the states' right to regulate by arbitral jurisprudence over the last two decades. However, an evaluation of individual aspects with regard to support schemes established by law, has proven to be difficult. In their assessment of legitimate expectations, tribunals have considered both specific as well as general representations to be a self-imposed limitations right to regulate of the host states. Nonetheless, often were these representations reviewed in conjunction and individual evaluations have been rare.

In general, the analysis demonstrated that expectations deriving from state representations are more likely to be qualified as legitimate if the underlying commitment was formal and specific.[1182] Tribunals have also continuously taken general and informal commitments into account and assessed whether they were in their entirety sufficient to induce a diligent investor to rely on the commitments.[1183] Although such commitments might not have been persuasive individually, general and informal commitments have proved to be a supplementary factor that tipped the balancing test towards the investors in the context of more specific conduct or a greater overall policy trend in the host state.[1184]

Regarding representations made to renewable energy producers, the Tribunal in *NextEra v. Spain* found that the legal framework and the regis-

---

1182 *See* Ch. 4 I 1) d).

1183 *See* LG&E Energy Corp. LG&E Capital Corp. and LG&E International, Inc. v. The Argentine Republic, Decision on Liability, 3 October 2006 ICSID Case No. ARB/02/1, para. 50, 175; BG Group Plc. v. The Argentine Republic, Award, 24 December 2007 UNCITRAL, para. 305, 306; InfraRed Environmental Infrastructure GP Limited and others v. Kingdom of Spain, Award, 2 August 2019 ICSID Case No. ARB/14/12, para. 430.

1184 In line with recent decisions, the Tribunal in *El Paso* found that different measures, individually not violating the legitimate expectations of the investor, may accumulate to a breach of the FET standard greater overall policy trend in the host state, in particular if the investor can demonstrate "a reiteration of the same type of commitment in different types of general statements", El Paso Energy International Company v. The Argentine Republic, Award, 31 October 2011 ICSID Case No. ARB/03/15, para. 337, 517, refering to Continental Casualty Company v. The Argentine Republic, Award, 5 September 2008 ICSID Case No. ARB/03/9, para. 261. Also cited by Cavalum SGPS v. Kingdom of Spain, Decision on Jurisdiction, Liability and Directions on Quantum, 31 August 2020 ICSID Case No. ARB/15/34, para. 433.

tration on its own do not sufficiently constitute legitimate expectations.[1185] However, it was also conceded that the overall picture of the host state's conduct may allow investors to draw certain conclusions in regard to the stability of the legal framework.[1186] Such a conclusion may be that the regulatory framework would not be changed in a way that would undermine the security and viability of their investment.[1187] In contrast, a larger number of tribunals assessed the overall picture and concluded that the general commitment conveyed by the legal framework could be perfected (and specified) by the overall state conduct.[1188] Jurisprudence shows that such overall state conduct can consist, inter alia, of statements of authorities or openly communicated policy goals or administrative acts.[1189] If the

1185 NextEra Energy Global Holdings B.V. and NextEra Energy Spain Holdings B.V. v. Kingdom of Spain, Decision on Jurisdiction, Liability and Quantum Principles, 12 March 2019 ICSID Case No. ARB/14/11, para. 584.

1186 NextEra Energy Global Holdings B.V. and NextEra Energy Spain Holdings B.V. v. Kingdom of Spain, Decision on Jurisdiction, Liability and Quantum Principles, 12 March 2019 ICSID Case No. ARB/14/11, para. 594-596. *See also* InfraRed Environmental Infrastructure GP Limited and others v. Kingdom of Spain, Award, 2 August 2019 ICSID Case No. ARB/14/12, para. 427.

1187 NextEra Energy Global Holdings B.V. and NextEra Energy Spain Holdings B.V. v. Kingdom of Spain, Decision on Jurisdiction, Liability and Quantum Principles, 12 March 2019 ICSID Case No. ARB/14/11, para. 594-596. *See also* InfraRed Environmental Infrastructure GP Limited and others v. Kingdom of Spain, Award, 2 August 2019 ICSID Case No. ARB/14/12, para. 427.

1188 Novenergia II - Energy & Environment (SCA), SICAR v. The Kingdom of Spain, Award, 15 February 2018 SCC Case No. V 2015/063, para. 665-669; Masdar Solar & Wind Cooperatief U.A. v. Kingdom of Spain, Award, 16 May 2018 ICSID Case No. ARB/14/1, para. 512-520; Antin Infrastructure Services Luxembourg S.à.r.l. and Antin Energia Termosolar B.V. v. Kingdom of Spain, Award, 15 June 2018 ICSID Case No. ARB/13/31, para. 552; OperaFund Eco-Invest SICAV PLC and Schwab Holding AG v. Kingdom of Spain, Award, 6 September 2019 ICSID Case No. ARB/15/36, para. 483; Greentech Energy Systems A/S, NovEnergia II Energy & Environment (SCA) SICAR, and NovEnergia II Italian Portfolio SA v. Italian Republic, Award, 23 December 2018 SCC Arbitration V (2015/095), para. 453; CEF Energia B.V. v. Italian Republic, Award, 16 January 2019 SCC Arbitration No. 2015/158, para. 210-215, 222, 234; STEAG GmbH v. Kingdom of Spain, Decision on Jurisdiction, Liability and Directions on Quantum, 8 October 2020 ICSID Case No. ARB/15/4, para. 508, 520.

1189 Novenergia II - Energy & Environment (SCA), SICAR v. The Kingdom of Spain, Award, 15 February 2018 SCC Case No. V 2015/063, para. 665-669; Masdar Solar & Wind Cooperatief U.A. v. Kingdom of Spain, Award, 16 May 2018 ICSID Case No. ARB/14/1, para. 512-520; Antin Infrastructure Services Luxembourg S.à.r.l. and Antin Energia Termosolar B.V. v. Kingdom of Spain,

overall state conduct induced the impression in investors that they will find a stable investment environment in the host state, investors can have legitimate expectations that the regulatory framework will not be altered to a certain degree.[1190]

However, indications given by a number of general and informal commitments do not release investors from assessing the investment environment with precaution. As an example, reliance on the legal framework and the advertising campaign was not seen as sufficient, since a reasonably diligent investor could have foreseen that changes were possible through various indications.[1191] Hence, representations of weaker indicative effect, such as general or informal communication, only form additional elements on which investors may base their expectations.

Award, 15 June 2018 ICSID Case No. ARB/13/31, para. 552; OperaFund Eco-Invest SICAV PLC and Schwab Holding AG v. Kingdom of Spain, Award, 6 September 2019 ICSID Case No. ARB/15/36, para. 483; Greentech Energy Systems A/S, NovEnergia II Energy & Environment (SCA) SICAR, and NovEnergia II Italian Portfolio SA v. Italian Republic, Award, 23 December 2018 SCC Arbitration V (2015/095), para. 453; CEF Energia B.V. v. Italian Republic, Award, 16 January 2019 SCC Arbitration No. 2015/158, para. 210-215, 222, 234; STEAG GmbH v. Kingdom of Spain, Decision on Jurisdiction, Liability and Directions on Quantum, 8 October 2020 ICSID Case No. ARB/15/4, para. 508, 520.

1190 The majority in *Greentech* held with regard to the Energy Account decrees and the GSE Conventions that the "combined weight of the evidence" demonstrated a commitment on the side of the state to refrain from subsequent changes of the regulatory framework Greentech Energy Systems A/S, NovEnergia II Energy & Environment (SCA) SICAR, and NovEnergia II Italian Portfolio SA v. Italian Republic, Award, 23 December 2018 SCC Arbitration V (2015/095), para. 453. Simlarly, the Tribunal in *Antin* assessed the various types of representations by the Spanish State and used the metaphor of the *leitmotiv* to determine the overall object and purpose of the host state's actions, Antin Infrastructure Services Luxembourg S.à.r.l. and Antin Energia Termosolar B.V. v. Kingdom of Spain, Award, 15 June 2018 ICSID Case No. ARB/13/31, para. 548. *See also* Novenergia II - Energy & Environment (SCA), SICAR v. The Kingdom of Spain, Award, 15 February 2018 SCC Case No. V 2015/063, para. 674; NextEra Energy Global Holdings B.V. and NextEra Energy Spain Holdings B.V. v. Kingdom of Spain, Decision on Jurisdiction, Liability and Quantum Principles, 12 March 2019 ICSID Case No. ARB/14/11, para. 587.

1191 Charanne and Construction Investments v. Kingdom of Spain, Award, 21 January 2016 SCC Case No. V 062/2012, para. 505. *See also* Masdar Solar & Wind Cooperatief U.A. v. Kingdom of Spain, Award, 16 May 2018 ICSID Case No. ARB/14/1, para. 494.

It follows that there is no prerequisite that legitimate expectation must always be based on contractual or formal administrative guarantees.[1192] Solely the overall legal picture of the state's legal framework and its conduct must be sufficiently clear as to whether the state intends to commit to certain actions or omissions in the future.[1193]

In conclusion, the jurisprudence shows that tribunals have been measuring the legal force of state representations as commitments in accordance with the question of whether the representations were aimed at the purposeful and specific inducement of an investment. The majority of tribunals did this by assessing not only the state measures individually, but in light of the overall conduct, i.e. the state's *leitmotiv*.

II. The Due Diligence Obligation imposed by the Notion of Legitimate Expectations

In order to exercise the right of legitimate expectations, arbitral tribunals require investors to make a diligent analysis of the legal framework for the investment.[1194] This requires investors to gather all relevant information and make a reasonable business decision based on the overall investment environment prevailing in the host state at the time of the investment.[1195]

1192 *Gary Born* formulated that "[t]he decisive question is not the form of a state's representations, but whether the content and character of those representations is sufficiently clear to give rise to legitimate investor expectations that the state will abide by its commitments", Antaris Solar and Dr. Michael Göde v. Czech Republic, Dissenting Opinion, 2 May 2018 PCA Case No. 2014-01, para. 45.

1193 The Tribunal in *Novengia* found that a considerable number of investors in the renewable energy sector invested in reliance on the statements and assurances given by the host, which "could not have been clearer", Novenergia II - Energy & Environment (SCA), SICAR v. The Kingdom of Spain, Award, 15 February 2018 SCC Case No. V 2015/063, para. 667.

1194 Invesmart v. Czech Republic, Award, 26 June 2009 UNCITRAL, para. 254; Frontier Petroleum Services Ltd. v. The Czech Republic Final, Award, 12 November 2010, para. 287; Parkerings-Compagniet AS v. Republic of Lithuania, Award, 11 September 2007 ICSID Case No. ARB/05/8, para. 333; Rusoro Mining Ltd. v. Bolivarian Republic of Venezuela, Award, 22 August 2016 ICSID Case No. ARB(AF)/12/5, para. 525. *See also* UNCTAD, 'Fair and Equitable Treatment', p. 70.

1195 The Tribunal in *Frontier* concurred, "a foreign investor has to make its business decisions and shape its expectations on the basis of the law and the factual situation prevailing in the country as it stands at the moment of the invest-

Thus, the doctrine of legitimate expectations also requires a certain level of due diligence by the investors, both prior to and during the investment.[1196] The recent cases in the renewable energy sector differ in regard to the time of the investment, as well as the level of due diligence applied. Therefore, it is necessary to assess which factors the tribunals in the respective cases deemed necessary for sufficient due diligence.

1) General Standard for Due Diligence

Tribunals observed that legitimate expectations may only be violated if the regulatory measures had not been "reasonably foreseeable by a prudent investor at the time of the investment".[1197] This is generally not the case if the legal framework of the host state leaves open at least the possibility that the support system is subject to future revision and modification.[1198] Therefore, due diligence requires the investors to familiarise themselves with the regulatory legal framework and understand its application and its effect on the investment.[1199]

Arbitral jurisprudence constantly stressed the fact that the expectations of the investor cannot be analysed in the abstract nor can they be based on

---

ment", Frontier Petroleum Services Ltd. v. The Czech Republic Final, Award, 12 November 2010, para. 287. Similarly, the Tribunal in *Parkerings* observed that "[t]he investor will have a right of protection of its legitimate expectations provided it exercised due diligence and that its legitimate expectations were reasonable in light of the circumstances", Parkerings-Compagniet AS v. Republic of Lithuania, Award, 11 September 2007 ICSID Case No. ARB/05/8, para. 333.

1196 Rusoro Mining Ltd. v. Bolivarian Republic of Venezuela, Award, 22 August 2016 ICSID Case No. ARB(AF)/12/5, para. 525.

1197 Charanne and Construction Investments v. Kingdom of Spain, Award, 21 January 2016 SCC Case No. V 062/2012, para. 505 (unofficial translation). *See also* Isolux Netherlands, BV v. Kingdom of Spain Final, Award, 17 July 2016 SCC Case V2013/153, para. 781; Belenergia S.A. v. Italian Republic, Award, 6 August 2019 ICSID Case No. ARB/15/40, para. 584.

1198 Charanne and Construction Investments v. Kingdom of Spain, Award, 21 January 2016 SCC Case No. V 062/2012, para. 505. *See also* Ch. 4 III 2).

1199 Electrabel S.A. v. Republic of Hungary, Award, 25 November 2015 ICSID Case No. ARB/07/19, para. 7.78; Charanne and Construction Investments v. Kingdom of Spain, Award, 21 January 2016 SCC Case No. V 062/2012, para. 495, 505; Belenergia S.A. v. Italian Republic, Award, 6 August 2019 ICSID Case No. ARB/15/40, para. 583, 584.

the investor's subjective beliefs.[1200] Hence, a violation of the investor's legitimate expectations must be based on an objective standard, which must be assessed on a case-by-case basis.[1201] The assessment must evaluate the due diligence efforts of the investors in light of international law, i.e. the FET standard, not under domestic law.[1202] Moreover, the conclusion of the due diligence must be supported by representations made by competent authorities of the host state and must significantly estimate the level of risk before the investment is conducted.[1203]

a) The Authority Conducting the Due Diligence

In general, the arbitral jurisprudence shows a tendency to require investors to acquire external legal advice by law or consulting firms, that have experience and reputation in the host state.[1204] The Tribunal in *RWE v.*

1200 Antin Infrastructure Services Luxembourg S.à.r.l. and Antin Energia Termosolar B.V. v. Kingdom of Spain, Award, 15 June 2018 ICSID Case No. ARB/13/31, para. 536; Charanne and Construction Investments v. Kingdom of Spain, Award, 21 January 2016 SCC Case No. V 062/2012, para. 495; Belenergia S.A. v. Italian Republic, Award, 6 August 2019 ICSID Case No. ARB/15/40, para. 583, 584.

1201 Charanne and Construction Investments v. Kingdom of Spain, Award, 21 January 2016 SCC Case No. V 062/2012, para. 495; Belenergia S.A. v. Italian Republic, Award, 6 August 2019 ICSID Case No. ARB/15/40, para. 583, 584; Antin Infrastructure Services Luxembourg S.à.r.l. and Antin Energia Termosolar B.V. v. Kingdom of Spain, Award, 15 June 2018 ICSID Case No. ARB/13/31, para. 536.

1202 Cube Infrastructure Fund SICAV and others v. Kingdom of Spain, Decision on Jurisdiction, Liability and Partial Decision on Quantum, 19 February 2019 ICSID Case No. ARB/15/20, para. 401; Blusun S.A. Jean-Pierre Lecorcier and Michael Stein v. Italian Republic, Award, 27 December 2016 ICSID Case No. ARB/14/3, para. 385.

1203 Cube Infrastructure Fund SICAV and others v. Kingdom of Spain, Decision on Jurisdiction, Liability and Partial Decision on Quantum, 19 February 2019 ICSID Case No. ARB/15/20, para. 401; Blusun S.A. Jean-Pierre Lecorcier and Michael Stein v. Italian Republic, Award, 27 December 2016 ICSID Case No. ARB/14/3, para. 385.

1204 *See* inter alia Masdar Solar & Wind Cooperatief U.A. v. Kingdom of Spain, Award, 16 May 2018 ICSID Case No. ARB/14/1, para. 497; BayWa r.e. Renewable Energy GmbH and BayWa r.e. Asset Holding GmbH v. Kingdom of Spain, Decision on Jurisdiction, Liability and Directions on Quantum, 2 December 2019 ICSID Case No. ARB/15/16, para. 76; CEF Energia B.V. v. Italian Republic, Award, 16 January 2019 SCC Arbitration No. 2015/158, para. 224,

Spain considered the size of the investment and the previous experience of the investors in the Spanish renewable energy sector.[1205] It opined that the investor could not have reasonably relied on its internal lawyers' advice without charging them with a specific regulatory due diligence exercise obligation or seeking external legal expertise.[1206] Hence, the Tribunal found that internal due diligence is only sufficient if the person conducting the due diligence is legally qualified.[1207] This view, however, has been contrasted by the Tribunal in *Novenergia v. Spain*, which set the legal education of the person conducting the due diligence in proportion with the clarity of the legal framework.[1208]

Overall, it can be assumed that the requirements regarding the level of legal expertise of the authority conducting the due diligence rise with the size of the investment and the complexity of the regulatory framework in the host state.

225; SunReserve Luxco Holdings v. Italian Republic Final, Award, 25 March 2020 SCC Arbitration V (2016/32), para. 831; ESPF Beteiligungs GmbH et. al. v. Italian Republic, Award, 14 September 2020 ICSID Case No. ARB/16/5, para. 537.

1205 RWE Innogy GmbH and RWE Innogy Aersa S.A.U. v. Kingdom of Spain, Decision on Jurisdicition, Liability, and certain Issues of Quantum, 6 January 2020 ICSID Case No. ARB/14/34, para. 510. *See also* Antaris Solar and Dr. Michael Göde v. Czech Republic, Award, 2 May 2018 PCA Case No. 2014-01, para. 297, 395, 432; Cavalum SGPS v. Kingdom of Spain, Decision on Jurisdiction, Liability and Directions on Quantum, 31 August 2020 ICSID Case No. ARB/15/34, para. 472.

1206 RWE Innogy GmbH and RWE Innogy Aersa S.A.U. v. Kingdom of Spain, Decision on Jurisdicition, Liability, and certain Issues of Quantum, 6 January 2020 ICSID Case No. ARB/14/34, para. 510. *See also* Antaris Solar and Dr. Michael Göde v. Czech Republic, Award, 2 May 2018 PCA Case No. 2014-01, para. 297, 395, 432; Cavalum SGPS v. Kingdom of Spain, Decision on Jurisdiction, Liability and Directions on Quantum, 31 August 2020 ICSID Case No. ARB/15/34, para. 472.

1207 RWE Innogy GmbH and RWE Innogy Aersa S.A.U. v. Kingdom of Spain, Decision on Jurisdicition, Liability, and certain Issues of Quantum, 6 January 2020 ICSID Case No. ARB/14/34, para. 511.

1208 Novenergia II - Energy & Environment (SCA), SICAR v. The Kingdom of Spain, Award, 15 February 2018 SCC Case No. V 2015/063, para. 580, 679.

b) Shared Due Diligence

Another question arising is whether investors may share their due diligence obligation. It was accepted that the due diligence analysis may be spread among a group of companies or partners of a joint venture.[1209] Similarly, tribunals observed that it is sufficient to rely on the analysis provided by local investment banks, who did their own due diligence review.[1210]

Accordingly, the Tribunal in *Masdar v. Spain* held that, inter alia, the engagement of the investors in multiple discussions with its co-venturer, which had detailed knowledge of the regulatory framework, and extensive discussions with a consortium of seven Spanish banks, each of which conducted their own due diligence analysis, constituted, alongside external reports by law firms, proof of sufficient due diligence.[1211] With regard to associated banks, the Tribunal in *Eiser v. Spain* observed that neither the local counsel nor the local banks could identify any risk regarding any drastic changes of the legal framework, which would render the investment effectively useless.[1212]

In general, amendments to the legal framework amounting to the destruction of the investment's value were not regarded as foreseeable. With regard to the attainment of the relevant information for the due diligence analysis, it was also deemed sufficient to rely on the information provided

1209 The Tribunal in *Watkins* found it to be sufficed that the due diligence report on the Spanish legal framework was issued to a company of the same group and not to the claimant, Watkins Holdings S.à.r.l. and others v. Kingdom of Spain, Award, 21 January 2020 ICSID Case No. ARB/15/44, para. 578. The Tribunal in *Cube* concurred that it is not necessary for each joint-venture partner to conduct a due diligence analysis, Cube Infrastructure Fund SICAV and others v. Kingdom of Spain, Decision on Jurisdiction, Liability and Partial Decision on Quantum, 19 February 2019 ICSID Case No. ARB/15/20, para. 406. The Tribunal in *National Grid* also concluded that the overall due diligence can be spread amongst a consortium, National Grid P.L.C. v. The Argentine Republic, Award, 3 November 2008 UNCITRAL, para. 103.

1210 InfraRed Environmental Infrastructure GP Limited and others v. Kingdom of Spain, Award, 2 August 2019 ICSID Case No. ARB/14/12, para. 437, 438; Eiser Infrastructure Limited and Energía Solar Luxembourg S.à.r.l. v. Kingdom of Spain, Award, 4 May 2017 ICSID Case No. ARB/13/36, para. 119.

1211 Masdar Solar & Wind Cooperatief U.A. v. Kingdom of Spain, Award, 16 May 2018 ICSID Case No. ARB/14/1, para. 497.

1212 Eiser Infrastructure Limited and Energía Solar Luxembourg S.à.r.l. v. Kingdom of Spain, Award, 4 May 2017 ICSID Case No. ARB/13/36, para. 118, 119, 387.

by the bank that pre-structured the investment, as long as there no reason to suspect that the information was incorrect or outdated.[1213]

c) Proof of Due Diligence

In principle, the burden of proof lies with the investors, which must demonstrate that they properly familiarised themselves with the existing laws.[1214] Only in cases in which the investors conducted a due diligence analysis, but on a rather shallow level, tribunals have tended to find a secondary burden of proof on the side of the state.[1215] In such a case, the state has to demonstrate that a more thorough legal analysis would have produced a different understanding of the regulatory framework or the investment environment in total.[1216]

Investors must address the question of regulatory stability in their due diligence and must reach a proper understanding of the significance of the representations made by the host state by seeking expert advice.[1217] With regard to the formal requirements for due diligence analysis, it was considered beneficial for the investor's case, if the decision to invest was carefully recorded in order to prove the comprehension of the investor's

1213 OperaFund Eco-Invest SICAV PLC and Schwab Holding AG v. Kingdom of Spain, Award, 6 September 2019 ICSID Case No. ARB/15/36, para. 487.

1214 Masdar Solar & Wind Cooperatief U.A. v. Kingdom of Spain, Award, 16 May 2018 ICSID Case No. ARB/14/1, para. 494; Isolux Netherlands, BV v. Kingdom of Spain Final, Award, 17 July 2016 SCC Case V2013/153, para. 781; Belenergia S.A. v. Italian Republic, Award, 6 August 2019 ICSID Case No. ARB/15/40, para. 583, 584; SunReserve Luxco Holdings v. Italian Republic Final, Award, 25 March 2020 SCC Arbitration V (2016/32), para. 713.

1215 Cube Infrastructure Fund SICAV and others v. Kingdom of Spain, Decision on Jurisdiction, Liability and Partial Decision on Quantum, 19 February 2019 ICSID Case No. ARB/15/20, para. 401; Novenergia II - Energy & Environment (SCA), SICAR v. The Kingdom of Spain, Award, 15 February 2018 SCC Case No. V 2015/063, para. 679.

1216 Cube Infrastructure Fund SICAV and others v. Kingdom of Spain, Decision on Jurisdiction, Liability and Partial Decision on Quantum, 19 February 2019 ICSID Case No. ARB/15/20, para. 401; Novenergia II - Energy & Environment (SCA), SICAR v. The Kingdom of Spain, Award, 15 February 2018 SCC Case No. V 2015/063, para. 679.

1217 Cube Infrastructure Fund SICAV and others v. Kingdom of Spain, Decision on Jurisdiction, Liability and Partial Decision on Quantum, 19 February 2019 ICSID Case No. ARB/15/20, para. 396.

reasoning.[1218] However, the investors' understanding does not need to be necessarily confirmed in every point by external counsel, nor is there a specific requirement of detailed written analysis.[1219] Rather, it is sufficient that investors can prove that they obtained professional advice and took it into consideration when making their investment.[1220]

2) Scope of Due Diligence

Once the "if" of the due diligence has been clarified, the question has to be addressed as to what scope a due diligence analysis must have, in order to be considered adequate to protect the legitimate expectations of investors. Especially in cases in which the expectations are based on the legal framework of the host state, such expectations are often deemed legitimate, if the due diligence reports contained a thorough legal analysis of the provisions and an identification of regulatory risks.[1221]

In general, the investors are not required to perform a full and extensive due diligence of the entirety of the host state's legal and economic environment.[1222] Rather, tribunals must consider whether the alleged expectations are reasonable in light of the information that a prudent investor would have assessed at the time of the investment.[1223] With regard to the informa-

1218 CEF Energia B.V. v. Italian Republic, Award, 16 January 2019 SCC Arbitration No. 2015/158, para. 225.

1219 Cube Infrastructure Fund SICAV and others v. Kingdom of Spain, Decision on Jurisdiction, Liability and Partial Decision on Quantum, 19 February 2019 ICSID Case No. ARB/15/20, para. 304, 401.

1220 ibid, para. 304, 401.

1221 Watkins Holdings S.à.r.l. and others v. Kingdom of Spain, Award, 21 January 2020 ICSID Case No. ARB/15/44, para. 588; Cube Infrastructure Fund SICAV and others v. Kingdom of Spain, Decision on Jurisdiction, Liability and Partial Decision on Quantum, 19 February 2019 ICSID Case No. ARB/15/20, para. 393; Hydro Energy 1 S.A.R.L. and Hydroxana Sweden AB v. The Kingdom of Spain, Decision on Jurisdiction, Liability and Directions on Quantum, 9 March 2020 ICSID Case No. ARB/15/42, para. 617.

1222 Isolux Netherlands, BV v. Kingdom of Spain Final, Award, 17 July 2016 SCC Case V2013/153, para. 781; Belenergia S.A. v. Italian Republic, Award, 6 August 2019 ICSID Case No. ARB/15/40, para. 584.

1223 The Tribunal in *Belenergia* observed that "an investor cannot legitimately expect that the legal and regulatory framework will not change when any prudent investor could have anticipated this change before making its investment", Belenergia S.A. v. Italian Republic, Award, 6 August 2019 ICSID Case No. ARB/15/40, para. 584.

tion that investors need to consider, a foreign investor, who is investing in a highly regulated field as the energy sector, is required to conduct rather extensive due diligence.[1224] Where a preliminary and comprehensive legal framework applicable to the sector, investors must base their due diligence analysis on the host state's legal framework and the national jurisprudence.[1225] Without such a thorough analysis, investors may not legitimately expect that the regulatory framework will not be modified throughout the lives of the plants.

Tribunals also considered that the due diligence reports explicitly have to focus on the regulatory risk, particularly if the legal framework already had experienced regulatory changes.[1226] For example, the *Belenergia* Tribunal considered a due diligence report not supportive with regard to the expectation of regulatory stability, as the reports presented by the investors failed to examine Italian regulatory risks in relation to FITs and minimum prices.[1227] However, a due diligence analysis that focuses on economic aspects, rather than the legal environment prevailing in the host state, will not be sufficient to fulfil the due diligence requirement.[1228]

In sum, arbitral jurisprudence indicates that an investor is required to consider (1) the umbrella legislation setting out the specific provisions on which the investors relied, (2) which state agency was in charge of regulating the support scheme and for what purpose, and (3) jurisprudence of

---

1224 Charanne and Construction Investments v. Kingdom of Spain, Award, 21 January 2016 SCC Case No. V 062/2012, para. 507; Cavalum SGPS v. Kingdom of Spain, Decision on Jurisdiction, Liability and Directions on Quantum, 31 August 2020 ICSID Case No. ARB/15/34, para. 444.

1225 Charanne and Construction Investments v. Kingdom of Spain, Award, 21 January 2016 SCC Case No. V 062/2012, para. 507; Cavalum SGPS v. Kingdom of Spain, Decision on Jurisdiction, Liability and Directions on Quantum, 31 August 2020 ICSID Case No. ARB/15/34, para. 444.

1226 Hydro Energy 1 S.A.R.L. and Hydroxana Sweden AB v. The Kingdom of Spain, Decision on Jurisdiction, Liability and Directions on Quantum, 9 March 2020 ICSID Case No. ARB/15/42, para. 613, 614, 617; Belenergia S.A. v. Italian Republic, Award, 6 August 2019 ICSID Case No. ARB/15/40, para. 585.

1227 Belenergia S.A. v. Italian Republic, Award, 6 August 2019 ICSID Case No. ARB/15/40, para. 585.

1228 RWE Innogy GmbH and RWE Innogy Aersa S.A.U. v. Kingdom of Spain, Decision on Jurisdicition, Liability, and certain Issues of Quantum, 6 January 2020 ICSID Case No. ARB/14/34, para. 512-514; Belenergia S.A. v. Italian Republic, Award, 6 August 2019 ICSID Case No. ARB/15/40, para. 586-588.

domestic courts.[1229] Nonetheless, it is to take into account while assessing the scope of the investors' analyses that it is not the tribunals' duty to second-guess the investors' due diligence. Rather, the scope of review must be limited to the question of whether the information available to the investor in the given case contradicted the asserted expectations.[1230]

a) Sources to Take into Consideration

To assess whether investors have given due consideration to all information available to them, it is first necessary to determine which sources of information are relevant to investors. Generally, the legitimacy of the investors' expectations must be assessed against the background of information that the investor knew or should reasonably have known at the time of the investment and be based on the conduct of the host state.[1231]

Additionally, investors cannot derive legitimate expectations from sources that they did not consider before making the investment, even if the content of these statements contained guarantees or any specific commitment.[1232] Furthermore, any ex-post interpretations of the legal framework cannot be used to test the investors' ex-ante legitimate expectations.[1233] Investors cannot base a claimed expectation upon the content of documents or discussions, to which they were not privy at the time of

---

1229 Stadtwerke München GmbH and others v. Kingdom of Spain, Award, 2 December 2019 ICSID Case No. ARB/15/1, para. 281.

1230 Jürgen Wirtgen, Stefan Wirtgen, Gisela Wirtgen and JSW Solar (zwei) GmbH & Co. KG v. Czech Republic, Dissenting Opinion, 11 October 2017 PCA Case No. 2014-03, para. 98.

1231 Electrabel S.A. v. Republic of Hungary, Award, 25 November 2015 ICSID Case No. ARB/07/19, para. 7.78; Hydro Energy 1 S.A.R.L. and Hydroxana Sweden AB v. The Kingdom of Spain, Decision on Jurisdiction, Liability and Directions on Quantum, 9 March 2020 ICSID Case No. ARB/15/42, para. 599; RREEF Infrastructure (G.P.) Limited and RREEF Pan-European Infrastructure Two Lux S.à.r.l. v. Kingdom of Spain, Decision on Responsibility and on the Principles of Quantum, 30 November 2018 ICSID Case No. ARB/13/30, para. 397; Cavalum SGPS v. Kingdom of Spain, Decision on Jurisdiction, Liability and Directions on Quantum, 31 August 2020 ICSID Case No. ARB/15/34, para. 443.

1232 ibid, para. 423.

1233 The Tribunal in *Wirtgen v. Czech Republic* found that the investors cannot rely on statements and alleged representations by the host state, which they had not reviewed and taken into consideration before making their investments, Jürgen Wirtgen, Stefan Wirtgen, Gisela Wirtgen and JSW Solar (zwei) GmbH

the investment.[1234] If the investors still rely on such sources, they cannot use them as proof of its expectation at the time. It may only be used to confirm a claimed expectation, but they have to establish a particular factual element of the alleged expectation.[1235] It follows that investors may only base their due diligence analysis on sources that are publicly available at the time of the investment. If, however, they rely on sources not publicly available, such sources may strengthen their argument in the overall assessment of the foreseeability, but are not capable of establishing proof in the first place.

Tribunals also considered that investors have to investigate or seek advice on the host state's applicable law and affirm that official statements could reasonably be attributed to the host state.[1236] Proper sources for information regarding the regulatory framework were deemed to be found in the reports and communications by competent state bodies and organisations.[1237] Moreover, investors may rely on statements issued in meetings and letters with senior officials of the host state, to confirm their understanding of the regulatory regime in place.[1238] The host state in *Novenergia*

& Co. KG v. Czech Republic, Award, 11 October 2017 PCA Case No. 2014-03, para. 423.

1234 Invesmart v. Czech Republic, Award, 26 June 2009 UNCITRAL, para. 252, 253, cited by Jürgen Wirtgen, Stefan Wirtgen, Gisela Wirtgen and JSW Solar (zwei) GmbH & Co. KG v. Czech Republic, Award, 11 October 2017 PCA Case No. 2014-03, para. 421.

1235 Invesmart v. Czech Republic, Award, 26 June 2009 UNCITRAL, para. 252, 253; Jürgen Wirtgen, Stefan Wirtgen, Gisela Wirtgen and JSW Solar (zwei) GmbH & Co. KG v. Czech Republic, Award, 11 October 2017 PCA Case No. 2014-03, para. 421.

1236 Hydro Energy 1 S.A.R.L. and Hydroxana Sweden AB v. The Kingdom of Spain, Decision on Jurisdiction, Liability and Directions on Quantum, 9 March 2020 ICSID Case No. ARB/15/42, para. 601; Cavalum SGPS v. Kingdom of Spain, Decision on Jurisdiction, Liability and Directions on Quantum, 31 August 2020 ICSID Case No. ARB/15/34, para. 445.

1237 Jürgen Wirtgen, Stefan Wirtgen, Gisela Wirtgen and JSW Solar (zwei) GmbH & Co. KG v. Czech Republic, Award, 11 October 2017 PCA Case No. 2014-03, para. 422; Novenergia II - Energy & Environment (SCA), SICAR v. The Kingdom of Spain, Award, 15 February 2018 SCC Case No. V 2015/063, para. 666-669; SolEs Badajoz GmbH v. Kingdom of Spain, Award, 31 July 2019 ICSID Case No. ARB/15/38, para. 423, 424; Watkins Holdings S.à.r.l. and others v. Kingdom of Spain, Award, 21 January 2020 ICSID Case No. ARB/15/44, para. 527, 528.

1238 NextEra Energy Global Holdings B.V. and NextEra Energy Spain Holdings B.V. v. Kingdom of Spain, Decision on Jurisdiction, Liability and Quantum Principles, 12 March 2019 ICSID Case No. ARB/14/11, para. 588, 589.

v. Spain raised the objection that the investors did not take into account (1) statements of private renewable energy business associations, (2) statements by "relevant investors" and (3) "Omitted Spanish Declarations".[1239] With respect to the first category, the Tribunal observed that none of the documents originated from the host state or any entity attributable to the state and hence they were not sufficient to raise red flags for the investor.[1240] Neither did the Tribunal consider the second and third category as a relevant source for doubts concerning the stability of the regulatory framework, as these omitted declarations regarded legislation that had already been implemented at the time of the investment.[1241] Overall, due diligence reports must only draw from sources that can be attributable to the state. Investors are not obligated to take into account any private or non-official statements regarding the investment environment unless they raise serious doubts.[1242]

This notwithstanding, the majority of the tribunals have, in general, limited themselves to ascertaining whether investors have consulted one or more competent law firms for legal analysis prior to their investment.[1243] Such a view raises doubts, as it would allow investors to blindly rely on the reports of their legal advisors and thus "buy out" of the due diligence requirement. However, it has been confirmed that it is, under regular circumstances, sufficient to consult a competent law firm to confirm the investors' expectations, if there is no obvious alternative way to obtain information.[1244] In particular, due diligence was found to be sufficient, if the host state's authorities would not have been able to provide better

1239 Novenergia II - Energy & Environment (SCA), SICAR v. The Kingdom of Spain, Award, 15 February 2018 SCC Case No. V 2015/063, para. 676.

1240 ibid, para. 676.

1241 ibid, para. 678.

1242 *See below* Ch. 4 II 3) a).

1243 *For example*, the majority of the Tribunal in *Foresight* considered that "it is reasonable for an investor to assume that its legal advisors would have raised a red flag had they detected any risk of fundamental change to the regulatory regime", Foresight and others v. Kingdom of Spain Final, Award, 14 November 2018 SCC Case No. V 2015/150, para. 380.

1244 OperaFund Eco-Invest SICAV PLC and Schwab Holding AG v. Kingdom of Spain, Award, 6 September 2019 ICSID Case No. ARB/15/36, para. 487; Cube Infrastructure Fund SICAV and others v. Kingdom of Spain, Decision on Jurisdiction, Liability and Partial Decision on Quantum, 19 February 2019 ICSID Case No. ARB/15/20, para. 401.

information.[1245] Thus, it has been proven to be a test for the sufficiency of the due diligence applied by the tribunal, to ask whether the investors could have taken any further steps to achieve information that would have resulted in a change of expectation.

b) Clarity of the Legal Framework

As demonstrated above, tribunals tend to regard the legal framework as the basis for state commitments. If investors base their reliance on the law, the legal framework must have also been the core of the due diligence analysis. It is unclear, however, what level of due diligence must be applied. There is a strong indication in arbitral jurisprudence that the thoroughness of due diligence depends on how clear the legal framework was designed by the host state.

In particular, with regard to the Spanish support scheme, tribunals found that the object and purpose of the relevant provisions were clear and specific that there was no need for further due diligence regarding possible changes of the legal framework.[1246] Moreover, it was observed that the clearer the underlying legal framework, the less thorough and competent the legal due diligence analysis must be.[1247] If the wording of the crucial norms of the dispute is "adamantly clear" so that it could be understood by common readers, no particularly sophisticated analysis is

---

1245 OperaFund Eco-Invest SICAV PLC and Schwab Holding AG v. Kingdom of Spain, Award, 6 September 2019 ICSID Case No. ARB/15/36, para. 487.

1246 Novenergia II - Energy & Environment (SCA), SICAR v. The Kingdom of Spain, Award, 15 February 2018 SCC Case No. V 2015/063, para. 679; Cube Infrastructure Fund SICAV and others v. Kingdom of Spain, Decision on Jurisdiction, Liability and Partial Decision on Quantum, 19 February 2019 ICSID Case No. ARB/15/20, para. 401; OperaFund Eco-Invest SICAV PLC and Schwab Holding AG v. Kingdom of Spain, Award, 6 September 2019 ICSID Case No. ARB/15/36, para. 485, 487; Cavalum SGPS v. Kingdom of Spain, Dissenting Opinion of David R. Haigh, 31 August 2020 ICSID Case No. ARB/15/34, para. 44.

1247 The Tribunal in *Novenergia* faced the host state's allegation that the investor did not perform adequate due diligence, based on the fact that not one single member of the investor's board of directors had legal expertise and hence oversaw warning signs of potential drastic changes Novenergia II - Energy & Environment (SCA), SICAR v. The Kingdom of Spain, Award, 15 February 2018 SCC Case No. V 2015/063, para. 580.

required.[1248] Additionally, the specificity of the host state's commitment may outweigh deficiencies in the thoroughness of the due diligence analysis.[1249] The bar for a due diligence analysis of a clear legal framework may also be lowered, if the size of the investment is to be considered small in comparison to the diligence efforts it would require to examine the entire legal framework.[1250]

Conclusively, arbitral jurisprudence demonstrates the trend that there is no requirement for a particularly sophisticated analysis, if the underlying norms are so adamantly clear they can be easily understood by common readers.[1251] Hence, any criticism of the investors' due diligence must take

---

1248 Novenergia II - Energy & Environment (SCA), SICAR v. The Kingdom of Spain, Award, 15 February 2018 SCC Case No. V 2015/063, para. 679; Cube Infrastructure Fund SICAV and others v. Kingdom of Spain, Decision on Jurisdiction, Liability and Partial Decision on Quantum, 19 February 2019 ICSID Case No. ARB/15/20, para. 401 and Cavalum SGPS v. Kingdom of Spain, Dissenting Opinion of David R. Haigh, 31 August 2020 ICSID Case No. ARB/15/34, para. 44.

1249 InfraRed Environmental Infrastructure GP Limited and others v. Kingdom of Spain, Award, 2 August 2019 ICSID Case No. ARB/14/12, para. 441, 442, 447. *Gary Born* even expressed the view that the only time due diligence comes into play is when particular inquiries would have led an investor to alter its expectations about national law protection, which is not the case if the wording of the specific provisions relied on by the investors are clear enough, so that further due diligence would have revealed nothing different, Antaris Solar and Dr. Michael Göde v. Czech Republic, Dissenting Opinion, 2 May 2018 PCA Case No. 2014-01, para. 76.

1250 *Gary Born* opined that the investment in comparison rather small and hence concurred that the investors were not obligated to conduct extensive due diligence, Antaris Solar and Dr. Michael Göde v. Czech Republic, Dissenting Opinion, 2 May 2018 PCA Case No. 2014-01, para. 77. Similarly, the Tribunal in *RWE* took into consideration the vast size of the investment and concluded that in light of the capital at stake, the due diligence analysis should have been more detailed, RWE Innogy GmbH and RWE Innogy Aersa S.A.U. v. Kingdom of Spain, Decision on Jurisdicition, Liability, and certain Issues of Quantum, 6 January 2020 ICSID Case No. ARB/14/34, para. 510.

1251 Novenergia II - Energy & Environment (SCA), SICAR v. The Kingdom of Spain, Award, 15 February 2018 SCC Case No. V 2015/063, para. 679; Opera-Fund Eco-Invest SICAV PLC and Schwab Holding AG v. Kingdom of Spain, Award, 6 September 2019 ICSID Case No. ARB/15/36, para. 485, 487; Isolux Netherlands, BV v. Kingdom of Spain Final, Award, 17 July 2016 SCC Case V2013/153, para. 781, 794; Antaris Solar and Dr. Michael Göde v. Czech Republic, Dissenting Opinion, 2 May 2018 PCA Case No. 2014-01, para. 77; Cavalum SGPS v. Kingdom of Spain, Dissenting Opinion of David R. Haigh, 31 August 2020 ICSID Case No. ARB/15/34, para. 44-46.

both the nature of the investments and the clarity of the host state's commitments into account.

c) Relevance of Domestic Case Law

A reoccurring defence raised by the host states, particularly by Spain, was that domestic case law clearly indicated that the regulatory framework could be amended at any point during the lifetime of the investments.[1252] It is acknowledged that the role of investment law tribunals is not to second-guess the decisions of national courts and act as a court of appeal on questions on domestic law.[1253] However, with reference to Article 3 of the ILC Articles on State Responsibility, it was held that the conformity of a state's act with its own constitution does not indicate whether the act was also compatible with international law.[1254] Additionally, Article 27 VCLT stipulates that states may not rely on national law to justify the breach of international obligations.[1255] Thus, arbitral tribunals are in general entitled to evaluate state measures in light of international law, although national courts already decided on their compatibility with domestic law. There is a general consensus that the question of whether an act is in conformity

---

1252 *See for example* Foresight and others v. Kingdom of Spain Final, Award, 14 November 2018 SCC Case No. V 2015/150, para. 320; Cube Infrastructure Fund SICAV and others v. Kingdom of Spain, Decision on Jurisdiction, Liability and Partial Decision on Quantum, 19 February 2019 ICSID Case No. ARB/15/20, para. 299; InfraRed Environmental Infrastructure GP Limited and others v. Kingdom of Spain, Award, 2 August 2019 ICSID Case No. ARB/14/12, para. 391.

1253 Perenco Ecuador Ltd. v. Republic of Ecuador and Empresa Estatal Petróleos del Ecuador Decision on Remaining Issues of Jurisdiction and on Liability, 12 September 2014 ICSID Case No. ARB/08/6, para. 583; Mondev International Ltd. v United States of America, Award, 11 October 2002 ICSID Case No. ARB(AF)/99/2, para. 126. *See also* Miljenić, 'Energy Charter Treaty – Standards of Investment Protection', p. 64.

1254 The Tribunal in *Perenco* pointed out that "under well-established principles of international law, as codified in Article 3 of the ILC Articles on State Responsibility, the fact that a law has been declared constitutional by the local courts, even by the highest court of the land, is not dispositive of whether it was in conformity with international law", Perenco Ecuador Ltd. v. Republic of Ecuador and Empresa Estatal Petróleos del Ecuador Decision on Remaining Issues of Jurisdiction and on Liability, 12 September 2014 ICSID Case No. ARB/08/6, para. 583.

1255 Dörr and Schmalenbach, *Vienna Convention on the Law of Treaties*, p. 493.

with domestic law is quite separate from the question of conformity with international law.[1256] National case law is most relevant in determining whether investors could legitimately expect, at the time of the investment, that the legal framework would not change or whether a sufficient evaluation of the case law as part of an appropriate due diligence process would have made changes foreseeable.

A larger number of tribunals considered the cases of the Spanish Supreme Court presented to it as of limited assistance, since the Court applied domestic law and did not address the specific issues of conflict in the given case.[1257] Issues tried before arbitral tribunals concerned claims based on the FET standard entailed in the ECT, whereas the Spanish Supreme Court judgments dealt with the compatibility of the states' measures with Spanish law.[1258] In particular, the Spanish Supreme Court did not decide the question of legitimate expectations arising out of the provisions of RD 661/2007.[1259] Therefore, findings regarding domestic law that do not concern an analogous context do not have significant relevance in the as-

1256 RWE Innogy GmbH and RWE Innogy Aersa S.A.U. v. Kingdom of Spain, Decision on Jurisdicition, Liability, and certain Issues of Quantum, 6 January 2020 ICSID Case No. ARB/14/34, para. 525; Eiser Infrastructure Limited and Energía Solar Luxembourg S.à.r.l. v. Kingdom of Spain, Award, 4 May 2017 ICSID Case No. ARB/13/36, para. 373; Cube Infrastructure Fund SICAV and others v. Kingdom of Spain, Decision on Jurisdiction, Liability and Partial Decision on Quantum, 19 February 2019 ICSID Case No. ARB/15/20, para. 300; I.C.W. Europe Investments Limited v. The Czech Republic, Award, 15 May 2019 PCA CASE No 2014-22, para. 538.

1257 SolEs Badajoz GmbH v. Kingdom of Spain, Award, 31 July 2019 ICSID Case No. ARB/15/38, para. 430; OperaFund Eco-Invest SICAV PLC and Schwab Holding AG v. Kingdom of Spain, Award, 6 September 2019 ICSID Case No. ARB/15/36, para. 491; 9REN Holding S.a.r.l v. Kingdom of Spain, Award, 31 March 2019 ICSID Case No. ARB/15/15, para. 242; Cavalum SGPS v. Kingdom of Spain, Dissenting Opinion of David R. Haigh, 31 August 2020 ICSID Case No. ARB/15/34, para. 40, 41.

1258 Cube Infrastructure Fund SICAV and others v. Kingdom of Spain, Decision on Jurisdiction, Liability and Partial Decision on Quantum, 19 February 2019 ICSID Case No. ARB/15/20, para. 300; Masdar Solar & Wind Cooperatief U.A. v. Kingdom of Spain, Award, 16 May 2018 ICSID Case No. ARB/14/1, para. 579.

1259 Cube Infrastructure Fund SICAV and others v. Kingdom of Spain, Decision on Jurisdiction, Liability and Partial Decision on Quantum, 19 February 2019 ICSID Case No. ARB/15/20, para. 300; Masdar Solar & Wind Cooperatief U.A. v. Kingdom of Spain, Award, 16 May 2018 ICSID Case No. ARB/14/1, para. 579.

sessment of international law claims.[1260] Hence, the domestic case law was regarded as too general and not addressing the same issues tried before the tribunals, in order to rebut the investors' allegation of having conducted proper due diligence.

Nonetheless, tribunals also concluded that the domestic case law would have made diligent investors aware of the possible changes in the legal framework.[1261] A diligent investor must generally be aware of decisions of the highest national courts that concern the investment environment in the host state, and in particular the legal framework governing the investment.[1262] Tribunals made clear that the decisions of a national court have no binding effect in the international law context, but found them relevant for the assessment of the question of what degree of stability an investor may legitimately expect.[1263] The highest national courts can, in general, be regarded as "the best qualified to rule on what the meaning

---

1260 RWE Innogy GmbH and RWE Innogy Aersa S.A.U. v. Kingdom of Spain, Decision on Jurisdicition, Liability, and certain Issues of Quantum, 6 January 2020 ICSID Case No. ARB/14/34, para. 518.

1261 Stadtwerke München GmbH and others v. Kingdom of Spain, Award, 2 December 2019 ICSID Case No. ARB/15/1, para. 277, 278; Foresight and others v. Kingdom of Spain Final, Award, 14 November 2018 SCC Case No. V 2015/150, para. 374; Charanne and Construction Investments v. Kingdom of Spain, Award, 21 January 2016 SCC Case No. V 062/2012, para. 507; Isolux Netherlands, BV v. Kingdom of Spain Final, Award, 17 July 2016 SCC Case V2013/153, para. 793, 796; BayWa r.e. Renewable Energy GmbH and BayWa r.e. Asset Holding GmbH v. Kingdom of Spain, Decision on Jurisdiction, Liability and Directions on Quantum, 2 December 2019 ICSID Case No. ARB/15/16, para. 590(a).

1262 SolEs Badajoz GmbH v. Kingdom of Spain, Award, 31 July 2019 ICSID Case No. ARB/15/38, para. 429; RWE Innogy GmbH and RWE Innogy Aersa S.A.U. v. Kingdom of Spain, Decision on Jurisdicition, Liability, and certain Issues of Quantum, 6 January 2020 ICSID Case No. ARB/14/34, para. 517, 518; Cavalum SGPS v. Kingdom of Spain, Decision on Jurisdiction, Liability and Directions on Quantum, 31 August 2020 ICSID Case No. ARB/15/34, para. 515; OperaFund Eco-Invest SICAV PLC and Schwab Holding AG v. Kingdom of Spain, Dissenting Opinion Philippe Sands, 6 September 2019 ICSID Case No. ARB/15/36, para. 21.

1263 Charanne and Construction Investments v. Kingdom of Spain, Award, 21 January 2016 SCC Case No. V 062/2012, para. 508; Isolux Netherlands, BV v. Kingdom of Spain Final, Award, 17 July 2016 SCC Case V2013/153, para. 793. *See also* Cavalum SGPS v. Kingdom of Spain, Decision on Jurisdiction, Liability and Directions on Quantum, 31 August 2020 ICSID Case No. ARB/15/34, para. 531.

and effect of a provision of domestic law".[1264] If the national court addresses the state's power to regulate its legal framework in a general manner, the findings may be presumed to be valid.[1265] Various arbitral tribunals took guidance with regard to the interpretation of national law from domestic courts.[1266] While domestic court decisions were mostly used as a defence by respondent states, they may also serve as an indication of the legitimacy of the investor's expectations.[1267]

Notwithstanding the potential of domestic court decisions as guidance, there is no rule that the interpretation handed down by domestic courts is the only possible interpretation.[1268] It follows that a tribunal must, even in the face of clear domestic jurisprudence, assess whether such meaning and effect should have been apparent to a diligent investor at the time of

1264 RWE Innogy GmbH and RWE Innogy Aersa S.A.U. v. Kingdom of Spain, Decision on Jurisdicition, Liability, and certain Issues of Quantum, 6 January 2020 ICSID Case No. ARB/14/34, para. 525.

1265 The PV Investors v. Kingdom of Spain Final, Award, 28 February 2020 PCA Case No. 2012-14, para. 608.

1266 With regard to the qualification of the Czech Solar Levy, as a tax in the meaning of Article 21(1) ECT, a number of tribunals hearing the claims against the Czech Republic based their conclusions on decisions by the Czech Constitutional Court and the Czech Supreme Administrative Court, Jürgen Wirtgen, Stefan Wirtgen, Gisela Wirtgen and JSW Solar (zwei) GmbH & Co. KG v. Czech Republic, Award, 11 October 2017 PCA Case No. 2014-03, para. 469; Antaris Solar and Dr. Michael Göde v. Czech Republic, Award, 2 May 2018 PCA Case No. 2014-01, para. 430. In contrast, the Tribunal in I.C.W. Europe Investments Limited v. The Czech Republic, Award, 15 May 2019 PCA CASE No 2014-22, para. 538, considered that "little, if any, guidance on the question of legitimate expectations may be gleaned from the May 2012 Constitutional Court Judgment". Tribunals in cases against Italy took guidance from the Italian Constitutional Court, which had held that the GSE Conventions could be unilaterally modified in compliance with Italian law CEF Energia B.V. v. Italian Republic, Award, 16 January 2019 SCC Arbitration No. 2015/158, para. 255; Belenergia S.A. v. Italian Republic, Award, 6 August 2019 ICSID Case No. ARB/15/40, para. 579; SunReserve Luxco Holdings v. Italian Republic Final, Award, 25 March 2020 SCC Arbitration V (2016/32), para. 827.

1267 *See* Watkins Holdings S.à.r.l. and others v. Kingdom of Spain, Award, 21 January 2020 ICSID Case No. ARB/15/44, para. 605.

1268 RWE Innogy GmbH and RWE Innogy Aersa S.A.U. v. Kingdom of Spain, Decision on Jurisdicition, Liability, and certain Issues of Quantum, 6 January 2020 ICSID Case No. ARB/14/34, para. 534.

the investment.[1269] Therefore, arbitral tribunals preserve a certain margin of interpretation of domestic laws, in light of international law, despite existing jurisprudence of national courts.

Additionally, domestic jurisprudence may lose its relevance, in light of a specific commitment by the host state.[1270] However, tribunals show a tendency to confirm their findings with the holdings of domestic courts.[1271] Thus, decisions of national courts do not have a direct effect on the assessment of the violation of international obligations, but investors may not be able to legitimately expect a certain course of events or outcome, if national courts have decided differently in the past.[1272] At the very least, an investor cannot claim that the legal framework was "adamantly clear", if national courts issued decisions that conflict with the investor's interpretation.

The analysis of the recent decisions demonstrates that the tribunals do not disagree on the fact that investors should include domestic jurisprudence in their due diligence procedure. Rather, the views of the tribunals differ again in the subsumption of this rule in individual cases. Most commonly, tribunals dissented on the question of whether the decision sufficiently covered the issues relevant to the assessment of the regulatory changes in light of international law, i.e. specific promises or guarantees through legislation.[1273] Hence, decisions by domestic courts can be treated

---

1269 RWE Innogy GmbH and RWE Innogy Aersa S.A.U. v. Kingdom of Spain, Decision on Jurisdicition, Liability, and certain Issues of Quantum, 6 January 2020 ICSID Case No. ARB/14/34, para. 534.

1270 InfraRed Environmental Infrastructure GP Limited and others v. Kingdom of Spain, Award, 2 August 2019 ICSID Case No. ARB/14/12, para. 440.

1271 WA Investments-Europa Nova Limited v. The Czech Republic, Award, 15 May 2019 PCA CASE No 2014-19, para. 550; The PV Investors v. Kingdom of Spain Final, Award, 28 February 2020 PCA Case No. 2012-14, para. 603.

1272 Charanne and Construction Investments v. Kingdom of Spain, Award, 21 January 2016 SCC Case No. V 062/2012, para. 507; Isolux Netherlands, BV v. Kingdom of Spain Final, Award, 17 July 2016 SCC Case V2013/153, para. 793; RWE Innogy GmbH and RWE Innogy Aersa S.A.U. v. Kingdom of Spain, Decision on Jurisdicition, Liability, and certain Issues of Quantum, 6 January 2020 ICSID Case No. ARB/14/34, para. 525; Cavalum SGPS v. Kingdom of Spain, Decision on Jurisdiction, Liability and Directions on Quantum, 31 August 2020 ICSID Case No. ARB/15/34, para. 446.

1273 *See for example* RWE Innogy GmbH and RWE Innogy Aersa S.A.U. v. Kingdom of Spain, Decision on Jurisdicition, Liability, and certain Issues of Quantum, 6 January 2020 ICSID Case No. ARB/14/34, para. 518, disagreeing with the findings of the Tribunals in Charanne and Construction Investments v. Kingdom of Spain, Award, 21 January 2016 SCC Case No. V 062/2012,

as "facts" of the case, but have no binding effect on arbitral tribunals operating under international law.[1274] It follows that the disregard of the national court's decisions can be seen as a violation of the investors' due diligence requirement.[1275]

3) Risks Identified and Warning Signs

The due diligence analyses of investors in the renewable energy sector have partly delivered different results, with regard to the risk associated with an investment, depending on the respective country and the type of power technology employed. Thereby, it is noticeable that in the Spanish CSP sector, in particular, increased protection against legislative measures that would undermine regulatory stability was found.[1276] In general, even if the diligence of an investor is "due", it does not create legitimate expectations, if the investor is aware of possible changes in the future.[1277] Warning signs that could make an investor aware of possible changes in the future can be manifold. However, in most cases, especially the earlier ones, the respec-

---

para. 507, and Isolux Netherlands, BV v. Kingdom of Spain Final, Award, 17 July 2016 SCC Case V2013/153, para. 793.

1274 The PV Investors v. Kingdom of Spain Final, Award, 28 February 2020 PCA Case No. 2012-14, para. 603; Isolux Netherlands, BV v. Kingdom of Spain Final, Award, 17 July 2016 SCC Case V2013/153, para. 793; Cavalum SGPS v. Kingdom of Spain, Decision on Jurisdiction, Liability and Directions on Quantum, 31 August 2020 ICSID Case No. ARB/15/34, para. 446.

1275 Foresight and others v. Kingdom of Spain, Dissenting Opinion Raúl Emilio Vinuesa, 14 November 2018 SCC Case No. V 2015/150, para. 48-50.

1276 InfraRed Environmental Infrastructure GP Limited and others v. Kingdom of Spain, Award, 2 August 2019 ICSID Case No. ARB/14/12, para. 418; Masdar Solar & Wind Cooperatief U.A. v. Kingdom of Spain, Award, 16 May 2018 ICSID Case No. ARB/14/1, para. 359, 522; Antin Infrastructure Services Luxembourg S.à.r.l. and Antin Energia Termosolar B.V. v. Kingdom of Spain, Award, 15 June 2018 ICSID Case No. ARB/13/31, para. 562, 563; RREEF Infrastructure (G.P.) Limited and RREEF Pan-European Infrastructure Two Lux S.à.r.l. v. Kingdom of Spain, Decision on Responsibility and on the Principles of Quantum, 30 November 2018 ICSID Case No. ARB/13/30, para. 589; Eiser Infrastructure Limited and Energía Solar Luxembourg S.à.r.l. v. Kingdom of Spain, Award, 4 May 2017 ICSID Case No. ARB/13/36, para. 117, 418.

1277 RREEF Infrastructure (G.P.) Limited and RREEF Pan-European Infrastructure Two Lux S.à.r.l. v. Kingdom of Spain, Decision on Responsibility and on the Principles of Quantum, 30 November 2018 ICSID Case No. ARB/13/30, para. 398.

tive due diligence reports identified delays in the construction process of the power plants as the only major risk, and hence that the facilities cannot be registered in time to benefit from the respective support schemes.[1278]

Those reports, which detected a regulatory risk considered them relatively low, irrespective of the host state.[1279] In general, arbitral jurisprudence did not deem the fact that a hypothetical low regulatory risk was identified, sufficient to undermine the investors due diligence and eviscerate their legitimate expectations.[1280] The risk identified has to be imminent and must not lead a prudent investor to believe that the investment may

1278 Eiser Infrastructure Limited and Energía Solar Luxembourg S.à.r.l. v. Kingdom of Spain, Award, 4 May 2017 ICSID Case No. ARB/13/36, para. 118; Cube Infrastructure Fund SICAV and others v. Kingdom of Spain, Decision on Jurisdiction, Liability and Partial Decision on Quantum, 19 February 2019 ICSID Case No. ARB/15/20, para. 301-304; NextEra Energy Global Holdings B.V. and NextEra Energy Spain Holdings B.V. v. Kingdom of Spain, Decision on Jurisdiction, Liability and Quantum Principles, 12 March 2019 ICSID Case No. ARB/14/11, para. 440, 595; Masdar Solar & Wind Cooperatief U.A. v. Kingdom of Spain, Award, 16 May 2018 ICSID Case No. ARB/14/1, para. 359, 497; ESPF Beteiligungs GmbH et. al. v. Italian Republic, Award, 14 September 2020 ICSID Case No. ARB/16/5, para. 543.

1279 *For example*, the Tribunal in *Antin* found that the investors had gathered all relevant information of the legal framework of the host state, by ordering three due diligence reports in total, and were thus able to base a reasonable business decision on said information. Although the due diligence reports at the time of the investment had noticed a change in the legal framework, it was reasonable for an investor to believe that there would not be alteration, as drastic and radical as the abolishment of the whole *Special Regime*, as the regulatory risk in the CSP sector was regarded remote, Antin Infrastructure Services Luxembourg S.à.r.l. and Antin Energia Termosolar B.V. v. Kingdom of Spain, Award, 15 June 2018 ICSID Case No. ARB/13/31, para. 562, 563. *See also* Cube Infrastructure Fund SICAV and others v. Kingdom of Spain, Decision on Jurisdiction, Liability and Partial Decision on Quantum, 19 February 2019 ICSID Case No. ARB/15/20, para. 301; NextEra para. 440; Blusun S.A. Jean-Pierre Lecorcier and Michael Stein v. Italian Republic, Award, 27 December 2016 ICSID Case No. ARB/14/3, para. 384; Masdar Solar & Wind Cooperatief U.A. v. Kingdom of Spain, Award, 16 May 2018 ICSID Case No. ARB/14/1, para. 359; Eiser Infrastructure Limited and Energía Solar Luxembourg S.à.r.l. v. Kingdom of Spain, Award, 4 May 2017 ICSID Case No. ARB/13/36, para. 118; Cavalum SGPS v. Kingdom of Spain, Decision on Jurisdiction, Liability and Directions on Quantum, 31 August 2020 ICSID Case No. ARB/15/34, para. 521.

1280 CEF Energia B.V. v. Italian Republic, Award, 16 January 2019 SCC Arbitration No. 2015/158, para. 233; Antin Infrastructure Services Luxembourg S.à.r.l. and Antin Energia Termosolar B.V. v. Kingdom of Spain, Award, 15 June 2018 ICSID Case No. ARB/13/31, para. 562, 562.

incur legal or administrative difficulties, even if these difficulties could be theoretically overcome. Such a situation can occur, if the investment is at an early development stage[1281], or when it has been conducted at a time in which the regulatory framework had already been altered several times in the recent past[1282]. The Tribunal in *Blusun v. Italy* applied the standard that the success of the investment must be, in light of the risk identified, "by no means certain".[1283]

General warning signs can be contradictions of the law and any official statements with the investors' initial legal assumptions, and due diligence reports issued by competent law firms.[1284] Apart from the jurisprudence of the host state's supreme court and the applicable national and EU law, *Phillip Sands* identified the volatile evolution of the legal framework preceding the investment and the socio-economic circumstances, such as the global economic crisis, as major warning signs, which needed to be considered before conducting an investment.[1285] Hence, in order to give due consideration to the states' right to regulate, investors must pay close attention to the expected changes in the economic and social conditions prevailing in the host state and the evolution that a legal framework has already undergone, at the time of the investment.[1286]

1281 Blusun S.A. Jean-Pierre Lecorcier and Michael Stein v. Italian Republic, Award, 27 December 2016 ICSID Case No. ARB/14/3, para. 386.

1282 Isolux Netherlands, BV v. Kingdom of Spain Final, Award, 17 July 2016 SCC Case V2013/153, para. 784-787; Antaris Solar and Dr. Michael Göde v. Czech Republic, Award, 2 May 2018 PCA Case No. 2014-01, para. 431; Belenergia S.A. v. Italian Republic, Award, 6 August 2019 ICSID Case No. ARB/15/40, para. 594, 595; Watkins Holdings S.à.r.l. and others v. Kingdom of Spain, Dissenting Opinion Helene Ruiz Fabri, 21 January 2020 ICSID Case No. ARB/15/44, para. 15; Cube Infrastructure Fund SICAV and others v. Kingdom of Spain, Separate and Partial Dissenting Opinion Christian Tomuschat, 19 February 2019 ICSID Case No. ARB/15/20, para. 14.

1283 Blusun S.A. Jean-Pierre Lecorcier and Michael Stein v. Italian Republic, Award, 27 December 2016 ICSID Case No. ARB/14/3, para. 386.

1284 Cube Infrastructure Fund SICAV and others v. Kingdom of Spain, Decision on Jurisdiction, Liability and Partial Decision on Quantum, 19 February 2019 ICSID Case No. ARB/15/20, para. 396.

1285 OperaFund Eco-Invest SICAV PLC and Schwab Holding AG v. Kingdom of Spain, Dissenting Opinion Philippe Sands, 6 September 2019 ICSID Case No. ARB/15/36, para. 25-28.

1286 Hydro Energy 1 S.A.R.L. and Hydroxana Sweden AB v. The Kingdom of Spain, Decision on Jurisdiction, Liability and Directions on Quantum, 9 March 2020 ICSID Case No. ARB/15/42, para. 600.

a) Socio-Economic Environment

The political and socio-economic environment must be the "front and centre" for any diligent investor.[1287] Tribunals have assessed the political and socio-economic environment, while considering whether it was a reasonable business decision by the investor to expect regulatory stability over the lifetime of the investment.[1288]

The recent renewable energy investment disputes were mainly sparked by the 2007/2008 recession, which urged states to reform their support systems, in order to avoid huge tariff deficits. Signs emerged that states may not be able to cope with the financial burden in face of an economic crisis. Tribunals assessed statements by state officials, as well as newspaper articles, and qualified them as sufficient to raise doubts about the stability of the support schemes in the future.[1289]

Moreover, the Italian State argued that investors cannot legitimately expect that FITs and FITs would be maintained amidst a financial crisis, which could be considered a *force majeur* situation.[1290] The Tribunal in *Greentech v. Italy* found that the regulatory framework conveyed the promise that the investors will receive the prescribed subsidies over a

---

1287 InfraRed Environmental Infrastructure GP Limited and others v. Kingdom of Spain, Award, 2 August 2019 ICSID Case No. ARB/14/12, para. 446.

1288 Hydro Energy 1 S.A.R.L. and Hydroxana Sweden AB v. The Kingdom of Spain, Decision on Jurisdiction, Liability and Directions on Quantum, 9 March 2020 ICSID Case No. ARB/15/42, para. 673; Antaris Solar and Dr. Michael Göde v. Czech Republic, Award, 2 May 2018 PCA Case No. 2014-01, para. 368.

1289 The Tribunal in *Antaris* found that press releases by the Ministry of Finance, statements issued by many officials, including current and former ministers, as well as articles by major Czech newspapers, could have made a diligent investor aware of the problems of the solar boom already in 2009, Antaris Solar and Dr. Michael Göde v. Czech Republic, Award, 2 May 2018 PCA Case No. 2014-01, para. 425-429, 440. The practice of assessing financial newspaper articles, in order to determine whether the investors should have been aware of possible changes in the future, was also followed by subsequent tribunals, *see* Cube Infrastructure Fund SICAV and others v. Kingdom of Spain, Decision on Jurisdiction, Liability and Partial Decision on Quantum, 19 February 2019 ICSID Case No. ARB/15/20, para. 345-347; Voltaic Network GmbH v. Czech Republic, Award, 15 September 2019 PCA CASE No 2014-20, para. 478.

1290 Greentech Energy Systems A/S, NovEnergia II Energy & Environment (SCA) SICAR, and NovEnergia II Italian Portfolio SA v. Italian Republic, Award, 23 December 2018 SCC Arbitration V (2015/095), para. 451; ESPF Beteiligungs GmbH et. al. v. Italian Republic, Award, 14 September 2020 ICSID Case No. ARB/16/5, para. 426.

course of 20 years.[1291] Hence, when assessing what the investors could have reasonably foreseen, the Tribunal observed that investors may trust the specific commitment of the state, unless the economic environment would have indicated that the host state will face a severe crisis, which would amount to *force majeur*.[1292] This, however, also ties in with the timing of the investment, which will be discussed next.[1293]

Thus, diligent investors must at least screen the investment environment in the host state for signs, which may indicate that the expected stability may not last over the lifetime of the investment.

b) Previous Development of the Regulatory Framework

Investors cannot legitimately expect that certain specific features of a legal framework will not be drastically altered, if previous regulatory changes had already been implemented, and the modification of said framework is already in full swing.[1294] When crucial changes to the legal framework were already introduced and the possibility of future changes cannot be ruled out, any expectation of stability may be misplaced.[1295] The legitimacy

---

1291 Greentech Energy Systems A/S, NovEnergia II Energy & Environment (SCA) SICAR, and NovEnergia II Italian Portfolio SA v. Italian Republic, Award, 23 December 2018 SCC Arbitration V (2015/095), para. 447.

1292 ibid, para. 451.

1293 *See above* Ch. 4 II 3) b).

1294 Belenergia S.A. v. Italian Republic, Award, 6 August 2019 ICSID Case No. ARB/15/40, para. 591; Isolux Netherlands, BV v. Kingdom of Spain Final, Award, 17 July 2016 SCC Case V2013/153, para. 787, 788; OperaFund Eco-Invest SICAV PLC and Schwab Holding AG v. Kingdom of Spain, Dissenting Opinion Philippe Sands, 6 September 2019 ICSID Case No. ARB/15/36, para. 20; Cube Infrastructure Fund SICAV and others v. Kingdom of Spain, Decision on Jurisdiction, Liability and Partial Decision on Quantum, 19 February 2019 ICSID Case No. ARB/15/20, para. 356 (with regard to the Claimants' hydro investments).

1295 The Tribunal in *Isolux* found that the revision of the legal framework was already at full swing at the time of the investment, Isolux Netherlands, BV v. Kingdom of Spain Final, Award, 17 July 2016 SCC Case V2013/153, para. 787-792. Similarly, the *9Ren* Tribunal also held that the amendment of the *Special Regime* by RD 1578/2008 contemplated future revisions and made changes to the remuneration foreseeable, 9REN Holding S.a.r.l v. Kingdom of Spain, Award, 31 March 2019 ICSID Case No. ARB/15/15, para. 298. The *Belenergia* Tribunal observed that the investment was conducted at a late stage, when new incentives were already subject to reduction and annual cost caps

of such expectations can be further undermined, if the legality of these modifications has been confirmed in various Supreme Court decisions.[1296] Hence, the first indicator for future changes can be the fact that the regulatory framework had already been modified several times at the time of the investment.[1297] The second indicator can be case law of the domestic courts that had confirmed the right of the state to amend its regulatory framework at any time.[1298] Given the states' margin of discretion in regulating their economy in the public interest, investors may not legitimately rely on the state to always implement the least intrusive measure.[1299]

No other conclusion was reached by the Tribunal in *Antaris v. Czech Republic*, which observed that the investors made every effort to finish the PV power plants before the limitation of the support scheme by incoming changes, without conducting specific due diligence.[1300] This conduct of the investor was qualified as more opportunistic than diligent.[1301] However, such conduct cannot be regarded as a diligent business decision and may not be argued to be a violation of legitimate expectations.[1302]

It follows that investors, which foresaw, or could have foreseen, regulatory changes, cannot legitimately expect that the imminent changes will not affect their investments. If an investment is made despite such realisations, the expectations of the investors solely amount to speculative hope, as opposed to internationally-protected expectations.[1303]

---

set out by the law had already been reached, Belenergia S.A. v. Italian Republic, Award, 6 August 2019 ICSID Case No. ARB/15/40, para. 591.

1296 Isolux Netherlands, BV v. Kingdom of Spain Final, Award, 17 July 2016 SCC Case V2013/153, para. 787-792.

1297 ibid, para. 788.

1298 ibid, para. 789-792.

1299 ibid, para. 823.

1300 In the opinion of the Tribunal, the investors saw a window of opportunity and were aware, or should have been aware, that dealing with the solar boom was a fast-moving and controversial political issue, Antaris Solar and Dr. Michael Göde v. Czech Republic, Award, 2 May 2018 PCA Case No. 2014-01, para. 396, 431.

1301 ibid, para. 431.

1302 As phrased by the *Isolux* Tribunal "[a] party that decides to invest in a country that [...] lacks legal security, may not then turn to complain that such security was not provided", Isolux Netherlands, BV v. Kingdom of Spain Final, Award, 17 July 2016 SCC Case V2013/153, para. 818 (unofficial translation).

1303 Antaris Solar and Dr. Michael Göde v. Czech Republic, Award, 2 May 2018 PCA Case No. 2014-01, para. 435.

c) The Phenomenon of the Hindsight-Bias

Arbitral jurisprudence has demonstrated that the time of the investment is crucial, in order to determine whether a diligent investor could have had legitimate expectations. As the investment environment evolves, imminent changes may become more foreseeable at a later stage.[1304] This leads to another subtle, but important notion addressed by the Tribunal in *Antin v. Spain*, which should always be taken into account: The hindsight bias.[1305] The Tribunal observed that, when determining the sufficient level of due diligence, "tribunals must attempt to place themselves into the time of the investment and consider the information and conditions available at such time, and to refrain from appraising the investor's expectations with the benefit of hindsight".[1306]

The hindsight bias is a psychological phenomenon that occurs when evaluating events in hindsight. The effect is that the *ex-post* observer will be more inclined to find the particular event foreseeable, just based on the fact that it happened.[1307] It follows that an observer in an investment case, who is unaware of this phenomenon, may find *ex-post* that the investor should have or at least could have foreseen the chain of events that led to the alleged violation of the legitimate expectations. Thus, an investment tribunal should always try to take an *ex-ante* view, by following fixed requirements for the due diligence of an investor in the situation of the claimant.

4) Requirements for the Investor's Due Diligence

This Section revealed that a major question for the violation of the notion of legitimate expectations is whether diligent investors could have been

---

1304 In Isolux Netherlands, BV v. Kingdom of Spain Final, Award, 17 July 2016 SCC Case V2013/153 and Belenergia S.A. v. Italian Republic, Award, 6 August 2019 ICSID Case No. ARB/15/40 the respective tribunals deemed the investments to be conducted at time in which the change in the regulatory framework was already apparent.

1305 Antin Infrastructure Services Luxembourg S.à.r.l. and Antin Energia Termosolar B.V. v. Kingdom of Spain, Award, 15 June 2018 ICSID Case No. ARB/13/31, para. 537.

1306 ibid, para. 537.

1307 Biais and Weber, 'Hindsight Bias, Risk Perception, and Investment Performance' (2009) 55(6) Management Science 1018, p. 1019.

aware of any upcoming regulatory changes during the period relevant for their investments.[1308] In order to be diligent, investors need to consider parameters such as business risk or the industry's regular patterns before conducting their investments.[1309] Investors must be aware of political, socio-economic, cultural and historical conditions prevailing in the host state relevant in the context of the investment.[1310] Hence, the due diligence assessment of the investment environment must not only include simple business-related factors, but also the political situation of the host state itself. In case the investors encounter volatile political conditions in the host state, they cannot ignore the prevailing situation or rely legitimately on the stability and predictability of the host states conduct.[1311] If the investor does so regardless, this conduct may constitute a breach of its due diligence obligation and thus disqualify the investor from protection under international investment law.

As far as the reach of the legal due diligence analysis is concerned, the position of recent tribunals is supplemented by earlier case law.[1312] While it might seem excessive to impose strict and extensive requirements on the due diligence of the investor, it can be argued that an investor, which is conducting sizeable investments in a foreign country, is certainly capable of getting appropriate legal advice.[1313] Given the number of tribunals that rejected the legitimacy of the investors' expectations, when conducting none or very little due diligence, the rule can be deduced that investors

---

1308 Viñuales, 'Investor Diligence in Investment Arbitration: Sources and Arguments', p. 362.

1309 LG&E Energy Corp. LG&E Capital Corp. and LG&E International, Inc. v. The Argentine Republic, Decision on Liability, 3 October 2006 ICSID Case No. ARB/02/1, para. 130; Copper Mesa Mining Corporation v. Republic of Ecuador Award PCA No. 2012-2, para. 6.61.

1310 Duke Energy Electroquil Partners & Electroquil S.A. v. Republic of Ecuador, Award, 18 August 2008 ICSID Case No. ARB/04/19, para. 340. *See also* Ch. 4 II 3) a).

1311 Dolzer and Schreuer, *Principles of International Investment Law*, p. 148.

1312 *For example*, the Tribunal in *MTD* concurred that diligent investors are required to take into account not only the basic regulations applicable to foreign investment transactions, but also the entire legal framework potentially applicable to the investment (such as municipal zoning law), MTD Equity Sdn. Bhd. and MTD Chile S.A. v. Republic of Chile, Award, 25 May 2004 ICSID Case No. ARB/01/7, para. 176.

1313 RWE Innogy GmbH and RWE Innogy Aersa S.A.U. v. Kingdom of Spain, Decision on Jurisdicition, Liability, and certain Issues of Quantum, 6 January 2020 ICSID Case No. ARB/14/34, para. 510. *See also* Diehl, *The Core Standard of International Investment Protection*, p. 407.

must always conduct the diligence of an experienced business person. This gives the evaluation an objective scope, although the term "experienced business person" still remains a vague phrase. Nonetheless, jurisprudence made apparent that any diligent business person or investor knows, or should know, that laws will evolve over time. Thus, investors can never legitimately expect that the legal framework, which applies to their investment, will remain unaltered under all circumstances.

The only general exception is a specific commitment by the state to the stability of the legal framework. In the absence of a specific commitment, the investor must conduct a due diligence analysis and may only legitimately expect that the state does not act unfairly, unreasonably or inequitably in the exercise of its legislative power.[1314] However, if the due diligence obligation is severely disregarded, even a specific commitment of the state may not be sufficient to create legitimate expectations.[1315] Notwithstanding, this seems to be rather an exception and requires manifest disregard.[1316] Recent tribunals made clear that not every doubt or ambiguity created by the host state contradicting its former guarantee will render the expectations of the investor illegitimate.[1317]

Since legitimate expectations cannot be based on subjective hopes and perceptions, but rather on objectively verifiable facts[1318], the legal value of

---

1314 Parkerings-Compagniet AS v. Republic of Lithuania, Award, 11 September 2007 ICSID Case No. ARB/05/8, para. 332.

1315 Tribunals like *Bayindir* and *Electrabel* denied the legitimacy of certain expectations even in the presence of specific commitment by the state, if the investor had, or could have had, presented strong evidence that the specific commitment would not be honoured by the state due to a change in domestic policy or contradicting international obligations, Bayindir Insaat Turizm Ticaret Ve Sanayi A.S. v. Islamic Republic of Pakistan, Award, 27 August 2009 ICSID Case No. ARB/03/29, para. 193; Electrabel S.A. v. Republic of Hungary, Award, 25 November 2015 ICSID Case No. ARB/07/19, para. 7.78.

1316 The Tribunal in *Nykomb* held that a Contracting Party to the ECT cannot be relieved of its obligations for providing FET under the Treaty simply by announcing that legally binding commitments, upon which the foreign investor is relying, will not be honoured, Nykomb Synergetics Technology Holding AB v. The Republic of Latvia, SCC, Award, 16 December 2003 SCC, p. 37, 38.

1317 Novenergia II - Energy & Environment (SCA), SICAR v. The Kingdom of Spain, Award, 15 February 2018 SCC Case No. V 2015/063, para. 677; SolEs Badajoz GmbH v. Kingdom of Spain, Award, 31 July 2019 ICSID Case No. ARB/15/38, para. 439; Watkins Holdings S.à.r.l. and others v. Kingdom of Spain, Award, 21 January 2020 ICSID Case No. ARB/15/44, para. 579, 582, 588.

1318 Dolzer and Schreuer, *Principles of International Investment Law*, p. 145.

the relied-on sources is of importance. Private or unofficial sources do not have to be the subject of the due diligence report, except for extraordinary cases.[1319] Investors alien to the host states' business environment have to secure relevant information by either consulting specialised law firms or experienced business partners. The more states have substantiated their public interest objectives, through public debate and other means of information, the more likely it is that a tribunal will conclude that investors could have foreseen upcoming changes in the regulatory framework, with proper due diligence of the investment environment.[1320]

Regarding the volatile political conditions in the host state, it could be argued that the financial crisis in 2007/2008 and its economic impact was a state of political turbulence, which would have made the change in generous state subsidies likely. However, the only cases in which the respondent states—although only partly successfully—defended themselves with such an argument against alleged FET breaches were the claims against newly emerging former Soviet countries[1321], and the claims against Argentina, in the aftermath of its financial crisis[1322]. In recent cases, however, the economic difficulties in Italy were not qualified as so severe that a diligent investor would have had doubts that the state honoured its specific commitment.[1323]

1319 Novenergia II - Energy & Environment (SCA), SICAR v. The Kingdom of Spain, Award, 15 February 2018 SCC Case No. V 2015/063, para. 676-678. They may, however, play as role in the assessment of the socia-economic environment, *see* Ch. 4 II 2) b).

1320 Arriving at a similar conclusion: Levashova, *The Right of States to Regulate in International Investment Law*, p. 202.

1321 Alex Genin, Eastern Credit Limited, Inc. and A.S. Baltoil v. The Republic of Estonia, Award, 25 June 2001 ICSID Case No. ARB/99/2, para. 348; Parkerings-Compagniet AS v. Republic of Lithuania, Award, 11 September 2007 ICSID Case No. ARB/05/8, para. 335, 336; Tokios Tokelés v. Ukraine, Award, 26 July 2007 ICSID Case No. ARB/02/18, para. 7-11; Generation Ukraine, Inc. v. Ukraine, Award, 16 September 2003 ICSID Case No. ARB/00/9, para. 20.37.

1322 *For example* LG&E Energy Corp. LG&E Capital Corp. and LG&E International, Inc. v. The Argentine Republic, Decision on Liability, 3 October 2006 ICSID Case No. ARB/02/1; CMS Gas Transmission Company v. The Argentine Republic, Award, 21 May 2005 ICSID Case No. ARB/01/8; Metalpar S.A. and Buen Aire S.A. v. The Argentine Republic, Award, 6 June 2008 ICSID Case No. ARB/03/5.

1323 Greentech Energy Systems A/S, NovEnergia II Energy & Environment (SCA) SICAR, and NovEnergia II Italian Portfolio SA v. Italian Republic, Award, 23 December 2018 SCC Arbitration V (2015/095), para. 451.

The diligence must also be measured against the overall prudence of the investors in the process of the investment. A diligent investor must structure its investment in accordance with the apparent purpose of the legal framework.[1324] If the investor fails to do so, its investment is not (fully) protected against the revocation of the benefits gained from the exploit of the legal framework's flaws.

With regard to what an investor should have known at the time of the investment, the argument can be made that tribunals may only consider facts and circumstances that investors can prove to have known. The content of internal governmental or administrative communication, to which the investors were not privy at the time of the investment, cannot serve as a basis for legitimate expectations.[1325] Hence, any information that came to the investor's attention at a later stage, which would amplify their claim to legitimate expectations, may not be seen as proof of the expectation's legitimacy.

Moreover, the level of due diligence is strongly influenced by the legal framework regulating the investment. In a highly regulated field, such as the renewable energy sector, diligent investors are expected to conduct an extensive analysis of the law of the country, in which they plan to invest.[1326] In general, recent tribunals have been satisfied by the investors' due diligence, if the investors were able to demonstrate that they consulted competent law firms and made clear efforts to properly collect information regarding the possibility of changes in a regulatory framework.[1327]

1324 The Tribunal in *Yukos* held that the use of "tax optimisation schemes" by the investors triggered the host state's unfair behaviour and hence constituted at least contributory fault, Yukos Universal Ltd. (UK - Isle of Man) v. Russian Federation Final, Award, 18 July 2018 PCA Case No. AA 227, para. 1633, 1634. Similarly, albeit confronted with less severe misconduct, the Tribunal in *Antaris v. The Czech Republic* expressed that the investor may not legitimately expect to circumvent legal hurdles by using flaws in the legal framework, Antaris Solar and Dr. Michael Göde v. Czech Republic, Award, 2 May 2018 PCA Case No. 2014-01, para. 396, 431.

1325 Invesmart v. Czech Republic, Award, 26 June 2009 UNCITRAL, para. 252, 253; Jürgen Wirtgen, Stefan Wirtgen, Gisela Wirtgen and JSW Solar (zwei) GmbH & Co. KG v. Czech Republic, Award, 11 October 2017 PCA Case No. 2014-03, para. 421.

1326 Charanne and Construction Investments v. Kingdom of Spain, Award, 21 January 2016 SCC Case No. V 062/2012, para. 507.

1327 Foresight and others v. Kingdom of Spain Final, Award, 14 November 2018 SCC Case No. V 2015/150, para. 380; OperaFund Eco-Invest SICAV PLC and Schwab Holding AG v. Kingdom of Spain, Award, 6 September 2019 ICSID Case No. ARB/15/36, para. 487; Cube Infrastructure Fund SICAV and others

Although the host state's case law has no binding force in international law, and thus poses no precedent for the arbitral tribunals, it remains relevant as factual elements to determine the legitimate expectations of the investor. It follows that any diligent investor needs to make an extensive legal analysis of not only the statutory law but also of the relevant case law.

Another highly debated question is how a diligent business person should deal with legal uncertainty, when risk is spotted. Tribunals held that the simple awareness of potential risks is not harmful to the diligence of the investors, if the risk is regarded as remote or the changes were never expected to be that drastic or severe.[1328] In contrast, investors cannot be regarded as diligent, if the due diligence research revealed an imminent risk or the investors foresaw a potential change and tried to circumvent it.[1329]

The analysis of recent and earlier awards under and outside of the ECT has shown reoccurring themes. Thus, decisions in the renewable energy cases are in most respects in line with earlier arbitral decisions. Another facette of this conclusion is that there are no striking differences between

---

v. Kingdom of Spain, Decision on Jurisdiction, Liability and Partial Decision on Quantum, 19 February 2019 ICSID Case No. ARB/15/20, para. 401; Masdar Solar & Wind Cooperatief U.A. v. Kingdom of Spain, Award, 16 May 2018 ICSID Case No. ARB/14/1, para. 497.

1328 The Tribunal in *Antin* held that it was reasonable for an investor to believe that there would not be alteration as drastic and radical as in the present case, although the due diligence reports at the time of the investment had noticed a change in the legal framework, Antin Infrastructure Services Luxembourg S.à.r.l. and Antin Energia Termosolar B.V. v. Kingdom of Spain, Award, 15 June 2018 ICSID Case No. ARB/13/31, para. 548, 562. The Tribunal in *RREEF* found that it does not create legitimate expectations, if the investor is aware of possible changes in the future, but if the changes turned out to be so drastic and radical that the minimum expectation of a reasonable return was violated, RREEF Infrastructure (G.P.) Limited and RREEF Pan-European Infrastructure Two Lux S.à.r.l. v. Kingdom of Spain, Decision on Responsibility and on the Principles of Quantum, 30 November 2018 ICSID Case No. ARB/13/30, para. 398, 399, 589.

1329 The Tribunal in *Blusun* found that investors cannot legitimately expect that their investment remains unharmed by imminent risks, even though the due diligence analysis merely regards them as "remote", Blusun S.A. Jean-Pierre Lecorcier and Michael Stein v. Italian Republic, Award, 27 December 2016 ICSID Case No. ARB/14/3, para. 384-386. The Tribunal *Antaris* held the investor to be merely "opportunistic", when the investor tried to invest "last minute" before changes to the legal framework were implemented, Antaris Solar and Dr. Michael Göde v. Czech Republic, Award, 2 May 2018 PCA Case No. 2014-01, para. 435.

the "classic" fossil-fuelled energy sector and the renewable energy sector, as both sectors are highly regulated and therefore demand an equivalent high level of due diligence. Furthermore, it is noteworthy that in the recent renewable energy cases, the due diligence matters were only discussed at the merits stage.[1330] Previous tribunals, however, have tended to consider menial due diligence at the quantum stage and reduced the damages awarded to the investors significantly through the concept of contributory fault.[1331] Hence, the lack of due diligence may not necessarily lead to a loss of the right to FET in every case, although recent tribunals have tended to follow an "all or nothing" approach.

In conclusion, an investor must show a high level of due diligence, which has to be tested against the diligence of an experienced business person. The level of due diligence rises, the more money is invested. On the other hand, investors are not required to conduct extensive legal analysis, if the wording and the intentions of the legal framework are clear. Although the term "experienced business person" gives an objective scope to the analysis, it remains a vague and undefined legal concept. Thus, this issue has to be assessed on a case-by-case basis. The due diligence, however, must include four key features:

(1) The investor has to analyse the basic regulations applicable to foreign investment transactions and the entire legal framework potentially applicable to the investment.
(2) The investor has to analyse the investment environment including risks related to the business itself, as well as risks regarding the stability of the legal framework and the host state itself.
(3) The investor has to have realistic expectations about the profitability of the investment. While it is legitimate to expect a reasonable return in

---

1330 Due diligence was even refused to be taken in consideration while discussing the quantum, inter alia, by Greentech Energy Systems A/S, NovEnergia II Energy & Environment (SCA) SICAR, and NovEnergia II Italian Portfolio SA v. Italian Republic, Award, 23 December 2018 SCC Arbitration V (2015/095), para. 547, 548.

1331 Occidental Exploration and Production Company v. The Republic of Ecuador Final, Award, 1 July 2004 LCIA Case No. UN3467, para. 687; MTD Equity Sdn. Bhd. and MTD Chile S.A. v. Republic of Chile, Award, 25 May 2004 ICSID Case No. ARB/01/7, para. 242, 243; Yukos Universal Ltd. (UK - Isle of Man) v. Russian Federation Final, Award, 18 July 2018 PCA Case No. AA 227, para. 1637; Hesham T. M. Al Warraq v. Republic of Indonesia, Award, 15 December 2014 UNCITRAL, para. 683.

general, the investor is not protected under the FET, if the investment is undertaken in a "high-risk/high-return" environment.

(4) The investor has to base its analysis on facts and circumstances offered by the host state. Unofficial sources are supplementary at best.

If the investor assesses the risks or expected returns unreasonably, subsequent losses have to be qualified as simple business risks, which are not protected by the FET standard.

III. The Host State's Margin of Discretion when Changing the Legal Framework

It has been established that the legal framework of a state is by its nature subject to change.[1332] In particular, investors cannot expect the legal framework to remain unaltered if there have been previous amendments.[1333] However, if this contention was without limits, no legitimate expectations in regard to a regulatory framework, which has not been established from scratch, could exist. Instead, the better approach is that, in the absence of a specific commitment, there cannot be the expectation that the regulatory framework will never be changed, but a certain degree of stability can be expected.

The test for the violation of this general stability requirement and hence the legitimate expectations is two-fold: First, it must be examined whether the investor had legitimate expectations. Second, it must be assessed whether those expectations were frustrated. As demonstrated in this Chapter, tribunals in the renewable energy cases show the tendency to qualify the conduct of the state and the reliance of the investors as sufficient to create legitimate expectations. However, less conformity is demonstrated, when it comes to determining the content of legitimate expectations and which measures frustrated them.

Generally, the notion of legitimate expectations does not bar the states from introducing regulatory changes.[1334] Recent tribunals held

1332 *See* Ch. 2 VI 1).

1333 Isolux Netherlands, BV v. Kingdom of Spain Final, Award, 17 July 2016 SCC Case V2013/153, para. 784, 785, 787; Antaris Solar and Dr. Michael Göde v. Czech Republic, Award, 2 May 2018 PCA Case No. 2014-01, para. 431.

1334 *See for example* Electrabel S.A. v. Republic of Hungary, Award, 25 November 2015 ICSID Case No. ARB/07/19, para. 7.77; OperaFund Eco-Invest SICAV PLC and Schwab Holding AG v. Kingdom of Spain, Award, 6 September 2019 ICSID Case No. ARB/15/36, para. 485; RREEF Infrastructure (G.P.) Limited and RREEF Pan-European Infrastructure Two Lux S.à.r.l. v. Kingdom

unanimously that states are, in principle, free to change their regulatory framework for various business sectors in light of public interest.[1335] This notwithstanding, tribunals constantly grappled with finding a methodology for the evaluation of the implementation of regulatory measures in light of a violation of the FET standard.[1336] In recent decisions, the attention turned to the questions of whether the changes were reasonable, proportional, or necessary, in order to determine the impact of the measures on the investor in light of the interest at stake for the states.[1337] Another reoccurring factor was the predictability of the introduced changes, particularly the question of whether measures were of retroactive effect.[1338] Depending on the specificity of the states' commitments, tribunals have considered different degrees of impact on investors' investments to be acceptable, i.e. not violating the legitimate expectations of the investors.

1) Reasonableness and Proportionality of the State's Acts

Reasonableness and proportionality are two closely related concepts in domestic and international law. In investment law, both notions are implemented in the FET standard as a balancing mechanism, either as a

---

of Spain, Decision on Responsibility and on the Principles of Quantum, 30 November 2018 ICSID Case No. ARB/13/30, para. 315, 316; Blusun S.A. Jean-Pierre Lecorcier and Michael Stein v. Italian Republic, Award, 27 December 2016 ICSID Case No. ARB/14/3, para. 363.

1335 OperaFund Eco-Invest SICAV PLC and Schwab Holding AG v. Kingdom of Spain, Award, 6 September 2019 ICSID Case No. ARB/15/36, para. 509; Antin Infrastructure Services Luxembourg S.à.r.l. and Antin Energia Termosolar B.V. v. Kingdom of Spain, Award, 15 June 2018 ICSID Case No. ARB/13/31, para. 532; Charanne and Construction Investments v. Kingdom of Spain, Award, 21 January 2016 SCC Case No. V 062/2012, para. 500, Foresight and others v. Kingdom of Spain Final, Award, 14 November 2018 SCC Case No. V 2015/150, para. 363; Cavalum SGPS v. Kingdom of Spain, Decision on Jurisdiction, Liability and Directions on Quantum, 31 August 2020 ICSID Case No. ARB/15/34, para. 419; Photovoltaik Knopf Betriebs-GmbH v. The Czech Republic, Award, 15 May 2019 PCA CASE No 2014-21, para. 494.

1336 AES Summit Generation Limited et. al. v. The Republic of Hungary, Award, 23 September 2010 ICSID Case No. ARB/07/22, para. 9.3.38; Electrabel S.A. v. Republic of Hungary, Award, 25 November 2015 ICSID Case No. ARB/07/19, para. 180. *See also* Coop and Seif, *ECT and State's Right to Regulate*, para. 10.83-10.87.

1337 *See* Ch. 4 III 1) b) and c).

1338 *See* Ch. 4 III 2).

self-standing notion or as the core aspect of the legitimate expectations of an investor.[1339] Tribunals have emphasised that it is not sufficient that change in the regulatory framework had a detrimental effect on the investments to establish liability under the FET standard.[1340] Rather, some type of balancing act must reveal an imbalance of the state's measure to the detriment of the investor.[1341] Accordingly, the Tribunal in *Charanne v. Spain* found acceptance in arbitral jurisprudence and stated that investors must rather demonstrate that the changes were also "incompatible with a criterion of economic reasonableness, with public interest or with the principle of proportionality".[1342] Thereby, it is not necessary that each of the state's measures were unreasonable individually, but it is theoretically possible that numerous changes in the regulatory system could be tantamount to a violation of the obligation to afford FET to the investors.[1343] It must be noted, however, that recent tribunals demonstrated an awareness that the criterion of "unreasonableness" should not be construed in a way to give arbitral tribunals the authority to scrutinise the host states' policy decisions.[1344] In the same vein, it has been repeatedly cited that, although

---

1339 *See* Ch. 2 IV 3).

1340 El Paso Energy International Company v. The Argentine Republic, Award, 31 October 2011 ICSID Case No. ARB/03/15, para. 400; Parkerings-Compagniet AS v. Republic of Lithuania, Award, 11 September 2007 ICSID Case No. ARB/05/8, para. 332; Impregilo S.p.A. v. The Argentine Republic, Award, 21 June 2011 ICSID Case No. ARB/07/17, para. 291; The PV Investors v. Kingdom of Spain Final, Award, 28 February 2020 PCA Case No. 2012-14, para. 580-582.

1341 Saluka Investments B.V. v. The Czech Republic Partial, Award, 17 March 2006 UNCITRAL, para. 306; Electrabel S.A. v. Republic of Hungary, Award, 25 November 2015 ICSID Case No. ARB/07/19, para. 165; Rusoro Mining Ltd. v. Bolivarian Republic of Venezuela, Award, 22 August 2016 ICSID Case No. ARB(AF)/12/5, para. 525; The PV Investors v. Kingdom of Spain Final, Award, 28 February 2020 PCA Case No. 2012-14, para. 583.

1342 Charanne and Construction Investments v. Kingdom of Spain, Award, 21 January 2016 SCC Case No. V 062/2012, para. 514 (unofficial translation).

1343 Stadtwerke München GmbH and others v. Kingdom of Spain, Award, 2 December 2019 ICSID Case No. ARB/15/1, para. 257.

1344 Blusun S.A. Jean-Pierre Lecorcier and Michael Stein v. Italian Republic, Award, 27 December 2016 ICSID Case No. ARB/14/3, para. 318; RREEF Infrastructure (G.P.) Limited and RREEF Pan-European Infrastructure Two Lux S.à.r.l. v. Kingdom of Spain, Decision on Responsibility and on the Principles of Quantum, 30 November 2018 ICSID Case No. ARB/13/30, para. 468; Hydro Energy 1 S.A.R.L. and Hydroxana Sweden AB v. The Kingdom of Spain, Decision on Jurisdiction, Liability and Directions on Quantum, 9 March 2020 ICSID Case No. ARB/15/42, para. 676.

investors do not have an "unmodifiable right", the changes affecting their investments have to be within a reasonable and predictable frame.[1345]

This reflects a longstanding line of arbitral jurisprudence.[1346] In general, state measures can be qualified as "rational", if they are consistent with the public policy expressed prior to the investment by the host state.[1347] Hence, although investors do not have an immutable right to stability, the investors may legitimately expect that legislative acts or other state measures abide at least to some degree by the criteria of public interest, economic reasonableness and proportionality.[1348] If a state follows these criteria, a certain degree of stability and predictability of the legal environment can be guaranteed. However, it must be further determined under what circumstances these criteria are met.

1345 Charanne and Construction Investments v. Kingdom of Spain, Award, 21 January 2016 SCC Case No. V 062/2012, para. 500; Eiser Infrastructure Limited and Energía Solar Luxembourg S.à.r.l. v. Kingdom of Spain, Award, 4 May 2017 ICSID Case No. ARB/13/36, para. 382; RREEF Infrastructure (G.P.) Limited and RREEF Pan-European Infrastructure Two Lux S.à.r.l. v. Kingdom of Spain, Decision on Responsibility and on the Principles of Quantum, 30 November 2018 ICSID Case No. ARB/13/30, para. 315, 316; Watkins Holdings S.à.r.l. and others v. Kingdom of Spain, Award, 21 January 2020 ICSID Case No. ARB/15/44, para. 520, 521.

1346 The Tribunal in *Total* held that the investor's expectations may be frustrated even in the absence of specific commitments, when the host state performs acts incompatible with the principles of economic rationality, the public interest or the principle of rationality, Total S.A. v. The Argentine Republic, Decision on Liability, 27 December 2010 ICSID Case No. ARB/04/01, para. 333. Similarly, the Tribunal in *Electrabel* observed that "a measure will not be arbitrary if it is reasonably related to a rational policy", Electrabel S.A. v. Republic of Hungary, Award, 25 November 2015 ICSID Case No. ARB/07/19, para. 179. *See also* AES Corporation and Tau Power B.V. v. Republic of Kazakhstan, Award, 1 November 2013 ICSID Case No. ARB/10/16, para. 258; Continental Casualty Company v. The Argentine Republic, Award, 5 September 2008 ICSID Case No. ARB/03/9, para. 258; Parkerings-Compagniet AS v. Republic of Lithuania, Award, 11 September 2007 ICSID Case No. ARB/05/8, para. 332; Marvin Roy Feldman Karpa v. United Mexican States, Award, 16 December 2002 ICSID Case No. ARB(AF)/99/1, para. 103.

1347 AES Summit Generation Limited et. al. v. The Republic of Hungary, Award, 23 September 2010 ICSID Case No. ARB/07/22, para. 10.3.36.

1348 Parkerings-Compagniet AS v. Republic of Lithuania, Award, 11 September 2007 ICSID Case No. ARB/05/8, para. 332, 333.

a) The Link between the State's Actions and the Public Interest

The public interest, in which the state acts, is the starting point for every assessment of reasonableness or proportionality. There must be a link between the measure and the objective sought to be achieved by the state.[1349] Otherwise, the infringement of the investors' rights will always outweigh the motivation leading to the measures taken. On the contrary, states are afforded a broader margin of discretion, if they sought to protect public interests of paramount importance.[1350]

In general, recent tribunals addressed this indeterminate concept of public interest and the states' right to regulate, by establishing whether there was an appropriate correlation between the host state's objective and the measures it took, in light of the rights at stake for investors.[1351] Thereby, the state and the competent authorities are afforded a prerogative of assessment, which circumstances are to be considered relevant for the public interest.[1352] Tribunals have accepted that states act in the public interest, when the measures were implemented to reduce the costs of subsidies in order to shield the public from excessive electricity prices and secure the sustainability of support schemes.[1353] Even if the measures implement constituted a break with previous policy decisions, states have the continuing duty to protect the public and themselves from adverse effects

1349 Dolzer and Schreuer, *Principles of International Investment Law*, p. 148.

1350 *See* Ch. 2 III 1).

1351 Blusun S.A. Jean-Pierre Lecorcier and Michael Stein v. Italian Republic, Award, 27 December 2016 ICSID Case No. ARB/14/3, para. 318; SolEs Badajoz GmbH v. Kingdom of Spain, Award, 31 July 2019 ICSID Case No. ARB/15/38, para. 451; The PV Investors v. Kingdom of Spain Final, Award, 28 February 2020 PCA Case No. 2012-14, para. 595, 596. *See also* Ch. 2 IV 3) c).

1352 Blusun S.A. Jean-Pierre Lecorcier and Michael Stein v. Italian Republic, Award, 27 December 2016 ICSID Case No. ARB/14/3, para. 318; SolEs Badajoz GmbH v. Kingdom of Spain, Award, 31 July 2019 ICSID Case No. ARB/15/38, para. 451.

1353 Belenergia S.A. v. Italian Republic, Award, 6 August 2019 ICSID Case No. ARB/15/40, para. 602-610, 630; Charanne and Construction Investments v. Kingdom of Spain, Award, 21 January 2016 SCC Case No. V 062/2012, para. 535; Cube Infrastructure Fund SICAV and others v. Kingdom of Spain, Decision on Jurisdiction, Liability and Partial Decision on Quantum, 19 February 2019 ICSID Case No. ARB/15/20, para. 409; I.C.W. Europe Investments Limited v. The Czech Republic, Award, 15 May 2019 PCA CASE No 2014-22, para. 639.

of previous miscalculated policies.[1354] However, states may not arbitrarily implement changes as they deem appropriate, but must "act in accordance with the legal commitments that it has made and the obligations that bind it".[1355] For example, it could be argued that a state's tariff reduction as a reaction to declining installation costs can be reasonable, if the affected plants actually profited from the reduced installation costs. In contrast, the retroactive application of such changes to older power plants that were not able to profit from declining installation costs would constitute an unreasonable measure.

The Tribunal in *AES Summit v. Hungary* defined a "rational policy" as a policy "taken by a state following a logical (good sense) explanation, with the aim of addressing a public interest matter".[1356] Thereby, the measures implemented by the host state must address a matter of public interest and must demonstrate that the measures are properly justified by providing a record of the reform options and explanatory documents and discussions.[1357] Combatting excessively high returns of investors at the expense of the consumers can be regarded as a "perfectly valid and rational policy objective".[1358] Hence, any measures linked to this public interest matter are not a violation of the FET standard, as long as they also abide by the other criteria, i.e. economic reasonableness and proportionality.[1359]

From this line of jurisprudence, it can be deduced that states cannot simply justify any act adversely affecting investors' rights, by putting forth a public interest of importance. Rather, the adverse effects must not exceed the acceptable margin of discretion of the state.[1360] Consequently, the acts must be reasonably implemented and set into proportion with the effects they have on foreign investments. Economic hardship does not necessarily

---

1354 Cube Infrastructure Fund SICAV and others v. Kingdom of Spain, Decision on Jurisdiction, Liability and Partial Decision on Quantum, 19 February 2019 ICSID Case No. ARB/15/20, para. 409.

1355 ibid, para. 409.

1356 AES Summit Generation Limited et. al. v. The Republic of Hungary, Award, 23 September 2010 ICSID Case No. ARB/07/22, para. 10.3.8.

1357 ibid, para. 10.3.31, 10.3.32.

1358 ibid, para. 10.3.34.

1359 ibid, para. 10.3.36.

1360 Hydro Energy 1 S.A.R.L. and Hydroxana Sweden AB v. The Kingdom of Spain, Decision on Jurisdiction, Liability and Directions on Quantum, 9 March 2020 ICSID Case No. ARB/15/42, para. 676; Antaris Solar and Dr. Michael Göde v. Czech Republic, Award, 2 May 2018 PCA Case No. 2014-01, para. 360; SunReserve Luxco Holdings v. Italian Republic Final, Award, 25 March 2020 SCC Arbitration V (2016/32), para. 685, 735.

equal public interests of importance, such as public health, protection of the environment, and access to water.[1361] It is therefore not surprising that the notion of public interest has played only a subordinate role in recent tribunals' considerations.

b) Economic Reasonableness of the State Acts

In the context of economic reasonableness, tribunals have examined the effects of the state measures on the profitability of the investments. Tribunals have shown sympathy for the idea that states maintain the discretion to decide reasonable measures. However, the states must also abide by the rules they set themselves when expressly codifying guarantees in their legal framework.[1362] This holds especially true if investors relied on these express codifications in their investment decision and are unable to disinvest.[1363] It has been observed that it is a common practice among states to offer various incentives just to dismantle them for future investments.[1364] One particular sign of unreasonableness spotted is the alteration of the legal framework with retroactive effect.[1365] Another aspect of reasonableness is whether the issue the host state aims to combat a problem that had already existed before the investment was conducted.[1366] If so, drastic changes to the regulatory framework may not be seen as a sign of a rational policy.[1367]

1361 *See* Ch. 2 IV 2).

1362 OperaFund Eco-Invest SICAV PLC and Schwab Holding AG v. Kingdom of Spain, Award, 6 September 2019 ICSID Case No. ARB/15/36, para. 510.

1363 ibid, para. 510.

1364 ibid, para. 510.

1365 ibid, para. 510, 511.

1366 Watkins Holdings S.à.r.l. and others v. Kingdom of Spain, Award, 21 January 2020 ICSID Case No. ARB/15/44, para. 599.

1367 Watkins Holdings S.à.r.l. and others v. Kingdom of Spain, Award, 21 January 2020 ICSID Case No. ARB/15/44, para. 599. With regard to the 2010 amendments of the Spanish support scheme, the Tribunal in *Charanne* concluded that, in economic terms, both the temporal limitation, as well as the limitation of eligible hours, cannot be branded as irrational, Charanne and Construction Investments v. Kingdom of Spain, Award, 21 January 2016 SCC Case No. V 062/2012, para. 534.

Moreover, host states are prohibited from engaging in behaviour that can be categorized as "bait-and-switch" tactic.[1368] "Bait-and-switch" tactics in an investment context can be characterized by the host state introducing a legal system that provides for an above-average return in order to raise the hopes and expectations of investors.[1369] When the host state is then unable to deal with its budget deficit, partially or fully caused by the support systems, it adjusts the levels of remuneration in a drastic and fundamental manner.[1370] It is evident, that such "bait-and-switch" tactics, in which investors and their capital are lured in the host state with promises which are subsequently reversed, are contrary to the criterion of economic reasonableness.

The tribunals, particularly in the Italian renewable energy cases, generally accepted that regulatory measures, which were linked to a public interest of importance, afforded a wider margin of discretion to the host state.[1371] This wide margin of discretion allows states to introduce changes that reduce the investors' returns to a reasonable degree.[1372] Only if the

---

1368 The term „bait-and-switch" was introduced by Robert Volterra in RREEF Infrastructure (G.P.) Limited and RREEF Pan-European Infrastructure Two Lux S.à.r.l. v. Kingdom of Spain, Partially Dissenting Opinion of Robert Volterra, 30 November 2018 ICSID Case No. ARB/13/30, para. 26. *See also* Novenergia II - Energy & Environment (SCA), SICAR v. The Kingdom of Spain, Award, 15 February 2018 SCC Case No. V 2015/063, para. 705.

1369 *See Robert Volterras* characterization of the Spanish renewable energy support system in RREEF Infrastructure (G.P.) Limited and RREEF Pan-European Infrastructure Two Lux S.à.r.l. v. Kingdom of Spain, Partially Dissenting Opinion of Robert Volterra, 30 November 2018 ICSID Case No. ARB/13/30, para. 26.

1370 ibid, para. 26.

1371 Blusun S.A. Jean-Pierre Lecorcier and Michael Stein v. Italian Republic, Award, 27 December 2016 ICSID Case No. ARB/14/3, para. 318; SunReserve Luxco Holdings v. Italian Republic Final, Award, 25 March 2020 SCC Arbitration V (2016/32), para. 945, 946, 948; Belenergia S.A. v. Italian Republic, Award, 6 August 2019 ICSID Case No. ARB/15/40, para. 630.

1372 In light of the public interest matters at stake, the Tribunal in *CEF* observed that the options provided by the *Spalma Incentivi Decree* were in of themselves not per se economically unreasonable, CEF Energia B.V. v. Italian Republic, Award, 16 January 2019 SCC Arbitration No. 2015/158, para. 240-244. *See also* the dissenting opinion of *Boisson de Chazournes* and the contrasting view expressed by the majority in ESPF Beteiligungs GmbH et. al. v. Italian Republic, Award, 14 September 2020 ICSID Case No. ARB/16/5, para. 709. The *Spalma Incentivi Decree* provided for (1) the extension of the duration of incentives while reducing incentives proportionally investments lifetime, (2) the variation of the quantum of incentives throughout time, (3) or the reduction

state committed to certain conduct, is its margin of discretion limited to the scope of the commitment.[1373] Under what circumstances a commitment to specific conduct is given, was examined above.[1374] Such a commitment does usually not already exist, if the host state gives the prospect of a simple return of investment, without a profit element.[1375] If the host state did not give a commitment to specific remuneration, investors may only legitimately expect to receive a reasonable return, instead of a specific return. The question of whether a return is still reasonable focuses on the actual return from the individual power plants received after the regulatory changes in light of their economic impact.[1376]

c) Proportionality between the State's Acts and the Investor's Rights

In contrast to the notion of reasonableness, disproportionality is more determinate, due to built-in limitations.[1377] The acceptance of the concept of proportionality by domestic administrative law courts, human rights courts and other bodies of international law has been demonstrated *supra*.[1378] Recent tribunals also considered proportionality in the core of their assessment of the reasonableness of the states' measures.[1379]

---

of the incentives altogether proportionate to the PV plant's annual production capacity.

1373 The Tribunal in *CEF* took into consideration that the investment was still profitable and provided for a fair return over 20 years. The Tribunal found that these measures in themselves reasonable but still violated the specific commitment given by the host state, CEF Energia B.V. v. Italian Republic, Award, 16 January 2019 SCC Arbitration No. 2015/158, para. 240-244.

1374 *See* Ch. 4 I.

1375 Contrary thereto, *Gary Born* held that the simple prospect to of a return would normally not have been sufficient to induce investment. Hence the investors could have legitimately expected to receive more than just a "reasonable" return, but the specific and generous remuneration set out in the ERO regulations, Antaris Solar and Dr. Michael Göde v. Czech Republic, Dissenting Opinion, 2 May 2018 PCA Case No. 2014-01, para. 23.

1376 *See* Ch. 4 III 3).

1377 Blusun S.A. Jean-Pierre Lecorcier and Michael Stein v. Italian Republic, Award, 27 December 2016 ICSID Case No. ARB/14/3, para. 318. *See* Ch. 2 IV 3) c).

1378 *See* Ch. 2 IV 3) a).

1379 RREEF Infrastructure (G.P.) Limited and RREEF Pan-European Infrastructure Two Lux S.à.r.l. v. Kingdom of Spain, Decision on Responsibility and on the Principles of Quantum, 30 November 2018 ICSID Case No. ARB/13/30

In the examination of the proportionality of the measures, tribunals assessed whether the state states acted in light of a profound public interest.[1380] Within this assessment, the decisive hallmark was whether the changes to the regulatory regime had a severe, but not detrimental, impact on the investment.[1381]

However, a simple link between a matter of public interest and the state's measure is not sufficient, on its own, to justify the investor's loss in light of proportionality. If there were less intrusive means available, the measures implemented by the host state may not have been necessary to achieve the host state's objectives.[1382] Necessity of the measures, however, is a key aspect of the Continental European approach to proportionality.[1383] If following an approach that is more based on reasonableness, one

---

para. 464; Hydro Energy 1 S.A.R.L. and Hydroxana Sweden AB v. The Kingdom of Spain, Decision on Jurisdiction, Liability and Directions on Quantum, 9 March 2020 ICSID Case No. ARB/15/42, para. 573; Cavalum SGPS v. Kingdom of Spain, Decision on Jurisdiction, Liability and Directions on Quantum, 31 August 2020 ICSID Case No. ARB/15/34, para. 414.

1380 The Tribunal in *Antaris* considered measures to be appropriate, "if they do not exceed the exercise of the host State's normal regulatory power in the pursuance of public interest and do not modify the regulatory framework relied upon by the investor at the time of its investment outside the acceptable margin of change", Antaris Solar and Dr. Michael Göde v. Czech Republic, Award, 2 May 2018 PCA Case No. 2014-01, para. 360(7). Similarly, the *Blusun* Tribunal observed that, although the host state's measures were "quite substantial", the change in the regulatory framework was not disproportionate to the infringement, as investors' rights were introduced as a "response to a genuine fiscal need, given the large take-up under the earlier Energy Accounts", Blusun S.A. Jean-Pierre Lecorcier and Michael Stein v. Italian Republic, Award, 27 December 2016 ICSID Case No. ARB/14/3, para. 342.

1381 Blusun S.A. Jean-Pierre Lecorcier and Michael Stein v. Italian Republic, Award, 27 December 2016 ICSID Case No. ARB/14/3, para. 342.

1382 The Tribunal in *Watkins* made the remark that less intrusive means, such as a tax on all CO_2 emissions, has even been identified by state officials, Watkins Holdings S.à.r.l. and others v. Kingdom of Spain, Award, 21 January 2020 ICSID Case No. ARB/15/44, para. 602. The Tribunal in *BayWa* included necessity-considerations in their assessment of the host state's measures and concurred that the claw-back "has not been shown to have been necessary to resolve the tariff deficit problem, which would have been solved in any event by the Disputed Measures without much further delay and without the element of claw-back of payments earlier lawfully made", BayWa r.e. Renewable Energy GmbH and BayWa r.e. Asset Holding GmbH v. Kingdom of Spain, Decision on Jurisdiction, Liability and Directions on Quantum, 2 December 2019 ICSID Case No. ARB/15/16, para. 496.

1383 *See* Ch. 2 IV 3) b).

may consider that measures are not out of proportion to the problem that they were designed to solve, if investors still receive a reasonable return on their investment.[1384] In balancing the opposing interests, the principle of a "shared sacrifice", i.e. those benefiting from the system should contribute to its continued operation and financial stability, can be followed.[1385] Under such principle, the decrease of the investors' revenue may be considered reasonably proportionate to the aim and purpose of the measures implemented by the respondent state, depending on how severe the economic impact is.[1386]

In addition, proportionality requires that the states' measures are not random or arbitrary, provided that they do not significantly modify the legal framework.[1387] The appropriateness of the modification can then be determined by an empirical assessment of the damages incurred by the investor.[1388] At its core, a proportionality analysis should take into account the nature of the right and the specific context of the case.[1389] The burden borne by the investor must not exceed what can reasonably be expected, in light of the general invitation and encouragement by the host state, to invest in a particular sector by reference to benefits including a very favourable remuneration regime.[1390]

1384 The Tribunal in *Stadtwerke* linked the proportionality of the measures to the rate of return the investors received after the alteration of the *Special Regime* and observed that the return rate was still reasonable, Stadtwerke München GmbH and others v. Kingdom of Spain, Award, 2 December 2019 ICSID Case No. ARB/15/1, para. 300, 325.

1385 ibid, para. 354.

1386 ibid, para. 354.

1387 RREEF Infrastructure (G.P.) Limited and RREEF Pan-European Infrastructure Two Lux S.à.r.l. v. Kingdom of Spain, Decision on Responsibility and on the Principles of Quantum, 30 November 2018 ICSID Case No. ARB/13/30, para. 460.

1388 RREEF Infrastructure (G.P.) Limited and RREEF Pan-European Infrastructure Two Lux S.à.r.l. v. Kingdom of Spain, Decision on Responsibility and on the Principles of Quantum, 30 November 2018 ICSID Case No. ARB/13/30, para. 472. *See also* Stadtwerke München GmbH and others v. Kingdom of Spain, Award, 2 December 2019 ICSID Case No. ARB/15/1, para. 355.

1389 RWE Innogy GmbH and RWE Innogy Aersa S.A.U. v. Kingdom of Spain, Decision on Jurisdicition, Liability, and certain Issues of Quantum, 6 January 2020 ICSID Case No. ARB/14/34, para. 570, 598, 600.

1390 RWE Innogy GmbH and RWE Innogy Aersa S.A.U. v. Kingdom of Spain, Decision on Jurisdicition, Liability, and certain Issues of Quantum, 6 January 2020 ICSID Case No. ARB/14/34, para. 570, 598, 600. *See also* Cube Infrastructure Fund SICAV and others v. Kingdom of Spain, Decision on Jurisdiction,

Therefore, factors for the disproportionality can, inter alia, be (1) the loss of considerable revenue, (2) the burden on individual plants exceeding that of similar plants, and (3) shortfall of a minimum return of less than 7%.[1391] The overall assessment of recent jurisprudence reveals that a measure, in order to be appropriate, must also have a sufficient link to a matter of public interest. Moreover, it must be one of the least intrusive means to address the issue and must not be excessive with regard to the damages it causes the investors.

d) Development towards a Stronger Role of the Proportionality Test

The 2012 UNCTAD Report on the FET standard already recognized the trend in arbitral jurisprudence to approach the balancing test in the notion of legitimate expectations.[1392] The Report observed the tendency in arbitral jurisprudence to determine the reasonableness of the state's measure and the investor's expectations, in light of the public interest at stake.[1393] By doing so, tribunals assess the link between the investment and specific commitments made by the host state to the investor.[1394] As it has been demonstrated in this Chapter, the principles of economic rationality, public interest, reasonableness and proportionality are of crucial importance to the assessment of reasonableness and, hence, legitimate expectations.

In order to prove the unreasonableness of the state's measure, an investor must demonstrate that the measures implemented do not bear "a reasonable relationship to some rational policy".[1395] In turn, a rational policy requires that the states act through logical and good sense means, in the pursuit of a public interest matter.[1396] Whether the public interest pursued and the measures implemented were in an appropriate correlation

---

Liability and Partial Decision on Quantum, 19 February 2019 ICSID Case No. ARB/15/20, para. 431, 434

1391 RWE Innogy GmbH and RWE Innogy Aersa S.A.U. v. Kingdom of Spain, Decision on Jurisdicition, Liability, and certain Issues of Quantum, 6 January 2020 ICSID Case No. ARB/14/34, para. 599.

1392 UNCTAD, 'Fair and Equitable Treatment', p. 68.

1393 ibid, p. 68.

1394 ibid, p. 68.

1395 Saluka Investments B.V. v. The Czech Republic Partial, Award, 17 March 2006 UNCITRAL, para. 460.

1396 AES Summit Generation Limited et. al. v. The Republic of Hungary, Award, 23 September 2010 ICSID Case No. ARB/07/22, para. 10.3.8.

demands an examination, in light of the nature of the states' measures and how they were implemented in detail.[1397] Such an approach offers the states a wider margin of discretion in order to cope efficiently with public interest matters.[1398] This allows democratic states to address issues of public controversies, such as a high level of profit by energy producers, and precludes that measures implemented to remedy those issues are per se qualified as irrational or arbitrary.[1399] This reasoning even applies if the motivation of the state's action is simply populistic.[1400]

Arbitral jurisprudence uniformly demonstrated that economic reasons, such as the sustainability of the support schemes, may constitute a matter of public interest. This public interest concern can then be addressed by states through measures and regulatory changes, without being unreasonable or disproportionate. This notwithstanding, the states must still tailor their measures with due regard to the consequences imposed on investors.[1401] Thus, the states must find one of the less intrusive means, albeit not necessarily the least intrusive means, as long as the proportionality analysis does not reduce the state's margin of discretion to one single measure.[1402]

The analysis shows that the combined notion of reasonableness and proportionality has two dimensions: Firstly, a general view of the impact of changes in the legal framework by considering the public interest, i.e. the purpose of the governmental measure, and the interest of investors, measured by the depth of the intervention and the previous commitments of the host state. Thereby, it is assessed whether the changes were pre-

1397 ibid, para. 10.3.9.

1398 The Tribunal in *Electrabel* observed in regard to this that "the host State is entitled to maintain a reasonable degree of regulatory flexibility to respond to changing circumstances in the public interest", Electrabel S.A. v. Republic of Hungary, Award, 25 November 2015 ICSID Case No. ARB/07/19, para. 7.77.

1399 ibid, para. 8.23.

1400 ibid, para. 8.23.

1401 Ioan Micula, Viorel Micula, S.C. European Food S.A, S.C. Starmill S.R.L. and S.C. Multipack S.R.L. v. Romania, Award, 11 December 2013 ICSID Case No. ARB/05/20, para. 525.

1402 As demonstrated, recent tribunals have been explicitly or implicitly following these findings, *see for example* Charanne and Construction Investments v. Kingdom of Spain, Award, 21 January 2016 SCC Case No. V 062/2012, para. 513-514; Foresight and others v. Kingdom of Spain Final, Award, 14 November 2018 SCC Case No. V 2015/150, para. 358-363; Stadtwerke München GmbH and others v. Kingdom of Spain, Award, 2 December 2019 ICSID Case No. ARB/15/1, para. 316-322.

dictable and applied retroactively. Secondly, a purely economic analysis is conducted. A measure qualifies as "reasonable", if the investor is still able to receive a reasonable rate of return. Factors such as predictability and retroactive effect of the measures, as well as the impact of the changes, i.e. how strongly they affected the investors' rights, have played a repeated role in determining the states' margin of discretion.

2) Predictability and Retroactive Effect of the Measures

Sources of international law, such as the FET provisions in investment treaties, must be construed in light of good faith, pursuant to Article 31(1) VCLT. As demonstrated, the notion of legitimate expectations itself finds its roots in the good faith principle.[1403] The good faith principle, particularly the rule of *venire contra factum proprium non valet*, prohibits contradictory behaviour.[1404] Depending on the foregoing conduct of the state, it can be contradictory, if the host state repeals laws and regulations with retroactively impact on which the investors relied in their investment decision. In general, a legislative measure has a retroactive effect, if it revokes any rights acquired by the investor and applies not only to the future, but also the past.[1405]

In general, states are not barred from introducing retroactive changes in the legislation.[1406] Nonetheless, if a retroactive measure conflicts with the

---

1403 *See* Ch. 2 I.

1404 Mairal, *Legitimate Expectations and Informal Administrative Representations*, p. 422, 423; Parchomiuk, 'The Protection of Legitimate Expectations in Administrative Law: A Horizontal Perspective', p. 6. *See also* Sipiorski, *Good Faith in International Investment Arbitration*, para. 9.04, 9.08; Kläger, *'Fair and Equitable Treatment' and Sustainable Development*, p. 130.

1405 Charanne and Construction Investments v. Kingdom of Spain, Award, 21 January 2016 SCC Case No. V 062/2012, para. 546 and 548; Isolux Netherlands, BV v. Kingdom of Spain Final, Award, 17 July 2016 SCC Case V2013/153, para. 813, 814; Nations Energy Corporation, Electric Machinery Enterprises Inc. and Jamie Jurado v. The Republic of Panama, Award, 24 November 2010 ICSID Case No. ARB/06/19, para. 642, 644, 646.

1406 The Tribunal in *Hydro* observed that "[t]here is no general principle which prohibits the retroactivity of legislation, but it may depending on the context, be relevant to unreasonableness, breach of legitimate expectation or destruction of acquired rights", Hydro Energy 1 S.A.R.L. and Hydroxana Sweden AB v. The Kingdom of Spain, Decision on Jurisdiction, Liability and Directions on Quantum, 9 March 2020 ICSID Case No. ARB/15/42, para. 676. *See also* Cavalum SGPS v. Kingdom of Spain, Decision on Jurisdiction, Liability

investors' legitimate expectations, they may give rise to compensation.[1407] It is not necessary for legislative frameworks to specifically and explicitly exclude the possibility of its repeal by a later law.[1408] However, it is indicated that the investors must prove that there was at least an implicit commitment of the host state to refrain from retroactively altering the legislative framework.[1409]

Whether a retroactive measure violated the legitimate expectations, correlates with the qualification of the measure's effect as proper or improper retroactivity. Proper (impermissible) retroactivity, as a principle, covers the situation in which a rule is introduced and applied to events that have already been concluded.[1410] Proper retroactivity occurs usually in situations in which an act's effectiveness precedes its date of publication or where a regulation applies to circumstances that have actually been concluded.[1411] In contrast, improper (permissible) retroactivity exists, when an investor may have planned their actions based on certain representations by the state and seeks redress, when the chosen policy is altered, even though this alteration is only prospective and not retrospective.[1412] In the latter variant of retroactivity, the regulations are linked to current, not yet concluded, circumstances with legal consequences for the future, whereby the affected legal position acquired in the past is subsequently devalued.[1413]

The issue of proper or improper retroactivity was most prominent in the cases against Spain, as the 2010 Amendments introduced, inter alia, cutbacks in the bonus working for renewable energy producers.[1414] The measures from 2013 onwards also affected the rights of investors to receive

---

and Directions on Quantum, 31 August 2020 ICSID Case No. ARB/15/34, para. 417.

1407 Hydro Energy 1 S.A.R.L. and Hydroxana Sweden AB v. The Kingdom of Spain, Decision on Jurisdiction, Liability and Directions on Quantum, 9 March 2020 ICSID Case No. ARB/15/42, para. 684.

1408 Cube Infrastructure Fund SICAV and others v. Kingdom of Spain, Decision on Jurisdiction, Liability and Partial Decision on Quantum, 19 February 2019 ICSID Case No. ARB/15/20, para. 289.

1409 Charanne and Construction Investments v. Kingdom of Spain, Award, 21 January 2016 SCC Case No. V 062/2012, para. 544-546.

1410 Craig, 'Substantive Legitimate Expectations in Domestic and Community Law', p. 304.

1411 ibid, p. 304.

1412 Palombino, *Fair and Equitable Treatment and the Fabric of General Principles*, p. 110.

1413 ibid, p. 110.

1414 Garcia-Castrillon, *Spain and Investment Arbitration - The Renewable Energy Explosion*, p. 288.

the prescribed remuneration that was initially granted to them upon the registration of the power plants with the RAIPRE.[1415] However, the newer method of calculating the remuneration was only applied with effect for the future. Amounts already paid on the basis of RD 661/2007 were not recovered. The 2010 Amendments, i.e. the cutbacks in the bonus working hours, were only considered to have a prospective effect.[1416] With regard to the 2013 amendments, several tribunals rejected the allegation of proper retroactivity. It was argued that changes only affected future remuneration, regardless of whether previous regulations promised remuneration on the basis of an unaltered calculation method for a certain operational lifetime of the power plants.[1417]

In contrast, the majority of the tribunals qualified the changes as impermissible proper retroactivity, as the changes retroactively rewrote the legal framework.[1418] In particular, the calculation method shifted from a

---

1415 *See* Ch. 3 III 1) a) (3).

1416 The Tribunal in *Charanne* found that the cutbacks in bonus working hours only "applied immediately from their entry into force when the plants were already in operation, but did not apply retroactively to prior periods", Charanne and Construction Investments v. Kingdom of Spain, Award, 21 January 2016 SCC Case No. V 062/2012, para. 548 (unofficial translation).

1417 Charanne and Construction Investments v. Kingdom of Spain, Award, 21 January 2016 SCC Case No. V 062/2012, para. 548; RWE Innogy GmbH and RWE Innogy Aersa S.A.U. v. Kingdom of Spain, Decision on Jurisdicition, Liability, and certain Issues of Quantum, 6 January 2020 ICSID Case No. ARB/14/34, para. 617; Isolux Netherlands, BV v. Kingdom of Spain Final, Award, 17 July 2016 SCC Case V2013/153, para. 814. Similarly, the Tribunal in Antaris v. Czech Republic considerd "that the modifications to the support scheme and the tax measures were retroactive, and considers that they did not violate the principle of legitimate expectation", Antaris Solar and Dr. Michael Göde v. Czech Republic, Award, 2 May 2018 PCA Case No. 2014-01, para. 430.

1418 RREEF Infrastructure (G.P.) Limited and RREEF Pan-European Infrastructure Two Lux S.à.r.l. v. Kingdom of Spain, Decision on Responsibility and on the Principles of Quantum, 30 November 2018 ICSID Case No. ARB/13/30, para. 329, 330; Eiser Infrastructure Limited and Energía Solar Luxembourg S.à.r.l. v. Kingdom of Spain, Award, 4 May 2017 ICSID Case No. ARB/13/36, para. 400; Novenergia II - Energy & Environment (SCA), SICAR v. The Kingdom of Spain, Award, 15 February 2018 SCC Case No. V 2015/063, para. 697; OperaFund Eco-Invest SICAV PLC and Schwab Holding AG v. Kingdom of Spain, Award, 6 September 2019 ICSID Case No. ARB/15/36, para. 513; Masdar Solar & Wind Cooperatief U.A. v. Kingdom of Spain, Award, 16 May 2018 ICSID Case No. ARB/14/1, para. 651; 9REN Holding S.a.r.l v. Kingdom of Spain, Award, 31 March 2019 ICSID Case No. ARB/15/15, para. 307; Foresight and others v. Kingdom of Spain Final, Award, 14 November 2018 SCC Case No. V 2015/150, para. 389; Watkins Holdings S.à.r.l. and others v. Kingdom

plant-specific calculation to a "one size fits all" calculation, which significantly altered the core of the previous support scheme and therefore had proper retroactive effect.[1419] Although the regulatory changes in theory only applied to the calculation of future remuneration, they were designed in a way that allowed the state to subtract past remuneration from future remuneration.[1420] Tribunals further elaborated that clawing back profits, which were deemed "excessive", from an ex-post perspective, was incompatible with the principle of stability included in the FET standard under the ECT, if the measures fail the necessity test.[1421] However, for retroactive measures to violate the legitimate expectations of an investor, the possibility of a retroactive change in the legal framework must not have been foreseeable. Retroactive changes are, for example, foreseeable if they are indicated by national jurisprudence.[1422]

Similar, the *Spalma Incentivi Decree* was qualified as an impermissible retroactive measure, whereas the prior legislative amendments only applied prospectively.[1423] In particular, the original legislative framework had included a tariff-adjustment procedure.[1424] Hence, the law had already

of Spain, Award, 21 January 2020 ICSID Case No. ARB/15/44, para. para. 569; Cavalum SGPS v. Kingdom of Spain, Decision on Jurisdiction, Liability and Directions on Quantum, 31 August 2020 ICSID Case No. ARB/15/34, para. 637.

1419 Eiser Infrastructure Limited and Energía Solar Luxembourg S.à.r.l. v. Kingdom of Spain, Award, 4 May 2017 ICSID Case No. ARB/13/36, para. 400.

1420 Stadtwerke München GmbH and others v. Kingdom of Spain, Dissenting Opinion Kaj Hobér, 2 December 2019 ICSID Case No. ARB/15/1, para. 22.

1421 BayWa r.e. Renewable Energy GmbH and BayWa r.e. Asset Holding GmbH v. Kingdom of Spain, Decision on Jurisdiction, Liability and Directions on Quantum, 2 December 2019 ICSID Case No. ARB/15/16, para. 496; RREEF Infrastructure (G.P.) Limited and RREEF Pan-European Infrastructure Two Lux S.à.r.l. v. Kingdom of Spain, Decision on Responsibility and on the Principles of Quantum, 30 November 2018 ICSID Case No. ARB/13/30, para. 325, 328; The PV Investors v. Kingdom of Spain Final, Award, 28 February 2020 PCA Case No. 2012-14, para. 813.

1422 RWE Innogy GmbH and RWE Innogy Aersa S.A.U. v. Kingdom of Spain, Decision on Jurisdicition, Liability, and certain Issues of Quantum, 6 January 2020 ICSID Case No. ARB/14/34, para. 523.

1423 SunReserve Luxco Holdings v. Italian Republic Final, Award, 25 March 2020 SCC Arbitration V (2016/32), para. 815.

1424 The Tribunal in *Sunreserve* observed that the prior decrees "contained a scope for re-modulation of the incentive tariff regime, so long as the incentive regime ensured the purpose of a fair remuneration to the investors", SunReserve Luxco Holdings v. Italian Republic Final, Award, 25 March 2020 SCC Arbitration V (2016/32), para. 813.

included the possibility of retroactive modifications. Therefore, it is not sufficient that a legislative measure applies to plants already in existence. Rather, the subsequent change must not have been foreseen in the legislative framework from the outset, which is not the case if the legal framework is explicitly subject to possible amendments in the future. It follows that there cannot be proper retroactivity in cases in which the investors never had acquired an unmodifiable right because the legislative framework had the option for future amendments already included.

A subsequent question is under what circumstances a time period may constitute a concluded matter. Subtractions from past income constitute impermissible retroactivity, as they, inter alia, affect the right of the shareholder of a company to enjoy their dividends, which are distributed periodically.[1425] Similar, the revocation of tax incentives or deduction of tax from existing credits were seen as impermissible retroactive alteration of the law, if the tax year was already concluded.[1426] In general, a tendency can be observed to regard as unlawful and retroactive such measures, which intervene in an already completed matter and have an influence on payments (or deductions) already received.[1427]

The case law demonstrates that there is no impermissible retroactivity, if the circumstances the measures intervene in have not been concluded yet, or if the legislative framework explicitly left open the possibility of future amendments. The majority of the Spanish tribunals also found that there is impermissible retroactivity in cases in which future remuneration is deducted from remuneration already received, in order to lower the average return for the investor over the lifetime of the investment.

1425 RREEF Infrastructure (G.P.) Limited and RREEF Pan-European Infrastructure Two Lux S.à.r.l. v. Kingdom of Spain, Decision on Responsibility and on the Principles of Quantum, 30 November 2018 ICSID Case No. ARB/13/30, para. 329.

1426 Nations Energy Corporation, Electric Machinery Enterprises Inc. and Jamie Jurado v. The Republic of Panama, Award, 24 November 2010 ICSID Case No. ARB/06/19, para. 644, 647.

1427 RREEF Infrastructure (G.P.) Limited and RREEF Pan-European Infrastructure Two Lux S.à.r.l. v. Kingdom of Spain, Decision on Responsibility and on the Principles of Quantum, 30 November 2018 ICSID Case No. ARB/13/30, para. 328; BayWa r.e. Renewable Energy GmbH and BayWa r.e. Asset Holding GmbH v. Kingdom of Spain, Decision on Jurisdiction, Liability and Directions on Quantum, 2 December 2019 ICSID Case No. ARB/15/16, para. 491, 492. Contrary thereto Isolux Netherlands, BV v. Kingdom of Spain Final, Award, 17 July 2016 SCC Case V2013/153, para. 814.

3) Impact of the Changes on the Investment

Regulatory changes are generally permissible, during the lifetime of an investment, especially if the investment's expected lifespan covers several decades. Part of the arbitral jurisprudence considers changes exceeding the states' margin of discretion to constitute a violation of the FET standard, even in the absence of a specific stabilization clause.[1428] However, arbitral jurisprudence is not meant as an instance of revision for the state measures.[1429] In the absence of a specific promise, the states' margin of discretion is wide and only the most basic expectations of the investors can be protected.[1430] The previous analysis has shown that the states are afforded a wider margin of discretion in the regulation of their legal framework, when the rights at stake are of public interest. However, the states can commit to refrain from implementing any adverse changes to the legal framework by means of a stability commitment.[1431] This notwithstanding, recent case law demonstrated that stability commitments can have varying types of specificity, spanning from a promise to specific remuneration to the simple promise of "reasonable" remuneration.

Among the successful Spanish cases, a number of tribunals held that the host state entered into a specific commitment and the investors were entitled to the specific remuneration prescribed by the regulatory framework to be in place at the time of the investment.[1432] In contrast, a comparable

---

1428 *See* Ch. 4 I 2) b).

1429 The Tribunal in *Antaris* observed that "it does not matter whether a tribunal believes that a particular course of action is 'good' or 'bad', that a different solution might have been 'better', or that a State could have done 'more,' or that other States took different measures", Antaris Solar and Dr. Michael Göde v. Czech Republic, Award, 2 May 2018 PCA Case No. 2014-01, para. 443. *See also* Watkins Holdings S.à.r.l. and others v. Kingdom of Spain, Dissenting Opinion Helene Ruiz Fabri, 21 January 2020 ICSID Case No. ARB/15/44, para. 14.

1430 In absence of a specific commitment, the Tribunal in *Continental* considered aspects like good faith, the absence of discrimination, the public interest motivating the change, and profitability of the investment in its assessment of whether a regulatory amendment exceeded that states' margin of discretion, Continental Casualty Company v. The Argentine Republic, Award, 5 September 2008 ICSID Case No. ARB/03/9, para. 261(iv).

1431 *See* Ch. 4 III 1) a).

1432 Antin Infrastructure Services Luxembourg S.à.r.l. and Antin Energia Termosolar B.V. v. Kingdom of Spain, Award, 15 June 2018 ICSID Case No. ARB/13/31, para. 561-568; Masdar Solar & Wind Cooperatief U.A. v. Kingdom of Spain, Award, 16 May 2018 ICSID Case No. ARB/14/1, para. 521, 522;

number of tribunals found that the Spanish *Special Regime* only included the commitment to "reasonable return" or "reasonable profitability" by the host state.[1433] In particular, tribunals considered the hierarchy within the legal framework and found that the law, on which the regulatory framework built, only provided for a reasonable return.[1434] Hence, this overriding principle would be the standard on which subsequent Royal Decrees need to be measured.

Although the tribunals interpreted the underlying facts to a varying degree, almost all resorted to an impact assessment that took into consideration the interference of the state's measures with the investment and its profitability. The impact assessment was conducted either within the examination of the economic reasonableness or the proportionality of the host state's measures. Therefore, the broader question is whether investors may have had legitimate expectations that the regulatory frame-

---

Novenergia II - Energy & Environment (SCA), SICAR v. The Kingdom of Spain, Award, 15 February 2018 SCC Case No. V 2015/063, para. 666-669, 695-697; Eiser Infrastructure Limited and Energía Solar Luxembourg S.à.r.l. v. Kingdom of Spain, Award, 4 May 2017 ICSID Case No. ARB/13/36, para. 389-406; OperaFund Eco-Invest SICAV PLC and Schwab Holding AG v. Kingdom of Spain, Award, 6 September 2019 ICSID Case No. ARB/15/36, para. 489; Foresight and others v. Kingdom of Spain Final, Award, 14 November 2018 SCC Case No. V 2015/150, para. 533.

1433 RREEF Infrastructure (G.P.) Limited and RREEF Pan-European Infrastructure Two Lux S.à.r.l. v. Kingdom of Spain, Decision on Responsibility and on the Principles of Quantum, 30 November 2018 ICSID Case No. ARB/13/30, para. 384-386; Stadtwerke München GmbH and others v. Kingdom of Spain, Award, 2 December 2019 ICSID Case No. ARB/15/1, para. 275; Watkins Holdings S.à.r.l. and others v. Kingdom of Spain, Award, 21 January 2020 ICSID Case No. ARB/15/44, para. 498; The PV Investors v. Kingdom of Spain Final, Award, 28 February 2020 PCA Case No. 2012-14, para. 596; Cavalum SGPS v. Kingdom of Spain, Decision on Jurisdiction, Liability and Directions on Quantum, 31 August 2020 ICSID Case No. ARB/15/34, para. 601, 612.

1434 The majority of the Tribunal in *Stadwerke* took into account the legislative history of the RD 661/2007 and considered that "the overriding principle for the determination of the premium is to achieve 'reasonable rates of return' by taking into account, inter alia, the investment costs that have been incurred and the cost of money in the capital market", Stadtwerke München GmbH and others v. Kingdom of Spain, Award, 2 December 2019 ICSID Case No. ARB/15/1, para. 275. Similarly, the Tribunal in *PV Investors* identified a "cardinal principle" of a reasonable return, which had to be taken as a hallmark for the violation of the investors' legitimate expectations, The PV Investors v. Kingdom of Spain Final, Award, 28 February 2020 PCA Case No. 2012-14, para. 596.

work would not be changed in a way that would undermine the economic security set out by the host states specific support schemes.[1435]

a) Fundamental Change as a Threshold for the Violation of Basic Expectations

The analysis in this Chapter revealed that the measures implemented by the host state must not be viewed individually, but in the context of the overall legal framework and the influence the measures had on the investment. When assessing the impact of the measures, tribunals turned to the question of whether the changes adversely and unexpectedly affected the conditions of the investments and deprived investors of their investment's value.[1436] In the assessment, the changes that violated the investors' legitimate expectations were classified as "radical", "drastic", or "fundamental".[1437] Despite the different wording, the key aspect identified by arbitral jurisprudence is whether the underlying legal framework has

---

1435 NextEra Energy Global Holdings B.V. and NextEra Energy Spain Holdings B.V. v. Kingdom of Spain, Decision on Jurisdiction, Liability and Quantum Principles, 12 March 2019 ICSID Case No. ARB/14/11, para. 591.

1436 Eiser Infrastructure Limited and Energía Solar Luxembourg S.à.r.l. v. Kingdom of Spain, Award, 4 May 2017 ICSID Case No. ARB/13/36, para. 382; RREEF Infrastructure (G.P.) Limited and RREEF Pan-European Infrastructure Two Lux S.à.r.l. v. Kingdom of Spain, Decision on Responsibility and on the Principles of Quantum, 30 November 2018 ICSID Case No. ARB/13/30, para. 379, 399.

1437 The Tribunal in *Eiser* observed that the FET obligation in Article 10(1) ECT must be understood in a way that "regulatory regimes cannot be radically altered as applied to existing investments, in ways that deprive investors who invested in reliance on those regimes of their investment's value", Eiser Infrastructure Limited and Energía Solar Luxembourg S.à.r.l. v. Kingdom of Spain, Award, 4 May 2017 ICSID Case No. ARB/13/36, para. 382; also cited by Watkins Holdings S.à.r.l. and others v. Kingdom of Spain, Award, 21 January 2020 ICSID Case No. ARB/15/44, para. 562, 563. Similarly, the Tribunal in *NextEra* held that "[t]he denial of legitimate expectations is based on the failure to provide that certainty and security by changing fundamentally the regime under which remuneration was to be calculated", NextEra Energy Global Holdings B.V. and NextEra Energy Spain Holdings B.V. v. Kingdom of Spain, Decision on Jurisdiction, Liability and Quantum Principles, 12 March 2019 ICSID Case No. ARB/14/11, para. 600. *See also* RREEF Infrastructure (G.P.) Limited and RREEF Pan-European Infrastructure Two Lux S.à.r.l. v. Kingdom of Spain, Decision on Responsibility and on the Principles of Quantum, 30 November 2018 ICSID Case No. ARB/13/30, para. 379, 399.

been changed in such a way as to alter all, or at least most, of the premises on which investors have based their investments.[1438]

With regard to the amendments and the eventual abolishment of the Spanish *Special Regime*, tribunals demonstrated different views on whether the changes were radical and drastic. Only one tribunal considered both the 2010 Amendments, as well as the introduction of the new regime, as fundamental changes.[1439] The majority of tribunals qualified only the 2013 measures as a violation of the legitimate expectations of the investors.[1440] Only a small number of tribunals concluded that neither of the measures was unreasonably drastic and violated the stability aspect of the FET standard, in light of the time during which the investments were made.[1441]

1438 *See also* Cube Infrastructure Fund SICAV and others v. Kingdom of Spain, Decision on Jurisdiction, Liability and Partial Decision on Quantum, 19 February 2019 ICSID Case No. ARB/15/20, para. 354, 427; SolEs Badajoz GmbH v. Kingdom of Spain, Award, 31 July 2019 ICSID Case No. ARB/15/38, para. 462; SunReserve Luxco Holdings v. Italian Republic Final, Award, 25 March 2020 SCC Arbitration V (2016/32), para. 735.

1439 Only the Tribunal in *Opera* found that also some of the 2010 amendments constituted a violation of the FET standard, OperaFund Eco-Invest SICAV PLC and Schwab Holding AG v. Kingdom of Spain, Award, 6 September 2019 ICSID Case No. ARB/15/36, para. 513.

1440 Novenergia II - Energy & Environment (SCA), SICAR v. The Kingdom of Spain, Award, 15 February 2018 SCC Case No. V 2015/063, para. 688, 697; Eiser Infrastructure Limited and Energía Solar Luxembourg S.à.r.l. v. Kingdom of Spain, Award, 4 May 2017 ICSID Case No. ARB/13/36, para. 363, 387; Cube Infrastructure Fund SICAV and others v. Kingdom of Spain, Decision on Jurisdiction, Liability and Partial Decision on Quantum, 19 February 2019 ICSID Case No. ARB/15/20, para. 424, 425; Foresight and others v. Kingdom of Spain Final, Award, 14 November 2018 SCC Case No. V 2015/150, para. 387-390; SolEs Badajoz GmbH v. Kingdom of Spain, Award, 31 July 2019 ICSID Case No. ARB/15/38, para. 462; Cavalum SGPS v. Kingdom of Spain, Decision on Jurisdiction, Liability and Directions on Quantum, 31 August 2020 ICSID Case No. ARB/15/34, para. 622, 623; OperaFund Eco-Invest SICAV PLC and Schwab Holding AG v. Kingdom of Spain, Award, 6 September 2019 ICSID Case No. ARB/15/36, para. 513. The Tribunal in *Charanne* examined only the 2010 measures and found no violation of the FET standard, but left, however, explicitly open the possibility that the 2013 measures were drastic enough to constitute a liability of the host state, Charanne and Construction Investments v. Kingdom of Spain, Award, 21 January 2016 SCC Case No. V 062/2012, para. 539, 540.

1441 Stadtwerke München GmbH and others v. Kingdom of Spain, Award, 2 December 2019 ICSID Case No. ARB/15/1, para. 275; The PV Investors v. Kingdom of Spain Final, Award, 28 February 2020 PCA Case No. 2012-14, para. 596; BayWa r.e. Renewable Energy GmbH and BayWa r.e. Asset Holding

In general, newly introduced changes are considered not drastic or radical, as long as they were not capricious or unnecessary and simply diminished, but not eliminated, essential characteristics of the specific features of the legislative framework.[1442] In particular, the question of whether "essential characteristics" were abolished was repeatedly used as a hallmark for the violation of legitimate expectations.[1443] "Essentials characteristics" are abolished, when investors are deprived of the security and certainty offered by the regulatory framework, and lost a significant part of their projected revenues.[1444]

GmbH v. Kingdom of Spain, Decision on Jurisdiction, Liability and Directions on Quantum, 2 December 2019 ICSID Case No. ARB/15/16, para. 590. The Tribunal in *Isolux* considered the changes as drastic, but observed that the investor, at the time of the investment in October 2012, could not have legitimately expected that a drastic alteration of the regulatory framework would not occur during the lifetime of the investment, Isolux Netherlands, BV v. Kingdom of Spain Final, Award, 17 July 2016 SCC Case V2013/153, para. 796.

1442 Charanne and Construction Investments v. Kingdom of Spain, Award, 21 January 2016 SCC Case No. V 062/2012, para. 517, 518.

1443 *See* inter alia Eiser Infrastructure Limited and Energía Solar Luxembourg S.à.r.l. v. Kingdom of Spain, Award, 4 May 2017 ICSID Case No. ARB/13/36, para. 382; Blusun S.A. Jean-Pierre Lecorcier and Michael Stein v. Italian Republic, Award, 27 December 2016 ICSID Case No. ARB/14/3, para. 317; Foresight and others v. Kingdom of Spain Final, Award, 14 November 2018 SCC Case No. V 2015/150, para. 359; Novenergia II - Energy & Environment (SCA), SICAR v. The Kingdom of Spain, Award, 15 February 2018 SCC Case No. V 2015/063, para. 694, 695; OperaFund Eco-Invest SICAV PLC and Schwab Holding AG v. Kingdom of Spain, Award, 6 September 2019 ICSID Case No. ARB/15/36, para. 508; RREEF Infrastructure (G.P.) Limited and RREEF Pan-European Infrastructure Two Lux S.à.r.l. v. Kingdom of Spain, Decision on Responsibility and on the Principles of Quantum, 30 November 2018 ICSID Case No. ARB/13/30, para. 314.

1444 the Tribunal in *NextEra* held that the decisive hallmark for the fundamental and radical change was the deprivation of the investors of the "security and certainty that, in light of the assurances they had received from Spanish authorities about guaranteeing the legal security of investments underway as well as the forecasts under which the investments were made and affirming legal and regulatory stability, they could have expected", NextEra Energy Global Holdings B.V. and NextEra Energy Spain Holdings B.V. v. Kingdom of Spain, Decision on Jurisdiction, Liability and Quantum Principles, 12 March 2019 ICSID Case No. ARB/14/11, para. 599. Similarly, it was observed in *Foresight* found that the regulatory framework is fundamentally altered, when investors are deprived of a significant part of their projected revenues, Foresight and others v. Kingdom of Spain, Dissenting Opinion Raúl Emilio Vinuesa, 14 November 2018 SCC Case No. V 2015/150, para. 388.

This, however, was observed to not be the case, if the regulatory framework was governed by an "overriding" or "cardinal" principle of reasonable return that made legislative changes foreseeable.[1445] Investors must assess the hierarchy in the legislative framework applicable to the investment and must consider whether expectations of a specific return can be reasonable in light of the object and purpose of the law on which investors relied.[1446] If representations by state authorities conflict with those "overriding principles", diligent investors cannot expect these representations to be honoured.[1447] This concept of overriding principles was, however, not left without criticism, as it would leave states a wide margin of discretion, even in light of precise representations from state authorities.[1448]

1445 Stadtwerke München GmbH and others v. Kingdom of Spain, Award, 2 December 2019 ICSID Case No. ARB/15/1, para. 275, 282; The PV Investors v. Kingdom of Spain Final, Award, 28 February 2020 PCA Case No. 2012-14, para. 596; Foresight and others v. Kingdom of Spain, Dissenting Opinion Raúl Emilio Vinuesa, 14 November 2018 SCC Case No. V 2015/150, para. 33; Cube Infrastructure Fund SICAV and others v. Kingdom of Spain, Separate and Partial Dissenting Opinion Christian Tomuschat, 19 February 2019 ICSID Case No. ARB/15/20, para. 23; STEAG GmbH v. Kingdom of Spain, Dissenting Opinion Dupuy, 8 October 2020 ICSID Case No. ARB/15/4, para. 9.

1446 The Tribunal in *Stadtwerke* held that investors should have been aware that EL 54/1997 set out a support scheme, which was only designed to provide for a reasonable return and left the specifics of the scheme to regulations of the competent Ministry. This was sought to ensure that the Ministry is capable to give effect to changing market conditions for the calculation of the premium. From a hierarchical perspective, the Ministry could not have been able to effectively bind the Spanish Parliament to its decision, Stadtwerke München GmbH and others v. Kingdom of Spain, Award, 2 December 2019 ICSID Case No. ARB/15/1, para. 281. The hierarchy within the legislative framework was also assessed by the tribunals in BayWa r.e. Renewable Energy GmbH and BayWa r.e. Asset Holding GmbH v. Kingdom of Spain, Decision on Jurisdiction, Liability and Directions on Quantum, 2 December 2019 ICSID Case No. ARB/15/16, para. 473; Hydro Energy 1 S.A.R.L. and Hydroxana Sweden AB v. The Kingdom of Spain, Decision on Jurisdiction, Liability and Directions on Quantum, 9 March 2020 ICSID Case No. ARB/15/42, para. 618

1447 Stadtwerke München GmbH and others v. Kingdom of Spain, Award, 2 December 2019 ICSID Case No. ARB/15/1, para. 275, 282.

1448 *Kaj Hobér* criticised the notion of any "overriding" or "cardinal" principle on the basis that fundamental stability, with respect to the main characteristics of the legal and regulatory framework, is in itself a reasonable and legitimate expectation among investors, Stadtwerke München GmbH and others v. Kingdom of Spain, Dissenting Opinion Kaj Hobér, 2 December 2019 ICSID Case No. ARB/15/1, para. 7.

Nonetheless, it becomes evident that arbitral tribunals measure the degree of the changes (1) by assessing the amendments to the overall character and the specifics of the legal framework and (2) by determining the influence the changes had on the investors' investment.[1449]

b) Characteristics of Fundamental Change on the Example of the Spanish Regime

Tribunals have regularly emphasized that it is not sufficient to simply adversely affect existing investments.[1450] Therefore, the crucial question is under what circumstances changes have to be considered "fundamental", "abrupt", "radical", or "drastic". A basic idea has already been developed in the previous Section, but it requires further definition. The Spanish support scheme is a particularly illustrative case study, as it has undergone two different types of regulatory changes, i.e. the 2010 Amendments and the 2013 Regime change.

(1) The 2010 Amendments Were within the State's Margin of discretion

The essential characteristics of the *Special Regime* under RD 661/2007 were the offer of a guaranteed FIT or FIP for a period of 25 years, the privileged access to the electricity transmission and distribution grid without an

---

1449 Arriving at a similar conclusion: Levashova, *The Right of States to Regulate in International Investment Law*, p. 151; However, she concedes that "[t]hese conditions have not been applied cumulatively by the tribunals in the examined cases, satisfying one of the two mostly sufficed."

1450 Charanne and Construction Investments v. Kingdom of Spain, Award, 21 January 2016 SCC Case No. V 062/2012, para. 517, 519; Cube Infrastructure Fund SICAV and others v. Kingdom of Spain, Decision on Jurisdiction, Liability and Partial Decision on Quantum, 19 February 2019 ICSID Case No. ARB/15/20, para. 419, 420; BayWa r.e. Renewable Energy GmbH and BayWa r.e. Asset Holding GmbH v. Kingdom of Spain, Decision on Jurisdiction, Liability and Directions on Quantum, 2 December 2019 ICSID Case No. ARB/15/16, para. 590; The PV Investors v. Kingdom of Spain Final, Award, 28 February 2020 PCA Case No. 2012-14, para. 580; SunReserve Luxco Holdings v. Italian Republic Final, Award, 25 March 2020 SCC Arbitration V (2016/32), para. 688, 692.

hourly limit, and the guarantee to renewable energy producers a reasonable return.[1451]

The 2010 Amendments introduced a set of changes, which adversely affected renewable energy power plants. These changes, inter alia, cancelled the right of the PV operators to receive the prescribed tariff after 25 years of operating lifetime, limited the amount of electricity eligible for FITs by imposing annual operating hour restrictions on all PV facilities, and delinked the annual update of the FIT from the CPI.[1452] Thus, the amendments provided for a limitation of the annual operation hours, as well as a reduction of certain revenues and cost consignments.

Only a number of tribunals examined the 2010 Amendments and the modification through the 2013 Regime as two separate measures. It was observed that—despite the cut in revenue—the *Special Regime* maintained its essential characteristics, even after the 2010 Amendments.[1453] Despite the measures' adverse effect on the revenue of the investments, they were not drastic enough to constitute a violation of the investors' legitimate expectations.[1454]

However, it must be borne in mind that these regulatory amendments had varying effects, depending on the renewable energy technology used. The amendments to the PV sector had far less dramatic effects than those

1451 Charanne and Construction Investments v. Kingdom of Spain, Award, 21 January 2016 SCC Case No. V 062/2012 at para. 516-518; Novenergia II - Energy & Environment (SCA), SICAR v. The Kingdom of Spain, Award, 15 February 2018 SCC Case No. V 2015/063, para. 394; Watkins Holdings S.à.r.l. and others v. Kingdom of Spain, Award, 21 January 2020 ICSID Case No. ARB/15/44, para. 549.

1452 *See* Ch. 3 III 1 a) (2).

1453 Charanne and Construction Investments v. Kingdom of Spain, Award, 21 January 2016 SCC Case No. V 062/2012, para. 519, 520.

1454 The Tribunal in *Cube* considered the measures to be reasonable and "within the range of adjustments that a reasonable investor must be prepared to accept and accommodate", Cube Infrastructure Fund SICAV and others v. Kingdom of Spain, Decision on Jurisdiction, Liability and Partial Decision on Quantum, 19 February 2019 ICSID Case No. ARB/15/20, 420. *See also* Novenergia II - Energy & Environment (SCA), SICAR v. The Kingdom of Spain, Award, 15 February 2018 SCC Case No. V 2015/063, para. 688; Foresight and others v. Kingdom of Spain Final, Award, 14 November 2018 SCC Case No. V 2015/150, para. 388; Cube Infrastructure Fund SICAV and others v. Kingdom of Spain, Decision on Jurisdiction, Liability and Partial Decision on Quantum, 19 February 2019 ICSID Case No. ARB/15/20, para. 420; Cavalum SGPS v. Kingdom of Spain, Decision on Jurisdiction, Liability and Directions on Quantum, 31 August 2020 ICSID Case No. ARB/15/34, para. 564, 568.

to the CSP plants, which may lead to different results, taking into consideration the overall impact of the amendments on the profitability of the power plants.[1455]

(2) Why did the 2013 Regime Constitute Radical Changes?

In contrast, the 2013 Regime brought a wider range of changes. The amendments repealed the *Special Regime* applicable to previous investments and established a completely new remuneration system. The regulatory changes had a "significant harmful effect" on the cash flows of the PV plants and therefore changed the financial basis for the investments.[1456]

The majority of the tribunals found that the changes implemented by the host state were "unprecedented" and constituted a "wholly different regulatory approach, based on wholly different premises" that amounted to a "total and unreasonable change".[1457] Whereas the *Special Regime*, from its introduction to its abolishment, was an "at risk" model, i.e. investors

1455 Eiser Infrastructure Limited and Energía Solar Luxembourg S.à.r.l. v. Kingdom of Spain, Award, 4 May 2017 ICSID Case No. ARB/13/36, para. 368, 389.

1456 As claimed by the investors in Antin Infrastructure Services Luxembourg S.à.r.l. and Antin Energia Termosolar B.V. v. Kingdom of Spain, Award, 15 June 2018 ICSID Case No. ARB/13/31, para. 154.

1457 Eiser Infrastructure Limited and Energía Solar Luxembourg S.à.r.l. v. Kingdom of Spain, Award, 4 May 2017 ICSID Case No. ARB/13/36, para. 363, 365; Novenergia II - Energy & Environment (SCA), SICAR v. The Kingdom of Spain, Award, 15 February 2018 SCC Case No. V 2015/063, para. 688, 697; Foresight and others v. Kingdom of Spain Final, Award, 14 November 2018 SCC Case No. V 2015/150, para. 397; Cube Infrastructure Fund SICAV and others v. Kingdom of Spain, Decision on Jurisdiction, Liability and Partial Decision on Quantum, 19 February 2019 ICSID Case No. ARB/15/20, para. 425, 442; NextEra Energy Global Holdings B.V. and NextEra Energy Spain Holdings B.V. v. Kingdom of Spain, Decision on Jurisdiction, Liability and Quantum Principles, 12 March 2019 ICSID Case No. ARB/14/11, para. 599; SolEs Badajoz GmbH v. Kingdom of Spain, Award, 31 July 2019 ICSID Case No. ARB/15/38, para. 462; OperaFund Eco-Invest SICAV PLC and Schwab Holding AG v. Kingdom of Spain, Award, 6 September 2019 ICSID Case No. ARB/15/36, para. 496, 513; Antin Infrastructure Services Luxembourg S.à.r.l. and Antin Energia Termosolar B.V. v. Kingdom of Spain, Award, 15 June 2018 ICSID Case No. ARB/13/31, para. 560; Watkins Holdings S.à.r.l. and others v. Kingdom of Spain, Award, 21 January 2020 ICSID Case No. ARB/15/44, para. 508, 555, 570; Cavalum SGPS v. Kingdom of Spain, Decision on Jurisdiction, Liability and Directions on Quantum, 31 August 2020 ICSID Case No. ARB/15/34, para. 622, 623.

had to bear the downside in case of mismanagement, but could also enjoy the upside, if they structured their investments in a profitable way.[1458] The new regime was designed as a "regulated return" model.[1459] This led to a large post-tax reduction of the remuneration, which was achieved by applying a calculation method based on a "standard plant", instead of taking into account the unique characteristics of the individual power plant and the financial structure of the investment.[1460] The switch to remuneration based mainly on plant capacity rather than the volume of energy produced, as well as a correlation of the remuneration with the market price, instead of an FIT.[1461] Additionally, the payment for electricity generated through natural gas as a support fuel was restricted, which affected mostly CSP power plants due to technical necessities.[1462] Lastly, the already described clawback, on the basis of past remunerations, became a focus for the determination of a drastic and fundamental change, although various representation by the host state between 2004 and 2010 had implied that any change to the *Special Regime* would not affect existing projects.[1463] Considered collectively, these measures altered the legislative framework in a drastic and fundamental fashion, while the measures examined individually might not have constituted such a substantial change.[1464]

1458 Foresight and others v. Kingdom of Spain Final, Award, 14 November 2018 SCC Case No. V 2015/150, para. 391.

1459 ibid, para. 391.

1460 Foresight and others v. Kingdom of Spain Final, Award, 14 November 2018 SCC Case No. V 2015/150, para. 394-396; BayWa r.e. Renewable Energy GmbH and BayWa r.e. Asset Holding GmbH v. Kingdom of Spain, Dissenting Opinion Horacio A. Grigera Naón, 2 December 2019 ICSID Case No. ARB/15/16, para. 17.

1461 Foresight and others v. Kingdom of Spain Final, Award, 14 November 2018 SCC Case No. V 2015/150, para. 394-396; BayWa r.e. Renewable Energy GmbH and BayWa r.e. Asset Holding GmbH v. Kingdom of Spain, Dissenting Opinion Horacio A. Grigera Naón, 2 December 2019 ICSID Case No. ARB/15/16, para. 17.

1462 CSP plants have energy storages, for example molten salt, that allows electricity production over night and during cloudy periods. In order to maintain the liquid in a molten state, gas power stations are used during longer periods of low sun radiation. *See also* Stadtwerke München GmbH and others v. Kingdom of Spain, Dissenting Opinion Kaj Hobér, 2 December 2019 ICSID Case No. ARB/15/1, para. 20.

1463 Foresight and others v. Kingdom of Spain Final, Award, 14 November 2018 SCC Case No. V 2015/150, para. 395.

1464 NextEra Energy Global Holdings B.V. and NextEra Energy Spain Holdings B.V. v. Kingdom of Spain, Decision on Jurisdiction, Liability and Quantum Principles, 12 March 2019 ICSID Case No. ARB/14/11, para. 598. *Kaj Hobér*

In comparison with the essential characteristics set out by the *Special Regime* under RD 661/2007, it becomes apparent that the changes implemented by the 2013 Regime were more drastic than just reducing the investors' returns. The FIT and FIP options, the unlimited offtake volume, and in some cases even the reasonable remuneration were affected. This change was held to be "unprecedented internationally".[1465] Thus, it is not surprising that the changes to the remuneration method were perceived as drastic and fundamental. The stability of a support system is crucial to investments in the renewable energy sector because of the high upfront-investment and the high demand for debt capital. The Spanish government itself had expected in the PER 2005-2010 that debt financing would represent nearly 80% of the total capital investment needed in order to meet the objectives set out in Directive 2009/28/EC.[1466] As anticipated, the ratio of 80:20 for debt and equity have become industry standard.[1467] Therefore, stable cash flow is necessary for some investors to even pay the interest on the loans.

With regard to investments in the utility or general interest sectors, it has been early on acknowledged that stability in the remuneration system is crucial for any investor.[1468] Those sectors are, in general, characterised by strong governmental regulation. Additionally, operators cannot suspend the service and or disinvest without major difficulties, as investments are

---

in his dissent concurred that the change from remuneration based on actual costs and debts to a "standard model" was "seemingly intended significantly to reduce subsidies to existing plant", Stadtwerke München GmbH and others v. Kingdom of Spain, Dissenting Opinion Kaj Hobér, 2 December 2019 ICSID Case No. ARB/15/1, para. 21.

1465 Hydro Energy 1 S.A.R.L. and Hydroxana Sweden AB v. The Kingdom of Spain, Decision on Jurisdiction, Liability and Directions on Quantum, 9 March 2020 ICSID Case No. ARB/15/42, para. 683; Eiser Infrastructure Limited and Energía Solar Luxembourg S.à.r.l. v. Kingdom of Spain, Award, 4 May 2017 ICSID Case No. ARB/13/36, para. 365.

1466 IDEA, PER 2005-2010, p. 268, 269. *See also* 9REN Holding S.a.r.l v. Kingdom of Spain, Award, 31 March 2019 ICSID Case No. ARB/15/15, para. 96.

1467 *See for example* Foresight and others v. Kingdom of Spain Final, Award, 14 November 2018 SCC Case No. V 2015/150, para. 77; SolEs Badajoz GmbH v. Kingdom of Spain, Award, 31 July 2019 ICSID Case No. ARB/15/38, para. 141; OperaFund Eco-Invest SICAV PLC and Schwab Holding AG v. Kingdom of Spain, Award, 6 September 2019 ICSID Case No. ARB/15/36, para. 190. *See also* IDEA, PER 2005-2010, p. 268, 269.

1468 Total S.A. v. The Argentine Republic, Decision on Liability, 27 December 2010 ICSID Case No. ARB/04/01, para. 333. *See also* Blackaby, *Utilities, Government Regulations and Energy Investment Arbitrations*, p. 78.

running long-term.[1469] Arbitral tribunals considered the replacement of the current regulatory framework with a "wholly different regulatory approach" as an elimination of the framework's essential characteristics.[1470] In an international comparison, it can be observed that cost reductions on the side of the state can also be reached by using approaches, which are less detrimental to the overall profitability of the investments.[1471]

Some of the tribunals did not find a violation of the FET standard through the 2013 Regime.[1472] Among these tribunals, a number based their conclusions on the facts that the investment was conducted at a time in which such fundamental changes were foreseeable or the investors were

1469 Total S.A. v. The Argentine Republic, Decision on Liability, 27 December 2010 ICSID Case No. ARB/04/01, para. 333. *See also* Blackaby, *Utilities, Government Regulations and Energy Investment Arbitrations*, p. 78.

1470 The *Eiser* Tribunal observed, with regard to CSP plants, that "[t]his new system was profoundly unfair and inequitable as applied to Claimants' existing investment, stripping Claimants of virtually all of the value of their investment", Eiser Infrastructure Limited and Energía Solar Luxembourg S.à.r.l. v. Kingdom of Spain, Award, 4 May 2017 ICSID Case No. ARB/13/36, para. 365. *See also* Foresight and others v. Kingdom of Spain Final, Award, 14 November 2018 SCC Case No. V 2015/150, para. 397; Watkins Holdings S.à.r.l. and others v. Kingdom of Spain, Award, 21 January 2020 ICSID Case No. ARB/15/44, para. 508, 509.

1471 See the approach taken by the Czech State, Ch. 3 III 3. A less detrimental approach can also be observed in the case of *AES Summit*, where the Tribunal held that the development of a new regulatory system that sought to reduce excessive profits on the expense of the consumer in light of the characteristics of individual plants could not be qualified as a violation of the FET obligation, as it covered each generator's actual costs and still produced a 7.1% return on the investment, AES Summit Generation Limited et. al. v. The Republic of Hungary, Award, 23 September 2010 ICSID Case No. ARB/07/22, para. 9.3.53-9.3.55.

1472 BayWa r.e. Renewable Energy GmbH and BayWa r.e. Asset Holding GmbH v. Kingdom of Spain, Decision on Jurisdiction, Liability and Directions on Quantum, 2 December 2019 ICSID Case No. ARB/15/16, para. 590(f) (but finding that the clawback constituted a violation); Isolux Netherlands, BV v. Kingdom of Spain Final, Award, 17 July 2016 SCC Case V2013/153, para. 804; 9REN Holding S.a.r.l v. Kingdom of Spain, Award, 31 March 2019 ICSID Case No. ARB/15/15, para. 310 (at least with regard to one plant that has not been registered in time); Stadtwerke München GmbH and others v. Kingdom of Spain, Award, 2 December 2019 ICSID Case No. ARB/15/1, para. 275, 282; The PV Investors v. Kingdom of Spain Final, Award, 28 February 2020 PCA Case No. 2012-14, para. 596, 620.

still in possession of profitable investments.[1473] Therefore, the changes implemented through the 2013 Regime can, in general, be regarded as drastic and radical changes that violated the investors' expectations of basic regulatory stability.

c) Fundamental Change in Numbers

Arbitral jurisprudence often used the loss in revenue or the post-tax return by investors as a benchmark to measure whether changes to the legislative framework were drastic and against basic expectations.[1474] The overall picture shows that tribunals, in particular those which found that the investors were only entitled to a "reasonable" or "fair" return, took the total reduction in income of the power plants, as well as the final return on the investments into account.[1475] This allows for applying an objective standard of what is reasonable, rather than relying on the subjective hopes

1473 BayWa r.e. Renewable Energy GmbH and BayWa r.e. Asset Holding GmbH v. Kingdom of Spain, Decision on Jurisdiction, Liability and Directions on Quantum, 2 December 2019 ICSID Case No. ARB/15/16, para. 590; Isolux Netherlands, BV v. Kingdom of Spain Final, Award, 17 July 2016 SCC Case V2013/153, para. 804; 9REN Holding S.a.r.l v. Kingdom of Spain, Award, 31 March 2019 ICSID Case No. ARB/15/15, para. 310.

1474 Only the Tribunal in *SunReserve* preferred a "qualitative, as opposed to quantitative" assessment of the regulatory changes. In contrast to previous tribunals, it did not consider it appropriate or necessary to determine the precise percentage or range that satisfied the "fair remuneration" criteria set out by the Italian regulatory regime, for the purposes of determining Italy's liability under Article 10(1) ECT. Nonetheless, the Tribunal factored in the reduction of the incentive tariffs in its decision whether the legitimate expectations of the investors were violated, SunReserve Luxco Holdings v. Italian Republic Final, Award, 25 March 2020 SCC Arbitration V (2016/32), para. 845, 848.

1475 The Tribunal in *Hydro* declared that a violation of the FET standard under Article 10(1) ECT is to be found, "if and to the extent that the remuneration of each of the plants […] failed to accord with a reasonable post-tax rate of return", Hydro Energy 1 S.A.R.L. and Hydroxana Sweden AB v. The Kingdom of Spain, Decision on Jurisdiction, Liability and Directions on Quantum, 9 March 2020 ICSID Case No. ARB/15/42, para. 770(3). Similarly, *Philippe Sands* opined that the legitimate expectations require a balancing act and that the reception of a "reasonable return" is the very manifestation of such balancing. In light of the economic crisis, the reduction falls within the acceptable margin of change, if the plant still makes a reasonable profit, OperaFund Eco-Invest SICAV PLC and Schwab Holding AG v. Kingdom of Spain, Dissenting Opinion Philippe Sands, 6 September 2019 ICSID Case No. ARB/15/36,

and aspirations of investors investing in the host state.[1476] The following analysis will examine the different types of impacts, the host states' measures had on the investment to demonstrate why certain changes were perceived as drastic and radical.

(1) The Spanish Promise of a "Reasonable Return"

In the Spanish renewable energy saga, tribunals which found that investors may only expect a "reasonable" return, took into consideration representations by state officials to determine a reasonable return rate. During the period in which RD 661/2007 was in place, Spanish state authorities emphasized the possibility of returns for investors "well above 7%".[1477] After the abolishment of the *Special Regime*, Spain's own Ministerial Order IET 2014 fixed the reasonable rate of return at 7.398% pre-tax and 5.9% after-tax.[1478]

This, however, was construed by tribunals as the floor, but not the ceiling of returns. It was held that, due to the favourable conditions set out by the *Special Regime*, the expectations of a "reasonable" return would not be limited to a 7% return.[1479] Accordingly, the majority of tribunals found

para. 40, 42, citing Philip Morris Brands Sàrl et. al. v. Oriental Republic of Uruguay, Award, 8 July 2016 ICSID Case No. ARB/10/7, para. 422.

1476 SunReserve Luxco Holdings v. Italian Republic Final, Award, 25 March 2020 SCC Arbitration V (2016/32), para. 848; Charanne and Construction Investments v. Kingdom of Spain, Award, 21 January 2016 SCC Case No. V 062/2012, para. 495; RREEF Infrastructure (G.P.) Limited and RREEF Pan-European Infrastructure Two Lux S.à.r.l. v. Kingdom of Spain, Decision on Responsibility and on the Principles of Quantum, 30 November 2018 ICSID Case No. ARB/13/30, para. 388.

1477 *See* Foresight and others v. Kingdom of Spain Final, Award, 14 November 2018 SCC Case No. V 2015/150, para. 378; Novenergia II - Energy & Environment (SCA), SICAR v. The Kingdom of Spain, Award, 15 February 2018 SCC Case No. V 2015/063, para. 674.

1478 *See* Foresight and others v. Kingdom of Spain Final, Award, 14 November 2018 SCC Case No. V 2015/150, para. 392.

1479 The Tribunal in *9Ren* agreed with the expert witness on quantum, who found that the reasonable rate for renewable energy projects amounts to 7% post-tax 9REN Holding S.a.r.l v. Kingdom of Spain, Award, 31 March 2019 ICSID Case No. ARB/15/15, para. 390, 392. On the lower end of the spectrum, the Tribunal in *RREEF* considered the cost-structure of the investment and concluded that the reasonable return must not be below 6.86% post-tax RREEF Infrastructure (G.P.) Limited and RREEF Pan-European Infrastructure Two

a fundamental change that violated the investors' basic expectations, when the return rate fell significantly below 7%.[1480]

Criticism was also raised with regard to the method of calculating the remuneration. It was not deemed sufficient for a power plant to achieve reasonable returns based on the model of a "standard installation".[1481] Instead, it was seen as important that the investments generate actual returns of over 7% under the given conditions prevailing in the individual case.[1482] A return calculation decoupled from the actual remuneration impaired by the regulatory changes is to be considered "ill-adapted".[1483] This is not to be understood that investors should not bear a share of the burden,

---

Lux S.à.r.l. v. Kingdom of Spain, Decision on Responsibility and on the Principles of Quantum, 30 November 2018 ICSID Case No. ARB/13/30, para. 589. Also agreed to by Hydro Energy 1 S.A.R.L. and Hydroxana Sweden AB v. The Kingdom of Spain, Decision on Jurisdiction, Liability and Directions on Quantum, 9 March 2020 ICSID Case No. ARB/15/42, para. 757. Similarly, *Phillipe Sands* took the rates of return granted by other EU Member states as a reference point and considered that a reduction from 7.8% to 6.1% or 5.7% still aligned with the market and hence guaranteed reasonable profitability, OperaFund Eco-Invest SICAV PLC and Schwab Holding AG v. Kingdom of Spain, Dissenting Opinion Philippe Sands, 6 September 2019 ICSID Case No. ARB/15/36, para. 38. *See also* Foresight and others v. Kingdom of Spain, Dissenting Opinion Raúl Emilio Vinuesa, 14 November 2018 SCC Case No. V 2015/150, para. 31; Novenergia II - Energy & Environment (SCA), SICAR v. The Kingdom of Spain, Award, 15 February 2018 SCC Case No. V 2015/063, para. 674; Cube Infrastructure Fund SICAV and others v. Kingdom of Spain, Decision on Jurisdiction, Liability and Partial Decision on Quantum, 19 February 2019 ICSID Case No. ARB/15/20, para. 293.

1480 Eiser Infrastructure Limited and Energía Solar Luxembourg S.à.r.l. v. Kingdom of Spain, Award, 4 May 2017 ICSID Case No. ARB/13/36, para. 396; 9REN Holding S.a.r.l v. Kingdom of Spain, Award, 31 March 2019 ICSID Case No. ARB/15/15, para. 390, 392; The PV Investors v. Kingdom of Spain Final, Award, 28 February 2020 PCA Case No. 2012-14, para. 754, 847; RREEF Infrastructure (G.P.) Limited and RREEF Pan-European Infrastructure Two Lux S.à.r.l. v. Kingdom of Spain, Decision on Responsibility and on the Principles of Quantum, 30 November 2018 ICSID Case No. ARB/13/30, para. 589; Hydro Energy 1 S.A.R.L. and Hydroxana Sweden AB v. The Kingdom of Spain, Decision on Jurisdiction, Liability and Directions on Quantum, 9 March 2020 ICSID Case No. ARB/15/42, para. 757.

1481 RWE Innogy GmbH and RWE Innogy Aersa S.A.U. v. Kingdom of Spain, Decision on Jurisdicition, Liability, and certain Issues of Quantum, 6 January 2020 ICSID Case No. ARB/14/34, para. 587.

1482 ibid, para. 587.

1483 InfraRed Environmental Infrastructure GP Limited and others v. Kingdom of Spain, Award, 2 August 2019 ICSID Case No. ARB/14/12, para. 543.

in order to contribute to the sustainability of the support system.[1484] The reduction in remuneration may very well be significant, as long as the return can still be qualified as reasonable.[1485] However, if the host state perceived a certain return as reasonable and committed to it, the state must abide by its own standard.[1486]

Hence, the calculation method for a reasonable return must be linked to the cost structure of the individual investment. Despite the radical changes, tribunals may not be able to find a violation of the legitimate expectations when investors still achieve a return of over 7%.[1487]

(2) The Italian Incentive Reduction

In comparison, the changes introduced by the *Spalma Incentivi Decree* were also significant, but not as detrimental. Tribunals found "a modest 6% to 8% reduction" in returns to be within the state's margin of discretion,

1484 RWE Innogy GmbH and RWE Innogy Aersa S.A.U. v. Kingdom of Spain, Decision on Jurisdicition, Liability, and certain Issues of Quantum, 6 January 2020 ICSID Case No. ARB/14/34, para. 589.

1485 The Tribunal in *Charanne* found that the reduction in the profitability of the plants, under the 2010 amendments of 8.5%-10%, did not constitute a fundamental change, Charanne and Construction Investments v. Kingdom of Spain, Award, 21 January 2016 SCC Case No. V 062/2012, para. 284, 539. Similarly, *Philippe Sands* opined that a return reduction from 7.8% to 6.1% or 5.7% still left the investors with a reasonable profitability, OperaFund Eco-Invest SICAV PLC and Schwab Holding AG v. Kingdom of Spain, Dissenting Opinion Philippe Sands, 6 September 2019 ICSID Case No. ARB/15/36, para. 38.

1486 RWE Innogy GmbH and RWE Innogy Aersa S.A.U. v. Kingdom of Spain, Decision on Jurisdicition, Liability, and certain Issues of Quantum, 6 January 2020 ICSID Case No. ARB/14/34, para. 589. That such an "overshooting" of the host state in the cost reduction can have a devastating effect on the profitability of an investment can be seen in the case of *Eiser*, in which the investors reported a 66% loss in revenue after the regime-change, which essentially "washed away the financial underpinnings" of the investment, Eiser Infrastructure Limited and Energía Solar Luxembourg S.à.r.l. v. Kingdom of Spain, Award, 4 May 2017 ICSID Case No. ARB/13/36, para. 389.

1487 BayWa r.e. Renewable Energy GmbH and BayWa r.e. Asset Holding GmbH v. Kingdom of Spain, Decision on Jurisdiction, Liability and Directions on Quantum, 2 December 2019 ICSID Case No. ARB/15/16, para. 590; Stadtwerke München GmbH and others v. Kingdom of Spain, Award, 2 December 2019 ICSID Case No. ARB/15/1, para. 353, 354; The PV Investors v. Kingdom of Spain Final, Award, 28 February 2020 PCA Case No. 2012-14, para. 754, 847.

especially in light of the previous evolution of the support system and the state's objective to make the support system more sustainable.[1488] In particular, the reduction was appropriate considering the lowered expenses, since the operation and management costs of PV power plants were reduced over time and the overall impact on the investment was not significant.[1489] However, an equal number of tribunals concluded that even such a "modest" reduction had a significant impact on the investment and fell below what investors could legitimately expect at the time of the investment.[1490] Hence, one may come once again to the conclusion that the severity of the state's measure correlates with the individual cost structure and profitability of the investment.

(3) The Preservation of a Reasonable Return by the Czech Republic

The support scheme established by the Czech Republic initially provided for a return of about 7%.[1491] Due to the technological advancements in the renewable energy sector, prices for the installation and maintenance of PV plants dropped and hence profits for investors rose significantly.[1492] The amendments to the support schemes were aimed to reduce the returns for investors to the levels initially intended by the host state.[1493] Since the

1488 Belenergia S.A. v. Italian Republic, Award, 6 August 2019 ICSID Case No. ARB/15/40, para. 595; SunReserve Luxco Holdings v. Italian Republic Final, Award, 25 March 2020 SCC Arbitration V (2016/32), para. 852.

1489 SunReserve Luxco Holdings v. Italian Republic Final, Award, 25 March 2020 SCC Arbitration V (2016/32), para. 860, 884.

1490 CEF Energia B.V. v. Italian Republic, Award, 16 January 2019 SCC Arbitration No. 2015/158, para. 238, 241; ESPF Beteiligungs GmbH et. al. v. Italian Republic, Award, 14 September 2020 ICSID Case No. ARB/16/5, para. 578.

1491 WA Investments-Europa Nova Limited v. The Czech Republic, Award, 15 May 2019 PCA CASE No 2014-19, para. 574, 687. *See also* Antaris Solar and Dr. Michael Göde v. Czech Republic, Award, 2 May 2018 PCA Case No. 2014-01, para. 445.

1492 The Tribunal in *WA Investment* estimated that "the return for the reference plant without amendments would have been 8.4% in 2009 and 11.4% in 2010", WA Investments-Europa Nova Limited v. The Czech Republic, Award, 15 May 2019 PCA CASE No 2014-19, para. 687.

1493 The Tribunal in *WA Investment* estimated that the return "with the amendments amounted to 7% in 2009 and 8.4% in 2010". Thus, it was concluded that the returns received by the investors were exactly in line with or well above the promised 7% return rate, WA Investments-Europa Nova Limited v. The Czech Republic, Award, 15 May 2019 PCA CASE No 2014-19, para. 687.

returns were in line with what was originally promised, tribunals could not find any fundamental changes to the support scheme.[1494] In particular, the hallmark was established that the changes could not be unreasonable, if the investors received a "level of revenue through the FIT system that ensures a 15 year payback of capital expenses and a return on investment of at least 7% per year over a period of 15 (later 20) years".[1495] In conclusion, the support scheme—even after its amendments—offered sufficient remuneration to pay back the investment within 9.9 years.[1496] This fell far below what was promised by the regulatory framework in place at the time of the investment, and the overall lifetime of a PV plant.[1497] Although the numbers demonstrate that the legislative measures put the investments in a less favourable position, the return still exceeded the initial promise by the host state. Hence, it was found that the changes did not repeal the fundamental features of the support scheme.[1498]

4) Interim Conclusion on the Host State's Margin of Discretion

The findings of early tribunals are reflected in previous jurisprudence: In absence of a specific promise, legitimate expectations can only be violated in cases in which the underlying legal framework was altered in a fundamental and drastic fashion.[1499] Additionally, assessing the impact of the

---

1494 The Tribunal in *Wirtgen* found that neither the legislation nor the implementing framework put a cap on the renewable energy investments at 7%, which is demonstrated by the fact that the investors in the given case received a return of 7% and more before and after the measures, Jürgen Wirtgen, Stefan Wirtgen, Gisela Wirtgen and JSW Solar (zwei) GmbH & Co. KG v. Czech Republic, Award, 11 October 2017 PCA Case No. 2014-03, para. 374.

1495 ibid, para. 416.

1496 I.C.W. Europe Investments Limited v. The Czech Republic, Award, 15 May 2019 PCA CASE No 2014-22, para. 536.

1497 ibid, para. 536.

1498 Voltaic Network GmbH v. Czech Republic, Award, 15 September 2019 PCA CASE No 2014-20, para. 491.

1499 The Tribunal in *Toto* decided that the changes in the regulatory framework would, in the absence of a stabilisation provision or related commitment, only be considered as a violation of the FET standard in case of a drastic or discriminatory change in the essential features of the legal framework, Toto Costruzioni Generali S.p.A. v. The Republic of Lebanon, Award, 7 June 2012 ICSID Case No. ARB/07/12, para. 244. This view is also reflected in a series of decisions against Argentina, in which tribunals concluded that the FET standard was violated in cases in which the basic features of the legal and business

measures requires taking into consideration the effect on the investors' projects compared to their overall size, as well as whether investors are able to amortise their investment and achieve a reasonable return.[1500] Hence, a qualitative distinction must be made, whether an incentive regime is simply "trimmed down" or is "outright terminated".[1501] Moreover, a "roller-coaster-effect" of continuous legislative amendments due to policy changes contribute to unpredictability and instability may violate the expectations of basic stability.[1502] Lastly, the cumulative effect of the measures implemented by the host state that lead to a total alteration of the entire legal setup for foreign investors constitutes a breach of the FET standard.[1503]

---

environment were changed in total by radical state measures, BG Group Plc. v. The Argentine Republic, Award, 24 December 2007 UNCITRAL, para. 307; Total S.A. v. The Argentine Republic, Decision on Liability, 27 December 2010 ICSID Case No. ARB/04/01, para. 168; El Paso Energy International Company v. The Argentine Republic, Award, 31 October 2011 ICSID Case No. ARB/03/15, para. 374, 515; CMS Gas Transmission Company v. The Argentine Republic, Award, 21 May 2005 ICSID Case No. ARB/01/8, para. 275. While parts of the CMS award was annulled, the cited portion was upheld as "adequately founded on the applicable law and the relevant facts.", CMS Gas Transmission Company v. The Argentine Republic Decision of the ad hoc Committee on the Application for Annulment of the Argentine Republic, 25 September 2007 ICSID Case No. ARB/01/8, para. 85.

1500 The Tribunal in *Toto* concluded that the impact of the challenged measures was relatively small in comparison to the overall size of the investment, Toto Costruzioni Generali S.p.A. v. The Republic of Lebanon, Award, 7 June 2012 ICSID Case No. ARB/07/12, para. 244. In the same vein, the Tribunal in *Total* found that states may only implement such regulatory measures which allow the investor "to recover its operations costs, amortize its investments and make a reasonable return over time", Total S.A. v. The Argentine Republic, Decision on Liability, 27 December 2010 ICSID Case No. ARB/04/01, para. 122, 333. Also observing that the investor could only reasonably expect to receive fair treatment and just compensation: ADC Affiliate Limited and ADC & ADMC Management Limited v. The Republic of Hungary, Award, 2 October 2016 ICSID Case No. ARB/03/16, para. 423, 424.

1501 Ioan Micula, Viorel Micula, S.C. European Food S.A, S.C. Starmill S.R.L. and S.C. Multipack S.R.L. v. Romania, Award, 11 December 2013 ICSID Case No. ARB/05/20, para. 684.

1502 PSEG Global Inc and others v. Republic of Turkey, Award, 9 January 2007 ICSID Case No. ARB/02/5, para. 250, 255.

1503 El Paso Energy International Company v. The Argentine Republic, Award, 31 October 2011 ICSID Case No. ARB/03/15, para. 510, 517. *See also* LG&E Energy Corp. LG&E Capital Corp. and LG&E International, Inc. v. The Argentine Republic, Decision on Liability, 3 October 2006 ICSID Case No. ARB/02/1, para. 139.

Previous arbitral jurisprudence also considered the quantification of a "reasonable return". It was opined that "a reasonable rate of return on an investment" is an essential aspect of attracting foreign investment, as investors would not enter into long-term commitments, without appropriate profit prospects.[1504] However, the simple expectation of a reasonable return alone does not create liability for states under international law.[1505] Rather, not receiving a reasonable return is a business risk inherently contained in any investment.[1506] States cannot be held accountable for business risks, if they did not guarantee certain returns.[1507] Nonetheless, this does not apply without limitations. A distinction must be made between ordinary investments and investments in the public sector, whose profitability depends upon future actions by the government.[1508] In general, investment in such sectors, which naturally depend on the state to be profitable, may be protected by a higher degree of stability-expectations. In the energy sector, remuneration that guarantees each investor actual costs-coverage and still produces above 7% return can be regarded as reasonable.[1509]

1504 The Tribunal in *Walter Bau* also considered a 14% return as reasonable, which is debatable but ultimately depends on the risk involved with the investment, Walter Bau AG v. The Kingdom of Thailand, Award, 1 July 2009 UNCITRAL, para. 12.1-12.3.

1505 MTD Equity Sdn. Bhd. and MTD Chile S.A. v. Republic of Chile, Award, 25 May 2004 ICSID Case No. ARB/01/7, para. 178.

1506 MTD Equity Sdn. Bhd. and MTD Chile S.A. v. Republic of Chile, Award, 25 May 2004 ICSID Case No. ARB/01/7, para. 178; Hydro Energy 1 S.A.R.L. and Hydroxana Sweden AB v. The Kingdom of Spain, Decision on Jurisdiction, Liability and Directions on Quantum, 9 March 2020 ICSID Case No. ARB/15/42, para. 580; Cavalum SGPS v. Kingdom of Spain, Decision on Jurisdiction, Liability and Directions on Quantum, 31 August 2020 ICSID Case No. ARB/15/34, p. 422.

1507 Hydro Energy 1 S.A.R.L. and Hydroxana Sweden AB v. The Kingdom of Spain, Decision on Jurisdiction, Liability and Directions on Quantum, 9 March 2020 ICSID Case No. ARB/15/42, para. 580; Cavalum SGPS v. Kingdom of Spain, Decision on Jurisdiction, Liability and Directions on Quantum, 31 August 2020 ICSID Case No. ARB/15/34, p. 422.

1508 Walter Bau AG v. The Kingdom of Thailand, Award, 1 July 2009 UNCITRAL, para. 12.3. and 12.4.

1509 The Tribunal in *AES Summit* is prevailing, which held that legislative amendments are reasonable and compliant with the investors' legitimate expectations, if the state reviewed all electricity generators' financial statements for the last available reporting period and set price caps in a manner that would cover each generator's production costs and still produces a 7.1% return on assets,

Conclusively, it is to find that recent jurisprudence is to a vast degree in line with previous arbitral decisions. Investors must always expect regulatory change to some degree. In particular, if the legislative framework has already undergone adverse changes, it must be perceived as a clear indication that the current regime would not be maintained unchanged and that any change may make the regime less favourable and less secure.[1510] Nonetheless, the legitimate expectations include, even in the absence of an express stability promise, that the essential characteristics of the legal framework will remain intact.[1511] The essential characteristics are affected, if the host state adopts a "wholly different regulatory approach", which adversely affects the investments.[1512] In particular, host states violate the legitimate expectations of the investors in the regulatory framework, if they use a "bait-and-switch" tactic, in which they first offer a generous support system to induce investment in their country and then switch to a less favourable system that severely diminishes or abolishes the profitability of investments.[1513] Thus, host states fail to provide fair and equitable treatment, if they "dismantle" the regulatory framework in place at the time of the investment.[1514]

In cases in which there were specific commitments, tribunals only accepted changes to the legislative framework that cut the incentives to the promised level, if investors received an excessive return irrespective

AES Summit Generation Limited et. al. v. The Republic of Hungary, Award, 23 September 2010 ICSID Case No. ARB/07/22, para. 9.3.66, 9.3.67.

1510 Cube Infrastructure Fund SICAV and others v. Kingdom of Spain, Decision on Jurisdiction, Liability and Partial Decision on Quantum, 19 February 2019 ICSID Case No. ARB/15/20, para. 392, 421.

1511 Total S.A. v. The Argentine Republic, Decision on Liability, 27 December 2010 ICSID Case No. ARB/04/01, para. 168, 333; Charanne and Construction Investments v. Kingdom of Spain, Award, 21 January 2016 SCC Case No. V 062/2012, para. 539; Eiser Infrastructure Limited and Energía Solar Luxembourg S.à.r.l. v. Kingdom of Spain, Award, 4 May 2017 ICSID Case No. ARB/13/36, para. 365, 382; Antin Infrastructure Services Luxembourg S.à.r.l. and Antin Energia Termosolar B.V. v. Kingdom of Spain, Award, 15 June 2018 ICSID Case No. ARB/13/31, para. 556.

1512 Eiser Infrastructure Limited and Energía Solar Luxembourg S.à.r.l. v. Kingdom of Spain, Award, 4 May 2017 ICSID Case No. ARB/13/36, para. 362, 365.

1513 RREEF Infrastructure (G.P.) Limited and RREEF Pan-European Infrastructure Two Lux S.à.r.l. v. Kingdom of Spain, Partially Dissenting Opinion of Robert Volterra, 30 November 2018 ICSID Case No. ARB/13/30, para. 26.

1514 Enron Corporation and Ponderosa Assets, L.P. v. The Argentine Republic, Award, 22 May 2007 ICSID Case No. ARB/01/3, para. 264, 266, 275.

of whether the investments remained profitable.[1515] If there is only the promise of a "reasonable" or "fair" return, tribunals observed throughout the different legislative backgrounds of the cases that investors may only legitimately expect post-tax returns of around 7%. The Spanish cases demonstrate that this must be the actual return rate generated by the investment and not a theoretical return rate, based on the model of a "standard installation". In contrast, facilities that operate at an above-average efficiency level cannot claim compensation, if their actual return rate exceeds the 7% threshold.

IV. Summary of Recent Jurisprudence

The analysis of recent arbitral decisions and earlier jurisprudence revealed an overlap on many issues. States can restrict their right to regulate under international law by issuing a specific commitment.[1516] However, not all state acts, which give the prospect of a certain treatment in the future, can be regarded as proper commitments under the notion of legitimate expectations. State representations must be precise to their object and purpose and must be aimed at inducing foreign investment.[1517] These representations can be either directed explicitly at an individual investor or at a limited group of potential investors.[1518] They can also gain cumulative significance, even if they are individually not capable of creating any legally protected expectations. The trend also indicated that general commitments, in particular the legal framework, can form a basis for the investors' reliance.[1519] Moreover, investors are required to conduct a rather extensive form of due diligence, depending on the specificity of the commitment received and the size of the investment.[1520] Lastly, it must be assessed whether the host state overstepped its margin of discretion by

1515 ESPF Beteiligungs GmbH et. al. v. Italian Republic, Award, 14 September 2020 ICSID Case No. ARB/16/5, para. 580, 755; Antin Infrastructure Services Luxembourg S.à.r.l. and Antin Energia Termosolar B.V. v. Kingdom of Spain, Award, 15 June 2018 ICSID Case No. ARB/13/31, para. 532, 573; 9REN Holding S.a.r.l v. Kingdom of Spain, Award, 31 March 2019 ICSID Case No. ARB/15/15, para. 292, 294, 297.

1516 *See* Ch. 4 I 1).

1517 *See* Ch. 4 I 3).

1518 *See* Ch. 4 I 3).

1519 *See* Ch. 4 I 2).

1520 *See* Ch. 4 II.

implementing adverse measures. These state actions must be considered in light of the principles of reasonableness and proportionality, predictability and retroactivity, as well as the overall impact of the changes on the investment.[1521] When evaluating the impact of regulatory changes, tribunals examine whether the changes were fundamental, drastic, or radical. In general, fundamental changes are found when the essential characteristics of the regulatory framework are altered and the returns of the investment fall below the promised and/or a reasonable rate of return.[1522] In the energy sector, a profit of 7% p.a. was regularly regarded as a reasonable return, in absence of a more specific commitment.[1523]

1521 *See* Ch. 4 III 1) and 2).
1522 *See* Ch. 4 III 3 a) and b).
1523 *See* Ch. 4 III 4).

Chapter 5: Interpretation and Evaluation of Arbitral Jurisprudence

Despite the significant increase in cases, investment arbitration has experienced a strong backlash from states and the EU with regard to its legitimacy. Among other concerns, host states fear the decrease of their regulatory and administrative flexibility, which is threatened by the broad interpretation of indefinite legal concepts, such as the FET standard and the notion of legitimate expectations, by democratically non-legitimated arbitrators.[1524] States bear reservations that arbitral tribunals will give the investors' interest priority over competing public interests of the host states and will come to investor-friendly decisions.[1525]

In the past, however, there has not been proof that arbitral tribunals have given preferential treatment to investors over states.[1526] Nor has the analysis of recent cases in the renewable energy sector provided any evidence that the vast majority of arbitral tribunals have overly restricted the rights of states or interpreted the rights of investors excessively. Tribunals have demonstrated their understanding of the importance of the states' right to regulate, and do not unilaterally give the interests of foreign investors priority over considerations of public interest. Nonetheless, the concerns raised strain the legitimacy and the acceptance of investment treaty arbitration. Therefore, these concerns must be addressed by consistent and transparent decision-making on the side of the tribunals, which

1524 UNCTAD, 'Fair and Equitable Treatment', p. xiiv. *See also* Levashova, *The Right of States to Regulate in International Investment Law*, p. 3.

1525 Kläger, *Revising Treatment Standards— Fair and Equitable Treatment in Light of Sustainable Development*, p. 67; Levashova, *The Right of States to Regulate in International Investment Law*, p. 3.

1526 Strezhnev, 'Detecting Bias in International Investment Arbitration' (2016), p. 22 <https://scholar.harvard.edu/files/astrezhnev/files/are_investment_arbitrators_biased.pdf?m=1459524441> (accessed 3 May 2021). The win-rate of investors in the reviewed arbitration proceedings increased due to the large number of losses suffered by Spain. Considering that the Czech Republic defended itself successfully in most of its cases and Italy's win/loss-rate is evenly distributed, the Spanish cases can be regarded as an anomaly and should not be regarded as an implication to a change in trend.

requires that indefinite legal concepts have to be refined and decisions must follow mutual reasoning.

The fact that arbitral practice is actually moving towards a more consistent approach is especially illustrated by the case law on the FET standard. The research has also shown that arbitral tribunals, notably more recently, consistently used the FET standard and the notion of legitimate expectations to not only take into account the conflicting interests typically connected to transnational investments, but also afforded the host states a considerable level of discretion, in which the states' measures are accepted as reasonable.[1527] This may be partly due to the more frequent and thorough use of the principle of proportionality.[1528]

In addition, tribunals expressed the willingness to comply with previous decisions concerning similar facts and circumstances.[1529] They also emphasised that they have a duty to adopt principles established by arbitral jurisprudence, if the individual case at hand is not subject to compelling contrary grounds.[1530] Such a harmonious interpretation is not only welcomed under the aspect of legal certainty, but is necessary in light of systemic integration in international law prescribed in Article 31(3)(c) VCLT. Systemic integration requires a concise interpretation of basic principles,

1527 *See* Ch. 4 III 1).

1528 This notwithstanding, the individual application of the principle of proportionality has not yet achieved the appropriate level of sophistication and uniformity, which would be appropriate for a principle that plays such a central role. For the critique to the application of the proportionality test *see* Ch. 2 IV 3.

1529 The PV Investors v. Kingdom of Spain Final, Award, 28 February 2020 PCA Case No. 2012-14, para. 521; BayWa r.e. Renewable Energy GmbH and BayWa r.e. Asset Holding GmbH v. Kingdom of Spain, Decision on Jurisdiction, Liability and Directions on Quantum, 2 December 2019 ICSID Case No. ARB/15/16, para. 317; InfraRed Environmental Infrastructure GP Limited and others v. Kingdom of Spain, Award, 2 August 2019 ICSID Case No. ARB/14/12, para. 255.

1530 The Tribunal in *PV Investors* expressed the belief that "subject always to the specific text of the ECT, and with due regard to the circumstances of each particular case, it has a duty to contribute to the harmonious development of international investment law in furtherance of the certainty of the rule of law", The PV Investors v. Kingdom of Spain Final, Award, 28 February 2020 PCA Case No. 2012-14, para. 521. *See also* BayWa r.e. Renewable Energy GmbH and BayWa r.e. Asset Holding GmbH v. Kingdom of Spain, Decision on Jurisdiction, Liability and Directions on Quantum, 2 December 2019 ICSID Case No. ARB/15/16, para. 317; InfraRed Environmental Infrastructure GP Limited and others v. Kingdom of Spain, Award, 2 August 2019 ICSID Case No. ARB/14/12, para. 255.

such as the right to regulate, proportionality, and those fragments of the FET standard that are simultaneously protected by human rights law.[1531]

The core of this research was dedicated to finding patterns in the recent arbitral jurisprudence in order to determine more refined requirements for the notion of legitimate expectations. If the standard remains open-ended and ambiguous, it will not provide any immediate answers for resolving cases and continue to undermine the authority of investment law.[1532] On the contrary, it is not advisable to overly refine the FET standard in order to maintain its flexibility, in light of the multitude of possible situations investors may find themselves confronted with.[1533] Nonetheless, investment practice is far from becoming too precise on certain issues. The recent renewable energy cases have shed more light on topics like the qualification of administrative registration requirements, advertising campaigns, and general policy statements. However, there is still ambiguity regarding the legal framework as a source of legitimate expectations.

I. Specificity of the States' Commitments

The notion of legitimate expectations draws from and is supplemented by other universal principles of administrative law, such as the prohibition of proper retroactivity, the principle of *pacta sunt servanda*, and the protection of trust in the stability of administrative decision-making.[1534] Therefore, governmental and administrative representations can take a large variety of forms, such as registration confirmations, which promise a certain period of stable remuneration, administrative resolutions further clarifying the content of a legislative promise. Even advertising campaigns, policy plans and explanatory reports of a more general nature may contain some form of commitment by the state.[1535] Depending on their nature, they can either be qualified as specific or general. With regard to the legitimacy of expectations, based on such administrative representations, it can be argued that all of them are capable of creating reliance worthy of protection

1531 Dörr and Schmalenbach, *Vienna Convention on the Law of Treaties*, p. 603, 604.

1532 Sipiorski, *Good Faith in International Investment Arbitration*, para. 9.07.

1533 ibid, para. 9.07.

1534 Mairal, *Legitimate Expectations and Informal Administrative Representations*, p. 414.

1535 *See* Ch. 4 I.

under the FET standard, as they are an expression of an act of appreciation by the administrative body.

In general, arbitral jurisprudence demonstrated that the more specific their legal form, content and wording, the stronger is the legal force of a commitment.[1536] Taking into account the aforementioned, this is only consequential, as more specific representations are an expression of a higher degree of consideration by the state. According to the analysis undertaken in this study, the potential commitments can be roughly classified into three categories. First, there are the "classic" specific commitments, which are individualized representations addressed to a single individual or to a small group.[1537] Tribunals accepted that such representations may purport expectations to receive a specific remuneration, instead of simply a reasonable one.[1538] Since they are an expression of strong consideration, the state's margin of discretion when altering the content of the commitment is limited. Second, general representations can be found, which are addressed to a limited group of potential investors, but lack specificity, such as general policy reports or advertising campaigns but also the legislative framework in itself.[1539] Such representations are generally weaker and only basic expectations—if any—can be deemed legitimate, in reliance on them.[1540] Third, a bundle of more specific and less general representations vis-à-vis investors may cumulate to set out the leading principles of the host state's policy, which encumbers the expectation that the promised policy will be further followed.[1541] Such a cumulation of representations

---

1536 *See* Ch. 4 I 3). Arriving at a similar conclusion: Levashova, *The Right of States to Regulate in International Investment Law*, p. 115, Section 6.03; Kläger, *'Fair and Equitable Treatment' in International Investment Law*, p. 187. *See also* Total S.A. v. The Argentine Republic, Decision on Liability, 27 December 2010 ICSID Case No. ARB/04/01, para. 121.

1537 *See* Ch. 4 I 1). *See also* Mairal, *Legitimate Expectations and Informal Administrative Representations*, p. 426.

1538 Masdar Solar & Wind Cooperatief U.A. v. Kingdom of Spain, Award, 16 May 2018 ICSID Case No. ARB/14/1, para. 512, 521; SolEs Badajoz GmbH v. Kingdom of Spain, Award, 31 July 2019 ICSID Case No. ARB/15/38, para. 443, 444; Greentech Energy Systems A/S, NovEnergia II Energy & Environment (SCA) SICAR, and NovEnergia II Italian Portfolio SA v. Italian Republic, Award, 23 December 2018 SCC Arbitration V (2015/095), para. 450, 451; CEF Energia B.V. v. Italian Republic, Award, 16 January 2019 SCC Arbitration No. 2015/158, para. 222, 237.

1539 *See* Ch. 4 I 2).

1540 Mairal, *Legitimate Expectations and Informal Administrative Representations*, p. 426.

1541 *See* Ch. 4 I 3).

can be characterised as the "*leitmotiv*" of the host states conduct.[1542] These representations may compensate for their legal quality, i.e. informality or generality, by their quantity and cohesive recurrence.

The specificity of the underlying commitment correlates with the level of legitimacy tribunals attributed to the expectations. In the face of a specific commitment with clear content, the legitimate expectations shield investors from significant deviations from the promised remuneration.[1543] When confronted with simple general commitments, for example through a legislative promise, without any additional representations, tribunals found the lowest level of expectations, and held that the investors were only shielded from drastic and fundamental changes in the legal framework.[1544] Others found that investors could only rely on receiving a reasonable return, as this was the basic promise given by the states by their regulatory framework and auxiliary representations.[1545] Administra-

---

1542 Antin Infrastructure Services Luxembourg S.à.r.l. and Antin Energia Termosolar B.V. v. Kingdom of Spain, Award, 15 June 2018 ICSID Case No. ARB/13/31, para. 548.

1543 Novenergia II - Energy & Environment (SCA), SICAR v. The Kingdom of Spain, Award, 15 February 2018 SCC Case No. V 2015/063, para. 673; Masdar Solar & Wind Cooperatief U.A. v. Kingdom of Spain, Award, 16 May 2018 ICSID Case No. ARB/14/1, para. 512, 521; SolEs Badajoz GmbH v. Kingdom of Spain, Award, 31 July 2019 ICSID Case No. ARB/15/38, para. 443, 444; OperaFund Eco-Invest SICAV PLC and Schwab Holding AG v. Kingdom of Spain, Award, 6 September 2019 ICSID Case No. ARB/15/36, para. 489; Greentech Energy Systems A/S, NovEnergia II Energy & Environment (SCA) SICAR, and NovEnergia II Italian Portfolio SA v. Italian Republic, Award, 23 December 2018 SCC Arbitration V (2015/095), para. 450, 451; CEF Energia B.V. v. Italian Republic, Award, 16 January 2019 SCC Arbitration No. 2015/158, para. 222, 237.

1544 Charanne and Construction Investments v. Kingdom of Spain, Award, 21 January 2016 SCC Case No. V 062/2012, para. 518, 519; Eiser Infrastructure Limited and Energía Solar Luxembourg S.à.r.l. v. Kingdom of Spain, Award, 4 May 2017 ICSID Case No. ARB/13/36, para. 365; RREEF Infrastructure (G.P.) Limited and RREEF Pan-European Infrastructure Two Lux S.à.r.l. v. Kingdom of Spain, Decision on Responsibility and on the Principles of Quantum, 30 November 2018 ICSID Case No. ARB/13/30, para. 523; Foresight and others v. Kingdom of Spain Final, Award, 14 November 2018 SCC Case No. V 2015/150, para. 365.

1545 Stadtwerke München GmbH and others v. Kingdom of Spain, Award, 2 December 2019 ICSID Case No. ARB/15/1, para. 275, 282; The PV Investors v. Kingdom of Spain Final, Award, 28 February 2020 PCA Case No. 2012-14, para. 596; Foresight and others v. Kingdom of Spain, Dissenting Opinion Raúl Emilio Vinuesa, 14 November 2018 SCC Case No. V 2015/150, para. 33; Cube Infrastructure Fund SICAV and others v. Kingdom of Spain, Separate

tive registration confirmations, such as the RAIPRE Registration, have not been qualified uniformly as a specific commitment by tribunals. Some tribunals concluded that the registration confirmations were specific guarantees that the power plant would receive the prescribed remuneration for a fixed duration of time.[1546] The majority, however, simply categorized them as auxiliary administrative acts, which do not convey any commitments, other than what is already in the law.[1547] Regardless of the approach, registration confirmations have proven to be a decisive moment in the creation of legitimate expectations. They are either capable of creating legitimate expectations themselves or specify the general legislative promise.[1548] Investors that acquired shares in companies that had not yet received their final registration were found to not be protected by the FET standard.[1549]

---

and Partial Dissenting Opinion Christian Tomuschat, 19 February 2019 ICSID Case No. ARB/15/20, para. 23.

1546 Antin Infrastructure Services Luxembourg S.à.r.l. and Antin Energia Termosolar B.V. v. Kingdom of Spain, Award, 15 June 2018 ICSID Case No. ARB/13/31, para. 552; Greentech Energy Systems A/S, NovEnergia II Energy & Environment (SCA) SICAR, and NovEnergia II Italian Portfolio SA v. Italian Republic, Award, 23 December 2018 SCC Arbitration V (2015/095), para. 447, 450; CEF Energia B.V. v. Italian Republic, Award, 16 January 2019 SCC Arbitration No. 2015/158, para. 214.

1547 Charanne and Construction Investments v. Kingdom of Spain, Award, 21 January 2016 SCC Case No. V 062/2012, para. 510; NextEra Energy Global Holdings B.V. and NextEra Energy Spain Holdings B.V. v. Kingdom of Spain, Decision on Jurisdiction, Liability and Quantum Principles, 12 March 2019 ICSID Case No. ARB/14/11, para. 585; Stadtwerke München GmbH and others v. Kingdom of Spain, Award, 2 December 2019 ICSID Case No. ARB/15/1, para. 306; RWE Innogy GmbH and RWE Innogy Aersa S.A.U. v. Kingdom of Spain, Decision on Jurisdicition, Liability, and certain Issues of Quantum, 6 January 2020 ICSID Case No. ARB/14/34, para. 544; RREEF Infrastructure (G.P.) Limited and RREEF Pan-European Infrastructure Two Lux S.à.r.l. v. Kingdom of Spain, Decision on Responsibility and on the Principles of Quantum, 30 November 2018 ICSID Case No. ARB/13/30, para. 285; Cube Infrastructure Fund SICAV and others v. Kingdom of Spain, Decision on Jurisdiction, Liability and Partial Decision on Quantum, 19 February 2019 ICSID Case No. ARB/15/20, para. 453; 9REN Holding S.a.r.l v. Kingdom of Spain, Award, 31 March 2019 ICSID Case No. ARB/15/15, para. 346; SunReserve Luxco Holdings v. Italian Republic Final, Award, 25 March 2020 SCC Arbitration V (2016/32), para. 821, 823.

1548 The PV Investors v. Kingdom of Spain, Concurring and Dissenting Opinion of Charles N. Brower, 28 February 2020 PCA Case No. 2012-14, para. 14. *See also* Ch. 4 I 1) a).

1549 Blusun S.A. Jean-Pierre Lecorcier and Michael Stein v. Italian Republic, Award, 27 December 2016 ICSID Case No. ARB/14/3, para. 386, 394; CEF

The registration was perceived as a major legal hurdle to overcome before any investor could legitimately expect to be eligible according to the exact legal framework in place at the time.[1550]

In light of the position endorsed in this analysis, with regard to the capability of the legislative framework to create legitimate expectations, the latter of the two approaches seems more persuasive.[1551] The law sets out a promise addressed to an indefinite number of potential investors and may, therefore, be regarded as too general.[1552] These concerns can be allayed, if the state confirms by a declaratory act that the legal framework also applies to the individual investment. Under such circumstances, the auxiliary act has only a declaratory effect and does not raise any expectations above and beyond what was already in the law. The case is different, however, if the auxiliary act indeed provides for a guarantee that exceeds the scope of the legislative promise.[1553] In such a case, an auxilliary act going "above and beyond" the scope of the underlying law may only form the basis for legitimate expectations, if it bears all features of a freestanding commitment, i.e. it must be precise to its object and purpose. Only under these requirements, auxiliary acts may also constitute specific commitments if the legal framework does not convey a promise of a more general nature.

Moreover, tribunals showed the tendency to take into consideration general representations, such as advertising campaigns and policy reports, as sources for legitimate expectations.[1554] Although they found that such representations are too general to constitute a specific commitment, they nonetheless considered general representations, in order to interpret oth-

---

Energia B.V. v. Italian Republic, Award, 16 January 2019 SCC Arbitration No. 2015/158, para. 188; SunReserve Luxco Holdings v. Italian Republic Final, Award, 25 March 2020 SCC Arbitration V (2016/32), para. 777, 781.

1550 Blusun S.A. Jean-Pierre Lecorcier and Michael Stein v. Italian Republic, Award, 27 December 2016 ICSID Case No. ARB/14/3, para. 386, 394; CEF Energia B.V. v. Italian Republic, Award, 16 January 2019 SCC Arbitration No. 2015/158, para. 188; SunReserve Luxco Holdings v. Italian Republic Final, Award, 25 March 2020 SCC Arbitration V (2016/32), para. 777, 781.

1551 *See* Ch. E I 2 b 4) *supra* and Ch. F II *infra*.

1552 CEF Energia B.V. v. Italian Republic, Award, 16 January 2019 SCC Arbitration No. 2015/158, para. 222; Belenergia S.A. v. Italian Republic, Award, 6 August 2019 ICSID Case No. ARB/15/40, para. 580.

1553 *For example*, the GSE Conventions were partly considered to provide a wider guarantee than the underlying legislative promise, and hence conveyed more specific expectations, *see* Ch. 4 I 1 a) (3).

1554 *See* Ch. 4 I 2 a).

er types of commitments.[1555] These conclusions are in conflict with the findings of *Levashova*, which stated that commitments should be specific formal representations, which "excludes general statements, such as political speeches or general laws; these do not create a specific right on the part of the investor".[1556] However, this statement was made at a time in which only a few arbitral decisions in the renewable energy sector were rendered.[1557] The case law that developed subsequent to the statement clearly recognises political statements, in conjunction with other representations of lesser legal weight, as well as the legislative framework, applicable to the investment as a basis for legitimate expectations.[1558] This does not demonstrate divergence in the arbitral jurisprudence, as the first awards dealt with the minority of the cases in which the investors were not able to prove the existence and frustration of legitimate expectations due to particular factual circumstances.

Further on, *Levashova* concluded that "a specific representation is one that: (1) is provided by a competent authority with a relevant decision-making power over the investment; (2) is aimed at the express and specific inducement of investment that should be crystallised in an agreement or licence or other assurance in writing and constitutes an explicit right [...] and (3) is directed at the specific investor and is not aimed at a large or even small groups of potential investors".[1559] Again, recent arbitral decisions can only partly confirm these findings.

1555 Antin Infrastructure Services Luxembourg S.à.r.l. and Antin Energia Termosolar B.V. v. Kingdom of Spain, Award, 15 June 2018 ICSID Case No. ARB/13/31, para. 548; Novenergia II - Energy & Environment (SCA), SICAR v. The Kingdom of Spain, Award, 15 February 2018 SCC Case No. V 2015/063, para. 668, 669; NextEra Energy Global Holdings B.V. and NextEra Energy Spain Holdings B.V. v. Kingdom of Spain, Decision on Jurisdiction, Liability and Quantum Principles, 12 March 2019 ICSID Case No. ARB/14/11, para. 587; Watkins Holdings S.à.r.l. and others v. Kingdom of Spain, Award, 21 January 2020 ICSID Case No. ARB/15/44, para. 527, 530; SunReserve Luxco Holdings v. Italian Republic Final, Award, 25 March 2020 SCC Arbitration V (2016/32), para. 788.

1556 Levashova, *The Right of States to Regulate in International Investment Law*, p. 132.

1557 The the latest case included in the scope of the research of Levashova is Masdar Solar & Wind Cooperatief U.A. v. Kingdom of Spain, Award, 16 May 2018 ICSID Case No. ARB/14/1.

1558 *See* Ch. 4 I 2).

1559 Levashova, *The Right of States to Regulate in International Investment Law*, p. 246 and Ch. 6.02.

Regarding the first premise, some tribunals held that the representations must be made by state officials or entities having the authority to regulate.[1560] Others, however, did not make a distinction with regard to the actual competence of the authority, but simply assessed whether it was a representation by a state entity, including a clear and specific commitment.[1561] From a due diligence evaluation point, it should be obvious to an investor that a state authority, without any regulatory powers, can only issue a promise to a limited degree. Nonetheless, a state can be expected to act in a cohesive manner, as national rules on administrative competence have no effect on the obligations of a state under international law.[1562] Therefore, the competence of the entity representing the state should not make a difference whether it is a representation, which may constitute a commitment in the meaning of the notion of legitimate expectations. Under the requirement of due diligence, however, investors must assess the limited competence of the authority and consider whether the representations confirm or contradict the conduct of competent regulatory authorities.[1563] If the representations simply reinforce or specify previous conduct, there is no argument why states should not be bound by such representation under international law.

1560 Stadtwerke München GmbH and others v. Kingdom of Spain, Award, 2 December 2019 ICSID Case No. ARB/15/1, para. 286, 287; Hydro Energy 1 S.A.R.L. and Hydroxana Sweden AB v. The Kingdom of Spain, Decision on Jurisdiction, Liability and Directions on Quantum, 9 March 2020 ICSID Case No. ARB/15/42, para. 663.

1561 Novenergia II - Energy & Environment (SCA), SICAR v. The Kingdom of Spain, Award, 15 February 2018 SCC Case No. V 2015/063, para. 668, 669; Antin Infrastructure Services Luxembourg S.à.r.l. and Antin Energia Termosolar B.V. v. Kingdom of Spain, Award, 15 June 2018 ICSID Case No. ARB/13/31, para. 545, 548; Watkins Holdings S.à.r.l. and others v. Kingdom of Spain, Award, 21 January 2020 ICSID Case No. ARB/15/44, para. 527; NextEra Energy Global Holdings B.V. and NextEra Energy Spain Holdings B.V. v. Kingdom of Spain, Decision on Jurisdiction, Liability and Quantum Principles, 12 March 2019 ICSID Case No. ARB/14/11, para. 587.

1562 Mairal, *Legitimate Expectations and Informal Administrative Representations*, p. 430; LG&E Energy Corp. LG&E Capital Corp. and LG&E International, Inc. v. The Argentine Republic, Decision on Liability, 3 October 2006 ICSID Case No. ARB/02/1, para. 94. *See also* Ch. 2 III 2 a).

1563 International Thunderbird Gaming Corporation v. The United Mexican States Separate Opinion of Thomas Wälde, 26 January 2006 UNCITRAL, para. 93; Mairal, *Legitimate Expectations and Informal Administrative Representations*, p. 431.

With regard to the second premise, arbitral jurisprudence demonstrates that the representation must indeed be directed at the inducement of foreign investment.[1564] However, it is not necessary that the commitment must crystallize in form of an agreement or other type of insurance. Rather, the legal framework was found to be sufficient to induce FDI and hence constitute a commitment.[1565] In close connection with this, the third premise must also be opposed, as recent decisions show that the legal framework and other general representations are capable of raising legitimate expectations to the extent that they are clear as to their object and purpose.[1566]

To summarize the arbitral jurisprudence, two major conclusions can be drawn. First, registration confirmations and other auxiliary acts should, under regular circumstances, not constitute a specific commitment.[1567] This rule applies at least as long as they simply further perpetuate what is already in the law and do not contain a promise going beyond the scope of the underlying general legal framework.[1568] However, such administrative acts may serve as a decisive point in time, as a successful registration is frequently the confirmation for the investor that the investment is eligible for the promises granted by the legislative framework.[1569] Therefore, registration confirmations and other auxiliary acts narrow down the general legislative promise *erga omnes* to a specific investor. Accordingly, other types of agreements, such as the GSE Conventions, exceed the scope of the law, as they specify the benefits an investor can legitimately expect under the legal framework and demonstrate a level of consideration that is characteristic of a specific commitment. Hence, they can produce more specific expecta-

---

1564 *See* Ch. 4 I 1) and 2).

1565 ESPF Beteiligungs GmbH et. al. v. Italian Republic, Award, 14 September 2020 ICSID Case No. ARB/16/5, para. 515-517, 529; Antin Infrastructure Services Luxembourg S.à.r.l. and Antin Energia Termosolar B.V. v. Kingdom of Spain, Award, 15 June 2018 ICSID Case No. ARB/13/31, para. 532; 9REN Holding S.a.r.l v. Kingdom of Spain, Award, 31 March 2019 ICSID Case No. ARB/15/15, para. 294-296.

1566 *See* Ch. 4 I 2).

1567 *See* Ch. 4 I (5).

1568 SunReserve Luxco Holdings v. Italian Republic Final, Award, 25 March 2020 SCC Arbitration V (2016/32), para. 699-703, 817.

1569 Blusun S.A. Jean-Pierre Lecorcier and Michael Stein v. Italian Republic, Award, 27 December 2016 ICSID Case No. ARB/14/3, para. 386, 394; CEF Energia B.V. v. Italian Republic, Award, 16 January 2019 SCC Arbitration No. 2015/158, para. 188; SunReserve Luxco Holdings v. Italian Republic Final, Award, 25 March 2020 SCC Arbitration V (2016/32), para. 777, 781.

tions. Second, informal and general representations are only capable of creating legitimate expectations in extraordinary circumstances. However, when they occur in a cohesive and non-contradictory manner, such representations can nonetheless cumulatively attribute to the formation of legitimate expectations. A particular role is thereby played by legislative promises, which are reviewed in the next Chapter.

II. The Legal Framework as Basis for Legitimate Expectations

While the protection of legitimate expectations is by now firmly rooted in arbitral practice, the exact requirements for the states' commitment are not (yet).[1570] In particular, the question of whether the legal framework of the host state can be regarded as a source of legitimate expectations, that protect investors from certain regulatory changes, is controversial. The analysis revealed that arbitral tribunals show a strong tendency to consider legislative commitments in their assessment of the investors' legitimate expectations despite their general nature.[1571] Such an understanding, however, may conflict with the critique in investment arbitration from Member States of the ECT and other investment protection treaties, as well as their efforts to preserve the states' right to regulate in investment law. It has to be evaluated whether these developments pose a threat to the legitimacy of investment arbitration or whether jurisprudence is more considerate than the criticism may suspect.

1) State Efforts to Protect Regulatory Flexibility

Recent FTAs and IPAs concluded by the EU stipulate that a violation of the FET standard may be found when states committed, through their conduct, to refrain from a certain action or treatment of the investors. For example, the Comprehensive Economic and Trade Agreement between the EU and Canada (CETA) provides that "when applying the above fair and equitable treatment obligation, a Tribunal may take into account whether a Party made a representation to an investor to induce a covered investment, that created a legitimate expectation, and upon which the investor

1570 Dolzer and Schreuer, *Principles of International Investment Law*, p. 133, 134, 139.

1571 *See* Ch. 4 I 2) b).

relied in deciding to make or maintain the covered investment, but that the Party subsequently frustrated"[1572]. Similar wording can be found in the EU-Vietnam IPA.[1573] At first glance, this wording may indicate that future FET clauses intend to rule out the opportunity for investors to legitimately rely on legislative promises or other representations of a more general type. However, examining other recently concluded IIAs with more refined definitions reveals that the argument can be made that such an interpretation may be misleading. In the EU-Singapore IPA, the Parties agreed that "the tribunal may take into account, where applicable, whether a Party made specific <u>or</u> unambiguous representations to an investor so as to induce the investment, that created legitimate expectations of a covered investor and which were reasonably relied upon by the covered investor, but that the Party subsequently frustrate".[1574] This definition indicates that not only specific commitments, but also general unambiguous representations may create legitimate expectations.

In addition, the EU also strives to maintain regulatory space for its Member States, by explicitly including the states' right to regulate in the wording of newly established investment protection provisions.[1575] In line with this reformed approach on investment protection, the EU also mandated the European Commission to engage in reform discussions of the ECT to clarify that "investment protection provisions cannot be interpreted as a commitment by the Parties not to change their laws, including in a manner that may negatively affect the investor's expectations of profits".[1576] This trend has been followed by other countries as well.[1577]

Despite the EU's efforts to further perpetuate the states' right to regulate in investment protection treaties, the main issue is and remains the balancing aspect of the notion of legitimate expectations. Tribunals must identify the interests at stake and aim to find a fair balance, in light of the commitments entered by the state vis-à-vis the investors and the public

---

1572 Article 8.10(4) of the CETA (2016)

1573 Article 2.5(4) EU-Vietnam IPA (2020).

1574 Article 2.4(3) of the EU-Singapore IPA (2018) (emphasis added).

1575 *See* Article 8.9 CETA (2016); Article 2.2(1) EU-Singapore IPA (2018); Article 2.2(1) EU-Vietnam IPA (2020).

1576 Council of the EU, Negotiating Directives for the Modernisation of the Energy Charter Treaty, 2. July 2019, p. 3 <https://data.consilium.europa.eu/doc/document/ST-10745-2019-ADD-1/en/pdf> (accessed 3 May 2021).

1577 *See* for example Article 4 Colombia-France BIT (2014); Article 9.8 Australia-China FTA (2015); Preamble Australia-Urugay BIT (2019); Peamble Myanmar-Singapore BIT (2019).

interest. Hence, the threshold for representations of the state creating legitimate expectations must not set too high, nor too low. If tribunals set the threshold too low, the excessive application of the FET standard limits the states' flexibility to deal with events affecting the public interest.[1578] If tribunals overly extend the threshold, however, the trust of investors in cross-country investment would likely be diminished and sustainable development hindered.[1579] Therefore, it must be carefully assessed whether the tendency of arbitral jurisprudence to qualify general legislation as a source of legitimate expectations overly restrains the states' right to regulate.

2) Appraisal of the Prevailing View in Arbitral Jurisprudence

As acknowledged by United Nations Conference on Trade and Development (UNCTAD), arbitral jurisprudence indicated already before 2012 that not only specific commitments addressed to the individual investor can be regarded as a source for legitimate expectations.[1580] The analysis in Chapter 4 demonstrated that tribunals may (today) have a more cohesive opinion on this issue than one might initially suspect.[1581] Only a few of the recent tribunals rejected the claim that legitimate expectations were grounded on the legal framework of the host state at the time of the investment alone.[1582] The majority of the tribunals found that the legal framework can, in general, convey legitimate expectations, but must include a

1578 Knoll-Tudor, *The Fair and Equitable Treatment Standard and Human Rights Norms*, p. 318, 319.

1579 Trujillo, 'Balancing Sustainability, the Right to Regulate, and the Need for Investor Protection: Lessons from the Trade Regime', p. 2758, 2759; Sussman, *The Energy Charter Treaty's Investor Protection Provisions: Potential to Foster Solutions to Global Warming and Promote Sustainable Development*, p. 527.

1580 Also "rules that are not specifically addressed to a particular investor but which are put in place with a specific aim to induce foreign investments and on which the foreign investor relied in making its investment" were qualified as sources for legitimate expectations, UNCTAD, 'Fair and Equitable Treatment', p. 69.

1581 *See* Ch. 4 I 2) b) (4).

1582 Charanne and Construction Investments v. Kingdom of Spain, Award, 21 January 2016 SCC Case No. V 062/2012, para. 493; Blusun S.A. Jean-Pierre Lecorcier and Michael Stein v. Italian Republic, Award, 27 December 2016 ICSID Case No. ARB/14/3, para. 367, 371; Belenergia S.A. v. Italian Republic, Award, 6 August 2019 ICSID Case No. ARB/15/40, para. 580; Jürgen Wirtgen, Stefan Wirtgen, Gisela Wirtgen and JSW Solar (zwei) GmbH & Co. KG v. Czech Republic, Award, 11 October 2017 PCA Case No. 2014-03, para. 417;

legislative promise with a certain degree of specificity.[1583] The minority of tribunals that rejected the claim to legitimate expectations on the basis of the legal framework mostly argued that the underlying law was too vague and did not entail the type of commitment alleged by the investors, or based on other specific factors made the reliance on the legal framework by the investors illegitimate.[1584] Thereby, tribunals did not per se disregard legislative promises as a source of legitimate expectations. Additionally, these decisions denying the creation of legitimate expectations through the legal framework were accompanied by forceful dissents.[1585] This confirms the more liberal approach in recent investment arbitration, as hinted at by *Palombino* in 2018.[1586]

However, this trend cannot be left without criticism. In general, it is uncontested that general laws, due to their effect *erga omnes*, are not per se promises and regulatory change is a risk that any investor needs to assess

---

WA Investments-Europa Nova Limited v. The Czech Republic, Award, 15 May 2019 PCA CASE No 2014-19, para. 548, 549.

1583 Charanne and Construction Investments v. Kingdom of Spain, Dissenting Opinion Guido Santiago Tawil, 21 January 2016 SCC Case No. V 062/2012, para. 5; Isolux Netherlands, BV v. Kingdom of Spain Final, Award, 17 July 2016 SCC Case V2013/153, para. 775; 9REN Holding S.a.r.l v. Kingdom of Spain, Award, 31 March 2019 ICSID Case No. ARB/15/15, para. 299; NextEra Energy Global Holdings B.V. and NextEra Energy Spain Holdings B.V. v. Kingdom of Spain, Decision on Jurisdiction, Liability and Quantum Principles, 12 March 2019 ICSID Case No. ARB/14/11, para. 596; Cavalum SGPS v. Kingdom of Spain, Decision on Jurisdiction, Liability and Directions on Quantum, 31 August 2020 ICSID Case No. ARB/15/34, para. 432; SunReserve Luxco Holdings v. Italian Republic Final, Award, 25 March 2020 SCC Arbitration V (2016/32), para. 699-703, 817; ESPF Beteiligungs GmbH et. al. v. Italian Republic, Award, 14 September 2020 ICSID Case No. ARB/16/5, para. 512.

1584 *See* Ch. 4 I 2 b).

1585 *For example* Charanne and Construction Investments v. Kingdom of Spain, Dissenting Opinion Guido Santiago Tawil, 21 January 2016 SCC Case No. V 062/2012, para. 5, 6; Isolux Netherlands, BV v. Kingdom of Spain, Dissenting Opinion Guido Santiago Tawil, 17 July 2016 SCC Case V2013/153, para. 4; Jürgen Wirtgen, Stefan Wirtgen, Gisela Wirtgen and JSW Solar (zwei) GmbH & Co. KG v. Czech Republic, Dissenting Opinion, 11 October 2017 PCA Case No. 2014-03, para. 25; Antaris Solar and Dr. Michael Göde v. Czech Republic, Dissenting Opinion, 2 May 2018 PCA Case No. 2014-01, para. 12; Stadtwerke München GmbH and others v. Kingdom of Spain, Dissenting Opinion Kaj Hobér, 2 December 2019 ICSID Case No. ARB/15/1, para. 14; Cavalum SGPS v. Kingdom of Spain, Dissenting Opinion of David R. Haigh, 31 August 2020 ICSID Case No. ARB/15/34, para. 85-87.

1586 Palombino, *Fair and Equitable Treatment and the Fabric of General Principles*, p. 118.

and assume.[1587] It has been emphasised by a plethora of arbitral tribunals that laws and regulations are responses to economic, social, and environmental circumstances and challenges, and are therefore by their nature evolutionary.[1588] To be dynamic and be capable of reacting to changing circumstances is the central purpose of the states' right to regulate.[1589] It is elementary to the successful and sustainable provision of public infrastructure and public services.[1590] Nonetheless, if the law is clear enough in regard to the stability of the framework, investors undoubtedly place great reliance on the regulatory framework when making their investment decision.[1591] For example, the regulatory risk that materialised in the Spanish *Special Regime* including the support scheme's total elimination and replacement with a less favourable support system.[1592] This risk, however,

---

1587 Hydro Energy 1 S.A.R.L. and Hydroxana Sweden AB v. The Kingdom of Spain, Decision on Jurisdiction, Liability and Directions on Quantum, 9 March 2020 ICSID Case No. ARB/15/42, para. 586; Blusun S.A. Jean-Pierre Lecorcier and Michael Stein v. Italian Republic, Award, 27 December 2016 ICSID Case No. ARB/14/3, para. 367; 371; CEF Energia B.V. v. Italian Republic, Award, 16 January 2019 SCC Arbitration No. 2015/158, para. 222.

1588 Hydro Energy 1 S.A.R.L. and Hydroxana Sweden AB v. The Kingdom of Spain, Decision on Jurisdiction, Liability and Directions on Quantum, 9 March 2020 ICSID Case No. ARB/15/42, para. 587; Eiser Infrastructure Limited and Energía Solar Luxembourg S.à.r.l. v. Kingdom of Spain, Award, 4 May 2017 ICSID Case No. ARB/13/36, para. 362; Cavalum SGPS v. Kingdom of Spain, Decision on Jurisdiction, Liability and Directions on Quantum, 31 August 2020 ICSID Case No. ARB/15/34, para. 428; Mamidoil Jetoil Greek Petroleum Products Societe S.A. v. Republic of Albania, Award, 30 March 2015 ICSID Case No. ARB/11/24, para. 617; EDF (Services) Limited v. Romania, Award, 8 October 2009 ICSID Case No. ARB/05/13, para. 217. *See also* Ch. 2 IV 1.

1589 Rusoro Mining Ltd. v. Bolivarian Republic of Venezuela, Award, 22 August 2016 ICSID Case No. ARB(AF)/12/5, para. 525; El Paso Energy International Company v. The Argentine Republic, Award, 31 October 2011 ICSID Case No. ARB/03/15, para. 352, 365; International Thunderbird Gaming Corporation v. The United Mexican States, Award, 26 January 2006 UNCITRAL, para. 127; Mann, 'The Right of States to Regulate and International Investment Law', p. 5.

1590 Mann, 'The Right of States to Regulate and International Investment Law', p. 5.

1591 ESPF Beteiligungs GmbH et. al. v. Italian Republic, Award, 14 September 2020 ICSID Case No. ARB/16/5, para. 512.

1592 *See* inter alia Cube Infrastructure Fund SICAV and others v. Kingdom of Spain, Decision on Jurisdiction, Liability and Partial Decision on Quantum, 19 February 2019 ICSID Case No. ARB/15/20, para. 301; NextEra Energy Global Holdings B.V. and NextEra Energy Spain Holdings B.V. v. Kingdom of

was considered very unlikely by investors and legal experts, who issued the due diligence reports.[1593] Tribunals accepted that the remote or abstract risk of regulatory change was not sufficient to undermine the investors' confidence in the legal framework.[1594] Indeed, it would be contrary to the reality of economic life to assume that investors would not rely on a clear legal framework and constant and uniform representations by the state.[1595] Thus, investors are likely to develop certain expectations on the basis of such facts and circumstances created by the state. From an economic point of view, no investor would invest in a host state with a legal framework that can be altered at any time and in any manner, regardless of the explicitness of its specific features, basically treating the investor without any fairness.[1596] Additionally, the argument can be made that, if regulatory frameworks were effective only until the states exercised their undoubted legislative power to override, "it would be practically

---

Spain, Decision on Jurisdiction, Liability and Quantum Principles, 12 March 2019 ICSID Case No. ARB/14/11, para. 440; Masdar Solar & Wind Cooperatief U.A. v. Kingdom of Spain, Award, 16 May 2018 ICSID Case No. ARB/14/1, para. 359; Eiser Infrastructure Limited and Energía Solar Luxembourg S.à.r.l. v. Kingdom of Spain, Award, 4 May 2017 ICSID Case No. ARB/13/36, para. 118.

1593 *See* inter alia Cube Infrastructure Fund SICAV and others v. Kingdom of Spain, Decision on Jurisdiction, Liability and Partial Decision on Quantum, 19 February 2019 ICSID Case No. ARB/15/20, para. 301; NextEra Energy Global Holdings B.V. and NextEra Energy Spain Holdings B.V. v. Kingdom of Spain, Decision on Jurisdiction, Liability and Quantum Principles, 12 March 2019 ICSID Case No. ARB/14/11, para. 440; Masdar Solar & Wind Cooperatief U.A. v. Kingdom of Spain, Award, 16 May 2018 ICSID Case No. ARB/14/1, para. 359; Eiser Infrastructure Limited and Energía Solar Luxembourg S.à.r.l. v. Kingdom of Spain, Award, 4 May 2017 ICSID Case No. ARB/13/36, para. 118.

1594 Cube Infrastructure Fund SICAV and others v. Kingdom of Spain, Decision on Jurisdiction, Liability and Partial Decision on Quantum, 19 February 2019 ICSID Case No. ARB/15/20, para. 304; NextEra Energy Global Holdings B.V. and NextEra Energy Spain Holdings B.V. v. Kingdom of Spain, Decision on Jurisdiction, Liability and Quantum Principles, 12 March 2019 ICSID Case No. ARB/14/11, para. 595; Masdar Solar & Wind Cooperatief U.A. v. Kingdom of Spain, Award, 16 May 2018 ICSID Case No. ARB/14/1, para. 498.

1595 Palombino, *Fair and Equitable Treatment and the Fabric of General Principles*, p. 110; Kube, *Tensions Between the International Investment Regime and Human Rights: A Regulatory Tilt?*, p. 165.

1596 Jürgen Wirtgen, Stefan Wirtgen, Gisela Wirtgen and JSW Solar (zwei) GmbH & Co. KG v. Czech Republic, Dissenting Opinion, 11 October 2017 PCA Case No. 2014-03, para. 49.

impossible for a State ever to give an undertaking upon which anyone could rely, or for legitimate expectations ever to arise".[1597] Circling back to the domestic origins of the notion of legitimate expectations, one can find legal systems like German law, in which the notion of protection of trust (*Vertrauensschutz*) is not limited to administrative, but also extends to legislative acts.[1598] However, other domestic legal systems do not follow the same method of extensive protection of private parties' expectations.[1599] A cautious approach to the legal framework as a source of legitimate expectations is sensible, as "it is unthinkable that a State could make a general commitment to all foreign investors never to change its legislation whatever the circumstances, and it would be unreasonable for an investor to rely on such a freeze".[1600]

Thus, the arguments of the restrictive approach have force, and demand careful consideration. Although it has been found that investors may have some degree of legally protected expectations based on the legal framework alone, those expectations may, due to the broad nature of the representation, be vaguer than those derived from specific promises.[1601] Therefore, specific interests of investors are under such circumstances not

1597 Cube Infrastructure Fund SICAV and others v. Kingdom of Spain, Decision on Jurisdiction, Liability and Partial Decision on Quantum, 19 February 2019 ICSID Case No. ARB/15/20, para. 289.

1598 Calmes-Brunet, 'Rechtssicherheit und Vertrauensschutz im Verwaltungsrecht: Ein Vergleich zwischem deutschem und französischem Recht', p. 1077-1081.

1599 Snodgrass, 'Protecting Investors' Legitimate Expectations - Recognizing and Delimiting a General Principle', p. 27; Palombino, *Fair and Equitable Treatment and the Fabric of General Principles*, p. 87.

1600 El Paso Energy International Company v. The Argentine Republic, Award, 31 October 2011 ICSID Case No. ARB/03/15, para. 372, 374. *See also* Continental Casualty Company v. The Argentine Republic, Award, 5 September 2008 ICSID Case No. ARB/03/9, para. 258; Mobil Exploration and Development Inc. v. The Argentine Republic, Decision on Jurisdiction and Liability, 10 April 2013 ICSID Case No. ARB/04/16, para. 953; RREEF Infrastructure (G.P.) Limited and RREEF Pan-European Infrastructure Two Lux S.à.r.l. v. Kingdom of Spain, Decision on Responsibility and on the Principles of Quantum, 30 November 2018 ICSID Case No. ARB/13/30, para. 244, 245; Hydro Energy 1 S.A.R.L. and Hydroxana Sweden AB v. The Kingdom of Spain, Decision on Jurisdiction, Liability and Directions on Quantum, 9 March 2020 ICSID Case No. ARB/15/42, para. 585; Blusun S.A. Jean-Pierre Lecorcier and Michael Stein v. Italian Republic, Award, 27 December 2016 ICSID Case No. ARB/14/3, para. 368.

1601 Considering the legislative framework to convey „reduced expectations": Maynard, 'Legitimate Expectations and the Interpretation of the 'Legal Stability Obligation'', p. 104.

worthy of protection, as no experienced business person would reasonably rely on such a general *erga omnes* stabilisation promise.[1602] However, the analysis of the arbitral jurisprudence demonstrates that the FET standard and the balancing act within the notion of legitimate expectations demand that the states must not exceed their margin of discretion, when changing their legislation.[1603] In the absence of a specific stabilisation agreement, the case law revealed that there are minimum expectations that a clearly designed regulatory framework can induce. Such minimum expectations are, inter alia, that the legal framework will not be changed unreasonably or disproportionally, and/or with a proper retroactive application.[1604] An unreasonable or disproportionate change can be assumed, if the underlying legal framework has been altered fundamentally and drastically, depriving the investor of the opportunity for a reasonable return.[1605] However, investors may not blindly rely on assurances given through the legal framework, but must conduct extensive due diligence.[1606] In particular, the investors must assess the socio-economic environment.[1607] This includes consulting competent law firms, with experience in the host states that can shed light on the regulatory risks and other warning signs.[1608]

In light of the aforementioned and given the importance of the right to regulate, for states to maintain their regulatory flexibility in times of urgency, it can be concluded that the legal framework can only constitute a basis for legitimate expectations under limited circumstances. On the side of the state, the law must be sufficiently clear and openly declare the

1602 El Paso Energy International Company v. The Argentine Republic, Award, 31 October 2011 ICSID Case No. ARB/03/15, para. 372; Philip Morris Brands Sàrl et. al. v. Oriental Republic of Uruguay, Award, 8 July 2016 ICSID Case No. ARB/10/7, para. 426; Charanne and Construction Investments v. Kingdom of Spain, Award, 21 January 2016 SCC Case No. V 062/2012, para. 510; Blusun S.A. Jean-Pierre Lecorcier and Michael Stein v. Italian Republic, Award, 27 December 2016 ICSID Case No. ARB/14/3, para. 367.

1603 *See* Ch. 4 III 4).

1604 *See* Ch. 4 III 1) and 2).

1605 *See* Ch. 4 III 3).

1606 The Tribunal in *Masdar* concluded that "[i]f the general legislation is to be regarded as a source of an investor's legitimate expectations, the investor must demonstrate that it has exercised appropriate due diligence and that it has familiarised itself with the existing laws", Masdar Solar & Wind Cooperatief U.A. v. Kingdom of Spain, Award, 16 May 2018 ICSID Case No. ARB/14/1, para. 494. *See also* Stadtwerke München GmbH and others v. Kingdom of Spain, Award, 2 December 2019 ICSID Case No. ARB/15/1, para. 264.

1607 *See* Ch. 4 II 3) a).

1608 *See* Ch. 4 II 1) a).

purpose of creating a stable investment environment.[1609] Additional affirmative action like registration confirmations then determines the scope of the legislative promise, and the time from which investors may rely on the applicability of the regulatory framework to the investment.[1610] In the assessment of the scope of the legislative commitment, the overall picture of the states' conduct, the *leitmotiv*, is critical.[1611] On the side of the investor, appropriate due diligence must be carried out, which includes an assessment of the legislative framework applicable to the investment, as well as the prevailing case law and the socio-economic environment.[1612]

3) Why the States' Right to Regulate is Not Unduly Restricted

The states' right to regulate encompasses a broad spectrum, such as the protection of public health, public safety, the environment, consumer protection and labour standards, as well as economic development and sustainability.[1613] While the sovereignty allows states, in theory, to regulate their own markets as they wish, the right to regulate is limited to a certain degree once states have entered into an investment protection treaty. Extending the FET standard to also protect expectations conveyed by regulatory representations could put additional strain on the states' right to regulate.[1614] Such extension may find states unintentionally bind-

---

1609 Isolux Netherlands, BV v. Kingdom of Spain, Dissenting Opinion Guido Santiago Tawil, 17 July 2016 SCC Case V2013/153, para. 4.

1610 As in Antin Infrastructure Services Luxembourg S.à.r.l. and Antin Energia Termosolar B.V. v. Kingdom of Spain, Award, 15 June 2018 ICSID Case No. ARB/13/31, para. 553, 554.

1611 Antin Infrastructure Services Luxembourg S.à.r.l. and Antin Energia Termosolar B.V. v. Kingdom of Spain, Award, 15 June 2018 ICSID Case No. ARB/13/31, para. 548; Novenergia II - Energy & Environment (SCA), SICAR v. The Kingdom of Spain, Award, 15 February 2018 SCC Case No. V 2015/063, para. 674; NextEra Energy Global Holdings B.V. and NextEra Energy Spain Holdings B.V. v. Kingdom of Spain, Decision on Jurisdiction, Liability and Quantum Principles, 12 March 2019 ICSID Case No. ARB/14/11, para. 587. *See also* Ch. 4 I 3).

1612 Masdar Solar & Wind Cooperatief U.A. v. Kingdom of Spain, Award, 16 May 2018 ICSID Case No. ARB/14/1, para. 494. *See above* Ch. 4 II and *infra* Ch. 5 III.

1613 *See* Ch. 2 IV 1).

1614 Gaukrodger, 'The Balance Between Investor Protection and the Right to Regulate in Investment Treaties', p. 18.

ing future governments and thereby depriving them of their autonomy.[1615] However, it is the very nature of investment treaties, and the obligations on states codified within them, to bind future governments to the benefit of regulatory stability and consistency in the states' conduct, even in the face of a change of government.[1616] Moreover, tribunals have emphasized that the FET standard "preserves the regulatory authority of the host State to make and change its laws and regulations to adapt to changing needs, including fiscal needs".[1617] The degree of limitation to the right to regulate is determined by the legitimate expectations of the investor. In general, tribunals have afforded states a larger margin of discretion, if the infringing measures evidentially followed a public purpose of paramount importance.[1618]

As discussed, the EU shows a trend of perpetuating the states' right to regulate in the new generation of investment protection and free trade agreements. For example, CETA provides that "[f]or greater certainty, the mere fact that a Party regulates, including through a modification to its laws, in a manner which negatively affects an investment or interferes with an investor's expectations, including its expectations of profits, does not amount to a breach of an obligation under this Section".[1619] This can be interpreted as an attempt by the EU to minimise the risk that tribunals will disregard the states' right to regulate when assessing an alleged violation of the FET standard.[1620] While this may seem like a "revolutionary novelty" in international investment law at first glance, the contrary has been revealed in this analysis. The depicted development in recent arbitral jurisprudence shows that tribunals already implemented an understanding of the FET standard, which duly appreciates the right to regulate.[1621] Not any adverse effect on the investment is deemed sufficient to constitute a violation of the notion of legitimate expectations. Rather, the disadvan-

1615 ibid, p. 18.

1616 ibid, p. 18.

1617 Blusun S.A. Jean-Pierre Lecorcier and Michael Stein v. Italian Republic, Award, 27 December 2016 ICSID Case No. ARB/14/3, para. 319(4); Hydro Energy 1 S.A.R.L. and Hydroxana Sweden AB v. The Kingdom of Spain, Decision on Jurisdiction, Liability and Directions on Quantum, 9 March 2020 ICSID Case No. ARB/15/42, para. 588.

1618 *See* Ch. 2 IV 1) c). *See also* Levashova, *The Right of States to Regulate in International Investment Law*, p. 202.

1619 Article 8.9(2) CETA (2016).

1620 Levashova, *The Right of States to Regulate in International Investment Law*, p. 264.

1621 *See* Ch. 4 III 1 d) and 3 d).

tages incurred by the investors must be greatly disproportionate to the public interests states aim to protect, in the absence of a clear and explicit stabilisation promise. Arbitral jurisprudence has continuously expressed that the states' regulatory powers remain in any event in place in order to adapt to changing economic, political and legal circumstances.[1622] When balancing the right of the state to regulate against the investors' interests in a stable investment environment, one must always be aware that it is the very core of the principle of state sovereignty to be able to deal with situations and problems that may emerge over the time and were impossible to anticipate.[1623] It has been held, however, that the economic crisis which the countries faced at the time of the disputed measures, were not grave enough to constitute *force majeure*.[1624] Therefore, the changes were not demanded by a public interest of paramount importance. This notwithstanding, the renewable energy cases demonstrated that the states need flexibility in dealing with any issues endangering the public interest. It is therefore legitimate for the EU to focus on renegotiating the ECT, in order to firmly incorporate the existing case law on states' right to regulate into international investment law.

Nonetheless, recent trends in the new generation of investment protection treaties, as well as arbitral jurisprudence, both indicate a shift in the balancing act in the direction of the preservation of a state's policy space to regulate in the public interest. This, however, does not indicate that states have or will have an unlimited margin of discretion even in the face of a

1622 Parkerings-Compagniet AS v. Republic of Lithuania, Award, 11 September 2007 ICSID Case No. ARB/05/8, para. 332; BG Group Plc. v. The Argentine Republic, Award, 24 December 2007 UNCITRAL, para. 298; Continental Casualty Company v. The Argentine Republic, Award, 5 September 2008 ICSID Case No. ARB/03/9, para. 258; Eiser Infrastructure Limited and Energía Solar Luxembourg S.à.r.l. v. Kingdom of Spain, Award, 4 May 2017 ICSID Case No. ARB/13/36, para. 362; RREEF Infrastructure (G.P.) Limited and RREEF Pan-European Infrastructure Two Lux S.à.r.l. v. Kingdom of Spain, Decision on Responsibility and on the Principles of Quantum, 30 November 2018 ICSID Case No. ARB/13/30, para. 244; Cavalum SGPS v. Kingdom of Spain, Decision on Jurisdiction, Liability and Directions on Quantum, 31 August 2020 ICSID Case No. ARB/15/34, para. 429.

1623 Titi, *The Right to Regulate in International Investment Law*, p. 33.

1624 Cavalum SGPS v. Kingdom of Spain, Decision on Jurisdiction, Liability and Directions on Quantum, 31 August 2020 ICSID Case No. ARB/15/34, para. 621; Greentech Energy Systems A/S, NovEnergia II Energy & Environment (SCA) SICAR, and NovEnergia II Italian Portfolio SA v. Italian Republic, Award, 23 December 2018 SCC Arbitration V (2015/095), para. 451.

severe threat to the public interest. The states' right to regulate must find its boundaries in the rule of law and the principle of good faith.[1625]

Given the high value of the states' right to regulate as an expression of their sovereignty, commitments regarding regulatory stability "must be explicit and cannot be assumed through an implicit declaration, diluted in general expressions".[1626] This view has been reinforced by recent arbitral jurisprudence, which clearly correlated the specificity of the investors' legitimate expectations with the specificity of the promise received. Hence, the threshold for a specific commitment must be set high. The claim to legitimate expectations is stronger and the investors are not required to apply a high level of due diligence, if they individually received specifically formal assurances that display visibly an official character.[1627]

In the absence of a specific stabilisation commitment, tribunals found that investors are only protected against fundamental changes in the essential characteristics of the regulatory regime, if there was no indication that the legal framework in place at the time of the investment would be subject to such change in the foreseeable future.[1628] Such an expectation of fundamental stability can be conveyed by a general commitment in a legislative promise.[1629] As it has been shown, general commitments have the

1625 ADC Affiliate Limited and ADC & ADMC Management Limited v. The Republic of Hungary, Award, 2 October 2016 ICSID Case No. ARB/03/16, para. 423. *See also* Ch. 2 IV 1) b).

1626 RREEF Infrastructure (G.P.) Limited and RREEF Pan-European Infrastructure Two Lux S.à.r.l. v. Kingdom of Spain, Decision on Responsibility and on the Principles of Quantum, 30 November 2018 ICSID Case No. ARB/13/30, para. 244.

1627 Coming to a similar conclusion: International Thunderbird Gaming Corporation v. The United Mexican States Separate Opinion of Thomas Wälde, 26 January 2006 UNCITRAL, para. 32.

1628 Charanne and Construction Investments v. Kingdom of Spain, Award, 21 January 2016 SCC Case No. V 062/2012, para. 513-519; Eiser Infrastructure Limited and Energía Solar Luxembourg S.à.r.l. v. Kingdom of Spain, Award, 4 May 2017 ICSID Case No. ARB/13/36, para. 382, 387; Novenergia II - Energy & Environment (SCA), SICAR v. The Kingdom of Spain, Award, 15 February 2018 SCC Case No. V 2015/063, para. 654, 694-697; Masdar Solar & Wind Cooperatief U.A. v. Kingdom of Spain, Award, 16 May 2018 ICSID Case No. ARB/14/1, para. 484; OperaFund Eco-Invest SICAV PLC and Schwab Holding AG v. Kingdom of Spain, Award, 6 September 2019 ICSID Case No. ARB/15/36, para. 508, 509; Antin Infrastructure Services Luxembourg S.à.r.l. and Antin Energia Termosolar B.V. v. Kingdom of Spain, Award, 15 June 2018 ICSID Case No. ARB/13/31, para. 531-533.

1629 *See* Ch. 4 I 2).

least legal force. They may only give rise to general and basic expectations, if they set out an investment environment in which stability is a key aspect for the investors. Hence, the stability requirement in the FET standard must not be construed to freeze the legal framework of the host state, but to limit its regulatory power to a reasonable and predictable margin of discretion.[1630]

The analysis revealed that a vast number of tribunals in the recent renewable energy disputes accepted a violation of the investors' legitimate expectations in cases in which the remuneration fell below a reasonable level of return.[1631] The case can be made that in the absence of a specific stabilisation promise, a violation of the FET standard can only be claimed if the state's measures prevent investors from receiving a reasonable return.[1632] Jurisprudence indicates that—at least in the renewable energy sector under the ECT—a reasonable return is achieved, if the investors receive roughly a 7% p.a. of interest on their investment.[1633] If the remuneration remained at a reasonable level, however, tribunals found that the host state acted within its margin of discretion, in light of the economic hardship and the commitments given, when changing their policy towards electricity tariffs in favour of other fields of public interest.[1634] Since not receiving a reasonable return is an inherent business risk, investors must

1630 EDF (Services) Limited v. Romania, Award, 8 October 2009 ICSID Case No. ARB/05/13, para. 217; Charanne and Construction Investments v. Kingdom of Spain, Award, 21 January 2016 SCC Case No. V 062/2012, para. 503; Cavalum SGPS v. Kingdom of Spain, Decision on Jurisdiction, Liability and Directions on Quantum, 31 August 2020 ICSID Case No. ARB/15/34, para. 425. The Tribunal in *Antaris* held that "[a]n expectation may be engendered by changes to general legislation, but, at least in the absence of a stabilization clause, they are not prevented by the fair and equitable treatment standard if they do not exceed the exercise of the host State's normal regulatory power in the pursuance of a public interest and do not modify the regulatory framework relied upon by the investor at the time of its investment outside the acceptable margin of change", Antaris Solar and Dr. Michael Göde v. Czech Republic, Award, 2 May 2018 PCA Case No. 2014-01, para. 360(7), also cited by CEF Energia B.V. v. Italian Republic, Award, 16 January 2019 SCC Arbitration No. 2015/158, para. 221.

1631 *See* Ch. 4 III 3 d).

1632 *See* Diehl, *The Core Standard of International Investment Protection*, p. 395.

1633 *See* Ch. 4 III 3 d).

1634 *See* Ch. 4 III 3 d).

prove that the legislative framework explicitly promised at least for a reasonable return.[1635]

A further indication of a violation of the legitimate expectations created by a legislative promise is the retroactive change of the regulatory framework, on which the investors placed their reliance. Proper, and therefore impermissible, retroactive change in the legislative framework applicable to the investment can be assumed, when the state's measures interfere with circumstances that have already been concluded.[1636] From a due diligence perspective, a caveat must be made, however, if the retroactive changes were imminent and evident, or the legal framework itself left open the possibility of retroactive amendments.[1637] Additional elements of the stability aspects were found in the Spanish cases, in which the implementation of a "one size fits all" remuneration standard, without considering the specific features of each investment, constituted a violation of the investors' legitimate expectations.[1638] While it can be argued that applying an individual standard to each investment would require an excessive effort, the replacement of one regulatory approach with a completely different regulatory approach leaves the investors with no room to react to the changing circumstances.[1639] This argument again intensifies in the public utility sector, in which investors only have a decreased chance of successful disinvestment.[1640] Therefore, fundamental stability requires states to exercise their right to regulate in a manner that allows the investors to adapt to the changing circumstances and still maintain the profitability of the investments.[1641]

1635 Hydro Energy 1 S.A.R.L. and Hydroxana Sweden AB v. The Kingdom of Spain, Decision on Jurisdiction, Liability and Directions on Quantum, 9 March 2020 ICSID Case No. ARB/15/42, para. 580; Cavalum SGPS v. Kingdom of Spain, Decision on Jurisdiction, Liability and Directions on Quantum, 31 August 2020 ICSID Case No. ARB/15/34, p. 422.

1636 Craig, 'Substantive Legitimate Expectations in Domestic and Community Law', p. 304.

1637 *See* Ch. 4 III 2).

1638 Eiser Infrastructure Limited and Energía Solar Luxembourg S.à.r.l. v. Kingdom of Spain, Award, 4 May 2017 ICSID Case No. ARB/13/36, para. 400; Stadtwerke München GmbH and others v. Kingdom of Spain, Dissenting Opinion Kaj Hobér, 2 December 2019 ICSID Case No. ARB/15/1, para. 21.

1639 Blackaby, *Utilities, Government Regulations and Energy Investment Arbitrations*, p. 78.

1640 OperaFund Eco-Invest SICAV PLC and Schwab Holding AG v. Kingdom of Spain, Award, 6 September 2019 ICSID Case No. ARB/15/36, para. 510.

1641 *See* for example AES Summit Generation Limited et. al. v. The Republic of Hungary, Award, 23 September 2010 ICSID Case No. ARB/07/22,

Arbitral jurisprudence also implemented an additional threshold by requiring that regulatory changes must be unreasonable and disproportionate to the public interest it aims to protect, in order to constitute a violation of the investors' legitimate expectations. As revealed in the analysis, in the absence of an explicit stability commitment, the change of the regulatory framework must be fundamental and drastic, and must severely affect the investors' rights.[1642] Since simple adverse effects on the investments are not sufficient to constitute a violation of the FET standard, tribunals are required to delve into a wide-reaching assessment of the infringements incurred by the investors.[1643] Thereby, recent arbitral jurisprudence established a decently high threshold to avoid an overly excessive limitation of the states' right to regulate.[1644]

In light of the aforementioned, host states are by no means obligated to elevate the interests of the investor above all other considerations.[1645] This is the only sensible since the notion of legitimate expectations holds the balancing act, may it be named a test of reasonableness or proportionality or both, at its core.[1646] Thus, any adjudicative body assessing the measures of the respondent state is obligated to conduct its balancing exercise, in light of the broad margin of discretion afforded by the right to regulate. A legislative promise does not prohibit the states from amending their regulatory framework, in pursuance of a public interest. It leaves states with a wide margin of discretion, unless states have further specified the promise and committed to a specific course of action or omission.[1647] But

para. 9.3.53-9.3.55, 9.3.73, in which the state developed a new regulatory approach for electrical generators that assessed the characteristics of individual plants, which was held to be "suboptimal" but not a breach of treaty.

1642 *See* Ch. 4 III.

1643 *See* Ch. 4 III 4).

1644 Irrespective of the individual facts and circumstances of each case that may have motivated and justified the state's actions. Coming to a similar conclusion: Levashova, *The Right of States to Regulate in International Investment Law*Levashova, p. 169.

1645 Electrabel S.A. v. Republic of Hungary, Award, 25 November 2015 ICSID Case No. ARB/07/19, para. 165; Antaris Solar and Dr. Michael Göde v. Czech Republic, Award, 2 May 2018 PCA Case No. 2014-01, para. 360(9); CEF Energia B.V. v. Italian Republic, Award, 16 January 2019 SCC Arbitration No. 2015/158, para. 221; Cavalum SGPS v. Kingdom of Spain, Decision on Jurisdiction, Liability and Directions on Quantum, 31 August 2020 ICSID Case No. ARB/15/34, para. 421.

1646 *See* Ch. 2 IV 3).

1647 Hydro Energy 1 S.A.R.L. and Hydroxana Sweden AB v. The Kingdom of Spain, Decision on Jurisdiction, Liability and Directions on Quantum,

even in the face of a specific stabilisation commitment, arbitral jurisprudence showed a tendency that states maintain the freedom to regulate, even though it must be limited to particularly drastic cases.

Moreover, it could be argued from a perspective of equal treatment that investors, who did not receive a specific commitment, should not be treated alike investors who engaged with state authorities.[1648] Therefore, it would be an excessive extension of the notion of legitimate expectations, if investors who were able to obtain a specific commitment were put on an equal footing with those who invested without such assurance.[1649] This may put states in an excessively disadvantaged position, as they are unintendedly stripped of their regulatory power. However, this argument can be rebutted on the ground that in particular in the energy sector, investors only have limited options in obtaining a specific type of assurance. Generally, security and stability for investors in the energy sector can be reached either through PPAs by means of contract and FITs or FIPs provided by the law.[1650] While PPAs have been used frequently in the fossil fuel sector[1651], investors in the renewable energy sector in the EU are mostly confronted with a support system that only provides for incentives by law. Only a very limited number of investors were able to secure a specific commitment outside the procedure provided by the support systems.[1652]

---

9 March 2020 ICSID Case No. ARB/15/42, para. 590; Philip Morris Brands Sàrl et. al. v. Oriental Republic of Uruguay, Award, 8 July 2016 ICSID Case No. ARB/10/7, para. 422-423, 426-427. *See also* Ch. 2 IV 1).

1648 Snodgrass, 'Protecting Investors' Legitimate Expectations - Recognizing and Delimiting a General Principle', p. 38; Maynard, 'Legitimate Expectations and the Interpretation of the 'Legal Stability Obligation'', p. 105; Vigotop Limited v. Hungary, Award, 1 October 2014 ICSID Case No. ARB/11/22, para. 625.

1649 Snodgrass, 'Protecting Investors' Legitimate Expectations - Recognizing and Delimiting a General Principle', p. 38; Vigotop Limited v. Hungary, Award, 1 October 2014 ICSID Case No. ARB/11/22, para. 625.

1650 Blackaby, *Utilities, Government Regulations and Energy Investment Arbitrations*, p. 78, 79.

1651 *See for example* Electrabel S.A. v. Republic of Hungary, Award, 25 November 2015 ICSID Case No. ARB/07/19, para. 5.56, 5.57; AES Summit Generation Limited et. al. v. The Republic of Hungary, Award, 23 September 2010 ICSID Case No. ARB/07/22, para. 4.4; El Paso Energy International Company v. The Argentine Republic, Award, 31 October 2011 ICSID Case No. ARB/03/15, para. 405, 407.

1652 *See for example* Masdar Solar & Wind Cooperatief U.A. v. Kingdom of Spain, Award, 16 May 2018 ICSID Case No. ARB/14/1, para. 515-521. In Italy, the support system that provided for PPAs before 1999 was repealed and replaced

This comparison shows that, at least in the energy sector, contractual and legislative promises are used equally to provide regulatory safety. In general, a legislator can bind a certain legal consequence, i.e. the receipt of FITs, to the existence of certain circumstances, namely the timely registration under the support system. By doing so, the state has already made the consideration that usually gives the administrative decision its character worthy of protection. Thus, expectations based on legislative promises cannot be seen as inferior, as opposed to a discretionary decision by the administration. However, legislative promises also tend to be vaguer in nature than a specific promise given by state authorities.[1653] Under such circumstances, legitimate expectations solely based on the legal framework may only be broad and general, and cannot preserve a specific position that is particularly favourable for the investor, as opposed to specific commitments.[1654]

It follows that the right to regulate can be limited by a legislative promise to the modification of the regulatory framework, but only within a reasonable margin of discretion.[1655] If states overstep their margin of discretion, when adapting their legal system to changing circumstances, they have the obligation to compensate investors for the losses unduly suffered.[1656] The gross yardstick for tribunals to measure whether the margin of discretion was exceeded, is the question of whether the legislative framework was changed in a fundamental and drastic manner, depriving investors of the legal basis for their investments.[1657] In such a case, it is the severity of the effect on the profitability of the investment that must be set in proportion to the public interest at stake.[1658] The proportionality analysis will then determine whether investors were overburdened by the

by the current system, *see* Belenergia S.A. v. Italian Republic, Award, 6 August 2019 ICSID Case No. ARB/15/40, para. 98-100.

1653 Maynard, 'Legitimate Expectations and the Interpretation of the 'Legal Stability Obligation'', p. 104.

1654 *See* Ch. 4 I 2) b).

1655 Antaris Solar and Dr. Michael Göde v. Czech Republic, Award, 2 May 2018 PCA Case No. 2014-01, para. 360.

1656 Saluka Investments B.V. v. The Czech Republic Partial, Award, 17 March 2006 UNCITRAL, para. 305; RWE Innogy GmbH and RWE Innogy Aersa S.A.U. v. Kingdom of Spain, Decision on Jurisdicition, Liability, and certain Issues of Quantum, 6 January 2020 ICSID Case No. ARB/14/34, para. 589.

1657 *See* Ch. 4 III 3).

1658 RWE Innogy GmbH and RWE Innogy Aersa S.A.U. v. Kingdom of Spain, Decision on Jurisdicition, Liability, and certain Issues of Quantum, 6 January 2020 ICSID Case No. ARB/14/34, para. 589.

state's measures.[1659] The measures implemented by the respondent states in recent cases affected the profitability of the investments to varying degrees. Whereas the Czech Republic introduced only mild regulatory changes that maintained a return of above 7% per year, the Spanish *Special Regime* was replaced with a completely new system that had adverse effects on the investments to a varying degree, as it fundamentally changed the characteristics of the support scheme.[1660] Accordingly, tribunals deciding on the Spanish cases showed a stronger tendency to accept a violation of the notion of legitimate expectations created by the Spanish *Special Regime*, whereas the Czech Tribunals were almost uniformly unable to identify any breach of the FET standard.[1661] In the Italian cases, the outcome of the proceedings was also influenced by the effect the regulatory measures had on the individual investment.[1662]

This demonstrates that the acceptance of the capability of legislative promises to create legitimate expectations is not an excessive limitation of the states' right to regulate. Rather, it compels states to abide by their own representations and leaves them a margin of discretion to act within.[1663] Hence, regulatory freedom is maintained as long as states refrain from introducing fundamental and drastic changes that unduly burden the investor and take away the profitability of their investments.

Moreover, a number of legal scholars have also developed additional legal approaches to limit any excessive restrictions on the states' right to regulate by the notion of legitimate expectations. As an example, it has been suggested by several authors that the strict application of the proportionality test is a proper means to adjust the state's right to the severity of the crisis faced by the host state.[1664] The amount of damage—if

1659 ibid, para. 589.
1660 *See* Ch. 4 III 3) c) (1).
1661 *See* Ch. 4 III 3) c) (3).
1662 *See* Ch. 4 III 3) c) (2).
1663 Saluka Investments B.V. v. The Czech Republic Partial, Award, 17 March 2006 UNCITRAL, para. 305; Total S.A. v. The Argentine Republic, Decision on Liability, 27 December 2010 ICSID Case No. ARB/04/01, para. 115; Cavalum SGPS v. Kingdom of Spain, Decision on Jurisdiction, Liability and Directions on Quantum, 31 August 2020 ICSID Case No. ARB/15/34, para. 424.
1664 Titi, *The Right to Regulate in International Investment Law*, p. 35; Tudor, *The Fair and Equitable Treatment Standard in the International Law of Foreign Investment*, p. 215-228; Bücheler, *Proportionality in Investor-State Arbitration*, p. 281-287.

any breach can be found—must then be determined accordingly.[1665] Such an approach would allow states to introduce more intrusive measures, the more the public interest is at stake. Alternatively, the application of the doctrine of frustration (*Wegfall der Geschäftsgrundlage*) in international investment law, as proposed by *Bayrak*, would allow states to remain responsive when faced with an unforeseeable event.[1666]

In conclusion, the discipline demonstrated by the arbitral jurisprudence, in the protection of the states' interests without overburdening the investors, shows that the international investment law practice aims to preserve the states' right regulate. As the methodological approach taken by the majority of the tribunals offers the opportunity to evaluate the state's conduct in light of the hardship is faced, the claim can be made that international investment law does not overstep its boundaries by elevating the interests of the investors over the needs of the states, thereby maintaining the states' sovereignty.

4) The Special Role of the Legal Framework Applying to the Public Utility Sector

The examined cases all concerned investments in the renewable energy sector. The renewable energy sector, such as all economic sectors that can be attributed to the public utility sector, bear the specific feature that investors in such field are particularly reliant on the stability and predictability of the legal framework.[1667] The public utility sector is highly regulated and does not allow for investors to freely exit their investment, once adverse changes are implemented.[1668] A legislative promise purported by an incentive regime, which is addressed to a rather small group of investors, must be treated differently than general legislation which applies

1665 Titi, *The Right to Regulate in International Investment Law*, p. 35; Tudor, *The Fair and Equitable Treatment Standard in the International Law of Foreign Investment*, p. 227, 228; Bücheler, *Proportionality in Investor-State Arbitration*, p. 281-287.

1666 Orhan Bayrak, *Investitionsschutz und Geschäftsgrundlage* (Nomos 2019), p. 262-265.

1667 Blackaby, *Utilities, Government Regulations and Energy Investment Arbitrations*, p. 78.

1668 OperaFund Eco-Invest SICAV PLC and Schwab Holding AG v. Kingdom of Spain, Award, 6 September 2019 ICSID Case No. ARB/15/36, para. 510.

to a variety of facts and circumstances, such as construction law.[1669] Hence, investors usually place greater reliance on indications of a legislative promise in this type of economic sector, and are therefore more worthy of protection.

However, investing in the utility sector of the host state does not only automatically come with the protection of fundamental stability. While investors in the utility sector are particularly dependent on the state, the regulation of the utility sector and the level of profit taken by investors is also a public and political matter.[1670] Limiting excessive profits by investors that weigh heavily on the state budget is a legitimate aim, in light of the public interest.[1671] Hence, investors in the utility sector may legitimately expect a certain degree of regulatory stability, but must also be aware that they have to endure changes to the legislative framework in the public interest, as long as they are not excessive.[1672]

Taking into consideration recent jurisprudence, it is notable that the majority of tribunals found a promise of basic stability within the different support schemes. This allows the conclusion that the regulatory framework applicable to the public utility sector may be more likely to create the legitimate expectations that the host state will refrain from any fundamental and drastic changes to the legal framework. This, of course, is under the caveat that the legislative promise is sufficiently clear to its

1669 Cube Infrastructure Fund SICAV and others v. Kingdom of Spain, Decision on Jurisdiction, Liability and Partial Decision on Quantum, 19 February 2019 ICSID Case No. ARB/15/20, para. 388; Isolux Netherlands, BV v. Kingdom of Spain Final, Award, 17 July 2016 SCC Case V2013/153, para. 775 and ESPF Beteiligungs GmbH et. al. v. Italian Republic, Award, 14 September 2020 ICSID Case No. ARB/16/5, para. 535. Contrary thereto: Charanne and Construction Investments v. Kingdom of Spain, Award, 21 January 2016 SCC Case No. V 062/2012, para. 493.

1670 Blackaby, *Utilities, Government Regulations and Energy Investment Arbitrations*, p. 78, 79.

1671 The Tribunal in *Electrabel* concurred that "politics is what democratic governments necessarily address; and it is not, ipso facto, evidence of irrational or arbitrary conduct for a government to take into account political or even populist controversies", Electrabel S.A. v. Republic of Hungary, Award, 25 November 2015 ICSID Case No. ARB/07/19, para. 8.23. Similarly, the Tribunal in *AES Summit* observed that the reduction of excessive profits in the public utility sector is a "perfectly valid and rational policy objective", AES Summit Generation Limited et. al. v. The Republic of Hungary, Award, 23 September 2010 ICSID Case No. ARB/07/22, para. 10.3.34.

1672 Blackaby, *Utilities, Government Regulations and Energy Investment Arbitrations*, para. 78.

object and purpose and there are no contradicting representations by the host state that would undermine the expectation of stability.[1673]

As the ECT only applies to investments in the public utility sector, i.e. the energy sector, the claim can be made that the FET standard included in Article 10(1) ECT protects expectations based on the legal framework to a higher degree than it might be under regular BITs. However, the level of protection offered by the regulatory framework and thus the legitimacy of the expectations must be assessed on a case-by-case basis.[1674] Particular focus must be set on the wording of the respective FET provision and the legislative promise relied on the investor.[1675] Therefore, the conclusions reached in this analysis are not unique to the ECT, but can be analogously applied in any other case involving the FET standard, if the wording of the particular BIT allows for such application.

III. Due Diligence Requirement under International Investment Law

Lastly, the notion of legitimate expectations also compels investors to act with due diligence when investing. Investors may not blindly rely on commitments on the side of the host state, may they be specific or of a more general nature. Jurisprudence demonstrated that proper due diligence requires investors not only to assess the risk associated with the entire legal framework potentially applicable to the investment.[1676] Investors must also consider domestic case law and the socio-economic environment prevailing in the host state in place, at the time of the investment.[1677] This rather extensive due diligence obligation on the side of the investors has also found acceptance in scholarly writings.[1678] While it might seem

1673 *See* Ch. 4 I 2) b) 4).

1674 Hobe, *The Development of the Law of Aliens and Emergence of General Principles of Protection under International Law*, p. 18.

1675 ibid, p. 18.

1676 Levashova, *The Right of States to Regulate in International Investment Law*, p. 163, 164. *See* Ch. 4 II 2.

1677 Hydro Energy 1 S.A.R.L. and Hydroxana Sweden AB v. The Kingdom of Spain, Decision on Jurisdiction, Liability and Directions on Quantum, 9 March 2020 ICSID Case No. ARB/15/42, para. 673; Antaris Solar and Dr. Michael Göde v. Czech Republic, Award, 2 May 2018 PCA Case No. 2014-01, para. 368. *See* Ch. 4 II 4).

1678 *See also* Viñuales, 'Investor Diligence in Investment Arbitration: Sources and Arguments', p. 362; Levashova, *The Right of States to Regulate in International Investment Law*, p. 171.

excessive to impose strict and extensive requirements on the due diligence of the investor, it can be argued that an investor, who invests considerable amounts of money in a foreign country, is certainly capable of getting appropriate legal advice.[1679] Therefore, investors are generally required to obtain external legal advice by law firms, which are able to prove a high degree of expertise in the host state's legal framework.[1680] It follows that investors may not solely rely on internal assessments or informal or general information of state authorities.[1681] The socio-economic environment and the previous developments of the legal framework also play a key role in a proper due diligence analysis, as "it would not be reasonable for an investor investing in a highly volatile political environment, whatever the assurances received, that the investment will no longer be affected by further disruptions".[1682] This view has been reflected in various arbitral decisions, which denied the investors any right to rely in their claim on legitimate expectations, if their investments were made at a time in which regulatory changes were imminent or already in full swing.[1683] However,

---

1679 RWE Innogy GmbH and RWE Innogy Aersa S.A.U. v. Kingdom of Spain, Decision on Jurisdicition, Liability, and certain Issues of Quantum, 6 January 2020 ICSID Case No. ARB/14/34, para. 510; Antaris Solar and Dr. Michael Göde v. Czech Republic, Award, 2 May 2018 PCA Case No. 2014-01, para. 297, 395, 432; Diehl, *The Core Standard of International Investment Protection*, p. 407; Mairal, *Legitimate Expectations and Informal Administrative Representations*, p. 443.

1680 *See* inter alia Masdar Solar & Wind Cooperatief U.A. v. Kingdom of Spain, Award, 16 May 2018 ICSID Case No. ARB/14/1, para. 497; BayWa r.e. Renewable Energy GmbH and BayWa r.e. Asset Holding GmbH v. Kingdom of Spain, Decision on Jurisdiction, Liability and Directions on Quantum, 2 December 2019 ICSID Case No. ARB/15/16, para. 76; CEF Energia B.V. v. Italian Republic, Award, 16 January 2019 SCC Arbitration No. 2015/158, para. 224, 225; SunReserve Luxco Holdings v. Italian Republic Final, Award, 25 March 2020 SCC Arbitration V (2016/32), para. 831. *See* Ch. 4 II 1) a).

1681 *See* Ch. 4 II 2). *See also* Mairal, *Legitimate Expectations and Informal Administrative Representations*, p. 420.

1682 Viñuales, 'Investor Diligence in Investment Arbitration: Sources and Arguments', p. 362, 263. *See also* Levashova, *The Right of States to Regulate in International Investment Law*, p. 163.

1683 Belenergia S.A. v. Italian Republic, Award, 6 August 2019 ICSID Case No. ARB/15/40, para. 591; OperaFund Eco-Invest SICAV PLC and Schwab Holding AG v. Kingdom of Spain, Dissenting Opinion Philippe Sands, 6 September 2019 ICSID Case No. ARB/15/36, para. 20; Cube Infrastructure Fund SICAV and others v. Kingdom of Spain, Decision on Jurisdiction, Liability and Partial Decision on Quantum, 19 February 2019 ICSID Case No. ARB/15/20, para. 356 (with regard to the Claimants' hydro investments).

not every issue spotted by the due diligence reports of an external law firm must necessarily deprive the investors of their legitimate expectation, as long as the risk is qualified as remote. On the one hand, any other conclusion would render it almost impossible for investors to reasonably rely on any commitment aside from crystal clear stability promises.[1684] On the other hand, external law firms often draft their legal opinions conservatively, in order to avoid liability and would thereby put any type of legitimate expectations at risk.[1685]

Although the due diligence analysis must cover a broad spectrum of elements, the information gathered for the assessment must not exhaustive in every aspect, but "ought to be measured against the information the investor ought (reasonably) to have known prior to investing".[1686] It must nonetheless extend to the legal framework and the national case law applying to the underlying case.[1687] Generally, it can be stated that the clearer the legal framework is phrased, the less effort is required from the investor.[1688] With regard thereto, it is reasonable for tribunals to assume that investors must prove that they took all relevant general information into consideration.[1689] On the contrary, states must demonstrate that a more

---

1684 *See* Ch. 4 II 3).

1685 Mairal, *Legitimate Expectations and Informal Administrative Representations*, p. 443.

1686 Power and Baker, 'Energy Arbitrations', *GAR, The European Arbitration Review 2018* (Law Business Research Ltd 2017), p. 3.

1687 *See* Ch. 4 II 2).

1688 *See* Novenergia II - Energy & Environment (SCA), SICAR v. The Kingdom of Spain, Award, 15 February 2018 SCC Case No. V 2015/063, para. 679; OperaFund Eco-Invest SICAV PLC and Schwab Holding AG v. Kingdom of Spain, Award, 6 September 2019 ICSID Case No. ARB/15/36, para. 485; Isolux Netherlands, BV v. Kingdom of Spain Final, Award, 17 July 2016 SCC Case V2013/153, para. 781; Antaris Solar and Dr. Michael Göde v. Czech Republic, Dissenting Opinion, 2 May 2018 PCA Case No. 2014-01, para. 77; The PV Investors v. Kingdom of Spain Concurring and Dissenting Opinion of Charles N. Brower, 28 February 2020 PCA Case No. 2012-14, para. 14-16. *See also* Ch. 4 II 2) b).

1689 Cube Infrastructure Fund SICAV and others v. Kingdom of Spain, Decision on Jurisdiction, Liability and Partial Decision on Quantum, 19 February 2019 ICSID Case No. ARB/15/20, para. 401; Novenergia II - Energy & Environment (SCA), SICAR v. The Kingdom of Spain, Award, 15 February 2018 SCC Case No. V 2015/063, para. 679.

thorough legal analysis would have produced a different understanding of the regulatory framework or the investment environment in total.[1690]

This allows the conclusion that the due diligence required under the notion of legitimate expectations, in accordance with arbitral jurisprudence, is extensive, but does not overburden investors. As demonstrated, the level of due diligence is a matter for a case-by-case assessment and must be objectively measured against what an "experienced business person" would have or should have known at the time of the investment.[1691] In particular, the test of an "experienced business person" obligates investors to (1) analyse the basic regulations applicable to the investment, (2) assess the socio-economic environment in the host state, (3) calculate the expected return reasonably in light of the regulatory and economic risk associated with the investment, and (4) only base its analysis on facts and circumstances offered by the host state.

1690 Cube Infrastructure Fund SICAV and others v. Kingdom of Spain, Decision on Jurisdiction, Liability and Partial Decision on Quantum, 19 February 2019 ICSID Case No. ARB/15/20, para. 401; Novenergia II - Energy & Environment (SCA), SICAR v. The Kingdom of Spain, Award, 15 February 2018 SCC Case No. V 2015/063, para. 679.

1691 *See* Ch. 4 II 4).

Summary

The FET standard did not become the focus of investment law practice until the late 1990s. Soon after its development began, it became clear that further definitions were necessary, in order to deal with the extensive nature of the FET standard. In addition to many individual aspects, in the early 2000s, it was above all the notion of the legitimate expectations that stood out. In order to carry out the balancing act, the principle of proportionality migrated shortly afterwards from constitutional and human rights law to investment law.[1692]

There is a reason why the FET standard became the most important investor protection right in international law, after it slumbered in investment treaties for several decades. The reason is not that tribunals only in more recent history discovered the hidden meaning of "fair" and "equitable". Rather, it is the case that the FET standard is a compilation of legal notions, which have existed in domestic and international law systems long before the conclusion of the first investment treaty.[1693] Administrative law, human rights, and general considerations of good faith all have contributed to the evolution of what the FET standard has become today.[1694] It must be understood that comparative law analysis does not always add to legal certainty, as slightly different principles are imported by tribunals from different jurisdictions and legal understanding.[1695] However, it contributes to the multi-layered nature of the FET and its legitimacy as an overarching principle of international law. Therefore, tribunals have moved towards defining the FET standard by breaking it down into several concrete principles.[1696] While this adds to the complexity of the

1692 Vadi, *The Migration of Constitutional Ideas: The Strange Case of Proportionality in International Investment Law and Arbitration*, p. 349; Stone Sweet, 'Investor-State Arbitration: Proportionality's New Frontier', p. 63.

1693 *See* Ch. 1 II.

1694 *See* Ch. 1 II.

1695 *For example* the similar, yet different notions of proportionality and reasonableness that lead to a varying approaches by tribunals depending on their legal educaton and background. *See* Ch. 2 IV 3) b).

1696 Gazzini, *Interpretation of International Investment Treaties*, p. 98; Levashova, *The Right of States to Regulate in International Investment Law*, p. 74.

FET standard, it makes decisions of arbitral tribunals more predictable for international investment law practitioners.[1697]

Despite the advancements in the development of the FET standard, concerns to the legitimacy of investment arbitration can be raised with regard to the quasi-legislative role of the arbitral practice.[1698] However, states have started to perpetuate the aspects of the FET standard which they deemed most important, in the new generation of BITs as well as the modernization of the ECT.[1699] Thereby, the states, as the "legislators" in international law, take an active role in the establishment of the normative content of the FET standard and guidelines adjudicative bodies interpreting IIAs are obligated to respect.[1700] As long as states maintain the undefined form of the FET standard in their IIAs, they deliberately grant arbitral tribunals a margin of discretion.[1701] Thus, investment law practice only fills out the margin of discretion, in order to be capable of dealing with violations of the FET standard of an infinite number and undefined form. Even though originating from different jurisdictions with different views on particular legal concepts, the arbitral practice has widely managed to develop a common understanding of the vague concept of the FET standard.

I. Fair and Equitable Treatment as a "Black Box"?

In the introduction to this research, *Kläger* was cited, who stated that the FET standard is a "black box".[1702] After the intensive analysis of the recently developed jurisprudence, the question is whether this statement still

---

1697 Dolzer, 'Fair and Equitable Treatment: Today's Contours', p. 15; Kläger, *'Fair and Equitable Treatment' and Sustainable Development*, p. 242; Maynard, 'Legitimate Expectations and the Interpretation of the 'Legal Stability Obligation'', p. 99, 100.

1698 Bücheler, *Proportionality in Investor-State Arbitration*, p. 66; Norton, 'The Role of Precedent in the Development of International Investment Law', p. 300; Schill, *Sources of International Investment Law: Multilateralization, Arbitral Precedent, Comparativism, Soft Law*, p. 11.

1699 For example by explicitly addressing the right to regulate, *see* Ch. 5 II.

1700 Knoll-Tudor, *The Fair and Equitable Treatment Standard and Human Rights Norms*, p. 319.

1701 Mondev International Ltd. v United States of America, Award, 11 October 2002 ICSID Case No. ARB(AF)/99/2, para. 118; Knoll-Tudor, *The Fair and Equitable Treatment Standard and Human Rights Norms*, para. 318.

1702 Kläger, *'Fair and Equitable Treatment' and Sustainable Development*, p. 242.

holds true today. The answer is—as always in law—depending on various facts and circumstances surrounding each case. The very basic principle of "hard cases make bad law" definitely applies as well in investment arbitration. However, the analysis has shown that especially in recent cases a clear system of soft precedent has evolved, which gives significant guidance to states which try to balance between the right to regulate and observe the rights granted to investors under the FET standard.[1703] While the cases demonstrated a divergence in the systematic and methodical approaches by different tribunals, the decisions can vastly be seen as the "correct"[1704] solution of the dispute, considering the specific features of each individual case. What has to be understood is that arbitral tribunals reached different findings in light of varying laws and regulations at the time of the specific investment. Albeit being superficially alike, tribunals found ample opportunity to distinguish their case from previous decisions on factual divergences.[1705] Nonetheless, tribunals have proved that they follow, in their majority, basic principles and interpretations of the FET standard.[1706] It is noteworthy that investment practice did manage to do so without any uniform instance of review. However, with those systematic shortcomings, investment practice still has to develop and consolidate further before an acceptable degree of legal certainty can be reached.

While assessing the consistency of the arbitral jurisprudence, one has to also keep in mind that consistency is not equal to correctness. Members of the *UNCITRAL Academic Forum on ISDS* found that "states are more concerned about consistently incorrect arbitral decisions than inconsistent but correct ones".[1707] As it was pointed out, "while consistency is a systemic notion, correctness is a decision-specific one, i.e., about the substantive

1703 If previous jurisprudence was disregarded, dissenters heavily objected: The PV Investors v. Kingdom of Spain, Concurring and Dissenting Opinion of Charles N. Brower, 28 February 2020 PCA Case No. 2012-14, para. 16; Cavalum SGPS v. Kingdom of Spain, Dissenting Opinion of David R. Haigh, 31 August 2020 ICSID Case No. ARB/15/34, para. 82-84.

1704 "Correct" at least in light of the conclusions drawn in the analysis.

1705 *See for example* InfraRed Environmental Infrastructure GP Limited and others v. Kingdom of Spain, Award, 2 August 2019 ICSID Case No. ARB/14/12, para. 390-405; Foresight and others v. Kingdom of Spain Final, Award, 14 November 2018 SCC Case No. V 2015/150, para. 367; 9REN Holding S.a.r.l v. Kingdom of Spain, Award, 31 March 2019 ICSID Case No. ARB/15/15, para. 299.

1706 *See* Ch. 5.

1707 Malcolm Langford, Daniel Behn and Maria C Malaguti, 'The Quadrilemma: Appointing Adjudicators in Future Investor-State Dispute Settlement' (13 Oc-

quality of a specific decision".[1708] Therefore, while consistent case law may be beneficial to the overall legitimacy of investment arbitration, it is more important to achieve "correct" decisions. Moreover, it is crucial to differentiate between correctness in a legal and a political understanding. While a decision could be correct from a legal technical perspective, particularly investment law must consider political public interests of the host state going beyond the simple application of the law.[1709] Therefore, arbitral investment arbitration practice must often engage in "trade-offs between a correct legal result and placation of parties".[1710] From a political standpoint, it is noteworthy that the renewable energy transition turned the tables, with regard to the defence of environmental protection. Whereas environmental protection has been used as a defence on the side of the states in order to justify their actions, it might obligate the states, to a certain degree, to assist in the transition to renewable energies, and hence tip the balancing test towards the investors of the renewable energy sector. Sustainable development, in particular in the renewable energy sector, is difficult to realise without foreign investment.[1711] Thus, regulatory stability is of crucial importance to ensure a transition to environmentally friendly renewable energy technologies, without taking away resources from economic, cultural and social development.[1712]

Power and *Baker* raised the question of whether the availability of investor-state arbitration, under treaties such as the ECT, dissuades states from offering incentives in respect of the initial capital inflow for renewable energy projects.[1713] The vague character of the FET is conceived as the threat to the states right to regulate, and has provoked criticism in literature and among respondent states alike.[1714] However, the majority of the

---

tober 2019) Concept Paper 2019/12, p. 24 <http://www.jus.uio.no/pluricourts/english/projects/leginvest/academic-forum/> (accessed 3 May 2021).

1708 ibid, p. 24.

1709 Blackaby, *Utilities, Government Regulations and Energy Investment Arbitrations*, p. 80, 81.

1710 Langford, Behn and Malaguti. Langford, Behn et al. 13.10.2019 – The Quadrilemma, p. 26.

1711 *See* Part III of the Introduction.

1712 Sussman, *The Energy Charter Treaty's Investor Protection Provisions: Potential to Foster Solutions to Global Warming and Promote Sustainable Development*, p. 529.

1713 Power and Baker, *Energy Arbitrations*, p. 5.

1714 *See* for example Muchlinski, "Caveat Investor'? The Relevance of the Conduct of the Investor Under the Fair and Equitable Treatment Standard', p. 530; Tudor, *The Fair and Equitable Treatment Standard in the International Law of Foreign Investment*, p. 109, 110; Schill, *Fair and Equitable Treatment, the Rule*

recent tribunals have emphasized that the reference to stability under the ECT must not be understood as a special stability obligation.[1715] Rather, it is an illustration of the obligation to honour the investors' legitimate expectations under the FET standard.[1716] This demonstrates a willingness among arbitral tribunals to react to criticism by balancing the interests of state and investors, in light of the principles of reasonableness and proportionality.[1717]

Investment arbitration can only look back at a relatively short history, starting with the first arbitral awards in the early 1990s.[1718] Given this relatively short timeframe, the progress in the development of the FET standard by arbitral jurisprudence is remarkable.[1719] In 2005, *Franck* used the metaphor of investment arbitration being "still in its infancy but in the middle of its first 'growing pains'".[1720] Today, 16 years later, investment arbitration and respectively investment law have undergone significant maturing. At the time of *Franck*'s writing, the notion of legitimate expectations was developed to further refine the FET standard. In present times the renewable energy cases have attributed, and continue to attribute, to further significant development of the notion of legitimate expectations and its components. In light of this rapid development and the non-bind-

---

of Law, and Comparative Public Law, p. 157; Dolzer, 'Fair and Equitable Treatment: Today's Contours', p. 33.

1715 *See* Isolux Netherlands, BV v. Kingdom of Spain Final, Award, 17 July 2016 SCC Case V2013/153, para. 764-766; Eiser Infrastructure Limited and Energía Solar Luxembourg S.à.r.l. v. Kingdom of Spain, Award, 4 May 2017 ICSID Case No. ARB/13/36, para. 382; Novenergia II - Energy & Environment (SCA), SICAR v. The Kingdom of Spain, Award, 15 February 2018 SCC Case No. V 2015/063, para. 646. Contrary, Plama Consortium Limited v. Republic of Bulgaria, Award, 27 August 2008 ICSID Case No. ARB/03/24, para. 173.

1716 Isolux Netherlands, BV v. Kingdom of Spain Final, Award, 17 July 2016 SCC Case V2013/153, para. 765; Eiser Infrastructure Limited and Energía Solar Luxembourg S.à.r.l. v. Kingdom of Spain, Award, 4 May 2017 ICSID Case No. ARB/13/36, para. 382; Novenergia II - Energy & Environment (SCA), SICAR v. The Kingdom of Spain, Award, 15 February 2018 SCC Case No. V 2015/063, para. 646.

1717 Zarra, 'Right to Regulate, Margin of Appreciation and Proportionality: Current Status in Investment Arbitration in Light of Philip Morris v. Uruguay', p. 96. *See also* Ch. 4 III 1).

1718 Franck, 'The Legitimacy Crisis in Investment Treaty Arbitration: Privatizing Publlic International Law through Inconsistent Decisions', para. 1522.

1719 Relativising his own position, Kläger, *Revising Treatment Standards— Fair and Equitable Treatment in Light of Sustainable Development*, p. 67.

1720 Franck, 'The Legitimacy Crisis in Investment Treaty Arbitration: Privatizing Publlic International Law through Inconsistent Decisions', p. 1523.

ing nature of arbitral decisions on subsequent tribunals, it is even more impressive that the disagreements between tribunals or members of a tribunal in the reviewed cases seldom regard general issues of law, but more often a different evaluation and qualification of the facts.[1721] In particular, the notion of legitimate expectations evolved from a potentially limitless catch-all provision towards a more "coherent and rigorous" interpretation, whose boundaries are accepted by arbitral jurisprudence.[1722] Although arbitral jurisprudence still experiences divergent rulings, the majority of the tribunals follow a reasonably straight line of arguments. As the analysis revealed, the application has shifted from a simple assessment of whether the states' measures were "reasonable" to a more systematic balancing of the rights at stake, by assessing the states' commitments, the investors' due diligence, and the overall impact of the investment, in light of the importance of the public interest sought to be protected.

Therefore, the underlying question of this research can be answered positively. A system of soft precedent has developed. Arbitral jurisprudence has not yet found a consistent direction on all issues. However, the decisions to date indicate that a uniform line will be found there as well, as the number of cases increases.

II. Future Challenges in the Application of the Fair and Equitable Treatment Standard

Still, international investment law practice faces structural issues in the application of a uniform and cohesive understanding of the notion of legitimate expectations.[1723] Article 31(1) VCLT requires the rights and obligations, such as the FET standard, to be interpreted in the context of the international treaty it is applied in. This may add to regulatory complexity as slight variations in the wording of each treaty may lead to a divergence in the interpretation of the investors' rights.[1724] With regard thereto, arbitral tribunals expressed the "duty to contribute to the

1721 *See* in particular the evaluation of the legal framework as a basis of legitimate expectations, Ch. 4 I 2) b).

1722 Potestà, 'Legitimate Expectations in Investment Treaty Law: Understanding the Roots and the Limits of a Controversial Concept', p. 122.

1723 Levashova, *The Right of States to Regulate in International Investment Law*, p. 270.

1724 Gaukrodger, 'The Balance Between Investor Protection and the Right to Regulate in Investment Treaties', p. 18.

harmonious development of international law and thereby to meet the legitimate expectations of the community of States and investors towards certainty and the rule of law", subject to the specificities of the treaty the FET provision is applied in.[1725]

In the recent renewable energy cases, it has been shown that not only developing countries may have difficulties complying with the legitimate expectations of the investors. Any divergence in the rights of the investors consequentially leads to immense complications in the host states' efforts to comply with all FET obligations.[1726] This is particularly relevant when states face complicated decisions on policy changes that potentially impose high costs on investors.[1727] Equally difficult is the appraisal of the investors' rights under international investment law by arbitral tribunals. Nonetheless, when considering that international investment law consists of around 3,000 legal texts, arbitral jurisprudence developed a relatively high degree of consistency.[1728] As revealed in the analysis, consistency even rises when the cases are decided on the same FET provision and underlying national law. Divergence in the decisions mainly occurred due to a differing evaluation of the facts, rather than a differing interpretation of the law.[1729]

However, a caveat may have to be made that when applying the conclusions drawn, particularly with regard to the legal framework as a basis for legitimate expectations. Investments in the renewable energy sector can be distinguished from "ordinary" investments, by virtue of their more narrow scope of application and the stronger dependence of the investment's profitability on the state actions.[1730] In general, the public utility sector is highly regulated and whether an investment is profitable or not strongly depends on the conduct of the state and less on the individual structure of

1725 Saipem S.p.A. v. The People's Republic of Bangladesh, Award, 30 June 2009 ICSID Case No. ARB/05/07, para. 90.

1726 Gaukrodger, 'The Balance Between Investor Protection and the Right to Regulate in Investment Treaties', p. 18.

1727 ibid, p. 18.

1728 *See also* Levashova, *The Right of States to Regulate in International Investment Law*, p. 245.

1729 Concluding the same with regard to the earliest cases: Baumgart and Mantilla Blanco, 'Eneuerbare Energien und "legitime Erwartungen" in der neueren Schiedspraxis zum Vertrag über die Energiecharta: Die Entscheidungen im Verfahren Charanne, Isolux und Eiser', p. 244.

1730 *See* in particular Ch. 5 II 4).

the investment.[1731] If it is clear from the outset that an investment can only be profitable when receiving a certain level of subsidies by the state, then the reliance by the investor on the regulatory framework providing for those subsidies is particularly high.[1732] In addition, the legislative representations to the energy sector are more specific than the general legal framework, as it is addressed to a more limited number of potential investors. Thus, investors in the energy sector are more dependent on legislative stability and must at least partly rely on legislative promises. If investors extensively rely on the legal framework, they must, however, conduct due diligence regarding the laws and regulations and may not be protected against each and every detrimental change.[1733]

Notwithstanding this rather positive outcome of this research, the developing system of soft precedent must be used to further flesh out the requirements for situations in which the investors' trust is legally protected by the FET standard. It was demonstrated that there are certain requirements for specific and general representations by the state, due diligence of the investors, as well as the impact of the states' measures in light of the public interest at stake.[1734] Tribunals must now further develop more defined requirements for the specificity of certain standardised state conduct based on the legal framework, such as registration confirmations, or a more concise approach to balancing. However, this cannot be left solely to arbitral tribunals, when the legitimacy concerns of ISDS should be alleviated. States must work on further solidifying their vision of the FET standard's scope of protection under the ECT and other IIAs. As the legislators in investment law, they can and must aid in the development of this standard by limiting the tribunals' margin of discretion.

1731 Blackaby, *Utilities, Government Regulations and Energy Investment Arbitrations*, p. 78, 79.

1732 *See* Ch. 5 II. 4).

1733 *See* Ch. 5 III.

1734 *See* Ch. 5.

Bibliography

Literature

Azad KA, *Advances in Clean Energy Technologies* (Academic Press 2021).

Baetens F, 'The Kyoto Protocol in Investor-State Arbitration: Reconciling Climate Change and Investment Protection Objectives' in Marie-Claire Cordonier Segger, Markus W Gehring and Andrew Newcombe (eds), *Sustainable Development in World Investment Law* (Global Trade Law Series vol. 30, Kluwer Law International 2010).

Baltag C, *The Energy Charter Treaty: The Notion of Investor* (International Arbitration Law Library, Wolters Kluwer Law & Business; Kluwer Law International 2012).

Baumgart M and Mantilla Blanco S, 'Eneuerbare Energien und „legitime Erwartungen" in der neueren Schiedspraxis zum Vertrag über die Energiecharta: Die Entscheidungen im Verfahren Charanne, Isolux und Eiser' (2018) Recht der Energiewirtschaft 242.

Bayrak O, *Investitionsschutz und Geschäftsgrundlage* (Schriften zur Europäischen Integration und Internationalen Wirtschaftsordnung vol. 46, Nomos 2019).

Benson C, Yim C and Orlowski V, 'The Energy Charter Treaty' in J. W Rowley, R. D Bishop and Gordon E Kaiser (eds), *The Guide to Energy Arbitrations* (Second Edition, Law Business Research Ltd 2017).

Biais B and Weber M, 'Hindsight Bias, Risk Perception, and Investment Performance' (2009) 55(6) Management Science 1018.

Blackaby N, 'Utilities, Government Regulations and Energy Investment Arbitrations' in J. W Rowley, R. D Bishop and Gordon E Kaiser (eds), *The Guide to Energy Arbitrations* (Second Edition, Law Business Research Ltd 2017).

Bonnitcha J, *Substantive Protection under Investment Treaties: A Legal and Economic Analysis* (Cambridge Studies in International and Comparative Law).

Brownlie I and Crawford J, *Brownlie's Principles of Public International Law* (Ninth Edition, Oxford University Press 2019).

Bücheler G, *Proportionality in Investor-State Arbitration* (Oxford University Press 2015).

Calmes-Brunet S, 'Rechtssicherheit und Vertrauensschutz im Verwaltungsrecht: Ein Vergleich zwischem deutschem und französischem Recht' (2014) 54(12) Juristische Schulung 1077.

Cameron PD, *International Energy Investment Law: The Pursuit of Stability* (Oxford University Press 2010).

Campbell C, 'House of Cards: The Relevance of Legitimate Expectations under Fair and Equitable Treatment Provisions in Investment Treaty Law' (2013) 30(4) Journal of International Arbitration 361.

Cheng T-H, 'Precedent and Control in Investment Treaty Arbitration' (2007) 30(4) Fordham International Law Journal 1014.

Commission JP, 'Precedent in Investment Treaty Arbitration' (2007) 24(2) Journal of International Arbitration 129.

Coop G and Seif I, 'ECT and State's Right to Regulate' in Maxi Scherer and Catherine Amirfar (eds), *International Arbitration in the Energy Sector* (Oxford University Press 2018).

Cottier T and others, 'The Principle of Proportionality in International Law: Foundations and Variations' (2017) 18 The Journal of World Investment & Trade 628.

Craig PP, 'Substantive Legitimate Expectations in Domestic and Community Law' (1996) 55(2) Cambridge Law Journal 289.

'De Brabandere, Host States Due Diligence Obligations in International Investment Law'.

Dias Simões F, 'When Green Incentives Go Pale: Investment Arbitration and Renewable Energy Policymaking' (2017) 45(2) The Denver Journal of International Law and Policy 251.

Diehl A, *The Core Standard of International Investment Protection: Fair and Equitable Treatment* (International Arbitration Law Library, 2012).

Dolzer R, 'Fair and Equitable Treatment: Today's Contours' (2014) 12(1) Santa Clara Journal of International Law 7.

Dolzer R and Schreuer C, *Principles of International Investment Law* (Second Edition, Oxford University Press 2012).

Dörr O and Schmalenbach K, *Vienna Convention on the Law of Treaties* (Springer 2018).

Dudas S, 'A Sovereign's Broken Promise: the Golden Ticket to a Billion-Dollar Award?' (2016) <http://arbitrationblog.kluwerarbitration.com/2016/06/21/a-sovereigns-broken-promise-the-golden-ticket-to-a-billion-dollar-award/>.

Dumberry P, 'Has the Fair and Equitable Treatment Standard Become a Rule of Customary International Law?' (2016) J Int Disp Settlement 155-178.

Dupuy F, 'La ´Protection de l'Attente Légitime des Parties au Contrat: Etude de Droit International des Investissements à la Lumière du Droit Comparé' (Dissertation (Ph.D) Paris-Panthéon-Assas 30 November 2007).

Dupuy P-M, 'Unification Rather Than Fragmentation of International Law? The Case of International Investment Law and Human Rights Law' in Pierre-Marie Dupuy, Ernst-Ulrich Petersmann and Francesco Francioni (eds), *Human Rights in International Investment Law and Arbitration* (Oxford University Press 2009).

Energy Charter Secretariat, *The Energy Charter Treaty: A Reader's Guide* (Energy Charter Secretariat 2002).

Espa I, 'Promoting Renewables in the Energy Union: Current Strategies and the Challenges Ahead' (2017) 2(1) Eur Invest Law Arbitr Rev 225.

Fanou M and Tzevelekos VP, 'Shared Territory of the ECHR and International Investment Law' in Yannick Radi (ed), *Research Handbook on Human Rights and Investment* (Research Handbooks in International Law Series, Edward Elgar Publishing 2018).

Franck SD, 'The Legitimacy Crisis in Investment Treaty Arbitration: Privatizing Public International Law through Inconsistent Decisions' (2005) 73 Fordham Law Review 1521.

Frauenhofer, EEG, BBH, IASA, SEI, 'Final Report on Renewable Energy Progress and Biofuels Sustainability' (Ecofys 2014).

Gallagher N, 'ECT and Renewable Energy Disputes' in Maxi Scherer and Catherine Amirfar (eds), *International Arbitration in the Energy Sector* (Oxford University Press 2018).

Garcia-Castrillon CO, 'Spain and Investment Arbitration - The Renewable Energy Explosion' in Armand de Mestral (ed), *Second Thoughts: Investor-State Arbitration between Developed Democracies* (Centre for International Governance Innovation 2017).

Gaukrodger D, 'The Balance Between Investor Protection and the Right to Regulate in Investment Treaties' (2017) OECD Working Papers on International Investment.

Gazzini T, 'General Principles of Law in the Field of Foreign Investment' (2009) 10(1) The Journal of World Investment & Trade 103.

•*Interpretation of International Investment Treaties* (Hart Publishing 2016).

Happ R, 'The Energy Charter Treaty' in Marc Bungenberg and others (eds), *International Investment Law: A Handbook* (Nomos 2015).

Henckels C, *Proportionality and Deference in Investor-State Arbitration: Balancing Investment Protection and Regulatory Autonomy* (Cambridge Studies in International and Comparative Law vol 122, CUP 2015).

Hendel CJ and Pérez AM, 'The Past, Present and Possible Future of the Spanish Remewable Energy Arbitration Saga' (2018) 31(1) International Law Practicum 96.

Hernández-Moro J and Martínez-Duart JM, 'Analytical model for solar PV and CSP electricity costs: Present LCOE values and their future evolution' (2013) 20 Renewable and Sustainable Energy Reviews 119.

Hirsch M, 'Investment Tribunals and Human Rights: Divergent Paths' in Pierre-Marie Dupuy, Ernst-Ulrich Petersmann and Francesco Francioni (eds), *Human Rights in International Investment Law and Arbitration* (Oxford University Press 2009).

Hobe S, 'The Development of the Law of Aliens and Emergence of General Principles of Protection under International Law' in Marc Bungenberg and others (eds), *International Investment Law: A Handbook* (Nomos 2015).

Hobér K, Dahlquist Cullborg J, *Investment Treaty Arbitration: Problems and Exercises* (Edward Elgar Publishing 2018).

•'Overview of Energy Charter Treaty Cases' in Maxi Scherer and Catherine Amirfar (eds), *International Arbitration in the Energy Sector* (Oxford University Press 2018).

Hobér K and Fellenbaum J, 'Political Risk Insurance and Investment Treaty Protection' in Marc Bungenberg and others (eds), *International Investment Law: A Handbook* (Nomos 2015).

ICSID Secretariat, 'Possible Improvements of the Framework for ICSID Arbitrations' (2004) <https://icsid.worldbank.org/sites/default/files/Possible%20Improvements%20of%20the%20Framework%20of%20ICSID%20Arbitration.pdf>.

IFC Performance Standard 1 - Assessment and Management of Environmental and Social Risks (IFC 2012) <https://www.ifc.org/wps/wcm/connect/topics_ext_content/ifc_external_corporate_site/sustainability-at-ifc/policies-standards/performance-standards/ps1>.

International Energy Agency, 'Energy Technology Perspectives 2014: Harnessing Electricity's Potential' (2014) <https://cleanenergysolutions.org/sites/default/files/documents/2014_05_12_iea_energy_technology_perspectives_webinar_transcript.pdf>.

International Law Commission, 'Guiding Principles Applicable to Unilateral Declarations of States Capable of Creating Legal Obligations, With Commentaries Thereto' (2006) <https://legal.un.org/ilc/texts/instruments/english/commentaries/9_9_2006.pdf>.

•'Report on Fragmentation of International Law: Difficulties arising from the Diversification and Expansion of International Law' (2006) <https://legal.un.org/ilc/documentation/english/a_cn4_l682.pdf>.

International Renewable Energy Agency, 'Renewable Power Generation Costs in 2019' (IRENA 2020) <https://www.irena.org/publications/2020/Jun/Renewable-Power-Costs-in-2019>.

IPPC, 'Special Report "Global Warming 1,5 °C" (Summary for Policy Makers)' (IPPC Publishing 2019) <https://www.ipcc.ch/sr15/>.

Kalicki J and Medeiros S, 'Fair, Equitable and Ambiguous: What Is Fair and Equitable Treatment in International Investment Law?' (2007) 22(1) ICSID Review 24.

Karl J, 'FDI in the Energy Sector: Recent Trends and Policy Issues' in Eric d Brabandere and Tarcisio Gazzini (eds), *Foreign Investment in the Energy Sector: Balancing Private and Public Interests* (Nijhoff International Investment Law Series, Brill 2014).

Kaufmann-Kohler G, 'Arbitral Precedent: Dream, Necessity or Excuse?' (2007) 23(3) Arbitration International 357.

Kingsbury B and Schill SW, 'Public Law Concepts to Balance Investors' Rights with State Regulatory Actions in the Public Interest—the Concept of Proportionality' in Stephan W Schill (ed), *International Investment Law and Comparative Public Law* (Oxford University Press 2010).

Kläger R, "'Fair and Equitable Treatment' and Sustainable Development' in Marie-Claire Cordonier Segger, Markus W Gehring and Andrew Newcombe (eds), *Sustainable Development in World Investment Law* (Global Trade Law Series vol 30, Kluwer Law International 2010).

– 'Fair and Equitable Treatment A Look at the Theoretical Underpinnings of Legitimacy and Fairness' (2010) 11(3) The Journal of World Investment & Trade 435.

– *'Fair and Equitable Treatment' in International Investment Law* (CUP 2011).

– 'Revising Treatment Standards— Fair and Equitable Treatment in Light of Sustainable Development' in Steffen Hindelang and Markus Krajewski (eds), *Shifting Paradigms in International Investment Law* (Oxford University Press 2016).

Knoll-Tudor I, 'The Fair and Equitable Treatment Standard and Human Rights Norms' in Pierre-Marie Dupuy, Ernst-Ulrich Petersmann and Francesco Francioni (eds), *Human Rights in International Investment Law and Arbitration* (Oxford University Press 2009).

Kolb R, *Good Faith in International Law* (Hart Publishing 2017).

Kriebaum U, 'Regulatory Takings: Balancing the Interests of the Investor and the State' (2007) 8(5) Journal of World Investment and Trade 717.

– 'Arbitrary/Unreasonable or Discriminatory Measures' in Marc Bungenberg and others (eds), *International Investment Law: A Handbook* (Nomos 2015).

Kube V, 'Tensions Between the International Investment Regime and Human Rights: A Regulatory Tilt?' in Vivian Kube (ed), *EU Human Rights, International Investment Law and Participation* (Interdisciplinary Studies in Human Rights, Springer International Publishing 2019).

Langford M, Behn D and Malaguti MC, 'The Quadrilemma: Appointing Adjudicators in Future Investor-State Dispute Settlement' (13 October 2019) Concept Paper 2019/12 <http://www.jus.uio.no/pluricourts/english/projects/leginvest/academic-forum/>.

Lasse Langfeldt, 'Proportionality in Investment Treaty Arbitration and the Necessity for Tribunals to Adopt a Clear Methodology' (Unpublished 2019).

Leonhardsen EM, 'Looking for Legitimacy: Exploring Proportionality Analysis in Investment Treaty Arbitration' (2012) 3(1) Journal of International Dispute Settlement 95.

Levashova Y, *The Right of States to Regulate in International Investment Law: The Search for Balance Between Public Interest and Fair and Equitable Treatment* (Wolters Kluwer Law & Business 2019).

Lo C-F, *Treaty Interpretation under the Vienna Convention on the Law of Treaties: A New Round of Codification* (Springer 2017).

Mairal HA, 'Legitimate Expectations and Informal Administrative Representations' in Stephan W Schill (ed), *International Investment Law and Comparative Public Law* (Oxford University Press 2010).

Mann H, 'The Right of States to Regulate and International Investment Law' (2002).

Mathews J, 'Reasonableness and Proportionality' (2016) <https://papers.ssrn.com/sol3/papers.cfm?abstract_id=2836264>.

Mayeda G, 'Playing Fair: The Meaning of Fair and Equitable Treatment in Bilateral Investment Treaties' (2007) 41(2) Journal of World Trade Law, Economics, Public Policy 273.

Maynard S, 'Legitimate Expectations and the Interpretation of the 'Legal Stability Obligation'' (2016) 1(1) Eur Invest Law Arbitr Rev 99.

Mbengue MM and Raju D, 'Energy, Environment and Foreign Investment' in Eric d Brabandere and Tarcisio Gazzini (eds), *Foreign Investment in the Energy Sector: Balancing Private and Public Interests* (Nijhoff International Investment Law Series, Brill 2014).

McLachlan C, Shore L and Weiniger M, *International Investment Arbitration: Substantive Principles* (Oxford International Arbitration Series, Second Edition, Oxford University Press 2017).

MIGA, *World investment and political risk 2013* (The World Bank 2014).

Miljenić O, 'Energy Charter Treaty – Standards of Investment Protection' (2018) 24(83) Croatian International Relations Review 52.

Mir-Artigues P, Cerdá E and del Río P, 'Analysing the Economic Impact of the New Renewable Electricity Support Scheme on Solar PV Plants in Spain' (2018) 114 Energy Policy 323.

Monebhurrun N, 'Gold Reserve Inc. v. Bolivarian Republic of Venezuela Enshrining Legitimate Expectations as a General Principle of International Law?' (2015) 32(5) Journal of International Arbitration 551.

Mouyal LW, *International Investment Law and the Right to Regulate: A Human Rights Perspective* (Routledge Research in International Economic Law, Routledge 2016).

Muchlinski P, ''Caveat Investor'? The Relevance of the Conduct of the Investor Under the Fair and Equitable Treatment Standard' (2006) 55(3) ICLQ 527.

Norton PM, 'The Role of Precedent in the Development of International Investment Law' (2018) 33(1) ICSID Review 280.

OECD, '"Indirect Expropriation" and the "Right to Regulate" in International Investment Law' (2004) <http://www.oecd.org/daf/inv/investment-policy/WP-2004_4.pdf>.

– *Guidelines for Multinational Enterprises, 2011 Edition* (OECD Publishing 2011).

Ortino F, 'Investment Treaties, Sustainable Development and Reasonableness Review: A Case Against Strict Proportionality Balancing' (2017) 30(1) Leiden Journal of International Law 71.

– 'The Obligation of Regulatory Stability in the Fair and Equitable Treatment Standard: How Far Have We Come?' (2018) 21(4) Journal of International Economic Law 845.

Palombino FM, *Fair and Equitable Treatment and the Fabric of General Principles* (T.M.C. Asser Press 2018).

Panizzon M, *Good Faith in the Jurisprudence of the WTO: The protection of Legitimate Expectations, Good Faith Interpretation and Fair Dispute Settlement* (Studies in International Trade Law vol 4, Hart 2006).

Panosch L, *Das Menschenrecht auf Wasser im internationalen Investitionsrecht* (Schriften zur Europäischen Integration und Internationalen Wirtschaftsordnung vol. 58, Nomos 2021)

Paparinskis M, *The International Minimum Standard and Fair and Equitable Treatment* (Oxford Monographs in International Law, Oxford University Press 2013).

Parchomiuk J, 'The Protection of Legitimate Expectations in Administrative Law: A Horizontal Perspective' (2017) 10(2) Baltic Journal of Law & Politics 1.

Patrizia CA and others, 'Investment Disputes Involving the Renewable Energy Industry Under the Energy Charter Treaty' in J. W Rowley, R. D Bishop and Gordon E Kaiser (eds), *The Guide to Energy Arbitrations* (Second Edition, Law Business Research Ltd 2017).

Potestà M, 'Legitimate Expectations in Investment Treaty Law: Understanding the Roots and the Limits of a Controversial Concept' (2013) 28(1) ICSID Review 88.

Power R and Baker P, 'Energy Arbitrations', *GAR, The European Arbitration Review 2018* (Law Business Research Ltd 2017).

Prieto Muñoz JG, 'El precedente en el derecho internacional de inversiones: el valor argumentativo de decisiones arbitrales previas' (2018) 22(22) IU.

Restrepo T, 'Modification of Renewable Energy Support Schemes Under the Energy Charter Treaty: Modification of Renewable Energy Support Schemes Under the Energy Charter Treaty: Eiser and Charanne in the Context of Climate Change' (2017) 8(1) Goettingen Journal of International Law 101.

Scheu J, *Systematische Berücksichtigung von Menschenrechten in Investitionsschiedsverfahren* (Studien zum Internationalen Investitionsrecht, Nomos 2017).

Schill SW, 'Fair and Equitable Treatment, the Rule of Law, and Comparative Public Law' in Stephan W Schill (ed), *International Investment Law and Comparative Public Law* (Oxford University Press 2010).

– 'Sources of International Investment Law: Multilateralization, Arbitral Precedent, Comparativism, Soft Law' in Samantha Besson and Jean d'Aspremont (eds), *The Oxford Handbook of the Sources of International Law* (Oxford University Press 2018).

Schønberg S, *Legitimate Expectations in Administrative Law* (Oxford University Press 2000).

Schreuer C, 'Fair and Equitable Treatment in Arbitral Practice' (2005) 6(3) The Journal of World Investment & Trade 357-386.

Schreuer C and Kriebaum U, 'At What Time Must Legitimate Expectations Exist?' (2012) Transnational Dispute Management 265.

Selivanova YS, 'Changes in Renewables Support Policy and Investment Protection under the Energy Charter Treaty: Analysis of Jurisprudence and Outlook for the Current Arbitration Cases' (2018) 33(2) ICSID Review - Foreign Investment Law Journal 433.

Simões FD, 'Blusun S.A. and others v Italy: Legal (in)stability and renewable energy investments' (2017) 26(3) RECIEL 298.

Sipiorski E, *Good Faith in International Investment Arbitration* (Oxford International Arbitration Series, 2019).

Snodgrass E, 'Protecting Investors' Legitimate Expectations - Recognizing and Delimiting a General Principle' (2006) 21(1) ICSID Review 1.

Stone Sweet A, 'Investor-State Arbitration: Proportionality's New Frontier' (2010) 4(1) Law & Ethics of Human Rights.

Stone Sweet A and Mathews J, 'Proportionality Balancing and Global Constitutionalism' (2008) 47(1) Columbia Journal of Transnational Law 73.

Strezhnev A, 'Detecting Bias in International Investment Arbitration' (2016) <https://scholar.harvard.edu/files/astrezhnev/files/are_investment_arbitrators_biased.pdf?m=1459524441>.

Sussman E, 'The Energy Charter Treaty's Investor Protection Provisions: Potential to Foster Solutions to Global Warming and Promote Sustainable Development' in Marie-Claire Cordonier Segger, Markus W Gehring and Andrew Newcombe (eds), *Sustainable Development in World Investment Law* (Global Trade Law Series Vol 30. Kluwer Law International 2010).

The World Bank, 'Inclusive Green Growth: The Pathway to Sustainable Development' (The World Bank 2012) <https://openknowledge.worldbank.org/bitstream/handle/10986/6058/9780821395516.pdf?sequence=1>.

Thirlway HWA, *The Sources of International Law* (Second Edition, 2019).

Tienhaara K and Downie C, 'Risky Business? The Energy Charter Treaty, Renewable Energy, and Investor-State Disputes' (2018) 24(3) Global Governance 451.

Titi A, *The Right to Regulate in International Investment Law* (Studien zum Internationalen Investitionsrecht, Nomos 2014).

Trujillo E, 'Balancing Sustainability, the Right to Regulate, and the Need for Investor Protection: Lessons from the Trade Regime' (2018) 59(8) Boston College Law Review 2735.

Tudor I, *The Fair and Equitable Treatment Standard in the International Law of Foreign Investment* (Oxford Monographs in International Law, Oxford University Press 2008).

UNCTAD, 'World Investment Report 2016', UNCTAD Series on Issues in International Investment Agreements II (United Nations Publication 2016).

– 'Fair and Equitable Treatment', UNCTAD Series on Issues in International Investment Agreements II (United Nations Publication 2012).

– 'Investment Policy Framework for Sustainable Development' UNCTAD Series on Issues in International Investment Agreements II (United Nations Publication 2015).

– 'World Investment Report 2019' UNCTAD Series on Issues in International Investment Agreements II (United Nations Publication 2019).

Vadi V, 'Proportionality, Reasonableness, and Standards of Review in Investment Treaty Arbitration' in Andrea K Bjorklund (ed), *Yearbook on International Investment Law and Policy 2013-2014* (Oxford University Press 2015).

– 'The Migration of Constitutional Ideas: The Strange Case of Proportionality in International Investment Law and Arbitration' in Andrea K Bjorklund (ed), *Yearbook on International Investment Law and Policy 2013-2014* (Oxford University Press 2015).

Valenti M, 'The Protection of General Interests of Host States in the Application of the Fair and Equitable Treatment Standard' in Giorgio Sacerdoti and others (eds), *General Interests of Host States in International Investment Law* (CUP 2014).

Vávra J, Cudlínová E and Miloslav L, 'Green Growth from the Viewpoint of the Czech Republic' in Jan Vávra, Miloslav Lapka and Eva Cudlínová (eds), *Current challenges of Central Europe* (Varia vol 29. Univ. Karlova Filozoficka Fak 2015).

Viñuales JE, 'Investor Diligence in Investment Arbitration: Sources and Arguments' (2017) 32(2) ICSID Review - Foreign Investment Law Journal 346.

– 'Sources of International Investment Law: Conceptual Foundations of Unruly Practices' in Samantha Besson and Jean d'Aspremont (eds), *The Oxford Handbook of the Sources of International Law* (Oxford University Press 2018).

Weeramantry JR, *Treaty Interpretation in Investment Arbitration* (Oxford University Press 2012).

Wood T, 'Political Risk or Political Right? Reconciling the International Legal Norms of Investment Protection and Political Participation' (2015) 30(3) ICSID Review 665.

Yannaca-Small K, 'Fair and Equitable Treatment Standard: Recent Developments' in August Reinisch (ed), *Standards of Investment Protection* (Oxford University Press 2008).

Zarra G, 'Right to Regulate, Margin of Appreciation and Proportionality: Current Status in Investment Arbitration in Light of Philip Morris v. Uruguay' (2017) 14(2) RDI.

Arbitral Awards

9REN Holding S.a.r.l v. Kingdom of Spain Award, 31 March 2019 ICSID Case No. ARB/15/15.

Abaclat and Others v. Argentine Republic Decision on Jurisdiction and Admissibility, 4 August 2011 ICSID Case No. ARB/07/5.

ADC Affiliate Limited and ADC & ADMC Management Limited v. The Republic of Hungary Award, 2 October 2016 ICSID Case No. ARB/03/16.

ADF Group Inc. v. United States of America Award, 9 January 2003 ICSID Case No. ARB (AF)/00/1.

AES Corporation and Tau Power B.V. v. Republic of Kazakhstan Award, 1 November 2013 ICSID Case No. ARB/10/16.

AES Corporation v. Argentine Republic Decision on Jurisdiction, 26 April 2005 ICSID Case No ARB/02/17.

AES Summit Generation Limited et. al. v. The Republic of Hungary Award, 23 September 2010 ICSID Case No. ARB/07/22.

Alasdair Ross Anderson et al v. Republic of Costa Rica Award, 19 May 2010 ICSID Case No. ARB(AF)/07/3.

Alex Genin, Eastern Credit Limited, Inc. and A.S. Baltoil v. The Republic of Estonia Award, 25 June 2001 ICSID Case No. ARB/99/2.

Antaris Solar and Dr. Michael Göde v. Czech Republic Award, 2 May 2018 PCA Case No. 2014-01.

Antaris Solar and Dr. Michael Göde v. Czech Republic Dissenting Opinion, 2 May 2018 PCA Case No. 2014-01.

Antin Infrastructure Services Luxembourg S.à.r.l. and Antin Energia Termosolar B.V. v. Kingdom of Spain Award, 15 June 2018 ICSID Case No. ARB/13/31.

Apotex Holdings Inc. and Apotex Inc. v. United States of America Award, 25 August 2014 ICSID Case No. ARB(AF)/12/1.

Associated Provincial Picture Houses Ltd. v. Wednesbury Corporation Judgment, 10 November 1947 [1948] 1 KB 223.

AWG Group Ltd. v. The Argentine Republic Decision on Liability, 30 June 2010 ICSID Case No. ARB/03/19.

AWG Group Ltd. v. The Argentine Republic Award, 9 April 2015 ICSID Case No. ARB/03/19.

Azurix Corp. v. Argentine Republic 14.7.2006, Award ICSID Case No. ARB/01/12.

Bayindir Insaat Turizm Ticaret Ve Sanayi A.S. v. Islamic Republic of Pakistan Award, 27 August 2009 ICSID Case No. ARB/03/29.

BayWa r.e. Renewable Energy GmbH and BayWa r.e. Asset Holding GmbH v. Kingdom of Spain Dissenting Opinion Horacio A. Grigera Naón, 2 December 2019 ICSID Case No. ARB/15/16.

BayWa r.e. Renewable Energy GmbH and BayWa r.e. Asset Holding GmbH v. Kingdom of Spain Decision on Jurisdiction, Liability and Directions on Quantum, 2 December 2019 ICSID Case No. ARB/15/16.

Belenergia S.A. v. Italian Republic Award, 6 August 2019 ICSID Case No. ARB/15/40.

BG Group Plc. v. The Republic of Argentina Award, 24 December 2007 UNCITRAL.

Biwater Gauff (Tanzania) Ltd. v. United Republic of Tanzania Award, 24 July 2004 ICSID Case No. ARB/05/22.

Blusun S.A. Jean-Pierre Lecorcier and Michael Stein v. Italian Republic Award, 27 December 2016 ICSID Case No. ARB/14/3.

Brazil - Measures Affecting Imports of Retreaded Tyres - AB-2007-4 Report of the Appellate Body, 3 December 2007 WT/DS332/AB/R.

Burlington Resources Inv. v. Republic of Ecuador Decision on Jurisdiction, 2 June 2010 ICSID Case No. ARB/08/5.

Cavalum SGPS v. Kingdom of Spain Dissenting Opinion of David R. Haigh, 31 August 2020 ICSID Case No. ARB/15/34.

Cavalum SGPS v. Kingdom of Spain Decision on Jurisdiction, Liability and Directions on Quantum, 31 August 2020 ICSID Case No. ARB/15/34.

CEF Energia B.V. v. Italian Republic Award, 16 January 2019 SCC Arbitration No. 2015/158.

Charanne and Construction Investments v. Kingdom of Spain Award, 21 January 2016 SCC Case No. V 062/2012.

Charanne and Construction Investments v. Kingdom of Spain Dissenting Opinion Guido Santiago Tawil, 21 January 2016 SCC Case No. V 062/2012.

Chemtura Corporation v. Canada Award, 2 August 2010 UNCITRAL.

CME Czech Republic B.V. v. The Czech Republic Final Award, 14 March 2013,

CMS Gas Transmission Company v. The Republic of Argentina Award, 21 May 2005 ICSID Case No. ARB/01/8.

CMS Gas Transmission Company v. The Republic of Argentina Decision of the ad hoc Committee on the Application for Annulment of the Argentine Republic, 25 September 2007 ICSID Case No. ARB/01/8.

Continental Casualty Company v. The Argentine Republic Award, 5 September 2008 ICSID Case No. ARB/03/9.

Copper Mesa Mining Corporation v. Republic of Ecuador Award PCA No. 2012-2.

Crystallex International Corporation v. Bolivarian Republic of Venezuela Award, 4 April 2016 ICSID Case No. ARB(AF)/11/2.

Cube Infrastructure Fund SICAV and others v. Kingdom of Spain Decision on Jurisdiction, Liability and Partial Decision on Quantum, 19 February 2019 ICSID Case No. ARB/15/20.

Cube Infrastructure Fund SICAV and others v. Kingdom of Spain Separate and Partial Dissenting Opinion Christian Tomuschat, 19 February 2019 ICSID Case No. ARB/15/20.

Daimler Financial Services AG v Argentine Republic Award, 22 August 2012 ICSID Case No. ARB/05/1.

Duke Energy Electroquil Partners & Electroquil S.A. v. Republic of Ecuador Award, 18 August 2008 ICSID Case No. ARB/04/19.

Eastern Sugar B.V. (Netherlands) v. The Czech Republic Partial Award, 27 March 2007 SCC Case No. 088/2004.

EDF (Services) Limited v. Romania Award, 8 October 2009 ICSID Case No. ARB/05/13.

Eiser Infrastructure Limited and Energía Solar Luxembourg S.à.r.l. v. Kingdom of Spain Award, 4 May 2017 ICSID Case No. ARB/13/36.

Eiser Infrastructure Limited and Energía Solar Luxembourg S.à.r.l. v. Kingdom of Spain Decision of Annullment, 11 June 2020 ICSID Case No. ARB/13/36.

El Paso Energy International Company v. The Argentine Republic Award, 31 October 2011 ICSID Case No. ARB/03/15.

Electrabel S.A. v. Republic of Hungary Award, 25 November 2015 ICSID Case No. ARB/07/19.

Enron Corporation and Ponderosa Assets, L.P. v. Argentine Republic Award, 22 May 2007 ICSID Case No. ARB/01/3.

Eskosol S.p.A. in liquidazione v. Italian Republic Award, 4 September 2020 ICSID Case No. ARB/15/50.

ESPF Beteiligungs GmbH et. al. v. Italian Republic Award, 14 September 2020 ICSID Case No. ARB/16/5.

European Communities—Customs Classification of Certain Computer Equipment, Report of the Appellate Body Report of the Appellate Body, 5 June 1998 WT/DS62/AB/R, WT/DS67/AB/R, WT/DS68/AB/R.

Foresight and others v. Kingdom of Spain Final Award, 14 November 2018 SCC Case No. V 2015/150.

Foresight and others v. Kingdom of Spain Dissenting Opinion Raúl Emilio Vinuesa, 14 November 2018 SCC Case No. V 2015/150.

Frontier Petroleum Services Ltd. v. The Czech Republic Final Award, 12 November 2010,

Gami Investments, Inc. v.The United Mexican States Final Award, 15 November 2004 UNCITRAL.

Generation Ukraine, Inc. v. Ukraine Award, 16 September 2003 ICSID Case No. ARB/00/9.

Glamis Gold, Ltd. v. The United States of America Award, 8 June 2009 UNCITRAL.

Gold Reserve Inc. v. Bolivarian Republic of Venezuela Award, 22 September 2014 ICSID Case No. ARB(AF)/09/1.

Greentech Energy Systems A/S, NovEnergia II Energy & Environment (SCA) SICAR, and NovEnergia II Italian Portfolio SA v. Italian Republic Award, 23 December 2018 SCC Arbitration V (2015/095).

Greentech Energy Systems A/S, NovEnergia II Energy & Environment (SCA) SICAR, and NovEnergia II Italian Portfolio SA v. Italian Republic Dissenting Opinion of Giorgio Sacerdoti, 23 December 2018 SCC Arbitration V (2015/095).

Hesham T. M. Al Warraq v. Republic of Indonesia Award, 15 December 2014 UNCITRAL.

Hydro Energy 1 S.A.R.L. and Hydroxana Sweden AB v. The Kingdom of Spain Decision on Jurisdiction, Liability and Directions on Quantum, 9 March 2020 ICSID Case No. ARB/15/42.

I.C.W. Europe Investments Limited v. The Czech Republic Award, 15 May 2019 PCA CASE No 2014-22.

Impregilo S.p.A. v. Argentine Republic Award, 21 June 2011 ICSID Case No. ARB/07/17.

India—Patent Protection for Pharmaceutical and Agricultural Chemical Products Report of the Appellate Body, 19 December 1997 WT/DS50/AB/R.

InfraRed Environmental Infrastructure GP Limited and others v. Kingdom of Spain Award, 2 August 2019 ICSID Case No. ARB/14/12.

International Thunderbird Gaming Corporation v. The United Mexican States Separate Opinion of Thomas Wälde, 26 January 2006 UNCITRAL.

International Thunderbird Gaming Corporation v. The United Mexican States Award, 26 January 2006 UNCITRAL.

Invesmart v. Czech Republic Award, 26 June 2009 UNCITRAL.

Ioan Micula, Viorel Micula, S.C. European Food S.A, S.C. Starmill S.R.L. and S.C. Multipack S.R.L. v. Romania Award, 11 December 2013 ICSID Case No. ARB/05/20.

Isolux Netherlands, BV v. Kingdom of Spain Final Award, 17 July 2016 SCC Case V2013/153.

Isolux Netherlands, BV v. Kingdom of Spain Dissenting Opinion Guido Santiago Tawil, 17 July 2016 SCC Case V2013/153.

Joseph Charles Lemire v. Ukraine Decision on Liability, 14 January 2010 ICSID Case No. ARB/06/18.

Joseph Charles Lemire v. Ukraine Award, 28 March 2011 ICSID Case No. ARB/06/18.

Joy Mining Machinery Limited v. Arab Republic of Egypt Award on Jurisdiction, 6 August 2004 ICSID Case No. ARB/03/11.

Jürgen Wirtgen, Stefan Wirtgen, Gisela Wirtgen and JSW Solar (zwei) GmbH & Co. KG v. Czech Republic Award, 11 October 2017 PCA Case No. 2014-03.

Jürgen Wirtgen, Stefan Wirtgen, Gisela Wirtgen and JSW Solar (zwei) GmbH & Co. KG v. Czech Republic Dissenting Opinion, 11 October 2017 PCA Case No. 2014-03.

Korea — Measures Affecting Imports of Fresh, Chilled and Frozen Beef Report of the Appellate Body - *AB-2000-8* -,11 December 2000 WT/DS161/AB/R; WT/DS169/AB/R.

L.E.S.I. S.p.A. and ASTALDI S.p.A. v. République Algérienne Award, 12 November 2008 ICSID Case No. ARB/05/3.

LG&E Energy Corp. LG&E Capital Corp. and LG&E International, Inc. v. Argentine Republic Decision on Liability, 3 October 2006 ICSID Case No. ARB/02/1.

Liberian Eastern Timber Corporation v Republic of Liberia Award, 31 March 1986 ICSID Case No ARB/83/2.

Liman Caspian Oil BV and NCL Dutch Investment BV v. Kazakhstan Award, 22 June 2010 ICSID Case No. ARB/07/14.

Loewen Group, Inc. and Raymond L. Loewen v. United States of America Award, 26 June 2003 ICSID Case No. ARB(AF)/98/3.

Mamidoil Jetoil Greek Petroleum Products Societe S.A. v. Republic of Albania Award, 30 March 2015 ICSID Case No. ARB/11/24.

Marvin Roy Feldman Karpa v. United Mexican States Award, 16 December 2002 ICSID Case No. ARB(AF)/99/1.

Masdar Solar & Wind Cooperatief U.A. v. Kingdom of Spain Award, 16 May 2018 ICSID Case No. ARB/14/1.

Metalclad Corporation v. The United Mexican States Award, 30 August 2000 ICSID Case No. ARB(AF)/97/1.

Metalpar S.A. and Buen Aire S.A. v. The Argentine Republic Award, 6 June 2008 ICSID Case No. ARB/03/5.

Methanex Corporation v. United States of America Final Award, 3 August 2005 UNCITRAL.

Mobil Exploration and Development Inc. Suc. Argentina Decision on Jurisdiction and Liability, 10 April 2013 ICSID Case No. ARB/04/16.

Mobil Investments Canada Inc. and Murphy Oil Corporation v. Canada Decision on Liability and on Principles of Quantum, 22 May 2012 ICSID Case No. ARB(AF)/07/4.

Mondev International Ltd. v United States of America Award, 11 October 2002 ICSID Case No. ARB(AF)/99/2.

MTD Equity Sdn. Bhd. and MTD Chile S.A. v. Republic of Chile Award, 25 May 2004 ICSID Case No. ARB/01/7.

MTD Equity Sdn. Bhd. and MTD Chile S.A. v. Republic of Chile Decision on Annulment, 21 March 2007 ICSID Case No. ARB/01/7.

National Grid P.L.C. v. The Argentine Republic Award, 3 November 2008 UNCITRAL.

Nations Energy Corporation, Electric Machinery Enterprises Inc. and Jamie Jurado v. The Republic of Panama Award, 24 November 2010 ICSID Case No. ARB/06/19.

NextEra Energy Global Holdings B.V. and NextEra Energy Spain Holdings B.V. v. Kingdom of Spain Decision on Jurisdiction, Liability and Quantum Principles, 12 March 2019 ICSID Case No. ARB/14/11.

Noble Ventures, Inc. v. Romania Award, 12 October 2005 ICSID Case No. ARB/01/11.

Novenergia II - Energy & Environment (SCA), SICAR v. The Kingdom of Spain Award, 15 February 2018 SCC Case No. V 2015/063.

Nykomb Synergetics Technology Holding AB v. The Republic of Latvia, SCC Award, 16 December 2003 SCC.

Occidental Exploration and Production Company v. The Republic of Ecuador Final Award, 1 July 2004 LCIA Case No. UN3467.

Occidental Petroleum Corporation and Occidental Exploration and Production Company v. The Republic of Ecuador Award, 5 October 2012 ICSID Case No. ARB/06/11.

OperaFund Eco-Invest SICAV PLC and Schwab Holding AG v. Kingdom of Spain Award, 6 September 2019 ICSID Case No. ARB/15/36.

OperaFund Eco-Invest SICAV PLC and Schwab Holding AG v. Kingdom of Spain Dissenting Opinion Philippe Sands, 6 September 2019 ICSID Case No. ARB/15/36.

Parkerings-Compagniet AS v. Republic of Lithuania Award, 11 September 2007 ICSID Case No. ARB/05/8.

Perenco Ecuador Ltd. v. Republic of Ecuador and Empresa Estatal Petróleos del Ecuador Decision on Remaining Issues of Jurisdiction and on Liability, 12 September 2014 ICSID Case No. ARB/08/6.

Philip Morris Brands Sàrl et. al. v. Oriental Republic of Uruguay Award, 8 July 2016 ICSID Case No. ARB/10/7.

Photovoltaik Knopf Betriebs-GmbH v. The Czech Republic Award, 15 May 2019 PCA CASE No 2014-21.

Plama Consortium Limited v. Republic of Bulgaria Award, 27 August 2008 ICSID Case No. ARB/03/24.

Portigon AG v. Kingdom of Spain Pending Proceeding ICSID Case No. ARB/17/15.

PSEG Global Inc and others v. Republic of Turkey Award, 9 January 2007 ICSID Case No. ARB/02/5.

Romak S.A. (Switzerland) v . The Republic of Uzbekistan Award, 26 November 2009 PCA Case No. AA280.

Ronald S. Lauder v. The Czech Republic Award, 3 September 2001 UNCITRAL.

RREEF Infrastructure (G.P.) Limited and RREEF Pan-European Infrastructure Two Lux S.à.r.l. v. Kingdom of Spain Decision on Responsibility and on the Principles of Quantum, 30 November 2018 ICSID Case No. ARB/13/30.

RREEF Infrastructure (G.P.) Limited and RREEF Pan-European Infrastructure Two Lux S.à.r.l. v. Kingdom of Spain Partially Dissenting Opinion of Robert Volterra, 30 November 2018 ICSID Case No. ARB/13/30.

Rupert Joseph Binder v. Czech Republic Final Award, 15 July 2011 UNCITRAL.

Rusoro Mining Ltd. v. Bolivarian Republic of Venezuela Award, 22 August 2016 ICSID Case No. ARB(AF)/12/5.

RWE Innogy GmbH and RWE Innogy Aersa S.A.U. v. Kingdom of Spain Decision on Jurisdicition, Liability, and certain Issues of Quantum, 6 January 2020 ICSID Case No. ARB/14/34.

S.D. Myers, Inc. v. Government of Canada Partial Award, 13 November 2000 UNCITRAL.

Saipem S.p.A. v. Bangladesh Decision on Jurisdiction and Recommendation on Provisional Measures, 21 March 2007 ICSID Case No. ARB/05/07.

Saipem S.p.A. v. The People's Republic of Bangladesh Award, 30 June 2009 ICSID Case No. ARB/05/07.

Salini Costruttori S.p.A. and Italstrade S.p.A. v. Kingdom of Morocco Decision on Jurisdiction, 23 June 2001 Case No. ARB/00/4.

Saluka Investments B.V. v. The Czech Republic Partial Award, 17 March 2006 UNCITRAL.

Sempra Energy International v. The Argentine Republic Award, 28 September 2007 ICSID Case No. ARB/02/16.

SGS Société Générale de Surveillance S.A. v. The Republic of Paraguay Award, 10 February 2012 ICSID Case No. ARB/07/29.

Siemens A.G. v. The Argentine Republic Award, 17 January 2007 ICSID Case No. ARB/02/8.

SolEs Badajoz GmbH v. Kingdom of Spain Award, 31 July 2019 ICSID Case No. ARB/15/38.

Stadtwerke München GmbH and others v. Kingdom of Spain Award, 2 December 2019 ICSID Case No. ARB/15/1.

Stadtwerke München GmbH and others v. Kingdom of Spain Dissenting Opinion Kaj Hobér, 2 December 2019 ICSID Case No. ARB/15/1.

Stati and others v. Kazakhstan Award, 19 December 2013 SCC Case No. 116/2010.

STEAG GmbH v. Kingdom of Spain Dissenting Opinion Pierre-Marie Dupuy, 8 October 2020 ICSID Case No. ARB/15/4.

STEAG GmbH v. Kingdom of Spain Decision on Jurisdiction, Liability and Directions on Quantum, 8 October 2020 ICSID Case No. ARB/15/4.

Suez, Sociedad General de Aguas de Barcelona, S.A. and Vivendi Universal, S.A. v. Argentine Republic Decision on Liability, 30 July 2010 ICSID Case No. ARB/03/19.

SunReserve Luxco Holdings v. Italian Republic Final Award, 25 March 2020 SCC Arbitration V (2016/32).

Técnicas Medioambientales Tecmed, S.A. v. The United Mexican States Award, 29 May 2003 ICSID Case No. ARB (AF)/00/2.

The PV Investors v. Kingdom of Spain Final Award, 28 February 2020 PCA Case No. 2012-14.

The PV Investors v. Kingdom of Spain Concurring and Dissenting Opinion of Charles N. Brower, 28 February 2020 PCA Case No. 2012-14.

Tokios Tokelés v. Ukraine Award, 26 July 2007 ICSID Case No. ARB/02/18.

Total S.A. v. The Argentine Republic Decision on Liability, 27 December 2010 ICSID Case No. ARB/04/01.

Total S.A. v. The Argentine Republic Award, 27 November 2013 ICSID Case No. ARB/04/01.

Toto Costruzioni Generali S.p.A. v. The Republic of Lebanon Award, 7 June 2012 ICSID Case No. ARB/07/12.

Tulip Real Estate and Development Netherlands B.V. v. Republic of Turkey Award, 10 March 2014 ICSID Case No. ARB/11/28.

Urbaser SA and Consorcio de Aguas Bilbao Bizkaia, Bilbao Biskaia Ur Partzuergoa v The Argentine Republic Award, 8 December 2016 ICSID Case No ARB/07/26.

Venezuela Holdings et. al. v. Venezuela, Award, 9 October 2014 ICSID Case No. ARB/07/27.

Vigotop Limited v. Hungary Award, 1 October 2014 ICSID Case No. ARB/11/22.

Voltaic Network GmbH v. Czech Republic Award, 15 September 2019 PCA CASE No 2014-20.

WA Investments-Europa Nova Limited v. The Czech Republic Award, 15 May 2019 PCA CASE No 2014-19.

Walter Bau AG v. The Kingdom of Thailand Award, 1 July 2009 UNCITRAL.

Waste Management, Inc. v. United Mexican States Award, 30 April 2004 ICSID Case No. ARB(AF)/00/3.

Watkins Holdings S.à.r.l. and others v. Kingdom of Spain Dissenting Opinion Helene Ruiz Fabri, 21 January 2020 ICSID Case No. ARB/15/44.

Watkins Holdings S.à.r.l. and others v. Kingdom of Spain Award, 21 January 2020 ICSID Case No. ARB/15/44.

William Nagel v. The Czech Republic Final Award, 9 September 2003 SCC Case No. 049/2002.

Yukos Universal Ltd. (UK - Isle of Man) v. Russian Federation Final Award, 18 July 2018 PCA Case No. AA 227.

Court Judgments

CJEU Judgment *Rewe-Zentral AG v Bundesmonopolverwaltung für Branntwein,* 20 February 1979 Case 120/78.

CJEU Judgment *The Queen v Minister of Agriculture, Fisheries and Food and Secretary of State for Health,* 13 November 1990 Case C-331/88.

CJEU Judgment *Atlanta v European Community,* 14 October 1999 C-104/97 P.

CJEU Judgment *Grundstückgemeinschaft Schloßstraße GbR v Finanzamt Paderborn,* 8 June 2000 C-396/98.

CJEU Judgment *Marks & Spencer plc v Commissioners of Customs & Excise,* 11 July 2002 Case C-62/00.

CJEU Judgment *Di Lenardo and Dilexport,* 15 July 2004 C-37/02 and C-38/02.

CJEU Judgment *Commission of the European Communities v Federal Republic of Germany,* 14 December 2004 Case C-463/01.

CJEU Judgment *HLH Warenvertriebs GmbH and Orthica BV v Germany,* 9 June 2005 C-17/03.

ECtHR Judgment *Handyside v. United Kingdom,* 7 December 1976 Application No. 5493/72.

ECtHR Judgment *Dudgeon v. United Kingdom,* 22 October 1981 Application No. 7525/76.

ECtHR Judgment *James and others v. United Kingdom,* 21 February 1986 Application No. 8793/79.

ECtHR Judgment *Matos e Silva, Lda. and Others v. Portugal,* 16 September 1996 Application No. 15777/89.

ECtHR Judgment *AD & OD v. United Kingdom,* 16 March 2010 Application No. 28680/06.

ECtHR Judgment *Oao Neftyanaya Kompaniya Yukos v. Russia,* 8.3.2012 Application No. 14902/04.

ECtHR Judgment *Centro Europa 7 srl and di Stefano v. Italy*,7 June 2012 Application No. 38433/09.

PCIJ Judgment *The S.S. "Wimbledon", Britain et al. v. Germany*,17 August 1923 PCIJ Series A01.

PCIJ Judgment *The Case of the S.S. "Lotus" (France v. Turkey)*,7 September 1927 PCIJ Series A10.